CHINA'S TRANSITION FROM SOCIALISM

Statist Legacies and Market Reforms

1980-1990

Dorothy J. Solinger

An East Gate Book

M. E. Sharpe
ARMONK, NEW YORK
LONDON, ENGLAND

9-8-94

An East Gate Book

Copyright © 1993 by M. E. Sharpe, Inc.

Library of Congress Cataloging-in-Publication Data

Solinger, Dorothy J.
China's transition from socialism: statist legacies and market reforms, 1980–1990/
Dorothy J. Solinger.
p. cm.—(The Political economy of socialism)
Includes bibliographical references and index.
ISBN 1-56324-067-X (cloth)
ISBN 1-56324-068-8 (pbk)
1. China—Economic policy—1976–
2. Central planning—China.
3. Socialism—China.
I. Title.
II. Series.
HC427.92.S63   1993
338.951—dc20
92-43250
CIP

Printed in the United States of America

The paper used in this publication meets the minimum requirements of
American National Standard for Information Sciences—
Permanence of Paper for Printed Library Materials,
ANSI Z39.48–1984.

∞

BM (c)   10 9 8 7 6 5 4 3 2 1
BM (p)   10 9 8 7 6 5 4 3 2

Table of Contents

Part III: Reforms in Restructuring Regions

Part IV: State Cadres and Urban Entrepreneurs

Acknowledgments

THE PIECES that make up this volume were written over the course of a decade. Most of them were originally presented at conferences; all of them were previously published, either in journals or in conference volumes. In some cases the papers benefited from readers' comments before the meetings were held or the volumes published, and in those cases I thank those readers on the title page of each individual essay. I am also glad to take this opportunity to express my gratitude to the conveners of these various meetings for giving me a chance to prepare a paper.

Despite attributions in a few of the chapters for the help given me by the Wuhan City Foreign Affairs Bureau in arranging interviews with city officials and enterprise managers, I would like to restate my thanks again here, especially for assistance in collecting the material that appears in chapters 4, 5, 6, 8, and 9. The office of the U.S. Consulate in Shenyang was very helpful during my time in that city in 1988.

The funds for making these various trips to China (in 1983, 1984, 1985, 1987, and 1988) were generously provided by the University of Pittsburgh's University Center for International Studies (its Contemporary China Program and its Asian Studies Program) and by its Research Development Fund, and by the School of Social Sciences at the University of California, Irvine.

For the idea to bring all these pieces together between two covers I feel a particular sense of appreciation. On separate occasions in early 1990 both Rick Baum and Tom Bernstein suggested that I undertake this project. And a special thanks to Doug Merwin and Mark Selden for allowing me to bring Rick and Tom's suggestion to fruition. Finally, without Ziggy Bates's tireless and efficient word processing this project could not have been completed.

D.J.S.

CHINA'S TRANSITION
FROM SOCIALISM

Introduction

THE 1980s were the decade of economic reform in China. The reform campaign was launched at the end of the 1970s with the contracting of agricultural production to households and the subsequent dissolution of the communes in the countryside, modest experiments in enterprise autonomy in the cities, the legitimation of petty private sectoral trading, and a sudden surge in China's participation in the global economy. The use of market mechanisms to supplement the state plan that lay at the core of these initiatives seemed to promise that the country had embarked on a process that, with time, would result in China's economic system eventually evolving into one in which the plan had been totally overtaken by the market. Indeed, in many ways, the results and achievements were remarkable, the changes startling.[1]

In fact, the increasingly extensive application of market tools over the decade—an application that became even more dramatic with preeminent leader Deng Xiaoping's much-celebrated southern inspection tour in early 1992—convinced many observers that the Chinese people would soon be living under a capitalist system. This volume seeks to demonstrate that that capitalism, when it emerges, will be distinctive. It does so by documenting the specific content and kind of capitalistic measures undertaken in China's urban economic reforms of the 1980s, and by explicating the concerns that lay behind them.

Accordingly, this collection of essays begins from a particular assumption: its guiding theme is the *statism* behind the reform effort. Starting from this statist perspective, this work, unlike much of the literature on the first decade of the Chinese reforms, does not envision reform of the economy—and the predominance of market-oriented institutions and behavior that this would usher in—as a goal in itself at that time. Rather, the picture here is one of reform as merely a *means*, a set of tools to be manipulated in the service of a few fundamental and overarching statist ends: the modernization, invigoration, and enhanced efficiency of the national economy and its consequent heightened capacity to boost

3

both productivity and returns to the central state treasury.

A related goal was to raise living standards, to improve the state's ability to address social needs, and to ensure social stability. These goals, and not marketization per se, constituted the "project" of the decade of economic reform in China. And it is against these aims that the political elite consistently assessed—and periodically curtailed or revamped—its program of urban reforms.

In this view, reform was not an objective to which a wavering commitment obtained; it represented instead a package of measures valued for their potential to improve the workings of and to increase the state's receipts from the national economy. The fundamental commitment supporting reform, then, was a contingent and not an absolute one. In fact, the critical October 1984 decision on the reform of the urban economy reached at the Third Plenum of the Twelfth Party Congress attests to this interpretation. As explicated in the mid-1980s by a top Chinese economist who was one of the leading proponents of reform, that resolution underlined the continuing prominence of the system of state ownership and of the core purposes of the political elite:

> Only by fully developing a commodity economy is it possible truly to invigorate the economy, spur an increase in productivity . . . and be sensitive to the complex and varied needs of society. . . . It is necessary to establish a commodity economy based on a system of public ownership. To understand a socialist planned economy clearly, it is necessary to apply consciously the law of value [—essentially, the workings of supply and demand—] and to establish a commodity economy based on the system of public ownership.[2]

This reading of the reforms' intentions is consistent with the other major party meeting concerned with the urban reform program, the opening session of the Thirteenth Party Congress, held in autumn 1987. Here even then party leader Zhao Ziyang, who all through the decade had been the chief proponent of reform, affirmed the pledge to use market reforms not for the purpose of creating a market, but in order to supplement and revitalize—but never to jettison—the socialist command economy.[3]

The period in which the eleven essays that follow were written coincides exactly with the decade of reform: the first was done in February 1980, the last completed in February 1990. They begin with the theoretical and policy conflicts that attended the birth and early stages of the reforms and go on to examine a range of reforms in the cities, including those in industry, commerce, regional restructuring, and ownership; there are also two that consider the place of the new entrepreneurial class emerging from the reform era, in both its small- and large-scale guises.

Except for the first two chapters, the consistent effort is to explore how plan and market were combined in practice. For this reason, many of the pieces draw upon local data, using material on the implementation of reforms in one particular city, Wuhan. Wuhan, the "central city" of central China, had a long history of experience as a commercial entrepôt and transport node before the Communists conquered it in 1949; its role as one of the principal national models in the reform era grew out of this history as well as being tied to the city's advantageous geographical position at the point where the Yangtze crosses the trunkline Beijing–Guangzhou railroad. Much of the data come from interviews conducted with economic bureaucrats, factory managers, and scholars in Wuhan during six visits to the city between 1983 and 1988; I also used local newspapers and journals from Wuhan as well as national sources.

The volume is organized by category; within each category I have arranged the articles chronologically. Thus, through these studies one may read of the gradual progression of urban reform, from the time in 1979 when a handful of firms in one province began to trade independently some of their surplus products (produced above the amount scheduled by the plan for delivery to the state), to the far more radical trials of bankruptcy, stock markets, and enterprise mergers in the late 1980s, even as the leadership's purposes behind the various initiatives remained surprisingly constant. One may also note the continuity in the new business class's dependence on cadres' goodwill, beginning with the obstructions cadres placed in the way of the activities of petty merchants in the early 1980s and culminating in the symbiotic dependence that grew up between bureaucrats and those capitalists with enough assets to form software companies by the end of the decade.

Chapters 1 and 2 highlight the leadership's ideas that initially shaped the reforms and the sorts of debate that attended their discussions in the early reform years. The first chapter locates the origin of the reform blueprints in designs first advanced nearly a generation before their emergence in 1979. It was already clear by early 1980 when the piece was composed that this time the experiment would be far more daring and multifaceted than similar trials in the mid-1950s and early 1960s had been. Yet it is interesting that even then, in that first fresh flush of loosening the plan, brakes were being applied; just as in 1956 measures that might alter the taxation system threatened reformers, whose fear of a potential loss of state income resulted in programs that limited but did not replace the plan.

The second chapter, on the debates over reform that took place at the meetings of the Fifth National People's Congress from 1978 through 1981, continues to illustrate the competition between plans for reform and strategies meant to enable the central government to capture more resources for itself. Though the chapter notes that a leadership consensus existed in the early 1980s on the priorities of economic modernization, upgrading the management and the performance of the economy, and improving the people's livelihood, worries about the social effects of state economic policies, about inflation, and about consequences for the state's financial receipts fueled much controversy and reconsideration in the short space of three years.

In one of the meetings the chapter describes, then Premier Zhao Ziyang advocated reform precisely because he believed the incentives it offered would increase production and revenue, thereby solving problems of state finance. The conclusion to the essay summarizes all the sessions of the Fifth National People's Congress up through December 1981 as evidencing a shared focus on the goal of economic growth among the political elite, but a standoff between plan and market as to how best to achieve that growth.

The second set of essays is about experiments in the urban state economic bureaucracy. Chapter 3, written at the end of 1983, discusses organizational rearrangements in the procedures and networks used in conducting state-run trade in the early 1980s. It begins from the premise that politicians had reached broad agreement that rigidities in the commercial bureaucracy and in its manner of conducting business had subverted proper socialist goals, namely, enhancing productivity and bettering the people's living standards. Reforms were necessary, all concurred, to stimulate growth through more flexible forms of trading. But the article stresses that any differences existing among the elite as to how great a role to accord the market dissolved when state power and state capacity to dominate the management of state assets and revenue were challenged.

Because of the mutual commitment to a state-run economic system, at such moments of challenge those of a bureaucratic leaning could easily convince their more marketeer-type colleagues that reforms should be curtailed, at least for a time. Furthermore, in that era, the professed objectives of the commercial system's reform were markedly statist: to encourage more output, which could then be siphoned off by state procurement agents; and, through the action of competition, to spur state-managed firms more effectively to corner the newly activated market.

Indeed, as one Chinese reformer points out, in those days state-operated planned wholesale trade was still viewed as the key for leading and managing the national market. Thus, for many, the function of this reform was yet to serve the plan: the chapter closes with a 1983 paraphrase of Deng Xiaoping that claims that the aim of reform is "to perfect, consolidate, and develop the basic system of socialism . . . and to promote the continuous development of the social productive forces."[4]

The fourth chapter, on the operation of the urban industrial bureaucracy as reforms got under way, draws heavily on interviews conducted in Wuhan in the spring of 1984. This piece considers the hypothesis that economic reforms—specifically, decentralization of economic powers and resources and redistribution of state benefits—might be leading to privatization and pluralization, respectively. But the essay concludes that in the local industrial economy economic actors were not adopting new forms of political behavior. Instead, they were simply adapting and retaining familiar behaviors as the structure of reward and opportunity, which remained vertically configured, was essentially unchanged.

That is, since neither state ownership, shortage, local officials' responsibility for the fulfillment of regime-set success indicators (and the assessment of such officials on this basis), branch-type disbursal of materials and capital, nor soft budgets had undergone any substantial alteration, the behavioral correlates of these principles and conditions had not shifted either. Again the theme of the central leaders' efforts to retain financial controls at the top of the system reappears.

Thus, despite the fact that managers were then judged not as to whether they met quantitative targets but as to whether they reached preset profit levels, the chief incentives to which they responded were still those laid down by their superiors and were not the product of horizontal, market-based interactions. The essay illustrates this point by discussing the mode of implementation in the city of a number of state economic policies in force as of mid-1984. The plan was receding, but the lessons it taught had yet to be unlearned.

The next essay, chapter 5, finds an irony at the heart of the reform program. This is that reformers assumed that market reforms would make it possible to overcome structural weaknesses associated with the planned economy, weaknesses that had produced inefficiencies and stagnation. But in fact, since three key infrastructural/developmental constraints persist in the Chinese economy—namely, shortage of productive inputs and capital goods, lack of design standardization, and inadequate channels of market information—firms have saved on transaction costs by frequently continuing to deal with the partners to exchange with whom the planning system had paired them for decades. In replacing prescriptive relational contracting with relational contracting by preference, firms are reproducing the essence of the old state plan. The moral here once again is the durability of the pathways left over by the plan.

The sixth chapter, based on interviews in both Wuhan and the northeastern city of Shenyang and on documentary materials from 1987 and 1988, takes a look at the most astonishing reforms attempted by this still allegedly socialist state: bankruptcy, the sale of state assets, enterprise mergers, and shareholding. It makes the argument, however, that even these most radical reforms were actually the product of statist goals, not an attempt to reorient the economy toward privatization or, despite claims to the contrary, even toward any genuine separation of management from ownership. In this case the critical goal was to recoup for the central budget losses sustained when the first stage of reform—which had sanctioned decentralization of resources and decision-making power and had disbursed higher wages and bonuses, all in the interest of invigorating the economy—had gone too far.

The objective informing this set of reforms was to manage the state's macro finances, so as to save funds and check inflation, all the while preserving state ownership. Instead of being capitalistic measures they were instead a bureaucratically arranged regrouping of state-owned assets in the interest of garnering larger returns to the treasury. Along the same lines, the article shows how official agents were injected into the new markets to act as supervisors and middlemen in order to administer all of the new experiments in the best interests of the state.

In the process, the political power of state bureaucratic offices and their cadres was if anything enhanced as it became translated into "market" power. The conclusion here is that these capitalistic practices were simply overlaid atop the state-owned economy. Rather than remolding the old system they instead took on its features, as they were forced to adapt to the state's fiscal needs and purposes and as they were directed by the state's officers and other employees.

Chapters 7, 8, and 9 look at the reforms connected with the restructuring of geographical regions. Chapter seven grounds its discussion in the concept of "uncertain paternalism," which describes the Chinese state's paternalistic impulses and its variable capacity to realize them. When the state succeeds in realizing its provisioning ambition, localities settle into dependency; but when it falters, the argument reads, localities fall back on strategies of encapsulation. The state plan over the years only acted to reinforce localities' inclination to turn inward, as it encouraged each separate little region to fulfill state-designated tasks, and also to protect itself against need.

The essay demonstrates how an endemic local particularism suits the decentralization components of the reform program but vitiates other reforms that aim at the activation of comparative advantage. A dialectic dangerous for the center also emerged from reform's decentralization. The program was meant to save the center expenses by devolving some investment responsibilities, and by permitting producers and exchange partners to work in part from their own profits rather than just from state disbursements. But the localities' instinct to amass resources for themselves eventually came to threaten the key objective of revenue accumulation at the central state level. Thus, the leadership, in essaying to create wealth through state withdrawal, instead found itself bested.

Chapter 8 takes a look at a group of reforms piloted in Wuhan, all aimed at replacing the old economic system's vertical, bureaucratically organized channels of command and coordination with lateral, market-type linkages. Wuhan, as a historically experienced commercial entrepôt, transport node, and financial center, seemed eminently suited to become a showcase that could lend credence to the potential of the reform program as a whole.

Accordingly, in mid-1984 Wuhan became the first provincial capital nationwide to be granted economic powers equal to those of a province. Reformist leaders in the capital evidently hoped that the empowerment of this city could underline the overall reform program's dramatic shift in emphasis toward commerce as the source of economic vigor and toward decentralized decision making as the most potent incentive. But an investigation of how a number of reforms in the Wuhan urban economy have actually worked out in practice—reforms connected with the new economic powers, those in enterprise autonomy, those entailing the creation of new investment sources, and those creating new modes of circulation and exchange—once again reveals a statist underpinning that hobbled the formation of something like a genuine market. For here again, those in charge of reform in the locality were able simply to turn the old structure to advantage, by only ever so slightly adapting old offices, channels, behavior, and relationships to fit the new system.

With the state's own cadres as watchdogs, it often became possible to use the state's offices to channel, compete with, or control new institutions. Thus, looking closely, one found that the reforms presented a double image: there were free-wheeling ventures, but they were accompanied either by state oversight and intervention or by political facilitation. I conclude this chapter by commenting that the reorientation of the bureaucratic organization of business works where it does because the plan and its patterns prepared the way.

Chapter 9 concentrates on one particular urban reform among those sketched out in chapter 8, the creation of "central cities," again drawing on materials from Wuhan in the late 1980s. Here I show how the urban economic reform was motivated by the idea of shifting the defining principle of urbanism away from hierarchy and toward network, and of transforming the producer city into the commercial city. Once more the impetus was to stimulate growth: policy makers believed that bursting through the bureaucratic barriers put up by the plan would do this. Cities such as Wuhan were encouraged to emphasize their potential as centers of circulation so that horizontal linkages between cities and larger regions could replace the mandatory vertical ties of the plan.

Unfortunately, however, the endurance of a jealous administrative power at the next higher level, the province, and the absence of a fully operative market worked to deprive cities like Wuhan of the clout they should have won, and only tied the city more tightly to the center in defense. The persistence of vertical hierarchies of power, in short, limited the city's ability to organize its own, much less any larger regional economy. The upshot was that Wuhan became the center of a set of truncated networks ensnared within the old hierarchies.

The last two chapters, 10 and 11, turn to the treatment of the new merchant class, the putative "private sector," that has grown up with the reforms. Chapter 10, written in mid-1983, is about the small businesspeople who began to emerge in the early 1980s, and it tells of their sufferings as they attempted to gather a bit of capital of their own. Although the chapter sets out three disparate standpoints among the leadership (and among local cadres as well) as to how to handle the private sector, it highlights the persistent ambivalence among the central elite as to how unreservedly it ought to promote an active small trade sector.

Even those most favorable to the little capitalists supported them for their ability to foster economic growth, not out of any principled stand in favor of private enterprise. Moreover, the essay shows how, even at that early stage, the discovery of state deficits and inflation already led to clampdowns in the interest of better meeting what were thought to be social needs. In pointing to the shared commitment to socialist values among politicians, the article addresses the connection between state control and the people's sustenance in the minds of those shaping economic policy, and thereby comments on the linkage between bureaucratic values and methods on the one side and a notion of positive state power on the other.

Chapter 11, prepared in early 1990, examines the place of the successful

urban bourgeoisie in the Chinese social order at the end of the decade. In expos-
ing how its success has hinged on symbiotic ties its members have been able to
forge with state bureaucrats, the piece reveals the continuing prominence and
domination of the state, despite reform, and its unaltered social hegemony a full
decade after the reforms began.

For the state and its institutions for the most part remained the principal
source of start-up capital, the only owner of the means of production, and the
chief purveyor of market information. But, since bureaucrats had grown dependent on the skills and energies of the new capitalists, offering them opportunities
in order to coopt them into the state's structures, there was an implicit pact
between the two groups to sustain the stasis of this so-called transitional phase.

As the essays overlap and expand upon each other, a clear image emerges
from their data: the urban economic reform in China in the 1980s was designed
as an instrument to fine-tune a decrepit machine. But since the wielders assigned
to manipulate this tool grasped it with untrained hands, they were bound to use it
crudely, to resort to practices familiar to them, and to rely on associates with
whom they had worked before. And each time the tool faltered, those who had
bestowed it saw fit to take it back again, as they sought other modes of temporarily tinkering with their machine. But through it all, they never meant to trade the
new tool for their own machine.

Notes

1. For some of the recent literature on the reforms, see the following edited collections:
Victor Nee and David Stark, eds., *Remaking the Economic Institutions of Socialism:
China and Eastern Europe* (Stanford: Stanford University Press, 1989); Gene Tidrick and
Chen Jiyuan, eds., *China's Industrial Reform* (New York: Oxford University Press, 1987);
Richard Baum, ed., *Reform and Reaction in Post-Mao China: The Road to Tiananmen*
(New York: Routledge, 1991); Bruce L. Reynolds, ed., *Reform in China: Challenges and
Choices* (Armonk, NY: M. E. Sharpe, 1987); Bruce L. Reynolds and Ilpyong J. Kim, eds.,
Chinese Economic Policy (New York: Paragon House, 1989); and Peter Van Ness, ed.,
Market Reforms in Socialist Societies: Comparing China and Hungary (Boulder: Lynne
Rienner, 1989).

2. Gao Shangquan, "The Reform of China's Industrial System," in Tidrick and Chen,
eds., *China's Industrial Reform*, p. 135. At the time that he wrote these words, Gao was
vice-chairman of the State Commission for Restructuring the Economic System and chairman of the Editorial Board of the journal *China's Economic System Reform*. The reform
document itself can be found translated into English in *China Daily*, October 23, 1984.

3. Zhao's speech was translated in *Beijing Review*, November 9–15, 1987, pp. i–xxvii.

4. As summarized in Ma Hong, "Reform Is Also a Revolution: A Discussion on
Studying 'Deng Xiaoping's Selected Works' on Economic System Reform," *Hongqi* (Red
flag), no. 20 (1983): 28.

Part I

Policy Making and Policy Conflict over Reform

1
Economic Reform via Reformulation: Where Do Rightist Ideas Come From?

In the social struggle, the forces representing the advanced class sometimes suffer defeat not because their ideas are incorrect but because, in the balance of forces engaged in struggle, they are not as powerful for the time being as the forces of reaction; they are therefore temporarily defeated, but they are bound to triumph sooner or later.

—Mao Zedong, 1967
"Where Do Correct Ideas Come from?"

Any ordinary reader of the Western press has long since divined that the "pragmatic" economic reform proposals now being floated and tested in China would not have been Mao's vision of "correct ideas." Nevertheless, the views emerging recently are reruns, now being played through the system for the third time. The purpose of this chapter is simply to document the early PRC sources of some central tenets of the reform agenda that first resurfaced in 1978 and to inform observers of these reforms that China is not, as some have assumed, just now drawing up its plans by looking outward to Eastern Europe for inspiration for change. Rather, at least some of the more crucial recommendations and experiments being thrust centerstage over the past

This article was originally written in February 1980. A more sophisticated treatment of the issues addressed here appears in chapter 5 of my book on the commercial system and its politics, *Chinese Business Under Socialism* (Berkeley: University of California Press, 1984).

The following people read and commented on this paper: Shun-hsin Chou, Gardel Feurtado, C. Thomas Fingar, David S. G. Goodman, Richard C. Kraus, Jan S. Prybyla, Thomas G. Rawski, Bruce Reynolds, and Andrew G. Walder. I appreciate all of their suggestions, even though some did not find their way into my revisions.

few years are in fact closely tied to suggestions made in China as early as 1955, a few of which were even tested in 1956 and in the early 1960s.

The reforms were first aired this time around as early as March 1978, when discussions of the Yugoslav economy began to appear publicly. By the time of the Third Plenum of the Eleventh Central Committee held in December 1978, market-oriented politicians, most notably Chen Yun (named a vice-chairman of the party at that meeting, and within six months made head of the State Council's powerful newly created Finance and Economic Commission),[1] had managed to incorporate into the meeting's decisions the view that enterprises ought to have greater rights of self-determination.[2]

Since late 1978, an array of interrelated proposals has come forward, all of which revolve around the themes of indirect planning, enterprise autonomy, and the use of economic measures (fluctuating prices to reflect supply and demand; bonuses, wages, employment, and profits to act as incentives; bank loans, as against direct allocations, for investment; taxation of fixed assets; competition among firms; profit retention by enterprises; and interest rates) rather than administrative commands for managing the economy. Reformist and anti-Maoist as these suggestions may appear, for the most part the leadership of the late 1970s has been rehashing and reviewing, not first considering, much of their substance.[3]

Chen Yun and Xue Muqiao

One striking example of the parallels between ideas propounded by economists today and those of a generation past can be found in two major documents. The first is a speech given by (then and now) Vice-Premier Chen Yun at the Eighth Congress of the Chinese Communist Party in September 1956; the second, an article that received much publicity in mid-1979 by noted economist and State Planning Commission adviser Xue Muqiao.[4] Not only are nearly all the important measures that Xue puts forward contained in Chen's 1956 address, but several of these are couched, word-for-word (but without any reference to the past), in the very terms Chen Yun himself once used.[5] These measures, if put into effect, would constitute a major underpinning for a whole cluster of corollary policies.

Four key proposals in the Xue article are taken directly from the 1956 piece. First and most important, perhaps, is the theme of indirect planning. For the industrial sector, this opens up the pivotal notion of enterprise autonomy. Xue begins by telling his readers that it is impossible to include all kinds of products in the state plan, and he goes on to note that, "for the most part, state plans for state enterprises on matters of production, marketing, and so on are only for reference purposes." On this point, we find Chen Yun in 1956 lobbying at the party Congress for the view that "norms in the plan should be for reference only; let factories, according to the situation in the market, set their own norms in carrying out production, not restrained by the norms in the plan. Then, based on their end-of-the-year achievements, they should hand over profits."

Second, both men extend this proposition of indirect and partial planning to agriculture. Chen says that unified purchase will still be necessary in future for grain, economic crops, and important sideline products. However, small local sideline products, in 1956 monopolized by local supply and marketing cooperatives (SMCs), ought to be purchased as well by state stores, co-op stores, and co-op small teams so that goods can circulate freely. Similarly, Xue in 1979 advises sticking, for the present, to unified and negotiated purchase quotas only for grain and other principal agricultural products.

From here Xue leads into his third restated point, in his discussion of price policy. "Make use of the pricing policy," he advocates. "We must learn to regulate agricultural production by means of the law of value," he goes on. A look at the position Chen Yun advanced over two decades before quickly shows us that Xue has nothing in mind that would be new for China. In fact, even when Chen wants to "make price policy beneficial to production" and complains that the stable, frozen, and unified prices then in use are "a phenomenon bad for production," he too is only harking back to practices already implemented in the early 1950s.[6]

On this issue both men conclude with the same observation: Chen notes that "prices will eventually stabilize, and free buying and selling will lead to an increase in production and the balance of supply and demand; only production increases can guarantee price stability." In the same vein, Xue argues that "if the law of value were used to readjust prices . . . commodity prices would not go up universally. Instead, some prices will rise and some will fall. This rise and fall will bring the prices of various commodities closer to their real value."

The fourth area where Xue repeats the ideas of 1956 is in the relations between industry and commerce, or production and marketing. Here Xue recalls a scheme originally put forward by Chen, and first enunciated publicly by him on June 30, 1956, at the Third Session of the First National People's Congress.[7] This scheme, entitled "selective purchase" (xuangou), has been referred to by a Western observer as "an invention of Chinese right-wing communism."[8] When Chen proposed the scheme in June, he seemed a bit impatient, as he noted that nothing yet had been done along these lines. For, he reminded his listeners, he had already raised the intimately linked notion of specialized industrial marketing companies at a meeting of the National Association for Industry and Commerce held in November 1955.

Selective purchase, as Chen outlined it at the June 1956 convention (and reiterated three months later as his opening proposal at the Eighth Party Congress), was to entail the following. First, for products closely related to the national economy and the people's livelihood and having simple specifications, such as cotton yarn and cloth, charcoal, and sugar, the method then practiced of unified purchase of factory output and its guaranteed sale by state commercial departments should be preserved, to ensure supplies and stabilize the market. Toward ordinary articles of daily use, on the other hand, that method should be abolished, and the selective purchase system should be introduced (a system similar to the one in use before 1956). For these goods, commercial departments would be able to exercise preferences in their purchases, making their choices in accord with the quality of the goods and market demand. Items that remained unpurchased after this selection would be left to the factories either to sell on their own or to entrust to commercial departments to sell as the factories' commission agents.

Also, factories could freely select and buy raw materials that were not in short supply, and lower-level shops were to be permitted to select and purchase stocks from any wholesale organ and directly from factories anywhere in the country, rather than being the passive recipients of goods from their superior wholesale companies. The purpose was to make factories concerned about the marketability of their products and so to raise quality and suit consumers' needs. In Xue's 1979 reintroduction of this plan, both the scheme and its rationale are nearly verbatim.

A subsidiary suggestion is Chen's June 1956 plan (which he said then he had introduced the autumn before) for industry to organize specialized companies to manage factories' production and sales instead of relying on commerce to handle all processing, ordering, unified purchase, and guaranteed sales. Such companies were in fact instituted in late 1955,[9] but, as if they had never existed before, Xue's 1979 article contains a request that such companies be created. "Departments in charge of goods and materials may set up companies specializing in various kinds of goods and materials to provide consumers with what they need," he proposed. "Certain trades may establish specialized companies for marketing their own products, and contracts on the supply and marketing of goods may be signed between suppliers and marketing agents, giving scope to various forms of circulation."

Chen Yun first envisaged this arrangement as a necessary component of his selective purchase program.[10] These companies, once in use, were compared to the socialist industrial trusts of the Soviet Union.[11] It seems likely that Chen's design of late 1955 laid the seed that grew to be the Chinese trusts of the early 1960s for which Liu Shaoqi was given the blame during the Cultural Revolution. Thus this key address that Chen delivered a generation ago, resurrected recently by the pen of Xue Muqiao, offers the essential blueprint for many of the changes the Chinese have been considering: indirect planning, enterprise autonomy, fluctuating prices, and response to the market.

This fascinating incident of Xue's wholesale reintroduction of old ideas needs to be put into a broader context, which can be done by posing several questions. First, how widespread were ideas such as those promoted by Chen Yun in the mid-1950s? The relative prevalence of reform proposals then will make today seem even less exceptional. Second, did any of the proposals of that earlier period actually influence the economic policies of the day or at any other time between the mid-1950s and the present? Third and last, to what extent have the recent reform proposals been put into effect? Each of these issues is a large one, and this article will provide only indications as to their answers.

Proposals for Reform in the Mid-1950s
(with an Aside on the Writings of Xue Muqiao)

The first point concerns the climate in which Chen laid out his proposals a generation ago. It is clear from even a cursory retrospect that the period surrounding the Eighth Party Congress, where Chen delivered his seminal proposals, was a very open one for market-oriented economists. At the Party Congress itself, Chen's ideas carried the day, and in November 1956 he was named minister of commerce. Evidence of his victory appears in the Congress proposals for the Second Five-Year Plan, where his method of selective purchase for certain goods was to have been combined, just as he had suggested, with the continuation of unified purchase for grain, edible oils, and cotton.[12]

At the same meeting, Li Fuchun, then chairman of the State Planning Commission, like Chen took up the theme of indirect planning, calling for less detailed plans and more flexibility at the lower levels. In particular, Li proposed allowing lower echelons to set their own targets.[13] The reports of others at the Congress suggested that profit be made the main plan target for evaluating enterprises.[14]

Following the meeting, in the first nine months of 1957 official economic journals became arenas for the discussion of many promarket proposals, the topics of which are all echoed in the reform plans of today. Xue Muqiao himself foreshadowed his June 1979 article in early 1957 in a contribution to *Jihua jingji* (Planned economy) in which he advocated reducing the scope of planned management, which he said (as he did again in June 1979) cannot be carried out in the collective ownership system; using price policy to adjust purchase and sales, while retaining planned distribution only for certain important products; implementing selective purchase by commercial units and factory sales; and changing from a tight, mandatory, thorough plan to an indirect one, written according to market needs.[15] Later in 1957 he wrote, again in that journal, that planning controls ought to cover only a small number of vital products and that production planning for all other products must be determined by the enterprises according to supply and demand.[16] Schurmann presents Xue as the spokesman for Chen Yun's plans at the time,[17] and it is indeed clear that Xue was largely repeating ideas that Chen had put forward a year earlier.

There is no way to know the relationship between Xue and these reform proposals. As an aside, however, it is intriguing to note a certain inconsistency in Xue's writings over the years. Two *Hongqi* (Red flag) articles show that on several occasions he has bent his published views to fit the political line of the time. Thus in May 1959, as the Great Leap Forward began to falter, Xue published an article clearly straddling the fence in economic theory.[18] Although he does tell readers that everything cannot be put into the plan, he criticizes "modern revisionists" for denying the plan. While he recognizes the need to use prices for consumer goods and to let such prices fluctuate and even rise, he also pays tribute to the continuing importance of rationing as a means of price control. And whereas he notes that investment must be set by the plan, a political tool, its proportions are to be decided through economic measures, such as price and economic accounting. The article also is liberally sprinkled with references to how different the economic system will become under communism, a polite and careful concession, no doubt, to the proponents of the Leap.

A 1963 article, criticized in early 1965 by economist Sun Yefang,[19] goes much further.[20] Here Xue comes down decisively on the side of the plan, saying, for example, that "our means of production are allocated and their price need not be influenced by supply and demand." This statement is not only in opposition to his view of 1979 that "it will be necessary to relax our planned management of the means of production, using less planned allocation," but it also contradicts his own earlier words. Even in the Leap-era article, Xue suggests using the market (and not allocation by the state) for exchange among state-operated enterprises when he maintains, if obliquely, that "some comrades wrongly think there are no value categories or exchange of equal values within the state sector."[21]

In this 1963 essay Xue also voices concern about the "possibility that high free-market prices would make the peasantry ignore collective production," and so he recommends the planned adjustment of such prices to keep price levels in the free market close to those set by the state. Finally, he also worries about inflation in a way that he did not either earlier or later: inflation helps those with higher incomes win out, he opines, in a vein quite foreign to his usual style.

Lest we should begin to lose faith in the integrity of Xue, two further notes offer some insight into the political pressures on economists in socialist China. Just as during the Cultural Revolution self-criticisms were de rigueur (then, for cooperation with past conservative policies), so they have become again today. In the foreword to one of his recent volumes (this one a collection of his previously published essays), Xue at least apologizes for his past "errors": "once we entered the 1960s, we overstressed class struggle and political thought education, and neglected developing the productive forces and the modernization of scientific technique. My essays could not help being influenced by that period."[22]

Xue's other remark, which I read as a piece of ironic commentary on the role of the economist in socialist China, appeared in an important article on the employment problem in the *People's Daily* in mid-1979. "Some people worry," he comments, "that using the collective enterprise system in the city may be committing a mistake in line. They hope that those in theoretical circles will write more articles to prove that this system does not amount to the capitalist road."[23] Perhaps where a flexible ideology can be used to justify major alterations in economic policy in this manner, such shifts are easier to absorb.

Returning to 1957, many other economists besides Chen and Xue wrote in the journals in favor of market strategies. To give only a taste of their range, Sun Yefang, who achieved fame as a Cultural Revolution scapegoat, was already concerned then that profits remitted upward should be based on the financial condition of the enterprise, rather than being fixed as they still were in mid-1957.[24]

Gu Zhun, expressing himself in June of that year in *Jingji yanjiu* (Economic research), was attacked six months later (after the political climate changed on the eve of the Great Leap) for having favored free competition; having advocated that individual enterprises arrange their own production plans and organizational measures; having viewed the plan as a forecast that would have no controlling function; having encouraged enterprises to calculate their own profits and losses independently; and having proposed price fluctuation as a means of regulating production and circulation.[25]

A last example of this promarket rhetoric is an article by Zhao Qingxin, also in an early 1957 issue of *Jingji yanjiu*. Here Zhao criticizes the state commercial system for its monopoly-like characteristics, and he also speaks out for freer prices as against the stable prices of which the new Communist regime was so proud.[26] In short, a brief scan reveals quickly that many of the central proposals au courant today also formed the framework for discussion in the very midst of the First Five-Year Plan period.

Implementation in the 1950s and 1960s

If one can judge from the press of the day, at least for a period in the autumn of 1956 in the wake of the Eighth Party Congress, experimentation with a measure of enterprise autonomy in marketing did occur, at least in the model factories whose stories were written up in the papers. Such trials, where they occurred, were closely linked to the institution of Chen Yun's selective purchase scheme, which forced factories to be buyer conscious since, if their products were not chosen by the commercial units either because of poor quality or because their specifications did not meet market needs, these goods would pile up in factory warehouses and become the responsibility of the factories.

The factories would then have a choice: they could set up their own retail outlets, or they could entrust the state commercial departments to buy and market their leftovers. Both alternatives, however, meant economic loss to the enterprise—the first entailed the expenditures of managing the business outlet; the second involved payment of commission fees to commercial units.[27] Incentives in 1956, then, were of a negative sort. That is, enterprise retention of increased profits was nowhere cited in the proposals or the anecdotal press accounts as a possibility; instead, the hope of avoiding financial loss was intended to motivate compliance.[28] In the end, then, an enterprise's ability to adapt to the market would influence whether it could fulfill its financial plan to the state, since only enterprises whose products were purchased could avoid these losses.[29] Here then was a market-oriented reform whose ultimate sanction was tied to satisfying planned norms. Concrete instances of experimentation in 1956 included a whole-sale station in Luda that collaborated with a factory in Dalien to trial produce new kinds of women's shoes on the basis of the new situation in the market;[30] tales of factories selling their own products, and so caring about increasing their colors and lowering costs to suit consumers' needs;[31] enterprises buying raw materials and selling industrial articles of daily use with prices that oscillated (if only within a range regulated by the state);[32] and commercial departments refus-ing inferior products that did not meet market needs, and replenishing their stocks from anywhere in the nation.[33] "Go beyond the plan," exhorted a local paper, "adapt to a shifting market."[34]

Chen Yun's plans, then, were picked up and saw a bit of practice soon after they were enunciated. Within a very few months, however, this episode came to a halt. In January 1957, a State Council directive suddenly ordered that the relations between industry and commerce were to remain as usual in 1957. The reason given was that the new selective purchase system would have required changes in the taxation system too cumbersome to undertake quickly. That is, the decision explained, part of the profits that had been submitted to the state by the commercial departments' wholesale organs would have been passed to the indus-trial departments from which the state would then have collected them in the form of taxes. The State Council decision voiced a fear that some state income might be lost should industry fail to hand over the requisite taxes in sufficient quantity.[35]

Thereafter, this minimarket experiment and, along with it, the prerogatives of the commercial units, were slowly snipped away. By May 1957, the local press began to print articles of complaint from a typical industrial planner's point of view. "Commerce only cares about sales," charged one, "and not about factories' needs for balance in production. Frequently changing the ordering plan makes it hard to raise the level of enterprise management."[36] In the same vein, another paper accused commercial departments of ordering goods and then not buying them when the slack season comes.[37] By March 1958 the *People's Daily* held that "commerce is no good at predicting needs," so that commercial units should, as they had before Chen's experiments, simply guarantee to purchase whatever industry produces.[38] This short-lived exercise in market freedom was apparently beaten back by the proponents of the plan, not to reemerge until the Great Leap Forward had played itself out.

The Ninth Plenum of the Eighth Central Committee in January 1961 again explored the concept of market coordination. Although in-depth analysis of this period is beyond the scope of this chapter, it is clear that no wholesale alteration of the economy took place. That party plenum mandated that even major indus-tries must reorient production to the needs of the consumer, and the "independent operational authority" of factory managers received emphasis. Enterprise profit, according to Schurmann, became the major success indicator of the enterprise, in contradistinction to the First Five-Year Plan's gross product value. Advertising media helped to connect supply with demand more than in the past, and some changes that Schurmann noted in the financial controls placed on enterprises indicated that these were substituting for detailed production targets. Such changes were much like those being suggested today: reforms in banking, restraints on loans, and investment quotas.[39] Also, above-target profits were to serve as a basis for additional rewards.[40]

Articles in both theoretical economic journals and the daily press did take a cue from these new policies, but the impression these give is that the extent of free expression, the degree of market experimentation, and the time period all were limited. For instance, an article by Xu Dixin in an early 1961 *Hongqi* overtly criticized the Guomindang's "state monopoly capitalism." But this article could well have been a covert appeal to loosen the exclusive control over marketing exercised by the Communist state in 1961.[41] Later in the year, socialist commerce was praised for "serving the consumers," a seemingly leftist slogan, in a *Hongqi* piece that managed to insert as well some references to limits on the possibilities of planning, along with advice to pay attention to business accounting and to market research.[42]

More explicit recommendations were made in these years, advising that profitability and efficiency be made the foundation for investment, and that the forces of supply and demand, rather than administrative commands, set prices.[43] But the most extreme positions, such as Sun Yefang's advocacy of using the profit norm as the sole criterion for evaluating enterprise operations, of giving jurisdiction over depreciation funds to basic-level enterprises, and of generally expanding enterprise autonomy were for the most part not issued publicly. It was only when Chen Boda printed Sun's essays in *Hongqi* as negative material for criticism on the eve of the Cultural Revolution that they saw the light of day.[44] Furthermore, the uncertainties of this period were such that by early 1963 Xue Muqiao had submitted his very leftist-leaning essay to *Hongqi*[45] and even Sun Yefang himself openly denied the need for a bonus system and for enterprise profit retention.[46]

In the daily press of this period there were stories about the marketing arrangements of factories. But throughout this time such reportage did not describe arrangements bestowing on factories the degree of freedom lent by the 1956 selective purchase venture. Instead, one finds a search for a formula whereby industry and commerce can collaborate on an equal footing so that industry need not submit fully to the demands of a shifting market, and yet some direct factory-shop linkages might lessen the cumbersome qualities of a planned purchase system. Nowhere do we see factories freely marketing their own commodities, and if the profit principle was truly in practice as an incentive for sales activity, there is no indication of it in the papers.[47] With the Cultural Revolution, of course, all advocacy of profits and markets quickly subsided, not to reemerge in any force until 1978.

The evidence from 1956 and from the early 1960s is similar: in both periods proposals surfaced and were even made into policy, as at the Eighth Party Congress and at that Congress's Ninth Plenum. But despite some theoretical advocacy and a certain degree of implementation, at neither time did these experiments reach full fruition before a countercurrent, favoring the plan, obstructed a further extension.

Implementation Today

This brief review of two earlier phases of reform formulations and their fates has sketched out the background against which the current critique of the planned economy must be viewed. Only about a year has passed since the recent recommendations were enunciated as policy. It is already clear, however, that this time the experimentation, while still not as far-reaching as the ideas of some theoretical economists, has gone further and is being taken more seriously than at any previous time.[48]

Receiving the most publicity have been the one hundred test-case factories in Sichuan.[49] Here factories that could increase their profits for two years were told they would not have to turn over the increased portion to the state; 5 percent of normal profits could be retained by factories and invested as they wish; after fulfilling state quotas, these units could sell their excess products; and finally, they could purchase their own raw materials wherever they chose.[50]

In other parts of the country, Chen Yun's 1956 selective purchase design has been revived, but, unlike in the earlier periods, this time profits are clearly being used as the incentive to lubricate the operation of the system.[51] Tales of factories selling articles outside the plan have dotted the papers: in Canton, for example, loss changed to profit when a factory trial-produced a new item and improved it to accord with market demands.[52] In Nanjing, factories rearranged the priorities assigned to their planned items in the order of their respective marketability.[53] Retail shops in Hangzhou were permitted to replenish their stocks on their own from production units and brigade enterprises.[54] Textile factories are vying for the market, and an enterprising Chinese medicine shop in Beijing did market research and thereby beat out its competitors.[55] Interestingly, however, this time again official policy in this area has not gone as far as Chen Yun proposed in 1956 (and as Xue Muqiao seconded in June 1979). Nearly a year after the experiment had begun, a Canton radio report announced that both domestic commerce and foreign trade departments must make their procurements of industrial products in accord with the specifications of the plan, and that state commercial departments must monopolize the purchase and sales of products that are covered in the state plan. Selective purchase by these departments, as well as sales by the factories themselves, may only come into play for products not covered by the plan, or for products produced in excess of the planned quota. A Chengdu broadcast on the same theme in March 1979 added that, even for commodities sold outside the plan, state-regulated prices must be observed.[56]

Thus, the reforms much heralded in the Western press of late not only are not new ones in China; neither are they an untrammeled flight into a total capitalistic departure from the plan; nor are they merely inspired and copied from the Yugoslav system or from the mid- to late 1960s reforms most extensive in Hungary but also undertaken elsewhere in Eastern Europe.[57] The death of Mao and the arrest of his leftist allies, along with China's concomitant expansion of its participation in the world market,[58] probably have made possible and perhaps necessary this dusting off and dressing up of measures devised long ago domestically that limit but do not replace the plan.

Notes

1. This commission seems to have been dissolved by mid-summer 1980, although no reason for this has been given.

2. China Journalist Group, "Report from Yugoslavia: A Visit to the Sarajevo Energoinvest," *Peking Review*, no. 12 (1978): pp. 41, 42; see also *China News Analysis* (hereafter *CNA*), no. 1165 (1979).

3. A December 1980 central party work conference reemphasized central government control over the economy, in the name of "readjustment" of the proportions of capital going to investment versus consumption, and of the percentage of investment to be used for agriculture and for light industry as against heavy industry. *Beijing Review* (hereafter *BR*), no. 14 (April 16, 1981), notes that this will entail slowing down the tempo of the recent reforms (p. 24) and states that the State Council has decided not to extend the experiment in enterprise autonomy to any additional enterprises for the time being (p. 29).

4. Chen Yun, "Guanyu zibenzhuyi gongshangye gaizao gaochao yihou di xin wenti" (New problems after the high tide of the transformation of capitalist industry and commerce), in *Renmin shouce* (People's handbook) (hereafter *RMSC*) (Beijing: Da Gong Bao She, 1957) pp. 85–88; Xue Muqiao, "Zenyang jinxing guomin jingji di jihua guanli" (How to effect planned management of the national economy), *Renmin ribao* (People's daily) [hereafter *RMRB*], June 15, 1979, translated in *Summary of World Broadcasts*, June 23, 1979, FE/6149/C1-C6, and in *BR*, no. 43 (1979): 14–20. On January 29, 1981, *RMRB* (p. 5) published an article specifically praising the ideas in Chen's 1956 speech.

5. Whether Chen was the original author of these ideas is irrelevant. It is possible that Xue was their creator, if one wishes to believe a Cultural Revolution attack on Xue as a "villainous adviser" of Liu Shaoqi, Deng Xiaoping, Chen Yun, and others, and as the "henchman" of Chen. See *Beijing gongshe* (Beijing commune) (a Red Guard tabloid), March 22, 1967, p. 2.

6. Dwight H. Perkins, *Market Control and Planning in Communist China* (Cambridge: Harvard University Press, 1966), chap. 3.

7. Chen Yun, "Guanyu shangye gongzuo yu gongshang guanxi wenti" (Questions in commercial work and industrial-commercial relations), *Guangming ribao* (Bright daily), July 1, 1956. (Hereafter Chen, *GMRB*, July 1, 1956.)

8. P. J. D. Wiles, *The Political Economy of Communism* (Cambridge: Harvard University Press, 1962), pp. 168, 173, 175, 182, 186. Wiles is a British economist who specializes in Soviet and Eastern European economies, and his comment that the plan is a

Chinese invention is thus informed by his intimate knowledge of these other systems. For more information on the details of and debates on this system, see Zhang Wen, "Dui gongye pin di ziyou shichang yu jiage guanli di yijian" (Opinions on the free market in industrial products and price management), *Da gong bao* (Impartial daily) (hereafter *DGB*), December 9, 1956. As Andrew Walder has pointed out, although some of the Chinese ideas may be original, in general the leadership is now looking squarely at ideas prevalent throughout the Communist world since Stalin's death (private communication).

9. See Wang Hung-ting, "The Nature and Functions of Industrial Special Companies," *Xin jianshe* (New construction), no. 101 (February 1957), translated in *Extracts from Chinese Mainland Magazines* (hereafter *ECMM*), no. 83 (1956), pp. 6–16.

10. Chen, *GMRB*, July 1, 1956.

11. Wang, "Nature and Functions," pp. 11–12; Xu Dixin, "Push to a New Stage the Transformation of Capitalist Industry and Commerce," *Xuexi* (Study), January 1956; and Guan Datong, "Zhuanye gongsi dui gongsi heying qiye di jingji gongzuo he zhengzhi gongzuo" (The economic and political work of specialized companies toward joint public-private enterprises), *Xin jianshe*, no. 6 (1956).

12. "Proposals of the Eighth National Congress of the Communist Party of China for the Second Five-Year Plan for the Development of the National Economy," in *Eighth National Congress of the Communist Party of China* (hereafter *Eighth National Congress*), vol. 1: *Documents* (Beijing: Foreign Languages Press, 1956), pp. 245–46.

13. *RMSC*, 1957, pp. 108–11, translated in *Eighth National Congress*, vol. 2: *Speeches*, p. 301; discussed in Franz Schurmann, "Economic Policy and Political Power in Communist China," *Annals of the American Academy of Political and Social Science*, vol. 349 (September 1963): 54.

14. Schurmann, "Economic Policy," p. 55.

15. Xue Muqiao, "Zai lun jihua jingji yu jiazhi guilu" (Again on planned management and the law of value), *Jihua jingji* (Planned economy) (hereafter *JHJJ*), February 1957.

16. In *JHJJ*, September 1957, pp. 20–24, discussed in Franz Schurmann, *Ideology and Organization in Communist China* (Berkeley: University of California Press, 1966), p. 197.

17. Schurmann, *Ideology and Organization*, p. 208.

18. Xue Muqiao, "Shehui zhuyi zhidu xia di shangpin shengchan he jiazhi guilu" (Commodity production and the law of value under the socialist system), *Hongqi* (Red flag) (hereafter *HQ*), no. 10 (1959), reprinted in *Xinhua banyuekan* (New China semi-monthly), no. 10 (1959): 165–70. This article was criticized by Sun Yefang in "Lun jiazhi" (On value) in *Jingji yanjiu* (Economic research) (hereafter *JJYJ*), no. 9 (1959).

19. Sun Yefang, "Yao quanmian tihui Mao zhuxi guanyu jiazhi guilu wenti di lunshu" (Fully understand Chairman Mao's theory on the law of value), reprinted in *JJYJ*, no. 11 (1978): 11, but originally written in late 1964 and revised in early 1965.

20. Xue Muqiao, "Jiazhi guilu he women di jiage zhengce" (The law of value and our price policy) *HQ*, no. 7, 8 (1963): 1–9.

21. Xue, "Shehui zhuyi," p. 168. Catchwords such as "value categories" and "exchange of equal values" refer to market relationships and thus prices.

22. Xue Muqiao, *Shehui zhuyi jingji lilun wenti* (Theoretical questions in socialist economy) (Beijing: Renmin chubanshe, 1979), p. 1.

23. *RMRB*, July 20, 1979, p. 2.

24. Sun Yefang, "Speaking about 'Gross Product Value' " *Tongji gongzuo* (Statistical work), 13 (1957): 8–14, discussed in Schurmann, "Economic Policy," pp. 53–54.

25. Gu Zhun, "Shi lun shehui zhuyi zhidu xia di shangpin shengchan he jiazhi guilu" (A preliminary discussion of commodity production and the law of value in a socialist system) *JJYJ*, June 1957, criticized in Zhang Chunyin et al., "Bochi Gu Zhun guanyu

jiazhi guilu di xiuzheng zhuyi guandian" (Refuting Gu Zhun's revisionist viewpoint on the law of value), *JJYJ*, no. 6 (1957), pp. 27–38.

26. Zhao Qingxin, "Guanyu kaifang guojia lingdao xia di ziyou shichang di zhubu yanjiu" (Initial research on opening free markets under state leadership), *JJYJ*, no. 2 (1957).

27. *DGB*, October 20, 1956.

28. Schurmann, in "Economic Policy," claims that the November 1957 decentralization in industry first established profit as a major production target for enterprises.

29. *Jiangxi ribao* (Jiangxi daily), December 9, 1956.

30. *Luda ribao* (Luda daily), November 18, 1956.

31. *Gongren ribao* (Worker's daily) (hereafter *GRRB*), October 16, 1956.

32. *DGB*, October 5, 1956.

33. *DGB*, October 20, 1956.

34. *Guangxi ribao* (Guangxi daily), November 18, 1956.

35. Survey of the *China Mainland Press*, no. 1473, pp. 10–11, and no. 1497, pp. 5–6 (both 1957). See note 48 below.

36. *Chengdu ribao* (Chengdu daily), May 24, 1957.

37. *Changjiang ribao* (Yangtze daily), May 31, 1957.

38. *RMRB*, March 12, 1958.

39. Schurmann, "Economic Policy," pp. 62–65.

40. Schurmann, *Ideology and Organization*, pp. 297–98.

41. Xu Dixin, "Concerning State Monopoly Capitalism in Old China," *HQ*, nos. 3–4 (1961), pp. 38–46. Translations from *Hung-ch'i, U.S. Joint Publications Research Service* (hereafter *JPRS*), no. 8123: 59–72.

42. "Think of the Consumers in Every Way Possible," *HQ*, no. 17 (1961), pp. 1–4. Translations from *Hung-ch'i*, no. 47, *JPRS*, no. 11021: 1–6.

43. Merle Goldman, "The Unique 'Blooming and Contending' of 1961–62," *China Quarterly*, no. 37 (1969): 63.

44. Sun Yefang, *Shehui zhuyi jingji di rogan lilun wenti* (Certain theoretical problems in socialist economy) (Beijing: Renmin chubanshe, 1979), pp. 1–2.

45. See note 20.

46. Sun, *Shehui zhuyi*, p. 3. Like Xue, Sun apologized for this "error" in this volume published in 1979.

47. Numerous articles over this period bear this out. See, for example, *DGB*, February 18, 1961, where commerce is urged to help industry improve quality; *DGB*, March 8, 1961, where commerce gives industry the results of its market research so that product designs can meet consumers' needs; *RMRB*, July 29, 1961, in which commerce helps industry draw up its plan; *RMRB*, August 13, 1962, where commerce and industry sign production/sales contracts and commerce does not just supply materials and take finished products as in the past, but helps to improve quality; *Nanfang ribao* (Southern daily), November 2, 1961, where both sides (industry and commerce) work together on good production; *GRRB*, January 17, 1963, in which the two hold periodic meetings to sign contracts: and *DGB*, January 18, 1963, February 12, 1963, and February 19, 1963, all of which describe various forms of direct links between commercial and industrial units, but only for small commodities that are outside the plan does any genuinely free market-type exchange occur.

48. Although talk of enterprise autonomy is still current in China as of this revision (mid-May 1981), restrictions harking back to 1957 and the mid-1960s have been applied in recent months. Also, a State Council directive of December 7, 1980 mandated that henceforth enterprises could set the prices for only minor industrial products (*RMRB*, December 8, 1980, p. 1); and a subsequent order by the State Council attacking speculation

and smuggling ruled that industrial commercial administrative management departments should "strengthen their guidance and control" over sales by industrial enterprises (*RMRB*, January 16, 1981, p. 1). Moreover, the State Council decision to restrict autonomy to those enterprises already granted it, mentioned in note 3, was justified on grounds hauntingly similar to those used in 1957: "Conditions are not ripe for a comprehensive reform of the whole economic structure ... [and] as no all-round reforms are being undertaken, the enthusiasm of the experimenting units will inevitably be hampered by outside conditions. For instance, there can be no immediate correction of certain irrational regulations in the state policies of taxation and prices."

49. Nationwide, something over 6,000 enterprises, or about 1.5 percent of China's 400,000 state-owned enterprises, had taken part in the experiment by the end of 1980.

50. See *CNA*, no. 1165, and *RMRB*, September 1, 1979. A more recent reference, on the by-then over 400 enterprises carrying out this experiment in Sichuan, is in *BR*, no. 14 (April 6, 1981): 21ff.

51. "Baoxiao gai wei xuangou" (Guaranteed sales changes into selective purchase), *Shichang* (Market), no. 5 (December 1, 1979).

52. *Guangzhou ribao* (Canton daily), November 9, 1979.

53. *RMRB*, November 12, 1979.

54. *RMRB*, December 5, 1979.

55. *RMRB*, December 18, 1979.

56. Chengdu Radio, March 11, 1979, and Guangzhou Radio, October 26, 1979.

57. This is not to say that Eastern Europe, and Yugoslavia in particular, have not served as models for China's economic thinkers. Articles describing the Yugoslav workers' council system and other aspects of its economy appeared in Chinese journals as early as 1957. See Schurmann, *Ideology and Organization*, p. 86, and, for one specific example, Fang Shan, "The Economic Development in Yugoslavia" *Shijie zhishi* [World culture], no. 4 (1957), translated in *ECMM* 84 (1957): 13–17. Also, the discussion of market and profit strategies of the early 1960s was nearly coincident in time with (but actually began more than one year earlier than) the publication of the famous September 1962 Liberman proposals in the Soviet Union (first discussed in 1955 or perhaps even earlier) on using profit as the basic criterion of enterprise success and allowing management to devise its own plans based on orders negotiated with customers. See Alec Nove, "The Liberman Proposals," *Survey*, no. 47 (1963): 112–18. The point here is that, while Chinese economists were undoubtedly aware of events in Yugoslavia in the 1950s, or proposals in the Soviet Union in 1962 and the 1965 reform there, and of the Hungarian overhaul of 1968, the Chinese have had their own history of reform and its defeat, and this history stretches back to late 1955.

58. The economist Gregory Grossman has argued that "to a significant extent, *all* of the recent economic reforms or proposed reforms in Eastern Europe though not in the Soviet Union have as a main purpose to render the given socialist economy more effective as an earner of foreign exchange and as a gainer from the international division of labor." See his "Foreign Trade of the USSR: A Summary Appraisal," in *International Trade and Central Planning: An Analysis of Economic Interactions*, ed. Alan A. Brown and Egon Neuberger (Berkeley: University of California Press, 1968).

2
The Fifth National People's Congress
and the Process of Policy Making:
Reform, Readjustment, and the Opposition

At once to persevere in the socialist system and to carry out reform of the economic system: this produces a question of the proper limits; to concentrate power and to decentralize authority, but how much to divide power? Planned adjustment and adjustment by the market, but to what degree should adjustment by the market be developed? Not abandoning administrative methods but also utilizing economic methods, but how to utilize economic methods? To what extent should they be utilized?

These really are problems puzzling domestic politicians and economists. A conclusion cannot be hastily reached, measures cannot be rashly adopted; this requires time for groping, experimenting, and summarizing, *but the daily moving economy cannot wait for their* "investigations," it obstinately continues in motion and development day and night, influencing the interests of a billion people.[1]

It is a well-known fact to those who have been paying attention that two policies—reform of the economic management system and readjustment of the proportionate relationships among sectors in the domestic economy—have been repeatedly proclaimed in China over the past four years. And students of the PRC have also

This chapter was originally prepared for the Eleventh Sino-American Conference on Mainland China, Taipei, Taiwan, June 7–13, 1982. I greatly appreciate the time and suggestions of the following people who read this manuscript in an earlier draft: David Bachman, Robert Dernberger, Thomas Fingar, Gregory Grossman, Nina Halpern, Harry Harding, Joyce Kallgren, Michael Lampton, John W. Lewis, Ramon Myers, Thomas Rawski, Susan Shirk, and Michael Weininger. That earlier version was presented at the UC-Berkeley Center for Chinese Studies Regional Seminar, February 27, 1982.

©1982 by the Regents of the University of California. Reprinted from *Asian Survey* 22, 12:1238–75, by permission of the Regents.

noted that efforts to achieve each of these goals have at times floundered in a seeming morass of opposition. By focusing on the changing policies enunciated at successive meetings of the National People's Congress (NPC) from early 1978 through 1981, this chapter will discuss the issues over which this conflict has been played out in this period and the positions the contenders have taken.

Specifically, it will address the shifting modernization policies of the Chinese economy at the most general level of the policy debate and will illuminate the particular clashes of opinion among policy makers that have attended and indeed produced these shifts. The work reports of the government at the NPC meetings over these years, along with relevant press articles preceding and following the sessions, provide an excellent data base for the analysis since they reveal the instability, opposition, reappraisal, and compromise that have characterized the design of economic strategy in recent years.

The analysis is based on an understanding of the nature of Chinese politics that posits that the game of politics in the PRC has a heavy rhetorical component; that change in policy occurs in response to a mix of causal factors, both political and economic; that the government organ, the NPC, at least in recent times has had a more active role to play in the formulation of economic policy than has previously been assumed; and that a form of coalition politics, organized in this instance around three broad bodies of opinion, structures the process of policy making.

The rhetorical aspect of Chinese politics includes a number of elements crucial both to shaping the type of policy that is produced and to deciphering the meaning of public pronouncements. First of all, it has been the style of those professing all shades of opinion to overstate their claims for any new departure and in the process to discredit thoroughly whatever was attempted in a previous stage but later seen as unsuccessful. As a Hong Kong commentator put it: "The situation in China is never as rosy as the official press describes it in one period, and never as gloomy as it describes it in another."[2] Sometimes the shifts are indeed dramatic; at other times it is important to look closely at what is in fact being proposed, since it may be less new than it appears. Moreover, continuity is often camouflaged as new beginnings, discontinuities as constancy.

Thus, the leadership (and the propaganda media) have frequently disguised some continuity in policy over the past few years by making it appear that the country is to embark on a new departure, when in fact a slogan that received little notice when it was first announced is simply being reiterated. For instance, the goal of reaching "good economic results," widely publicized as "a new path for development" after the fourth session of the Fifth NPC in late 1981, was actually first mentioned in the first session in February 1978, a meeting later castigated for setting overambitious targets.[3]

Also, achieving a "comprehensive balance" and making efforts "within the limits of our capabilities," offered as changes in direction at the time of the third session in September 1980, were both mandated as early as December 1978 at the Third Plenum of the Eleventh Central Committee of the Party (hereafter, the Third Plenum).[4] Since the structural conditions of the Chinese economy—an agricultural base, an insufficient supply of consumer goods, and a high rate of investment in producer goods, basic industries, and capital construction over the years—have not basically altered, and since the most fundamental goals of the leadership—economic modernization and improving the livelihood of the people—have not changed, it is not surprising to note that the same calls to action reemerge over and over. But, no doubt to inspire fresh mass commitments with each new meeting, these words are repeatedly offered up as if the elite had just reached novel insights. Another latent function of presenting old lines as new ones may be to conceal the fact that the goals they stress have not been met by earlier efforts.

At the same time, stark discontinuities in line have been presented as being merely a continuation or amplification of previous popular policies. The most obvious example of this is the frequent reference to the decisions of the Third Plenum, a meeting credited in 1979 and 1980 as being the fountainhead for all subsequent experiments with market reform, decentralization of authority, and enterprise autonomy. The public would have to forget all they had read in the preceding two years to accept at face value the claim of continuity with this meeting that was made after the December 1980 party work conference, for this conference reimposed administrative controls (rather than economic ones), centralization and unification (instead of autonomy for enterprises and localities), and increased governmental intervention into the economy. Nevertheless, an editorial in the *People's Daily* that appeared soon after the December 1980 conference was entitled "No Change in the Party's Guideline." It reinterpreted the message of the Third Plenum to have entailed nothing more than the "emancipation of the mind," being resourceful, "seeking truth from facts," and getting united to look ahead.[5] While these phrases did indeed embody the spirit of that earlier meeting, the leadership of two years later stressed these more ideological invocations but thereby masked what was in fact a radical reorientation of method. As one observer in Hong Kong put it, "In propaganda, again referring to the Third Plenum is done just to calm the people's minds."[6] Similarly, the eight-character direction for running the economy—readjustment, reform, consolidation, and improving standards (hereafter, the eight-character policy)—first publicized at the second session of the Fifth NCP in June 1979 contains such scope for flexibility that it has easily served as the reference point for an array of reformulations in the two-and-a-half years that followed its initial announcement. In short, in interpreting policy, it is often necessary to peel away the accompanying rhetoric in order to know where change is and is not occurring.

Another assumption about the rhetorical style of Chinese politics is that the members of the elite are themselves extremely careful about the various shades of meaning they are communicating by the use of particular phrases, listings of priorities, qualifications, and omissions. The fact that three different leaders can seem to concur on a specific policy at one time but still explain the need for this policy in strikingly different terms, or can advocate the use of a certain measure but qualify how this measure is to be used in radically disparate ways, suggests that these men are intentionally making a point through their choice of language. This aids one in fathoming the demarcations among groups and individuals in the policy process. Thus, the leadership's arrival at some "general line" has never prevented speakers at political meetings from inserting their own biases and concerns into their speeches in subtle ways, even as they seemingly support what is offered to the world as consensus. A last dimension of this theme about rhetoric flows from the assumption that leaders have a purpose in selecting their particular wording—that is, they intend to use the open forum of the NPC to address and perhaps mobilize supporters, and to make known their differences in approach. Thus, the policy debate, though often apparently highly ideological and seeming to end each time with participants in general agreement, in reality contains important conflicts deliberately made public.

The second element in the framework for understanding Chinese politics upon which this chapter rests concerns the nature of causality in propelling change in policy. Here the rhetorical component just outlined plays a role. That is, because much that has been stated and even attempted in a preceding period has been done in an extreme manner, policy change must often take the form of correcting the excesses. Whether or not leaders have carefully considered in advance the possible consequences of a particular radical proposal, time and again the brush of a new scheme with the real world of policy execution has produced unforeseen side effects. It has therefore been necessary to revamp or retrench what was only recently put forward.

Also, the presence within the elite of a range of contending formulas for economic change (to be spelled out more fully below) has meant that these leaders have found it difficult to settle upon one firm, unwavering direction in economic policy over the past few years, and this in turn has contributed to the short-term nature of any particular victory. Any given winning position, unless it has itself been a sort of hodgepodge compromise, has eventually become vulnerable to critics affiliated with another standpoint. Thus, both external feedback resulting from implementation and internal political infighting account for shifts in line after brief intervals.

This investigation also posits that the NPC, at least in recent years, has served as more than a rubber stamp on decisions reached at the previous party meeting. Although the NPC may have merely reissued party decisions on occasion,[7] it seems that the NPC has more often acted as a forum for hashing out significant differences—for evaluating recent economic performance, for responding to political feedback that appeared in the press in preceding months, and possibly for garnering the support of particular social constituencies.

The more detailed and down-to-earth declarations that have issued from the sessions of the legislative body have frequently been the culmination of a period of trial, sometimes following months after party plenary meetings and even party work conferences. During such phases of experimentation, reports of opposition and reappraisals have been permitted to appear in the press. The statements that have emerged from the NPC sessions as government work reports have always taken these premeeting views into account, so that the wording of the government work reports (or the remarks of different speakers at the same meeting) sometimes contain inconsistencies and always show evidence of compromise.

Finally, the analysis in this essay is rooted in an assumption that a set of opinion groups or political coalitions have taken definite positions in the debate over how to modernize China in this period. Rather than subscribing to the more simplified characterization of the present leadership as a "pragmatic" faction that has already bested its rivals, the ideologues, the research for this study has instead uncovered at least three broad lines of fissure within the policy-making elite in recent years, or three separate stances on a range of issues about how to develop the economy. One of these advocates readjustment of sectoral relationships in the economy, and its proponents are most concerned with central planning and with the promotion of light over heavy industry. A second faction favors reform or "restructuring" and sees experiments in decentralization and the use of market principles as the most important tenets of policy. A leftover or catchall group supports various elements of the status quo ante the Third Plenum and opposes some or all aspects of the other two strategies. The members of this third group include backers of heavy industry, particularly branches of heavy industry such as coal and machine-building that have been shortchanged by the new policies. Also included in this group for analytical purposes, though not necessarily in full agreement with it on all issues, are remnant radicals who fear the ideological corrosion and corruption they associate with liberalization of the economy. Those taking these various positions will be referred to respectively in the pages that follow as the Readjustment Group (Adjusters), the Reformers, and the Conservers. Key politicians associated with (and indeed, perhaps the head of) each are Chen Yun, Zhao Ziyang, and Yu Qiuli (for the proindustry contingent among the Conservers, at any rate).

It is true that by the time the Fifth National People's Congress met in February 1978, the remaining members of the central elite reached a broad consensus on the goal of pursuing economic development above any other ends and on upgrading the management and performance of the economy generally in the course of modernization. In China, however, as in the United States, leaders of all shades of social and economic philosophy agree that inflation and unemployment must be reduced, but because of their quite disparate values, perspectives, and analyses, they choose very different strategies to deal with these issues and at the same time modernize China's economy.

This analysis in terms of three separate positions unravels certain oppositions and alliances that, without the aid of this approach, seem to add up to only two points of view. For example, readjustment has been combated from two different angles. Those in charge of provinces where heavy industry, especially coal and machine-building, is prominent resent the cutbacks, but they do not agree with most of the positions taken by the Reformers, who are also resisting readjustment but prefer to direct investment away from heavy and into light industry.

In an echo of the industrialization debates of the 1920s in the Soviet Union, when politicians and economists argued over how and how fast to modernize the economy of that country, an array of issues has entered the arena of discussion. In brief, discussions have centered on questions of using administrative versus economic methods to guide the economy; between centralization and giving more decision-making powers to localities and enterprises; over how speedily economic growth should be forced to occur; over the treatment of heavy industry; over the extent of permissible foreign trade. The various sessions of the NPC have come down on different sides of these issues, in large part in response to the clout of different coalitions at different times. Later sessions sometimes reversed the pronouncements of earlier meetings and sometimes returned to positions once taken but rejected in the interim.

With regard to these issues, Adjusters and Reformers agree on slowing down growth and on putting more investment into light industry, but they differ on the importance of central planning and on the timing of decentralization. Reformers favor carrying it out sooner, and Adjusters, later. Adjusters are more concerned about deficits and inflation than Reformers are, and the Conservers generally pay less attention to this issue than Adjusters do. Conservers, like Adjusters, *usually* are more oriented toward planning and centralization than Reformers are, although this is not always the case with the Conservers, and the two disagree on the questions of speed and on whether or not to invest more in heavy industry. Finally, Reformers are the most prone to advocate foreign trade, with Adjusters worrying about its effect on the budget and Conservers uneasy about the possibility of importing machinery that could be made by the factories in China itself. (See Table 2.1)

Although the documents from China and the assessments from Hong Kong that form the data base for this study reveal the existence of these conflicting viewpoints, they do not make similarly clear who the members of each group may be, beyond the few central-level officials who speak out for the various positions. It is probably easiest to speculate about the opposition, the Conserver group, which appears to consist of those who belonged to the several concentric rings of progressively less "left" politicians that Deng Xiaoping has successively peeled away over the years in his battle to establish authority and power for himself and his followers.[8]

The various segments of this pro–status quo ante group may not view themselves as a coalition and at best may only ally in a fluid fashion on selective issues. They do, however, all support a mobilization approach to economic development and have all at times received the label of "leftism" from the Deng faction as it attached this term to groups further and further from Mao as the

Table 2.1

Three Positions on Economic Policy: Various Issues, 1978–81

	Speed	Investment in light industry vs. heavy	Central planning	Timing of decentralization	Deficits, inflation	Foreign trade	Administrative vs. economic regulation of the economy
Reformers	Slow*	Pro-light*	Anti	Sooner	Less concerned*	Pro	Economic primary
Adjusters	Slow*	Pro-light*	Pro*	Later*	Concerned	Have reservations*	Administrative* primary
Conservers	High	Pro-heavy	*Usually* pro	*Usually* later	Some in this group don't pay attention to this issue*; others do	Have reservations*	*Usually* favor administrative

*Indicates agreement between two stances on a given issue.

period of his death receded in time. Among those who are part of this generalized "leftist" or Conserver group, the most vocal have spoken out for the interests of the coal and machine-building industries and against the "chaos" of the so-called capitalist practices that have accompanied the market reforms of the past few years.

Deciding who might be represented by the spokespersons of the Reformer and Adjuster groups can best be done by inference. The most obvious bases determining which point of view a particular group or institution is prone to support are the province in which it is located and the branch of industry with which it is connected. Most simply put, it is likely that those from provinces where there is an economic surplus would favor the local autonomy that is associated with the decentralization proposals of the Reformers, while poorer provinces would prefer the guarantees in the planned approach of the Adjusters. Both Reformers and Adjusters, however, have advocated shifting investment away from heavy industry, so that areas where heavy industry predominates would not, as a whole, support either of these stances.

On the other hand, various factors differentiating the several branches of heavy industry could incline their proponents to take various stances on the reform proposals. For instance, industries such as the coal industry, which suffers from low prices and relatively high tax rates (8 percent),[9] would have a particular animus against the reform plans because they allow enterprises to retain profits, a

retention contingent in part on the present price and tax structure. Other industries, such as oil, have lower tax rates (5 percent)[10] or higher profit rates (e.g., the
processing and textile industries)[11] and so may find things to gain from reform.
Too, competition between branches of heavy industry—for central-level or foreign firms' investment, or for the right to import foreign equipment, for example—may pit representatives of one industrial branch or one plant against those
of another. But it seems that heavy industry speaks with one voice on behalf of
continuing the high levels of funding for heavy industry as a whole, for capital
accumulation, and for basic construction that has historically characterized the
central plan in socialist countries. Spokespersons for this sector also agree on the
importance of the *speedy* or accelerated approach to growth that has been linked
with greater allocations for heavy industrial departments in socialist economies.[12]

The narrative below will relate the story of changing Chinese economic policy from 1978 through 1981 as enunciated at meetings of the Fifth NPC and as
argued over by proponents of the three opinion groups identified above. It will
follow the assumption that the members of the Chinese leadership choose their
words and their wording cautiously, purposively, and with precision, and so will
draw on some implicit rules of evidence derived from a close reading of the
Chinese press.

These include the following: it is essential in understanding a given speaker's
position to examine the reasons he gives for the failure of a given policy; to note
the order in which he lists his priorities or the priority that he assigns to one
strategy over others (often expressed by the order in which he enumerates possible methods for solving problems); to pay attention to the qualifying phrases he
may use in presenting a new general line; to perform a rough content analysis by
actually counting the number of times he refers to particular policies (e.g., Xue
Muqiao mentioned using "economic levers" *seven* times in an article that appeared in January 1982, despite the general consensus then to shelve reform for
the time being and concentrate on planning);[13] to watch for the use of key
slogans (such as "mobilizing the initiative of the lower levels," which has frequently entered the speeches of Zhao Ziyang even after the December 1980 party
Work Conference that aimed to recentralize the economy); to look at the positions the speaker attributes to the "some people" who almost invariably are
attacked in any speech; to keep in mind important catchwords that embody the
essence of a policy (such as "administrative interference" or "economic levers")
and check whether the speaker has introduced these into his talk, or, as frequently occurs, entirely omitted a phrase that is a principal part of a new policy,
thereby signaling his disapproval of it. All of these strategies of analysis have
been used here to compare different speeches delivered at roughly the same time
and thereby to come to conclusions as to the presence of conflict. These strategies have also helped in assigning speakers, or the institutions, regions, or enterprises on whose behalf they speak, to one of the three "groups" identified above.

From the First to the Second Session
(February 1978–June 1979):
The Conservers and Readjustment

In the years that followed it, the hapless first session of the Fifth NPC, held from February 26 to March 5, 1978, came under much censure. Its decisions, including the Draft Outline of the Ten-Year Plan for the National Economy (1976–85) that it announced, were castigated for being overly ambitious, leftist, and adventuresome because they emphasized speedy growth pushed ahead through the promulgation of what were later considered to be excessively high production targets.[14] Premier Hua Guofeng was given the job of delivering the government work report at this meeting, so whatever errors that document was subsequently believed to contain were laid directly at his doorstep.

It is true that this report spoke of the "construction of an advanced heavy industry," of "speeding up the development of the basic industries," taking "steel as the key link," of building 120 new large-scale capital construction projects, of putting an amount of investment into capital construction over the plan period that would equal or exceed the total invested in that area for the entire time from 1949 to 1976, of turning out 400 billion kilograms of grain and 60 million tons of steel a year by 1985. These various dicta, along with the promotion of the machine-building and coal industries (among others), mark the report as the handiwork of the faction within the Conserver group that favored heavy industry.

But it is an oversimplification to state, as later analysts have done, that the Conserver group (the Petroleum Faction, headed by Yu Qiuli, was then at the core of this group) subscribed to the same basic economic strategy as did the leftist radicals who surrounded Mao Zedong. According to one interpretation, the Petroleum Faction worked through the use of mass movements, used politics to motivate economic work, favored command warfare for directing economic activity, stressed heavy industry to the neglect of light industry and agriculture, rejected balance, sought high targets, high speed, and high levels of accumulation, ignored the question of the people's livelihood, and used strict controls in management but took great risks. The writer of this characterization claimed that the speech at the First NPC carried this line.[15] But Hua informed his listeners right at the start that the draft outline plan he was presenting was one only slightly revised from a document written in 1975 and attacked then by the Gang of Four as "the source of the right deviationist wind" and "a revisionist document." Thus the pro–heavy industry (or Petroleum Faction) group among the Conservers must be differentiated from the Gang of Four leftists, with whom such analyses often confused them, since this Ten-Year Plan was anathema to the latter group.

Hua also revealed in his speech that the present plan was the product of the highest authorities in China. First of all, it reiterated and expanded upon a grand design for economic modernization advanced by Zhou Enlai at the Third (1964) and Fourth (1975) NPCs. The State Council had compiled it by revising an outline first prepared on the instructions of Zhou in the summer of 1975, which itself had been discussed and approved by the party's Politburo at that time. Perhaps to give credit for the plan where it was due, Hua noted in another part of his address that Deng Xiaoping had been in charge of the country in 1975 as Zhou Enlai lay dying. Thus, this plan, both when it was first laid out and most likely when it was revised by the State Council in late 1977 (just after Deng's second rehabilitation at the Eleventh Party Congress) must have received Deng's sponsorship.[16] By the time the plan was found unworkable in 1979, Deng had switched to a different camp.

A third misunderstanding later encouraged by the leadership about this meeting is that its directives ignored agriculture and light industry. In fact, its first point is to "mobilize the whole nation and go in for agriculture in a big way"; it also mandated "a vigorous development in light industry." And, unlike at some of the later meetings, the authors of this address called for an increase in investment for agriculture and for more mechanization in that sector as well as for following the example of Dazhai and using scientific methods.

Perhaps most interestingly, many of the ideas that were subsequently associated with both the reform and the readjustment policies (neither of which had been introduced as of early 1978) first got a hearing at this meeting in Hua Guofeng's speech. Hua suggested reliance on existing enterprises as the foundation (rather than putting investment mainly in new construction); coordination and specialization (belying the subsequent criticism that those who prepared this plan preferred generalists); planned, proportionate development; and equal pay for equal work. In this same vein, what has gone altogether unnoticed in the period since is that for the first time since the death of Mao, market principles were alluded to in a central forum. This was still months before the Third Plenum, which has popularly been considered the beginning of promarket policies, and even some time before Hu Qiaomu (in the next month to be appointed head of the Chinese Academy of Social Sciences) delivered to the State Council in July 1978 his famous speech on observing economic laws. Perhaps with some behind-the-scenes advising from Hu, Hua's talk mentioned that "the law of value [which applies to using economic criteria, such as price and profit, to direct economic activity rather than just following politically determined directives] must be consciously applied under the guidance of the unified state plan," and he maintained that it was necessary to "fully utilize finance, banking and credit [later referred to in Hu's address as "economic means"] in promoting and supervising economic undertakings to spur all enterprises to improve management."[17]

This early reference to market principles, though, was made in tandem with commands that seemed to contradict its spirit, probably an indication of continuing uncertainty and/or conflict within the elite over the shape that growth should take.[18] For instance, it gave directions to "bring all economic undertakings into the orbit of planned, proportionate development," and, while transferring certain enterprises to the localities, to ensure that "the central authorities, instead of washing their hands of these enterprises, . . . enthusiastically assist the local authorities to run them well; . . . the center and the localities should work for the strengthening of the unified leadership of the central authorities."[19] Thus, the conclusion to be drawn was that the heavy hand of the central plan was to remain at the helm.

In short, the first session of the Fifth NPC, though advocating in the main the ambitious approach of the Conserver group, contained as well a representation of the views of the Reformers, then rising into ascendance. Interesting too is that more than two years of investigation and study had been required before the plan presented here could be made public, during which time its proponents had to overcome resistance from the supporters of the Gang, and it also absorbed new opinions coming to the surface. Though its optimism about the capacity of the economy had later to be corrected, this plan itself carried the germ of many of the ideas later presented as modifications of it.

The Third Plenum, which met more than nine months later (December 18–22, 1978), picked up and emphasized these early sprouts of capitalism with which Hua had peppered his address. But for those who were watching closely, the switch from "leftism" to use of the market was not nearly so abrupt as the detractors of the first session's plan have propagandized. For one thing, in the talk entitled "Observe Economic Laws" that President of the Chinese Academy of Social Sciences Hu Qiaomu delivered to the State Council sometime in July, he explicated at some length the notions of reliance on "objective economic laws," planned proportionate development, the law of value, linking enterprise management with the material interests of the staff and workers in them, putting the people's livelihood ahead of the development of production, increased specialization and coordination, and reducing reliance upon purely administrative methods to carry out economic work; and he hinted at profit retention by the enterprises.[20] That these ideas, however, were in the air after the first session of the NPC but before Hu made his remarks to the State Council was evident from a perusal of the documents of the National Conference on Learning from Daqing and Dazhai in Finance and Trade, held in late June and early July. In Hua Guofeng's own speech at that meeting, he referred to economic levers, "objective economic laws," and the law of value, as did an article in the *People's Daily* that reported on the meeting.[21]

According to a Hong Kong journalist, conflict within the higher reaches of the party over Hu's talk delayed its publication in the pages of the *People's Daily* until October 6.[22] This account maintains that opposition throughout the party was rooted in habit, which it was difficult to reverse all at once, and also derived from the feeling of some bureaucrats, long acting as basically uneducated generalists, that this new policy would conflict with their personal interests. One early and immediate sign of resistance was the publication in the *People's Daily* of a Thirty-Point Decision on Industry in early July, which put far more emphasis on strengthening unified state planning than it did on market principles and economic laws.[23]

The Third Plenum has become famous for its call to "shift the emphasis of our party's work and the attention of the people of the whole country to socialist modernization."[24] As if the first NPC session had not also placed agriculture (and indeed even increased investment in agriculture) at the top of its list of priorities, this meeting stressed that "the whole party should concentrate its main energy and efforts on advancing agriculture as fast as possible."

As noted above, this convention made its mark by introducing to the nation the approach of the Reformers in its call to change the methods of management and in its dictum that "it is necessary boldly to shift [authority] under guidance from the leadership to lower levels so that the local authorities and industrial and agricultural enterprises will have greater power of decision in management under the guidance of unified state planning." Once again it took up the refrain of economic laws, the law of value, and economic methods; and, in its disapproval of the past policy of egalitarianism, it underlined Hua's concern about equal pay for equal work (from the First NPC speech) and Hu's mention of linking the enterprise's success with the material interests of the workers.

This meeting also contained a mixed message, however, and one that was not well publicized at the time or even soon thereafter. As well as being the forum that first explicitly formulated for the public the principles of the Reformers, it was also the place where the slogans of the Adjusters first had a hearing,[25] for its communiqué spoke of "comprehensive balance," laying a "solid foundation" for rapid development, working "within the limits of our capabilities to carry out capital construction actively and steadily and not rush things, wasting manpower and material"; and it referred to "some major imbalances" in the national economy that "have not been completely changed." Its line on the improvement of the people's livelihood is no different from that of Hua's February address, since it states that "it is imperative to improve the livelihood of the people in town and country step by step on the basis of the growth of production." With its focus on agriculture, this meeting made no determination on the relative weight to give to the separate branches within the industrial sector. Still, with its emphasis on market principles and decentralization, and its charge to avoid haste and waste, it does represent a shift from earlier in the year.

The need to readjust imbalances in the economy that the Third Plenum's communiqué hinted at received much more discussion in the months just after the issuance of that document. In the spring of 1979, the Politburo's Standing Committee held a meeting at which Vice-Premier Chen Yun proposed the notion of economic readjustment. According to a Hong Kong journal, Li Xiannian, representing the State Council, explained this direction at a Central Party Work Conference in April 1979.[26] Apparently, by that point it had become clear that the program propagated in early 1978 was too grandiose to be accomplished with China's scarce resources and present economic structures.[27]

Decisions were made to reduce the scale of capital construction; to shift the emphasis in development from steel production and heavy industry generally toward more investment in agriculture and light industry, thereby righting the proportionate relationships among branches in the economy; and to stress consumption proportionately more and accumulation relatively less. Top economic theorist Xue Muqiao wrote several years later that it was at this conference that the eight-character slogan—readjustment, reform, consolidation, and raising standards—was first enunciated, a slogan that would be the catchword for all economic policy pronouncements over the next few years. Xue credited this meeting with having rectified errors in the economic work of the preceding two years and with having cleared up mistaken leftist influences that had existed for a long time.[28] The Hong Kong source, however, commented that "most of the people within the party did not understand" this policy and that the deficit, inflation, and overissuance of currency that were uncovered in late 1980 were the result.[29]

Lack of understanding was probably not the major issue, for resistance to this new direction would have been the predictable position for those still tied to the Conservers' point of view. Even though the second session of the NPC that took place only two or three months later (June 18–July 1, 1979) took up and popularized the eight-character slogan from the April meeting, it appears that the major speakers here were not in accord with all of that April meeting's deliberations.

Thus, Hua carefully defined the term "readjustment" as meaning:

> making conscientious efforts to rectify the serious disproportions in our economy caused by long years of interference and sabotage by Lin Biao and the Gang of Four to bring about relatively good coordination in the growth of agriculture and light and heavy industries and of the various industrial branches and to maintain a proper ratio between accumulation and consumption.[30]

This formulation said nothing, however, about the decrease in the tempo of development or the reductions in heavy industry and in accumulation that the April meeting had mandated. Indeed, Hua actually continued to call for "high-speed development" and for expanding all branches of the economy, including heavy industry. He did say that throughout the next three years, the various sectors of the economy should develop "in a harmonious way." But he stated only that light industry and textile production would grow "in pace with or slightly faster than heavy" and that the output of major light and textile industry products should increase merely "as domestic purchasing power rises." At this meeting Hua gave permission to the machine-building industry, among others, to increase its output. He did call attention to "imbalance in many respects within and among industrial departments" and to the fact that in capital construction, which he noted needed to be curtailed, "far too many projects were being undertaken all at the same time." Still, it seems that these words belie his intent, if speed and the growth of heavy industry were to be permitted to go on.

Saying that "readjustment" was "crucial for the economy as a whole," Hua went on to speak of a need to rectify "shortcomings in the structure of the economy and of enterprise management." But at this point, when the Reformers, in the wake of the Third Plenum, were already beginning to popularize their new schemes for decentralization, his plan was quite cautious, as is apparent in his discussion of "restructuring":

> After exploration, experimentation, and practice over the coming three years, we must formulate a series of measures that will give industrial, agricultural, transport, communications, and cultural enterprises the necessary power to make their own decisions and take initiatives in production and management *in accord with the needs of society* [i.e., not in accord with the law of value; emphasis added].

Head of the State Planning Commission Yu Qiuli was even more emphatically unenthusiastic about readjustment.[31] He went so far as to praise the work that had been done in economic affairs over the past two years: "The planned rate of growth will be lower than that in the past two years. This is because the growth in those two years consisted to a considerable degree in economic recovery." His defense of that period when he was in charge of much of the economy[32] placed him squarely in opposition to both the Adjusters and the Reformers, who all wished to reorient the economy, expressly to rectify what they believed to be gross mistakes in the work of those years.[33]

In Yu's vision, heavy industry was to grow by 7.6 percent and light by 8.3 percent as part of a program of "sustained, proportionate and [again] high-speed development." He did admit that "a major aspect in readjustment work is the rational arrangement of the scope of capital construction and the proper allocation of investment in the light of our financial and material resources, so as to raise the efficiency of such investments." But he went on to add that "despite reduction, the scale of investment is still fairly large." He also noted that a major portion of investment would go to coal production, referring to key projects centered on the eight mining areas in Shanxi, Hebei, Liaoning, Anhui, and Shandong, which is of interest in the discussion of the third and fourth sessions below.

Another issue in Yu's address that bears on the continuing controversies in this period are his worries about the process of "consolidation," which entails suspending or merging inefficiently operating enterprises:

> Of course, the cessation or suspension of the construction of some projects will cause some losses. For instance, part of our construction workers will be left idle, as will some production equipment already arranged for. We should check and clear up orders contracted for equipment, readjust production plans,

divert construction workers to other projects and maintain and protect those projects whose construction is to be halted or put off for the time being, in order to reduce losses to the minimum.

This concern for the social effects of readjustment later fell subject to criticism from the Adjusters, as will be seen below.

And though Yu followed Hua's line in proposing an increase in funds for agriculture, along with the mechanization of this sector and in advocating faster growth in the light and textile industries, Yu had nothing whatever to say on the subject of reform, decentralization, and autonomy for the localities. Also, he expressed concern for stable and controlled prices, a preference that indicated his Conserver antimarket orientation. In contradistinction to Yu's approach, and even to some extent to Hua's, an article in *Beijing Review* that appeared as the Congress continued in session took quite a different emphasis.[34] For instance, it spoke of beginning to carry out reform simultaneously with readjustment, of integrating the adjustment of the plan with the regulation of the market, and of expanding the powers of the localities and of the enterprises. It went so far as to suggest that the state-owned enterprises "must become genuinely independent units of cost accounting responsible for their own profits and losses," a position more extreme than any yet proposed at an NPC meeting (the usual formulation terms them "relatively" independent). Though this article spoke as well of comprehensive balance, planned and proportionate development, and the consolidation of enterprises, its rather extreme statement on the subject of reform is evidence of the range of opinions current in summer 1979. In doing so, it helps to highlight the extent to which Yu Qiuli, for one, stood apart from both the Adjusters (to judge from what is known of the conclusions drawn at the April Party Work Conference) and the Reformers.

All in all, it seems that the second session was meant to retrench the plans laid out at the first by introducing into the public domain the concept of readjustment. This adjustment was meant both to temper reform and to cut back on excessive modernization goals enunciated in early 1978. However, since the speakers at this meeting were still the representatives of the Conserver group, neither readjustment nor reform received a full hearing at this time.

From the Second Session to the Third
(Summer 1979–September 1980):
The Uncertain Heyday of Reform

More than a year passed between the second and third sessions. A close reading of the press over this period reveals that much controversy among all three positions marked these months. This is corroborated in an analysis by a Hong Kong journalist who maintained that "after June 1979, following the implementation of the policy of readjustment, the weaknesses of the Petroleum

Faction's original designs for China's economic development—weaknesses in not fitting objective laws, and in not working within the limits of capabilities—were revealed, and the differences between the factions sharpened."[35] For one thing, during the autumn of 1979, an open debate appeared in the pages of the *People's Daily*, in which adjustment (centralization) was pitted against reform (decentralization).[36] By the following spring, the Ten-Year Plan that had been associated with the Conserver group and presented at the first NPC session in early 1978 was junked altogether, and Yu Qiuli lost his position as Head of State Planning to Vice-Premier Yao Yilin (who had long been affiliated with the domestic commercial sector), although these moves were not yet announced openly.[37]

Either as a form of self-criticism or in an effort to prove that his own style in planning work jibed with the values then being brought into vogue by the Adjusters, Yu Qiuli had an article printed in the *People's Daily* in May 1980 in praise of Li Fuchun. Li, by then deceased, had directed State Planning in the 1950s with the aid of Chen Yun and Zhou Enlai, according to the paper.[38] In Yu's account, Li (who, Yu noted, had been his mentor), had achieved good results in planning by stressing the Adjuster tactics of comprehensive balance, proportionate relations among economic sectors, and objective possibilities. Setbacks, he said, had come from not paying adequate attention to objective realities and from setting too high targets. Still, Yu managed to mention "high-speed growth" twice, thus inserting his own pet concerns. Though the article was said to have been written in honor of the eightieth anniversary of Li's birth, it certainly signaled that a change was being advocated in the sphere of state planning.

This bit of indirection, in its subtle reference to the disfavor in which Yu Qiuli and his methods then stood, represented the fact that Chen Yun and his Adjusters had at least overcome the Conserver group, if not yet the Reformers, for the paper at the same time also presented the views of the Adjusters in opposition to the Reformers. One article explicitly noted that "readjustment is key now," even though, it went on, "one kind of viewpoint thinks that weaknesses in our country's economic system are very many, and that this [readjustment] presently is the main obstruction to economic development. . . . [T]hey advocate making reform the keypoint of our eight-character direction . . . but this is one-sided." This stance on the primacy of readjustment held sectoral adjustment to be necessary to establish the requisite "external conditions" for reforms in management and enterprise autonomy. It also maintained that setting the proper conditions for the reforms, through readjustment, would require some seven to eight more years.[39] Previously the two strategies had been billed as taking place in tandem.

But in the same month, an essay in *Red Flag* journal, echoing a speech delivered in Sichuan in March by Zhao Ziyang, warned, in defense of the reforms, that one "should not use problems [in reform] as an excuse for going back to the old methods."[40] An additional piece of evidence that a high level of controversy characterized this period is the fact that although Chen Yun's views on behalf of readjustment, first enunciated at the Party Work Conference in April 1979, were now being reiterated in the paper, they had not yet been fully accepted at any NPC session.[41] Indeed, although another session (the third) was held in September 1980, Chen's proposals still did not gain a real hearing; they were not fully brought out into the open for another three months beyond that. Meanwhile, the State Council continued to endorse reform by passing a very liberal report of the State Economic Commission in August on expanding and extending the autonomy of industrial enterprises.[42]

Aside from these disagreements about the nature of planning (through high targets and speed, or with deliberation) and over readjustment versus reform, the expression of other sorts of unease, probably brought forward by an antimarket faction within the Conserver group, made its way into the political process during this time as well. Concerns about mounting inflation in the wake of the market reforms became serious enough that by April 1980 the party's Central Committee and the State Council issued a joint directive on strengthening price management.[43] In June, the *People's Daily* recommended a kind of "socialist competition," in opposition to the practice of "some districts and enterprises" that "keep secrets about progressive technique, not in the socialist spirit," a view that showed some displeasure with unchecked market freedoms.[44] Other articles from this period criticized behavior induced by the material incentives of the reform policies and so indirectly castigated profit-seeking. The acts censured ranged from short-weighting pastries, to destroying bamboo trees and other natural resources in order to sell them in the market, to polluting food products with coloring in order to solicit business.[45]

Similarities existed between the tone of this carping and earlier words of other Conserver spokespersons since both Yu Qiuli and Hua Guofeng had addressed the problem of price stability and price controls in mid-1979 at the second NPC session, before the market initiative had gotten far under way, and Hua had mentioned this issue in February 1978 as well, at the first session. In any event, the opponents of this pro–heavy industry group chose late summer 1980 to expose a costly and fatal disaster on an oil rig stationed in the Bohai Gulf—an incident that had actually occurred months before, in November 1979—for which the Petroleum Faction of the Conserver group could be held accountable. As one source put it, "The Bohai incident removed a great stumbling block from the implementation of the New Economic Policy."[46] Following this enormous humiliation for those in charge of oil drilling and for others associated with them in other fields of heavy industry and in state planning, Yu Qiuli could then openly be removed from his job without much public questioning. Soon thereafter, in late August 1980, the third session of the Fifth NPC was convened, and this was the session most prone to the promotion of reform.

This meeting, however, involved far more than the enthusiastic endorsement of free-market principles attributed to it by the Western press.[47] Major speeches by a number of top economic officials contained different emphases since each speech writer had to make choices about the extent to which his talk would or would not respond to the concerns that had surfaced in the media in the preceding months, even without the need any longer to respond to the recently vanquished Conserver group.[48] These concerns had found expression in the debate over the relative importance to accord to reform versus readjustment and to problems of inflation, and over whether competition was appropriate in a socialist setting—concerns documented above.

Both Premier Hua Guofeng and Yao Yilin, the newly named head of State Planning who now took the place of Yu Qiuli, delivered major addresses.[49] Neither evinced any particular worry about the problem of inflation, although each did mention unnamed difficulties in the experiment in structural reform. However, both introduced new formulations in their discussion of the market initiative, formulations that subtly limited the scope of the freedoms, even as they called for a further expansion of the program. In this regard, they did take account implicitly of the proreadjustment views advanced in the May *People's Daily* articles by implying that reforms could no longer be pushed full steam ahead. Also, both supported not the unadulterated competition of the early August State Economic Commission report,[50] but, in Yao's words, "the socialist cooperative spirit" and "competition under the guidance of the state plan," and, in Hua's, "competition . . . in conditions permissible under socialism."

On the subject of enterprise autonomy, Yao authorized it, but it was to be under the guidance of the plan and exercised only after state-set quotas for production had been met. Too, only one, and the sixth at that, of the eight tasks he listed was in support of market adjustment. But here again, his wording suggested a note of caution: "Carry out market adjustment under the guidance of the state plan. . . . [T]he state plan should do well the work of comprehensive balancing." Here it is apparent that, even though Yao wished to "expedite experiments in restructuring the economic managerial system," giving the enterprises greater power (under the plan's guidance) than they had at that time, he was mindful of the need for overarching direction and supervision from above. But Yao's assessment, on the whole, was that the economy was "livening up," and that the market reforms had produced good results—in increase of output, in output value and profits, in arousing the enthusiasm of workers and staff, in improving operational management, and in bettering the quality of products.

On the subject of the work done in readjustment, Yao was essentially optimistic, claiming "marked progress in economic readjustment." While he did take note of the deficit (which was 17 billion *yuan* in 1979, 12 billion in 1980), he seemed to excuse this: "Financially, we are still operating in the red. The readjustment of the national economy is a highly complex and difficult task and some contradictions and difficulties are bound to appear. . . . [T]hese problems can be solved step by step." And he simply advocated continuing to carry out the eight-character policy, to achieve a coordinated development of the various sectors in the economy.

A few of Yao's remarks on the theme of readjustment provide clues as to why representatives of the interests of heavy industry have been dissatisfied with this program: coal and oil production had slowed down (and here one must recall the emphasis that Yu Qiuli had directed to investment in coal production at the second session); machine-building was operating under capacity; and plants in the heavy industrial sector were told to transfer part of their productive capacity and of their technical forces to the production of consumer goods. In sum, Yao's speech exuded confidence about the overall state of the economy and favored a tempered continuation of reform.

Hua's speech had generally the same tone. However, it seems that, even as he endorsed an extension of the decision-making power of the enterprises, going so far as to call for giving them—"under the centralized leadership of the state"—the "necessary power for genuinely [not relatively, as was then the case] independent decisions," he managed to inject a bit of old leftist philosophy. For he, unlike any of the other speakers, but in reiteration of his own remarks at the second session, proposed that "an enterprise should have the right independently to carry on production, exchange and other economic activities *according to the needs of society* and the law of value" (note the order: society first, law of value second; emphasis added).

Among the other top central-level officials who spoke at the meeting, two took sanguine views of the state of the economy along the same lines as Hua and Yao. Thus, in an opinion that would soon be overridden by acclaim, Minister of Finance Wang Bingqian remarked that "China's financial deficit last year did not cause any big increase in the issue of paper money, nor did it bring serious difficulties to the economy."[51] And Vice-Premier Wan Li, whose name has repeatedly been associated with the design and propagation of the reform program, announced that "China will hold to her present course in economic reform so that the Chinese people may give full play to their initiative." Wan went on to reveal that the question of whether or not to report the deficit to the public had been discussed among the top leadership several times and that the conclusion had been, in short, that "the state has difficulties but the people's livelihood has improved."[52]

The words of others, though, foreshadowed what later appeared to observers to be an abrupt turnaround that came a mere three months later. Peng Zhen, in his capacity as vice-chairman of the Standing Committee of the NPC, delivered a report on the work of this body in which he conveyed the information that some members of that committee had been complaining about rising prices and the excessive issuance of bonuses by some areas. They demanded, he relayed, tighter price control in order to end these abuses.[53] More pointedly, Liu Zhongfu, director of the State Price Bureau, expressed explicit concern about the rises in prices, which he claimed had resulted from serious imbalance in the economy and from the gap between the availability of commodities and purchasing power as well as from the illicit behavior of enterprises in raising prices "at will" to earn greater profits or to create more funds for larger bonuses for their staff and workers.[54] Unlike Hua, Yao, Wang, and Wan, then, this man in charge of price stability proclaimed the "main task" now to be that of strengthening price control rather than simply carrying on along the present course. Thus, the speeches of top officials showed definite evidence of differences in viewpoint and perspective and of some stock-taking that had taken place in the period since the previous session. These occasional fine shades of distinction were enough to lend a tone of inconsistency to the totality of the pronouncements and to provide a sense of possibly unstable compromises having been struck.

Among the deputies, however, the disparities in position were glaring. Indeed, even within provinces, at times no effort was made to present a united block of opinion; different deputies from the same place voiced support for incompatible measures, probably representing the fact that each spoke for different economically based constituencies. The looseness of the eight-character slogan, which could be made to stand for many things, and the debates that had earlier appeared in the press, as well as the open atmosphere of the third session generally, no doubt all gave leeway for a range of views to be expressed. Again, drawing on the threefold distinction presented earlier in this chapter, the various views of the delegates on the topic of domestic economy can be subdivided into three stands: those who favored reform, those who represented heavy industry, and those who for one reason or another supported some aspect of readjustment. Though the top-level officials who had supported heavy industry had now lost their standing, spokesmen from the provincial level continued to speak on its behalf.

Supporters of reform generally came from areas that had benefited from the flexible economic policies of the past few years: a spokesman from Guangdong; a speaker for the Shanghai textile industry; deputies from Sichuan who listed the advantages of expanding the decision-making powers for enterprises; the chairman of the Anhui Provincial People's Congress, who declared that the policy of enterprise autonomy, in which one hundred enterprises in Anhui were participating, was paying off; and a representative from a machine-building plant in Liaoning, who claimed that, since the plan had cut back on the production tasks given to this plant under the terms of the readjustment policy, the flexibility of the reform policy allowed this firm to find profitable business to take up the slack. Two deputies used the occasion to demand even more autonomy for their units than the reform policy as then being implemented had given them to date. One was a cadre from an enterprise in Hunan that had been chosen for the experiment and who now demanded more decision-making power for his unit; the other was a speaker for Shanghai who requested greater financial power and maneuverability for the city and less "overbearing control" of its funds by the central authorities.[55]

Although the staff at the Liaoning machine-building plant were resourceful enough to use the reform policies to undo the damage that readjustment had visited upon their industry, other representatives from areas strong in heavy industry lobbied for more investment and more work and were clearly not doing well under the administration of either the reform or the readjustment policies.[56]

Deputies from Jilin, for example, in which Changchun is a major center of the machine-building industry, argued that "machines should not be imported if they can be built at home." Other delegates from Liaoning, a province important for machine-building and other heavy industry, spoke out for state investment in transforming old enterprises.

Deputies from Shanxi, Henan, and Anhui all took the floor on behalf of the coal industry, a branch of the economy particularly disadvantaged by both the reform and the readjustment policies.[57] The representative from Henan complained that the income of the localities engaged in coal production was too low and demanded subsidies from the state, along with a reversal of the then-current trend of reducing and even stopping coal production. The Anhui delegate made an interesting observation, at once throwing cold water on some foreign trade and rallying support for coal and domestic machinery: "The money spent on three imported sets of coal mining equipment," he calculated, "is enough to build a coal pit with an annual production capacity of 600,000 tons." These claims for coal and machine-building are to be expected, in light of Yao's admission that these two industries had suffered under the new economic policies, and they point to a significant source of opposition to both reform and readjustment.

As for the other provincial speakers who offered views on economic policy, only those from Anhui made remarks in support of readjusting the economy,[58] but this did not really amount to an endorsement of readjustment, as this policy had been presented by the central leadership. The Anhui group was led by Vice-Premier Wan Li, who is thought to have been a key shaper of the economic policies of the past few years. All of the others favored readjustment only in the hope that its implementation might lead to a solution to what each saw to be serious problems in the economy, either locally in their own provinces or on a national scale. Thus, speakers from Hunan, Shanghai, Jilin, Hebei, Jiangxi, and Shanxi all worried aloud about the deficit, excessive capital construction, imbalance, and inflation. The Shanxi speaker in particular drew attention to the fact that Yao Yilin had not even addressed the question of inflation, a problem about which "the masses are very unhappy and worried."

Delegates from Guangdong, Hubei, and Henan endorsed readjustment so long as it led, as promised, to actual increases in investment in the sectors about which they were concerned—light industry and agriculture. But, as Guangdong deputy Wu Lengxi pointed out, the reports of the central officials at this session had said "nothing concrete" about developing these sectors. Promises of heightened investment in agriculture and its mechanization, which the first and second sessions had foretold, were absent from this meeting's agenda. This was noted by the representative from Hubei, who commented that the amount of state investment planned for agriculture for 1981 accounted for only 8 percent of the total national expenditure, a drop from the 14 percent envisaged at the second session.[59] Finally, deputies from Shanghai and Jiangsu urged more investment in urban construction and less in capital construction. Thus, readjustment, because it represented a change from the past, mainly attracted attention from those who were discontented with their receipts from the state and those who used the occasion to press for a better deal.

The tone of the principal addresses at the third session reveal it as a forum at which reform-prone central officials hoped to stay the course. They tried to accomplish this safely by downplaying to their audience (and perhaps to themselves as well) the impact of deficit and inflation, and by tempering the force of free-market strategies through giving a nod in the direction of "comprehensive balance," increasing the guidance from the plan, and retrenching the investment in capital construction and heavy industry. But to judge from the words of those deputies who spoke out at the meeting, the fate of heavy industry and the economic problems in the provinces caused by deficit, inflation, and lowered central-level investment aroused more interest locally than the faltering reform campaign.

The Aftermath of the Third Session and the Fourth Session (Autumn 1980–December 1981): Readjustment Tempered by Reform

The sharp turnaround that these various signs of disquiet presaged came much more quickly than the optimism displayed by Yao and Hua would have led most outside observers to expect. Interestingly, when the occasion came for Yao to explain the shift, he made it appear that this decision rested solely on the new information that had become available with the analysis of the results of the 1980 economic plan ("the fulfillment of the 1980 national economic plan has revealed several problems that call for our serious consideration").[60] Casting a measure of doubt on this account of Yao's, however, is the admission by Premier Zhao Ziyang at the fourth session of the Fifth NPC, in December 1981, that after the third session the State Council had "made a further comprehensive analysis of the economic situation and identified some major problems calling for immediate solution."[61] The Council had done this almost immediately on the closing of the third session, Zhao explained, at meetings held in October and November 1980, followed by an authoritative work conference of the Party Central Committee in December—that is, *before* the 1980 economic data had been analyzed. This timing seems to indicate that a reappraisal, one that probably developed from differences of opinion made public at the September NPC session and not just from new data, spurred the change in line.

The line that emerged from this December Work Conference was the one that Chen Yun had been promoting since the Party Work Conference of April 1979— scaling down capital construction, shifting the proportion of investment toward light industry and away from heavy, and tightening central control through "comprehensive balance." At this December meeting, Chen delivered a speech consisting of fourteen points[62] that called for a definitive switch to readjusting and permitted only those aspects of reform (such as the use of bank loans to enterprises rather than the customary gratis dispersal of funds and equipment from the center) that posed no threat to overall central-level management of the economy.[63]

Though the readjustment was termed temporary, Chinese officials now recognized that it would require more than the additional three years predicted earlier. In opposition to the reform schemes that had been progressing despite Chen's repeated calls for putting readjustment first, this line mandated recouping the powers that had been lent to the localities and enterprises; halting the experiment in enterprise autonomy so that it would apply only to those 6,600 firms where it was already in effect; and restoring a greater degree of central control through administrative measures (as opposed to economic ones) and governmental (rather than market-type) intervention into the economy. The idea was to deal with deficits by diverting money and materials away from the lower levels and back into the central treasury.

The Chinese leaders used several arguments to justify the move away from reform. For instance, according to one of these, all the restructuring measures, including profit retention and price readjustments, depended on backing from the state in the form of financial power and material resources. The serious imbalance and the deficit were thought to preclude this upper-level support, and indeed, granting autonomy was thought to intensify the imbalance and increase the deficit, causing new fluctuations. Also, expanding the decision-making powers of the enterprises was said to work only in the presence of certain conditions external to the enterprises themselves, and these conditions were at present lacking in the Chinese economy: coordination among supplies, marketing, and production; a balance between supply and demand of goods; a rational tax system and a price structure that reflected relative costs; and a sufficiency of raw materials and power for the various enterprises at all administrative levels competing in the market.[64]

If the sources are accurate, this policy of readjustment aroused opposition from two factions: "A few people doubt and resent this decision . . . [and] some call it retreat, some even regard it as 'restoration.' " One of these was labeled leftist, followers of the Gang; the other was composed of "our comrades" who had not yet judged the situation soberly.[65] "Leftists," according to one account, were those who had rejected the cutback in capital construction. The body of opinion attacking these people attributed the deficit to the resulting imbalance between sectors in the national economy.[66] One might speculate that among these "leftists" were members of the Conserver group, people who saw that their own projects and enterprises were to receive diminished funding in the wake of this initiative. It is also possible, even though it was nowhere explicitly stated among the sources reviewed for this essay, that the opposition among "our comrades" was rooted in those who preferred to carry on with the reforms. Although some analyses blamed both excessive capital construction *and* the reforms for the crisis in the economy, some focused their fire on the reforms: "Thousands of units directly engaged in production and marketing carrying on their fervent activities separately cannot ipso facto insure the harmonious development of the whole national economy or attain the best macroscopic economic results."[67]

One source recounted the existence of two different views on why inflation had occurred. The first, attributed to Minister of Finance Wang Bingqian, pointed to wage increases and state subsidies used in raising the purchase prices paid to the peasants for their agricultural products, along with the costs of the Vietnam War.[68] Such an interpretation fits neatly with the argument noted above that restructuring requires funds that the state does not possess, a likely argument for one who is in charge of financial affairs. Such a position, present as well in Chen Yun's speech at the meeting,[69] appears to find fault with the incentives strategies of the Reformers. The other opinion on inflation's causes agrees with the gist of Zhao's speech,[70] since it blames disproportions in the economy and the overextended scale of construction. This perspective, while preserving the sanctity of the reform program, at the same time in effect attacks those who were advocating more investment in heavy industry. In any case, the facts that two alternative courses were criticized and that a strategy of readjustment was put forward to correct the two types of problems identified here do lend credence to an interpretation couched in terms of three lines of conflict.

These December 1980 decisions, along with the results of the 1980 plan, led to a revision of the 1981 national economic plan that amounted to a more extensive program for readjustment. Yao Yilin delivered a report on this revision to the seventeenth meeting of the Standing Committee of the Fifth NPC in late February 1981.[71] Here Yao echoed the calls for more centralization and for "necessary administrative measures to avoid anarchy," and he dictated a reduction in appropriations for capital construction by nearly one half (from 55 billion to 30 billion yuan) for 1981, along with a plan for the central government to borrow from the surpluses of the local governments.

However, Yao chose not to explain the economic "potential danger," as he referred to it, in terms of the reforms. Rather, he maintained that the danger arose from an increased amount of currency having been put into circulation and from the failure of the supply of commodities to rise along with mass purchasing power. This view, reiterated later in the year by economist Xue Muqiao,[72] has often been used before in China to suggest that the principal solution to economic problems is to increase production, usually through market incentives. And though Yao this time did mention "unhealthy price rises" and the excessive issuance of bonuses by some units, and endorsed the postponement of reforms that contradict readjustment, at the same time he spoke out in favor of encouraging reforms, even of undertaking new reforms under proper leadership, including (but, the implication was, not limited to) those in the original 6,600 firms.

In the wake of the December 1980 and February 1981 conferences devoted to installing a new economic strategy of radical retrenchment, during the first half of 1981 the leadership focused on macroeconomics. Before long, however, the elite was to discover that readjustment alone would not be sufficient for righting the ills in the national economy. Already at the State Council plenary meeting in mid-April, Zhao Ziyang put forward a nine-point proposal on tactics, which set the direction for the remainder of the year and became the basis for the line of the fourth session of the NPC held at the end of the year. It suggested increasing the production of consumer goods, relying on existing enterprises, and reorienting the output mix of enterprises in the heavy industrial sector. Underlying his words was his hope that, on the foundation of stabilizing the economy, it would be possible gradually to continue the experiment in reform, listed as his ninth point.[73]

Zhao's reintroduction of the reform theme was followed in the succeeding months by a number of developments that supported this thrust. In May, the State Council passed a report on enterprise autonomy directing that the micro economy should be enlivened even as macro guidance was strengthened over the economy as a whole, and mandated continuing with reform experiments that were efficacious.[74] Then, at the Sixth Plenum of the Eleventh Party Central Committee held in June, a new form of management, the responsibility system, was proposed for use in industrial and communications enterprises.[75] This scheme once again alerted the workers and staff in state enterprises that their own material interest would be tied to the successes of their firm. This time, however, a punitive element was added, since individuals were to be cashiered for any losses for which they could be held accountable but given bonuses for their successes.

Also in June, in a related development, the State Council officially approved the delegation of power to the lower levels of administration in conducting foreign trade exchanges, a power that the localities had already been given in 1979 and 1980 but which had been rescinded with the recentralization in February 1981.[76] By October, a leading Beijing newspaper had announced that power should be delegated to the lower levels and the enterprises, that the economy should once again be run mainly with economic levers, and that, as the reforms progressed, any problems they might induce could be solved through increased macrolevel guidance.[77]

Besides this new shift back in the direction of reform or "restructuring," a change in the still-young strategy of readjustment also marked the year 1981. This development entailed pressure from those responsible for heavy industry, along with a growing awareness in policy-making councils that the course had to be rewritten one more time in order to attend to certain serious effects that readjustment was visiting upon this sector.

Signs of trouble were clear by mid-year, when industry as a whole registered an increase of only 0.8 percent over the same period the year before (light industry increasing by 11.6 percent but heavy decreasing by 8.2 percent).[78] In particular, the output of heavy industry had dropped because the steel and machinery industries had been forced to reduce production.[79]

By early fall, broadcasts from the provinces that serve as bases for heavy industry began to champion the important contribution that this sector had made and, they claimed, could continue to make to the national economy. One report from Shandong termed it the key to the growth rate in all of industry and to overcoming the current financial difficulties, and pleaded for a guarantee that its output would fall as little as possible or not at all during the period of readjustment.[80] Other announcements, from Liaoning and Shanxi, castigated those who spread the "false impression" that readjustment meant that the output of light industry should be increased and that of heavy decreased. The report from Shanxi spoke too of a "state of mental depression and helplessness in the face of new conditions and problems emerging from readjustment." "At one time," it noted, "a major question was whether the machine-building industry could survive. . . . [T]he situation appeared quite hopeless." These writers also demanded raising the rate of development "to the highest degree possible" and developing that portion of the heavy industrial sector that was to be supported so that it "can maintain a definite speed."[81]

Perhaps these advocates obtained a hearing, for at the same time the *People's Daily* ran articles pointing out that without growth in heavy industry the state's financial income would be affected, and that without the work of the heavy industrial plants there would be no technological equipment, power, or raw and other materials for production of consumer goods.[82] It was becoming clear to central decision makers that the plants made idle by readjustment still had workers who needed to be paid and maintenance expenditures to be met.

When the elite recognized these difficulties, a debate ensued in which the Conserver group managed to show some clout.[83] This debate included a set of disagreements, centering on speed ("some sang the tune of high targets, high speed"); the question of whether heavy industry should not again receive priority treatment, as in the past; the rate of investment ("some want to raise [it], as they see too few orders, and productive capacity sitting idle"); and reform (some disapproved that the enterprises and localities were enriching themselves while the center could not make ends meet). Another argument arose then about the use of foreign capital since "some" feared that the import of large quantities of equipment and technology could harm China's own machine-building industry.[84] According to a commentator in Hong Kong, these views counted as "leftism" because their proponents used the pretext of problems in economic development to raise doubts about the present elite's overall strategy.[85] These "leftists," to judge from the interests they advanced, must have been members of the Conserver group.

Meanwhile, leftist thinking in another guise, from another sort of Conserver viewpoint, cropped up too, censuring the "sinister trend and unhealthy practices" associated with the relaxation in economic policy that was at the heart of reform.

These critics called for ideological work and even for class struggle, a term rarely heard in the past few years. Along this same line, leftists attacked the responsibility system as retrogression, a deviation from socialism, and maintained that profit ought not to be the only means of evaluating enterprises.[86] Whether these authors were also supporters of heavy industry cannot be discerned from their critiques. The fact is clear, however, that both readjustment and reform were subjected to onslaughts from what is considered the left today in China, and it is unlikely that these "leftists" would have felt free to speak or that their words would have seen print without patrons in high circles who permitted their views to surface.

Thus, in the period between the third and fourth sessions of the Fifth NPC, disagreement was rife over the question of centralization versus autonomy for the lower levels; over using mainly administrative versus economic methods; on the subjects of speedy growth and the place of heavy industry; and over how much weight to give to inflation, deficits, and profits. Against this background, it is obvious that the claims, made at the fourth meeting, of continuity in executing the eight-character direction and in carrying out readjustment papered over much reappraisal and conflict.

Premier Zhao Ziyang's address to the fourth session of the Fifth NPC (held in the first half of December 1981) followed essentially the same pattern that Yao Yilin's report had done during the third session more than a year before. That is, Zhao, like Yao, spoke in basically optimistic tones about the effectiveness of measures in the recent past on improving the economy.[87] He referred to the achievement of a "basic balance" between revenue and expenditure and between credit receipts and payments; pointed out that the data, once they were in, would probably show a drop in the 1981 deficit to 2.7 billion (the result of sharp reductions in spending, particularly in military spending, and greatly increased foreign loans);[88] and related that prices were "stable in the main." He attributed these improvements to the strengthened centralized leadership, price controls, and curtailment of capital construction that had been carried out over the preceding year.

Zhao did admit that minor problems still existed in each of these areas. But given the general cast of his remarks and the outlook on the state of the economy on which they were founded, it is clear that he believed that centralized controls had done their job for the time being. His "fundamental solution" to financial difficulties and lack of funds was to "adopt correct policies that will arouse the initiative of all the workers and staff, all enterprises and all local authorities so that they will work hard to increase production,"[89] a goal he hoped the country could attain through intensified use of market strategies. Perhaps the most pronounced evidence of his bias appears in the following quotation, in which he explicitly proposed the extension of the enterprise autonomy reforms with which his name has been linked from the start, reforms that had been confined to the initial experimental batch of 6,600 firms earlier in the year: "We must not, on account of financial difficulties, abandon reforms that not only help release the initiative of local authorities, enterprises and workers and staff members but also contribute to the overall interest. Otherwise we will block the channels for increasing production and revenue and thus aggravate problems of finance."[90]

It is striking to anyone who has been following the debates of the past few years to see Zhao claiming that an *obstruction* of reforms would be bad for China's financial situation because of the detrimental effect such obstruction would have on incentives, when so much of the literature in the media of the recent past has argued that reforms destroy financial stability. Moreover, he urged that "as soon as possible" an overall plan for restructuring the economy must be drawn up.[91]

Other themes in Zhao's report that events and press discussions of the months just preceding had anticipated included the place of heavy industry in the national economy, the treatment of the agricultural sector, the extent of permissible foreign trade, and corruption. Zhao definitely showed that the issue of the recent decline in heavy industry was serious and one to which the leadership had been giving careful thought. In the latter half of 1981, he revealed, much had been done to change its orientation and to increase exports from that sector so that its growth had begun to pick up by the end of the year. But, he admitted, "much work needs to be done" in this regard to "bring about a change in the present situation of the dearth of assignments to heavy industry." Thus, although the term "readjustment" was still the catchword, it now had new, added dimensions. Policy makers had definitely shifted away from the original meaning of simply investing less in heavy industry and more in agriculture and light industry.[92]

Though Zhao, like keynote speakers at all previous sessions, placed agriculture first in his list of (ten) priorities, he openly admitted that "the state will gradually increase its investment . . . but will not be able to increase it by much." He therefore mandated accelerated development in agriculture through reliance on "correct policies and on science." And with regard to foreign trade, though Zhao supported persistence in the open-door policy, he also endorsed enhancing "our capacity for self-reliant action."[93] Most significant in this area, he made a bow in the direction of those who had shown concern about imports that threatened China's own machinery industry: "From now on, China should mainly import technology and single machines or key equipment that cannot be produced domestically. We should not import complete sets of equipment every time."[94]

Finally, it was only at the very end of his discussion of economic matters that the premier raised the troublesome issue of "unhealthy tendencies" and "obnoxious practices" in economic work—those behaviors that had borne the brunt of attacks by opponents of the reforms, such as underhand connections, demanding commissions, embezzlement, speculation, and profiteering.[95] Besides showing the relatively low priority he attached to such problems, by putting them last, Zhao also failed to endorse the leftist analysis that these practices are the effect of profit-seeking and, thus, ultimately of market strategies. In short, Zhao

Ziyang, credited as the author of much of the economic liberalization of the past few years in China, used the opportunity of addressing the NPC to push for upgrading of the strategies in which he believes.

Compared with the third session, the atmosphere at the fourth was restrained, reflecting the generally less open political climate in late 1981. One Hong Kong–based observer characterized the speeches as having the air of one "trimming his sails" and remarked that the speakers were generally "obliging."[96] Indeed, a number of the deputies did express satisfaction with Zhao's report and relief at the reduction of the deficit, and noted improvements in the economic condition of their home provinces.[97]

Still, the representatives of heavy industry used this occasion to continue to express their discontent, reintroducing some themes first raised by Yu Qiuli at the second session in 1979. From Henan, one speaker demanded a national program to advance the interests of the machine-building industry, the readjustment of which he believed was going too slowly. He voiced concern for the large number of plants employing thousands of workers or even more than ten thousand workers each. "If no overall arrangements are made for such large plants' production, if they themselves have to 'obtain rice to cook' [here he refers to a fear among those in certain enterprises of having to fend for themselves on an open market, rather than receiving the guidance and protection of the plan], things will certainly be muddled, which will cause losses." Others said: "The machine-building industry hasn't suffcient production tasks, but we've imported a large number of machines from abroad."[98]

In a similar vein, a representative from Jiangsu implored the central government not to "wash its hands of enterprises practicing the planned economy." In the past, he noted, "the First Ministry of Machine Building exercised rigid control over its enterprises and one-sidedly stressed central control, but this year . . . it has instructed them to find their own way in production." This delegate pleaded for the reinstitution of unified, centralized distribution of key raw materials and implied that the decentralization measures had permitted "improper relationships" to guide local allocation of such necessities as wood and coal.[99]

Deputies from Beijing, Guangdong, Sichuan, Gansu, and other provinces seemed to disagree with Zhao Ziyang by stressing inflation, which they reported the masses to be grumbling over, and voiced "hope that the central and local authorities will continue to handle commodity prices as a major matter . . . and make efforts to stabilize commodity prices."[100] From Jiangsu, a delegate drew attention to "a tendency to stress too much the role of regulation by the market."[101] So, even in the rather more closed climate of the fourth session, it was clear that competing views of the state of the economy and of how best to run it were in the air.

Immediately following the conclusion of the convention, even more signs of controversy emerged in the press, a somewhat surprising development if one presumes that the convocation of a Congress session is in itself a symbol of compromise having been reached. The most explicit evidence of conflict appeared in an essay in the *People's Daily* by economist Ma Hong. "One more phenomenon" he considered "worthy of our attention" was that

> some comrades have not had a sufficient understanding of the necessity to readjust the service orientation and product mix of heavy industry. [This implies that these people were dissatisfied with the concessions given to heavy industry with the redefinition of readjustment at this time.] They have even resented the readjustment, saying that, "the orientation must not be altered; the product patterns must be preserved; the work force must not be dismissed; the equipment must be left untouched. We must hold out during the readjustment and stage a comeback soon."[102]

It is intriguing to speculate on the conniving of this cabal, dedicated to maintaining the old place of heavy industry in the economy, to which Ma refers.

At least two other crucial issues remained foci for contention. One of these was the question of the speed of development. Although authoritative pronouncements decreed that "the speed cannot be too quick,"[103] only days after the meeting closed, a radio broadcast from Shanxi (a province that over the past few years has repeatedly made the case for heavy industry and its rapid growth) exclaimed about the "great prospects for pursuing speed in the readjustment," urging the nation to "strive for a higher and suitable speed."[104]

Probably most significant, however, was unmistakable evidence of an ongoing battle over giving priority to reform or readjustment, or, in essence, to market-directed versus plan-directed economic activity. This conflict appears to be one joined by the very top officials in China, since Zhao Ziyang's report and his subsequent speech in early March 1982 give clear evidence of his continuing preference for market reforms.[105] Meanwhile, party Vice-Chairman Chen Yun, the revered economic policy maker, has placed himself firmly on the side of the plan. In late January, Chen invited the "responsible people" from the State Planning Commission (including its chairman, Yao Yilin) to a forum on the question of strengthening the planned economy.

The report on this little meeting that the public read in *People's Daily* is remarkable for its omission of any reference to market strategies, despite Chen's endorsement of the now newly coined formulation, "the planned economy is the key link, with the market economy playing a supplementary role." This past master at devising schemes for market freedoms for the firms has apparently changed his mind about how to solve China's economic problems, at least given the present context, for in one place in the article he is actually quoted as having said, "When we manage the enterprises we must *even more* strengthen planning, we must be particular about whether the products have a market, where raw materials will come from, and how to run management. Now we have some localities that are not particular about these problems."[106]

This cursory review of economic policy in the PRC over the past four years unquestionably shows much evidence of indecision, vacillation, and reversal, a great deal of which can be documented as deriving from disputes over perspective and approach. At least three key opinion groups have fought for different designs for organizing and running the national economy, and to date none of them has clearly emerged as dominant. In fact, as of early 1982 the voices of each group seem at least as strong and as much in conflict as at any time over the period under consideration.

In the midst of these changes, however, this factionalism has ironically introduced a constant factor into the councils of debate: that is, all sessions of the Fifth NPC, a congress born after the death of Mao Zedong, have been arenas where the focus has been economic growth and where there has occurred a sort of standoff between plan and market in the authoritative document (the government work report) and in inconsistencies that appeared in the speeches of key central officials or else among the addresses of the deputies from the localities.

Thus, though the first session has been noted for leftist adventurism, it was in fact a meeting whose work report paid most obeisance to the principle of tight central planning and was also the first forum where market principles were publicly enunciated. The second, known for introducing the eight-character policy that placed readjustment first, actually included some strongly promarket language (though not at all in the speech of Yu Qiuli). At the third, most of the key speakers called for extension of the market experiment, but now couched such cries within the context of the state plan. And at the fourth session, though the propaganda notices billed it as a continuation of readjustment, the premier's own biases, as well as reactions to new problems, belied this claim. The complicated interplay of Adjuster, Reformer, and Conserver viewpoints, as well as the intractability of the problems these several strategies essay to solve, has had a crucial role in delaying the design of a shared agenda.

A subtheme of this chapter has been a revised view of the role of the NPC in Chinese politics. Drafting the details of economic policy has historically been more the province of the government—of the State Council—than of the party in the PRC. But this study of the several sessions of the Fifth National People's Congress has shed much light on the processes of debate, opposition, and reappraisal that characterize the work of this larger legislative body in China in its effort to direct the economy.

Notes

1. *Zheng ming* (Contend) (Hong Kong) (hereafter *ZM*), no. 50 (December 1981): 21.

2. *China News Analysis* (hereafter *CNA*), no. 1196 (1980): 6.

3. *Peking Review* (hereafter *PR*), no. 10 (1978): 25, and *Beijing Review* (hereafter *BR*), no. 3 (1982): 3.

4. *PR*, no. 52 (1978): 12, and *Renmin ribao* (People's daily) (hereafter *RMRB*), September 1, 1980, p. 1.

5. *RMRB*, January 19, 1981, excerpted in *BR*, no. 7 (1981): 11.

6. Jiang Yi, "Can Chen Yun's Scheme Resolve the Difficult Problems in the Economy?" *ZM*, no. 4 (March 1981): 42.

7. *RMRB*, February 24, 1978, states that the Second Plenum of the Eleventh Party Congress passed all the documents later issued at the first session of the Fifth NPC.

8. See Lowell Dittmer, "China in 1981: Reform, Readjustment, Rectification," *Asian Survey* 22, 1 (1982): 33–35, for a brief summary of this process.

9. Xue Muqiao, "Problems to Be Solved in Reforming the Economic Management System," *Jingji yanjiu* (Economic Research), no. 1 (1982): 5.

10. Ibid.

11. Speech by Zhao Ziyang, in *Foreign Broadcast Information Service* (hereafter *FBIS*), April 22, 1980, p. L4.

12. Alex Nove and D. M. Nuti, eds. *Socialist Economics: Selected Readings* (Harmondsworth: Penguin Books, 1972): p. 13.

13. Xue Muqiao, "Problems."

14. For the text of the government work report delivered by Hua at this meeting, see *PR*, no. 10 (1978): 7–40.

15. Ju Zhongyi, "The 'New Economic Faction' Overturns the 'Petroleum Faction,'" *Dongxiang* (Trend) (hereafter *DX*), no. 24 (September 1980): 9–10.

16. *PR*, no. 10 (1978): 19, 10; see also *BR*, no. 38 (September 22, 1980): 16, where Hua implies at the third session that the plan presented in early 1978 had been devised in late 1975. See also *PR*, no. 52 (1978): 13, which notes that Deng was entrusted by Mao in 1975 with the responsibility of presiding over the work of the Central Committee.

17. *PR*, no. 10 (1978): 25. See also from this period *PR*, no. 9 (1978): 25–26, and no. 12 (1978): 41–42, which report on economically independent farms that work through contracts and worker self-management, respectively, in Yugoslavia.

18. See Robert F. Dernberger, "Prospects for the Chinese Economy," *Problems of Communism* (September–December 1979): 8; and *CNA*, no. 1157 (June 22, 1979): 3–4.

19. *PR*, no. 10 (1978): 25.

20. The text may be found in *RMRB*, October 6, 1978, translated in *FBIS*, October 11, 1978, pp. E1–E22.

21. *RMRB*, July 8 and 5, 1978.

22. Ju Zhongyi, "New Economic Faction," p. 10.

23. *RMRB*, July 3, 1978.

24. The Communiqué of the Third Plenum is found in *PR*, no. 52 (1978): 6–16.

25. Perhaps in an effort to add more legitimacy to the ideas of readjustment, *BR*, no. 27 (1981): 26–27, claims that it was the Third Plenum that first directed attention to readjustment.

26. Liu Ying, "The Retransformation of the Ownership System," *ZM*, no. 47 (September 1981): 22. See also *Issues and Studies* (hereafter *I & S*), 15, 9 (1979): 2–3; *ZM*, no. 20 (January 1979): 16; *Guangjiaojing* (Wide angle) (Hong Kong), no. 80 (1979): 4–8, 19; and *ZM*, no. 31 (1980): 12. Chen's speech is translated in *I & S*, 16, 4 (1980): 80–97. On a later occasion, Deng Xiaoping revealed that Chen had been in charge of financial and economic work after the Third Plenum and that it was he who had brought up the principle of readjustment in spring 1979. See the translation of Deng's speech to the December 1980 Party Work Conference in *I & S*, 17, 7 (1981): 102.

27. See Dernberger, "Prospects," p. 10; and Yuan Kuei-sheng, "The New Phase of Communist China's Economic Readjustment," *I & S*, 15, 11 (1979): 33, 35.

28. Xue Muqiao, "Postscript to *Investigations on Questions in China's Socialist Economy*," *Hongqi* (Red flag) (hereafter *HQ*), no. 21 (1981): 28–29.

29. Liu Ying, "Retransformation," p. 22.

30. The text of Hua's speech is in *BR*, no. 27 (1979).

31. The text of Yu's speech is in *BR*, no. 29 (1979): 7–16.

32. Ju Zhongyi, "New Economic Faction," p. 10, states that the members of the Petroleum Faction, who had long done the leadership work in finance and state planning, controlled the economy from 1976 to 1978. For a more explicit account of successes in 1977, see *RMRB*, October 25, 1977, where Yu is quoted as stating that after the fall of the Gang of Four, from June 1977, the total value of the country's industrial output per month exceeded the highest average in the past; that production targets were reached in most of eighty major projects; that grain production in twenty-nine provinces surpassed the 1976 level. Kinji Yajima, in "Communist China's Economic Modernization Program," *I & S*, 14, 7 (1978): 42, notes that contradictions appeared in articles in the media, so that sometimes excellent production results were listed and sometimes production was presented as being still in a state of stagnation in this period. See also Dernberger, "Prospects," p. 6, where he notes that there had been no growth in 1976 but that there had been industrial gain in 1977.

33. On failures in 1977–78, see Xue Muqiao's analysis referred to above (n. 28); and Deng's December 1980 speech, cited in n. 26, where he mentions (p. 102) "two years of confusion following the smashing of the Gang," which "developed into even greater imbalances."

34. Shi Zhengwen, "Readjusting the National Economy: Why and How?" *BR*, no. 26 (1979): 13–23. Here I assume that pro-Reform elements had more input into the media at this time than they did into the speeches delivered at the meeting.

35. Ju Zhongyi, "New Economic Faction," p. 11. I prefer to consider the Petroleum Faction, whose positions seem to be the same as those who represent heavy industry, as being only one segment of the Conserver group. I handle this faction in this manner since an important thrust of the Conserver group's position, for the purposes of this chapter and the debates it traces, is the group's defense of heavy industry.

36. *RMRB*, November 9, 1979, p. 3, contains one example. But the Conserver group stood to benefit neither from readjustment nor from reform, so this is another dimension of conflict.

37. Ju Zhongyi, "New Economic Faction," p. 11.

38. *RMRB*, May 22, 1980, p. 2.

39. *RMRB*, May 16 and 17, 1980, p. 5 in both issues.

40. Fang Fang, Song Fucheng, and Yu Chongguang, "Treat the Circulation Process Seriously, Make the Economy Lively," *HQ*, no. 10 (1980): 22–25. Zhao's speech is in *FBIS*, March 22, 1980, pp. Ll–L7.

41. An interesting, if typically indirect, comment to this effect is an *RMRB* article on August 14, 1980, p. 5, which noted that in January 1957 Chen Yun exposed his ideas on the economy, "a correct theory, that had been shelved for a long time." I take this reference to the past to be a critical statement about the present.

41. See *Zhonghua Renmin Gongheguo Guowuyuan gongbao* (Bulletin of the State Council of the PRC) (hereafter, *SC Bulletin*), November 20, 1980, which contains this report, dated August 9, 1980, on pp. 419–27. David Bachman kindly provided me with this and other copies of this bulletin. *RMRB*, September 1, 1980, indicated that the experiment in enterprise autonomy was to be spread nationwide by the end of 1981.

42. In *RMRB*, April 26, 1980, p. 1. This was only one instance of concern expressed over this issue over the years 1979–80. In the fall of 1979, state shops were charged with creating "disguised price increases." See, for example, *FBIS*, October 1, 1979, p. R5, and October 5, 1979, p. P9.

44. *RMRB*, June 12, 1980. The State Council passed regulations enforcing this "socialist competition" in October. See *SC Bulletin*, December 1, 1980, pp. 487–89.

45. RMRB, April 25, 1980, p. 3, and May 2, 1980, p. 3; *Shichang* (Market), no. 18 (June 25, 1980): 3.

46. Ju Zhongyi, "New Economic Faction," p. 11. See also Xu Xing, "Questions Raised at the 4th Session of the Fifth NPC," *ZM*, no. 51 (January 1982): 19.

47. See, for example, *New York Times*, August 31, 1980. The Western journalists were not totally aware of the nuances and longer-range context of the meeting, knowledge of which is needed for interpreting the meeting's documents fully.

48. Here I use the term "speech writer" guardedly. I hesitate to *assume* that the person who delivers a particular address was its author or its sole author, or even that he fully supports and believes what he is saying. One possibility, of course, is that a set of ideas was in the air, and these were distributed for presentation among the various speakers. At a minimum, however, I can certainly make the claims (1) that a group of different ideas existed, some of which directly contradicted other ideas on the same topic; and (2) that these ideas had been revealed through debates reported in the press between the time of this meeting and the second session, and also that these several different ideas were held by the various deputies, as will be seen below.

49. Hua's speech is in *BR*, no. 38 (1980): 12–29; Yao's is in *BR*, no. 38 (1980): 30–43. For a summary of Yao's points on structural reform, see *RMRB*, September 1, 1980, p. 1.

50. See note 42.

51. *FBIS*, September 2, 1980, p. L20.

52. *FBIS*, September 1, 1980, p. L28; September 12, 1980, p. L5.

53. Peng's report on the work of the Standing Committee of the NPC is in *BR*, no. 39 (1980); this remark is on p. 29.

54. *FBIS*, September 11, 1980, p. L17.

55. These views are in *FBIS*, September 2, 1980, p. L24 (Guangdong), p. L24 (Shanghai), p. L27 (Sichuan), and p. L28 (Anhui); September 15, 1980, p. L25 (Liaoning); September 16, 1980, p. L14 (Hunan); and September 24, 1980, pp. L10–L11, and September 25, 1980, p. L3 (Shanghai).

56. These are in *FBIS*, September 11, 1980, p. L23 (Jilin); September 12, 1980, p. L3 (Shanxi), pp. L18–L19 (Henan); September 15, 1980, p. L12 (Liaoning); and September 25, 1980, p. L8 (Anhui).

57. Henan is not a major producer of coal, as Anhui and Shanxi are, but it does turn out some coal.

58. These views are in *FBIS*, September 2, 1980, p. L27, and September 15, 1980, p. L13 (Hunan); September 2, 1980, p. L28 (Anhui); September 2, 1980, pp. L44–L45, September 11, 1980, p. L18, September 16, 1980, p. L13, September 18, 1980, p. L6, September 19, 1980, p. L9, and September 23, 1980, p. L5 (Shanghai); September 8, 1980, p. L28 (Guangdong); September 11, 1980, p. L22 (Jilin); September 12, 1980, p. L12 (Hubei), L17 (Hebei), and L18 (Jiangxi); September 18, 1980, p. L2 (Henan); September 24, 1980, p. L13 (Shanxi); and September 25, 1980, p. L11 (Jiangsu).

59. *BR*, no. 26 (1979): 9.

60. This report of Yao's is in *BR*, no. 11 (1981): 14–20, 27. This statement is on p. 15.

61. Zhao's work report at the fourth session is in *FBIS*, December 16, 1981, pp. K1–K35.

62. Jiang Yi, "Chen Yun's Scheme."

63. These decisions are reported in *BR*, no. 1 (1981): 3, no. 4 (1981): 3, no. 7 (1981): 11–12; *RMRB*, December 23, 1980, p. 5, in *FBIS*, January 6, 1981, pp. L18–L24; *RMRB*, December 30, 1980, p. 5, in *FBIS*, January 5, 1981, pp. L15–L20; *HQ*, no. 1 (1981): 28–30, in *FBIS*, January 29, 1981, pp. L23–L26, to list a few of the relevant articles.

64. One account claimed that more than five thousand small wine factories, managed

at the brigade level, had sprung up in Sichuan alone, snatching raw materials and markets away from bigger, state-run concerns. See Xiao Cheng, "Why Did the Economic Reforms Shift from Being Urgent to Following a Circuitous Route?" *ZM*, no. 41 (March 1981): 47.

65. *FBIS*, January 29, 1981, p. L26.

66. *BR*, no. 7 (1981): 11.

67. *RMRB*, December 23, 1980, p. 5, in *FBIS*, January 6, 1981, pp. L18–L24.

68. Xiao Cheng, "Why Did the Economic Reforms Shift?," p. 48. On p. 49 Xiao mentions that some people had directly censured the reforms for encouraging the pursuit of profit.

69. Chen's speech (along with those of Deng, Zhao, and Li Xiannian) is summarized and translated from *ZM*, no. 40 (1981), in *FBIS*, February 2, 1981, pp. U1–U15. Chen emphasized "mistakes in reform," that "we cannot afford high wages and commodity prices," and that it is "wrong to stress economic laws alone."

70. Zhao pinpointed the "major cause" of the troubles as being that "we did not grasp readjustment in industry," speaking as well of "the high accumulation rate," "huge investments," "high targets," and "serious dislocations." See *FBIS*, February 2, 1981, p. U10.

71. See note 60.

72. Xue Muqiao, "Postscript," p. 29.

73. Jiang Yi, "China's New Economic Situation and Difficult Problems," *ZM*, no. 47 (September 1981): 16–19, and Liu Ying, "Retransformation," pp. 22–23. This advocacy of limited reforms in the present in order to lay a foundation for a large-scale future reform is a persistent theme in Zhao's speeches over the past few years. See *FBIS*, April 22, 1980, p. L2, and April 1, 1982, p. K4.

74. See *SC Bulletin*, September 5, 1981, pp. 439–51. The document is dated May 20, 1981.

75. *FBIS*, August 6, p. T2.

76. Pauline Loong, "100 Companies Blossom," *Far Eastern Economic Review* (hereafter *FEER*), November 13, 1981, p. 76. See also *BR*, no. 11 (1981): 18, on the "eight unifications," the eighth of which states that "the unified management of foreign trade and foreign exchange must be strengthened."

77. In *Guangming ribao* (Bright daily), October 4, 1981, translated in *FBIS*, October 26, 1981, p. K3.

78. *ZM*, no. 47: 17. An article by Ma Hong in *RMRB*, December 29, 1981, p. 5, in *FBIS*, January 8, 1982, on p. K14, says that the planned rate had been for an increase of 3 percent for all of industry.

79. "Current Economic Situation on the Chinese Mainland," *I & S*, 17, 10 (1981): 9.

80. *FBIS*, September 15, 1981, p. O4.

81. For Liaoning, see *FBIS*, October 28, 1981, p. Sl, and *HQ*, no. 22 (1981): 20–23, in *FBIS*, December 10, 1981, pp. Sl–S7; also *Shanxi ribao*, November 20, 1981, in *FBIS*, December 9, 1981, pp. R3–R6.

82. *RMRB*, October 16, 1981, in *FBIS*, October 28, 1981, pp. K9–K12; and an undated *RMRB* editorial in *FBIS*, November 24, 1981, p. K4.

83. Zhang Rodan, "Three Answers, Three Questions: Assessing Zhao Ziyang's Economic Report," *ZM*, no. 51 (January 1982): 23.

84. *FBIS*, November 17, 1981, p. K5.

85. Zhang Rodan, "Three Answers," p. 24.

86. *FBIS*, August 30, 1981, p. P2; August 12, 1981, p. K7; *RMRB*, November 5, 1981, in *FBIS*, November 10, 1981, p. K4.

87. See note 61.

88. See Robert Delfs, "Carry on Tinkering," *FEER*, December 11, 1981, p. 65.

89. Zhao, work report, in *FBIS*, December 16, 1981, p. K19.

90. Ibid. (emphasis added).

91. Ibid., p. K22 (emphasis added).

92. Zhao himself admitted this change in the definition of readjustment (work report, p. K7): "It was at the Second Session of the Fifth National People's Congress held in June 1979, that the State Council proposed the task of readjusting, restructuring, consolidating and improving the economy within three years. Through practice, we have since gained a deeper understanding of this principle. As far as readjustment is concerned, we should not only readjust the proportions between industry and agriculture, between light and heavy industries and between accumulation and consumption; we should also readjust the product mix, the technological makeup, the line-up of enterprises and the organizational structure so as to rationalize the overall structure of our national economy. *Therefore, economic readjustment covers a much wider range than we first envisaged."* (Emphasis added.) This is the passage in which Zhao explained that implementation of the eight-character phrase would take another five years or a little longer, beginning in 1981.

93. In Zhao's speech to the National Industrial and Communications Work Conference three months later, he repeatedly referred to "the policy of opening the country externally and enlivening the economy internally," which he termed the present policy, and which was to create conditions for further reform. This phrase peppered his speech despite (and belying?) his claim that administrative interference and giving highest priority to planned economy were priorities. See *FBIS*, April 1, 1982, pp. K1–K13.

94. Ibid., p. K21.

95. Ibid., pp. K32–K33.

96. Xu Xing, "Questions Raised," pp. 18–19.

97. This was so for deputies from Heilongjiang (*FBIS*, December 7, 1981, pp. K10–K11); Zhejiang (*FBIS*, December 7, 1981, p. K9); Guangdong (*FBIS*, December 7, 1981, p. K12, and December 8, 1981, p. K4); Fujian (*FBIS*, December 8, 1981, pp. K5–K6); Shandong (*FBIS*, December 8, 1981, p. K5); and Jiangsu (*FBIS*, December 9, 1981, pp. K8–K9).

98. *FBIS*, December 7, 1981, pp. K9–K10.

99. *FBIS*, December 8, 1981, p. K3.

100. Ibid., December 8, 1981, p. K4.

101. *BR*, no. 1 (1982): 14.

102. Ma Hong, "Economic Readjustment and Rate of Development," *RMRB*, December 29, 1981, p. 5, in *FBIS*, January 8, 1982, p. K14.

103. *BR*, no. 1 (1982): 4.

104. Taiyuan Radio, December 29, 1981, in *FBIS*, January 18, 1982, p. R7.

105. See note 93. See also an article by Yan Lin on Chen Yun's promarket ideas of 1956 in *HQ*, no. 2 (1982): 31–34, translated in *FBIS*, February 12, 1982, pp. K5–K9, which echoes Zhao's call for "an overall plan for reform" in the shortest time possible; and one by Xue Muqiao ("Problems"), which mentions "economic levers" or "economic methods" seven times, and at the outset quotes a German economist who recommended reducing planning and controlling the economy by economic methods and economic legislation. Xue calls for "going further in extending enterprise autonomy" and makes no mention whatever of administrative interference in the economy, asking instead for state guidance by economic levers and legislation.

106. *RMRB*, January 26, 1982, p. 1 (emphasis added). Is it significant that while Chen spoke of the plan as key, the market as supplement, Yao Yilin at this forum put the two on a par, stating that the present system is one that is "built on the principle of combining the planned economy with regulation by the market" (*BR* no. 12 [1982]: 18), a slogan last in vogue in mid-1980.

Part II

Experiments in the Urban State Economic Bureaucracy

3

Commercial Reform and State Control: Structural Changes in Chinese Trade, 1981–83

Clearly a crucial component of the current economic reforms in the People's Republic of China is the one concerning commerce. Since late 1978, the majority of the top leadership has agreed that rigidities in China's socialist commercial bureaucracy have worked over time to subvert certain central socialist goals. That is, too much state control has denied the population the higher living standards that the revolution promised, while "impoverished" marketing channels may even have limited the state-led productivity that was also at the heart of the post-1949 leaders' plans. Accordingly, the political elite in recent years has largely shared a perception that freer, more flexible forms of trading ought to be allowed and even promoted, as an important means of stimulating economic growth and providing marketplaces that are better supplied with goods. And, indeed, the green light given to open markets and private trading has immeasurably enlivened commercial exchange in China and has permitted a new prosperity unprecedented in the People's Republic.

Limits to Commercial Reform at the Level of Policy

This common commitment to liberalize business practices has been accompanied, however, by two sorts of brakes. In the first place, harking back to age-old assumptions in China about the nature of state power and of the proper relationship

An earlier version of this chapter was presented at the Annual Meeting of the Association for Asian Studies, held in Washington, DC, March 1984. It was part of a panel entitled "The Political Economy of Reform in China," chaired by Thomas G. Rawski.

This paper first appeared in *Pacific Affairs* 58, 2 (Summer 1985): 197–215. Reprinted with permission of *Pacific Affairs*.

between the state and the economy, virtually all the key decision makers believe that, ultimately, it is the role of the central government to dominate the management of the greater bulk of national revenue. Therefore, at several junctures over the past five or six years when this domination seemed threatened, a basic elite consensus has emerged to tighten or reinstitute price controls and to strengthen the role of state-run marketing organs. At such times, too, politicians have ordered a heightened "supervision" over the conduct of business by nonstate actors (collectively run trade organizations and private peddlers and merchants).

The second kind of limit on liberalization comes from what I have elsewhere termed the "bureaucratic tendency" in commercial policy making.[1] While particular individuals may shift their allegiance to this "tendency" or policy standpoint—as the current economic context, their own bureaucratic position, or the sometimes Byzantine fluctuations in Chinese political alliance-formation undergo changes—this more conservative, control-focused strain has persistently been represented over the years in policy councils in the PRC.[2] In the current period, its principal adversary has been what I call the "marketeer" tendency, one that emphasizes not state control but the importance of incentives and market-like practices for enhancing output. In the discussions of commercial policy over the past half decade, bureaucrats (generally, those who adhere to the bureaucratic tendency at any given time) agree with marketeers (again, a category that particular people may or may not belong to at a given time) that state monopolies over the circulation of goods must be relaxed. The former, however, argue that it is at the same time essential to streamline and revivify the state commercial bureaucracy—the wholesale companies and the rural supply and marketing cooperatives (SMCs)—so that this bureaucracy has a better than even chance of besting nonstate actors in the marketplace. Temporary clampdowns on economic relaxation, then, are best explained with reference to periodic triumphs of the bureaucrats' continuing effort to ensure that the state treasury benefits from any increases in productivity that the new reforms may elicit. The presence of this bifurcation of outlook over market reform is alluded to in an essay in the *People's Daily* in late 1981: "Many see chaos in liveliness. But chaos is only the branch [i.e., it is a secondary, not a root, issue], and that chaos is found in management, not in circulation. Anyway, it is only a reflection of temporary contradictions within reform. Many others think that the problem of chaos can be solved by making the market lively, that at present it's not lively enough."[3]

This chapter assumes that, while both bureaucrats and marketeers are in accord over the idea that the state-dominated commercial network must be revamped, bureaucrats have balked if the incentives permitting private sales of "post-quota" products lead producers to fail to meet the procurement targets of the state plan. And because of the mutual commitment of the two tendencies to a state-run economic system, the bureaucrats have sometimes been able to convince marketeers that reforms interfering with state revenue collection and with the management of key commodities ought to be curtailed. This commitment and its concomitant dynamic account for a strong strain of state control in commercial reform policies, for switches in policy line, and for contradictory regulations, which have all marked this program of liberalization.

This explanation of the pitfalls of the reform program, drawing on two fundamental features of the policy process itself, is intended to supplement other sorts of analyses of "obstructions" to reform. For instance, some accounts—by outsiders as well as by the press in the PRC—call attention to "remnant Leftists," "radical elements" who censure current policies as capitalist. Others have pointed to lower-level functionaries who staff the state-owned units and see their own interest and jobs in jeopardy as the private sector expands and steals their business. Similarly, some believe that Beijing bureaucrats in charge of central planning find the new freedoms inimical to their own mission. While by no means discounting these other sorts of interpretation, all of which bode badly for a speedy thoroughgoing overhaul of China's socialist economic system, this paper offers another way of understanding the process of reform.

The notion of a dominant state sector combined with visions of reform comes naturally to the present politicians in Beijing. The concept of a state-led reform that helps fill state coffers lies squarely within Chinese tradition, being reminiscent, for example, of the eleventh-century reform effort undertaken by the Song dynasty statesman Wang Anshi. For Wang, too, hoped to steer the state toward expanding financing so that economic growth and general prosperity would be stimulated, while the state itself ultimately would derive a larger share from that increased productivity.[4]

Competing visions of reform have commonly cropped up in other socialist societies in periods of liberalization. As one author put it:

> no matter how successful it is in promoting greater efficiency, rationalization [promoted by many Soviet leaders] can only be insufficient as a policy answering the developmental needs of the Soviet system. Some would contend that not just the perfection of techniques, fine adjustments, and reform are needed, but indeed fundamental systemic change—even revolutionary change—is required. The demands of change go beyond efficiency.[5]

This same basic duality is reflected in a recent journalistic analysis of the late Soviet leader Yuri Andropov's December 1983 economic speech to the Central Committee of the Communist party of the Soviet Union. As one reporter put it, the emphasis "was all on discipline, on cracking down on those who fail to meet plans. There was not a hint of the far-reaching decentralization that many Soviet economists consider necessary." The critique Andropov presented to the party meeting inveighed against economic bottlenecks, planning errors, failures to meet targets, and waste. Although all these censures imply a need for improving economic efficiency, they symbolize a markedly different means of changing the economic system from the total attack on "the dead weight of the bureaucracy" that Andropov had initiated four months earlier. These alternatives highlight a contrast between *better* state control and *less* state control as alternative means of re-forming, but not revolutionizing, economic life in a socialist system.[6]

The central distinction between the two visions of reform, both of which favor making use of market strategies although neither abandons the plan, also comes through in comparing the two previous programs of economic liberalization in the PRC, as symbolized in the differing prescriptions for each of them, prepared by that old dean of economic policy, Chen Yun.[7] In late 1956, at the start of the more liberal period of the two, Chen, as the newly named minister of commerce, remarked on behalf of the (then) just-installed free markets: "We ought freely to adopt free trading, and should not worry if prices go up for a time to a certain degree. . . . We must avoid that kind of inflation that is due to decreased production. Only increase of production in large amounts can guarantee price stability." In that era, the first loosening of the planned economy after the completion of socialist transformation, commercial units were often also instructed "to utilize fully the small merchants and peddlers," another sign that more flexible strategies were in ascendance.

In the early 1960s, though, a perhaps wiser Chen Yun, or at any rate a man facing a severely damaged economy, spoke out for a more constricted form of loosening the bureaucracy. Although he suggested a "free market within a certain scope" as being "good for promoting production," he went on to add that "if the peasants get too much cash and we can't get it back, there will be no way to get them to sell [their produce] to the state." Thus, he concluded, "the supply and marketing cooperatives should compete with the speculators and control the free market." At the same time Chen advocated increasing the state's procurement prices for some agricultural products, expressly to entice the peasantry to sell more of their produce to the state and less on the free market.

In the present period, marketeers seek not just the efficiency of state-dominated trade (a main point for the bureaucrats), but greater efficiency of trading in general, throughout the entire economy in nonstate as well as official channels of business. Their strategy sees market forces as a necessary supplement to the plan, having its own life, pushing into corners that the plan cannot reach, rather than just using reformist methods mainly as a means to shore up the plan, or only to increase state receipts. And where bureaucrats hope reform can help the state to perfect itself, marketeers recognize the limits on state organization and state power. They know that there are things state organs are not equipped to do, gaps or lacks in the reach of the state bureaucracy that the private sector and the market can fill.

For bureaucrats, a crucial function of commercial reform (aside from its role in helping to promote production by providing a more open market for commodity exchange) is to enable state-run purchasing units to act as the state's instrument in—and check on reform in—other economic sectors. That is, in recent years the agricultural responsibility system in the countryside and factory sales in the cities have enhanced productivity. Bureaucrats believe that the state-managed trade organs—the SMCs and the state wholesale companies—ought to restructure their organization and rationalize their procedures so that they can dominate the collection of the new additional output. This would guarantee that the state would reap the maximum possible benefit from the increased production. In short, these organs are supposed to channel for the state the fruits of private freedoms in the other economic sectors. Obviously, the implicit message is that state-managed firms must learn to be better at procuring this output than the newly liberated private-sector businesses. Bureaucrats, then, gear their instructions about reform toward increasing the efficiency of the state-run commercial organs, through the use of less restrictive modes of operation than those they used in the past.

Where the marketeer approach recognizes that the state plan needs a private supplement, plan proponents stress the other side of the picture. That is, they emphasize what they claim to be the weakness of the private peasant sector in operating on its own. In this way bureaucrats justify the role they insist upon for state organs, as these lines from late 1983 issues of the *People's Daily* attest:

> To fully tap the potential of . . . the commodity economy, and promote the development of commodity production, it is necessary to grasp pre-, during, and post-production service. The peasants can't solve these problems [of market intelligence, the divorce between production and sales, and blockages in transport] themselves. . . . They have a pressing need for the government's economic departments to *supply* this kind of service.

And:

> Developing diversified operations is the intense demand in the rural areas. But without a commercial organ with its heart on the peasants' interests, actively developing production for them and supplying aid, seeking an outlet for their products, wholeheartedly serving them, their production will meet great difficulty.[8]

The data used in this chapter are taken from articles appearing in the official press over the years 1981–83, a period after the initial burst of experimentation had settled down. This phase began at a time when inflation, deficits, and declining central receipts caused concern at the top, and was just prior to a sudden reinvigoration of the reform thrust which followed a major party work conference in March 1984.[9] This juncture was on the whole one that was marked much more by the bureaucratic tendency than the period either right before it or immediately following it. Nonetheless, the insights that material from this time offers into the checks on reform in a supposedly reformist era might caution observers about the limited possibilities for any total or rapid departure from socialist practices in the PRC.

The remainder of this chapter will contain three sections. First, it will illustrate the way statist conceptions confined the design of concrete reform measures in the early 1980s. Next, it will provide examples of contradictions and shifts between bureaucratic and marketeer approaches to market liberalization in these years. And finally, it will evaluate the commercial reform program and suggest a more long-term prognosis, on the basis of the analysis of limits laid out above.

Bureaucratic Limits on Concrete Reform Measures

The guiding philosophy behind commercial reform as a whole was codified into the slogan "three manys, one fewer" sometime in 1983. These are many coexisting economic forms, many channels for circulation, and many styles of operations, along with fewer bureaucratic links in the circulation process.[10] Other similar, related directing principles over the past five years have included more flexible pricing; fewer rationed goods; promotion of contract systems of various sorts (instead of mandatory plans); authorization for using "economic methods" (in lieu of administrative commands) in commercial activity; basing production plans on market needs; and an overall increase in the number of sites for commercial exchange throughout society as a whole. These several standards for the program of reform are meant to apply to *all* firms engaged in trading, whether in the public or the private sector.

In addition, commercial reform policy is directed specifically at upgrading the performance of the organs within the *state-owned* commercial bureaucracy, as noted above. Measures with this aim involve instituting an "economic responsibility system" for state-owned commercial firms; experimenting with independent accounting systems for state-run stores; democratizing the management of SMCs and expanding their functions, so that they provide new services to rural households (a measure coupled with the spread of the agricultural responsibility system, which has reduced the role of the previous, collective style of organizing rural trade); simplifying the internal structure of the state wholesaling companies, while enlarging their field of operations; and encouraging state-operated trade offices to do more market investigation and forecasting. Additional measures include rationalizing the division of labor between organs doing state work in the cities and those in the rural areas; orienting marketing according to economically demarcated, traditionally (pre-1949) utilized trade routes, and centering it in the historic market towns, rather than along the lines of and at the sites of bureaucratic authority; separating government administration from enterprise management; and bringing wholesale and retail concerns together into jointly operating bodies. The overarching goal, toward which all of these schemes are aimed, is to "raise economic results." This dimension of the reform program, especially dominant in much of 1981 and 1983, is the one identified here as bureaucrat centered.

The other side of commercial reform, the one expressing more of a marketeer mentality, has two parts. First of all, as regards the state sector, its tenets permit units within the industrial and agricultural branches of the state-managed economy to participate in the market on their own. Such a reform grants the staffs of these productive units a degree of autonomy in obtaining inputs and in finding market outlets. This means that the many channels for trade and the many operating styles that are the hallmarks of the reform effort include some that diverge from the classical Soviet-type economy's marketing framework, which typically assigns production and marketing to separate sorts of firms situated in distinct hierarchies.

Moreover, fewer producer goods, raw materials for heavy industry, and consumer goods are now directly controlled by the state sector. Therefore, producer firms may procure from, and put onto, the open market (although, theoretically at least, within state-set price ranges) commodities that were previously available legally only through planned allocation. But even as these reforms proceed, and as the leadership sanctions a reduction in state-run wholesaling trade, this policy has been constrained at times by the bureaucrat approach. For policy makers have also encouraged what they term "direct link-ups" between production units and the state trade bureaucracy's retail outlets. Such arrangements are meant to ensure that the state continues to receive and control the commodities in question, undercutting productive units' right to make fully private deals on their own.

The second part of marketeer reform is the one that has probably attracted the most attention among visitors to China, and in the Western press. This is the new right given to the petty private sector—peasants, peddlers, handicraft workers, and stall-merchants, whether selling individually or joined in "collectives"—to market their wares with only minimal state intervention. Even in its most liberal guise, though, this policy demands that such traders pay taxes and management fees, obtain licenses, and observe whatever shifting regulations apply at any given moment. Related is the freedom bestowed on the populace at large to participate in open-air markets, in the cities as well as in the villages (again, on condition that rules presently in force be observed).

Here too, though, bureaucratic influences have crept in at times. Thus, state trade organs have been ordered to intervene in this form of trade as well, by making sure that taxes are paid;[11] by punishing "corrupt" elements among individual operators;[12] by having state organs settle accounts for cotton purchases with individual households,[13] so that they are forced to sell to the state; by supplying "leadership" over the collective enterprises and organizing them in cooperation with state-sector firms;[14] and by forming liaisons with communes and their subdivisions to "help" the individual peasants in them market their produce.[15] While the state is not always able to attain this control it is seeking, it is significant that even the most liberal facet of the policy of reform contains within itself this objective of having state-managed firms corner the newly active market, more forcefully at some junctures than at others.

A closer look at the structural reforms for upgrading performance within the state-run trade bureaucracy will bear out the contention that, although many of these measures do intend new flexibility for the units involved, their ultimate rationale in the early 1980s has generally been to increase state procurement.[16] The most basic of these structural reforms, the attack on the monopoly position of state-run commerce, is referred to in the press as one of "dredging circulation channels" and "allowing many channels to coexist." Proponents justify this policy as necessary to correspond to variations in the level of development of production among districts; to fit complicated exchange relations, both between and within ownership systems; and to match differences in the production and consumption of the many commodities on the market.[17]

But under this seemingly liberal rubric, even in progressive Shanghai many of the new channels suggested amount to different avenues for state organs to ensure that they themselves obtain new products. Commercial departments, for example, are instructed to set up "in a planned way" large agricultural trade centers in peripheral areas of the city; institute more departments in stores where prices are set by bargaining; expand the operations of state-governed warehouses; and designate more places for installing mobile vendors, supposedly to "facilitate" peasants' sales.[18] Moreover, SMCs are warned that "in the competition among channels," they are to "improve their own operations management [and] fully develop [their] function as the main channel in rural commodity circulation."[19]

There has been some modest adjustment of planned prices for some key raw materials; the prices of machinery and some consumer durables have been allowed to float downward; SMCs, grain departments, cooperative commerce, licensed peddlers, and peasants have been permitted to utilize "negotiated prices" after planned targets for procurement of key commodities have been fulfilled; industrial and commercial departments (instead of price organs) have been authorized to set prices for small commodities; higher-quality industrial goods are to become more expensive than inferior versions of the same product; and the State Council has given "free rein" in the pricing of over 350 commodities, including such items as small pottery, umbrellas, buttons, some vegetables and fruit, and some medicines.[20]

Nonetheless, even this last decision—which also granted producers "a free hand" in fixing prices ("in line with state policies," of course), and which let them consult with wholesalers in determining price levels—still noted that city and county price administrative departments will have certain important rights. Thus, price offices may enlarge or narrow the scope of the small commodities to be priced by the enterprises "when necessary"; may regulate profit levels for small commodities; and may put ceilings on interregional, purchase and sale, and wholesale and retail differentials. These offices are also charged with the job of keeping market prices stable.[21] Placing such powers in the hands of the units customarily responsible for price-control work seems likely to be a basis for jurisdictional conflicts, if not also vitiating somewhat the newly granted privileges for producers.

Despite the new policy of encouraging many operations styles, again we find a retained power for the state and its wonted trade organs. A multitude of new operational forms has been suggested for trade: collectively managed warehouses; supply-and-marketing management departments (*jinglibu*) in communes; individuals and groups of peasants engaging in trade; joint operations between commercial units, between commercial and industrial units, between agricultural and commercial units, among units from all three sectors, and between firms representing the various ownership systems; sales exhibitions; and trade on commission and agency bases.[22] Nonetheless, generally speaking, most of these new partnerships and arrangements will have a state-managed organ as a principal participant.[23] Also, as one commentator openly declared, "With many economic forms coexisting, we still need a primary one." His reference here is to state-operated, planned wholesale trade, which he labeled "the key for leading and managing the national market."[24]

As for the new use of "economic methods," their role for some publicists is, frankly, "to guarantee purchase by the state and the completion of the task of obtaining goods in demand for the state." In the countryside, the SMCs have been told to use economic methods to "adjust" the sales and marketing plan. This, in effect, simply means using state price policy rather than administratively organized compulsory purchases for an unchanged end: gathering up produce for the state.[25] Here again, for some the function of reform is mainly to serve the plan.

As for reform of the SMCs, here the effort to ensure state domination of the market by a state-directed organ has perhaps been more subtle, but it is still unmistakable. Orders to the coops to serve the people, to "help" the peasants develop commodity production—in supplying market intelligence, with obtaining means of production for them, with technical services, in processing their goods, and in fetching "rational prices" for their output—are aimed at making certain that the coops retain their hold on the rural market, as this quotation illustrates: "Competition has developed between various kinds of commerce . . . the peasants will sell popular goods to other commercial forms or sell it themselves when they can get a price higher than from selling to the SMC. . . . If we don't solve these problems [of the SMCs' conflicts with the peasantry], the SMC will be seriously divorced from the peasantry."[26]

Moreover, as the SMCs "help" peasants with their sales, they have been urged to "link scattered production with state plans," or to try to convince the peasantry to plant in accordance with the needs of the state.[27] Other ways in which the SMCs have openly been told to increase their powers and their activities in the recent past include commanding them to expand their operations and their services, by attempting to buy and market the products of the peasantry that are in excess of their quotas, as well as products that are not in the state plan (those the peasants would be prone to take to free markets).

One last example of this increasing strength being accorded the SMCs recently appeared in a story of a model county-level SMC in Shunde County,

Guangdong. This coop absorbed local peasants' idle funds in the form of shares, in order to run a trade company operated jointly with peasants of some means.[28] In all these ways, then, structural reform of the commercial system in the countryside is meant to increase the control of the usual state-directed organ, the SMC, even as it uses more "economic" and fewer administrative methods to attain such control.

This more careful look at the intent behind some of the more highly touted of the new reforms of the state commercial structure weakens the notion that something altogether new has emerged in the area of state-run commercial policy in the People's Republic since late 1978. A close study of the policy toward the private sector and trade fairs[29] reveals a similar ambivalence: while "liberalization" and "flexibility" are often catchwords, when applied to actual practice, many directives on reform betray a belief that freer markets should first unlock, but then deliver to the state, more goods and resources.

Contradictions and Policy Shifts in Implementation

The double edge of so many of the policies just reviewed helps to explain contradictions among directives on the reform program; shifts in specific components of the effort and in overall direction within relatively brief time periods; and what have been tagged by outside observers, and often by the press in the PRC as well, as "obstructions" to the reforms. As noted above, the usual explanation given by foreign analysts is that those with a self-interested stake in the old, bureaucratically organized arrangements are attempting to undermine the challenge to their positions posed by the new measures.

Obviously, there is a good measure of truth in such assessments. Two clearcut examples in the commercial sector are cases of opposition to the simplification of wholesaling structures and "locality blockades." According to critiques of the first form of resistance, various levels of government have each created their own set of wholesale organs over the years, because of the revenue to be squeezed from their operation. For each time that goods pass through a wholesale station, the government in the area may draw revenues from price differentials and fees, which it has been allowed to add to the price of such goods-in-transit. Also, having jurisdiction over these offices permits local governments to hire more personnel and to acquire new facilities. One journalist reported a calculation that Heilongjiang Province could save 2.5 million yuan a year in transport expenses and depletion alone by cutting down from three or four to only one the number of intermediary links in the circulation paths for marketing live pigs.[30] That sums of such magnitude are involved provides a good clue as to why lower levels of administration are loath to comply with these new regulations.

"Locality blockades," termed as "inconsistent with the demand of breaking through barriers and with the reform of the economic system," are similarly said to derive from the economic benefits that local offices of government acquire from maintaining their hold over commodities which originate in their area of jurisdiction. Reform goals of developing specialization and cooperation, and of expanding horizontal trade ties between enterprises at the same administrative level but in different geographic areas, are thwarted when local governments, anxious to pocket the profits of enterprises in their areas, oppose any changes in commodity flows or pricing patterns that might decrease their own revenues. This problem has apparently been intensified with the institution of financial reforms that link localities' revenue with enterprise profits.[31]

But apart from the foot-dragging and subversion of the reform program in which local governments and their cadres engage—a subject that has already received much scholarly attention, and which, therefore, will *not* be a focus of analysis here—"obstruction" is clearly also a function of elite ambivalence and discord about the extent of permissible reform. This is borne out by comparing quite disparate directives, and also moral tales, concerning nearly identical issues that have appeared in the press only a matter of months apart.

One such example concerns the changing line devised for new forms of trading outside the usual state commercial bureaucracy. Two articles, spaced about ten months apart, take quite different stands on the functions of this kind of commerce.[32] The first, from March 1982, attacked the "trust trade companies" (*xintuo maoyi gongsi*), of which Guangdong had 115 at that point, for paying too much attention simply to earning money. Their inclination toward profits, it charged, caused these new companies to favor dealings in foreign goods over local ones; to pursue only large business deals, rather than opening outlets for small commodities; and to overemphasize their own business, rather than fulfilling their proper role, which is to serve as commission agents for the state in sales, purchases, storage, and shipping. The criticism here is that this new form of marketing, despite its representing a mode of commercial flexibility, still ought to be operating under the plan's guidance, to help the localities in which it is situated to dispose of local goods that are in excess. Thus, one might conclude, even the new streams of trading must still flow toward the same main channel of the plan.

The second article, dated mid-January 1983, approached the issue of these new channels from just the opposite viewpoint, and defended trade warehouses (*maoyi zhanjing*) another "new" (actually, a traditional trade form restored and abolished several times since 1956) style of operating, in the face of resistance that they were meeting from state organs. Those putting limits on their operations were reminded that these bodies rightly have some of their own business to do, besides the commission work they engage in for the state. Their job of marketing things not in the state shops had been stymied, the article pointed out, by regulations commanding them to obtain approval for the prices they set, and placing limits on the scope of their operations. "If their operations scope is exactly the same as that of the state companies, they won't be able to develop their own function," the writer explained. It seems evident that these various enterprises operating outside the old state-run system are conceived of quite differently by disparate observers, and at various times.

Yet another example indicative of this sort of conflict of viewpoints relates to the legitimate bounds for long-distance trading of grain and other rural produce by nonstate merchants. In February 1983, Shanghai published a set of regulations on the reform of the commercial system that explicitly permitted communes, brigades, teams, and even individual peasants in the area to sell any products but cotton at market prices, after they had completed their compulsory sales to the state. Previous rulings that had required approval for shipping agricultural products to other areas for sale were canceled, and SMCs, cooperative commercial organs, and licensed peddlers were all also allowed to buy and sell grain at negotiated prices.[33]

In this same vein, and around the same time, the State Council, in conjunction with the Ministry of Commerce and the State Commission for Restructuring the Economic System, proclaimed that collective and individual commercial enterprises could send salesmen to sell in other counties or even other provinces, so long as they sold only surplus commodities after state plan obligations were fulfilled. This order also rescinded previous regulations stipulating that only food departments were authorized to act as agents in purchasing and marketing food grains at negotiated prices.[34]

But these directives, highly liberal for the PRC, were undone, at least in Shanghai, in less than six months. The municipal government there decreed in mid-July that punishments would be doled out for purchasing grain from local grain stores and then shipping it to other localities for resale at a profit.[35] It is true that the earlier order had not specified what the supply source for obtaining commercial grain must be. But it still seems that a part of what had been at least implicitly allowed earlier in the year had become illegal by summer.

In one last set of contrasting anecdotes, peasants engaging in trade on their own were defended in the press against local state trade organs that were trying to interfere with their business.[36] But on the other side of this issue, various departments and units, presented as competing with the SMC to acquire valued rural commodities, were criticized, and the SMC was presented as being in the right.[37] In a story of the first type, onion-growing peasants in Anhui were forced by the local state products wholesale company to sell their output to the company. Moreover, the local state company drastically lowered the usual procurement price and charged the peasants a commission and a management fee, all of which obstructive behavior was censored in the press.

But one cannot easily draw a moral to the effect that trade outside the customary state-managed circulation channels must always be protected in the face of state-sector attempts to intercept it. In both early and late 1981, articles appeared chastising noncommercial organs that competed with the SMC in procuring choice and scarce products, thereby making impossible the completion of the

SMC's purchase plan. Some of the other organs involved included commune enterprises, jointly operated companies, and foreign trade departments.

Each of these three sets of contrasting stances toward reform and its side effects reflects a basic ambivalence toward the program as a whole, as outlined above. It is true that many of these incidents or behavior patterns involved cases of local-level bureaucratic resistance and interference of one sort or another. But, more important for the argument here, these cases represent contrasts or shifts in *policy*, and not just problems in implementation. Thus, these episodes reveal a conflict between the inclination of some policymakers (marketeers) to rely on incentives to stimulate productivity, on the one hand, as against another group within the elite. This second group (the bureaucrats) is willing to tolerate the use of incentives up to a point, but will oppose the milieu of freer marketing within which they are set when it has the additional and usually linked effect of encouraging peasants, factory managers, and staff in state commercial organs and stores to ignore or sidestep the state's essential purchases. It seems from this review of the press of the past few years that at the point when the state begins to lose out from the release of market forces, bureaucrats can convince marketeers to pull in the reins on reform in various ways, at least for a time.

Evaluation and Prognosis

The final step of this analysis is to attempt an evaluation of the program. Such an assessment must take into account the presence within the policy-making elite of two separate stances. The whole elite of the present period seems to be in agreement that an enlivened commerce stimulates productivity, and also agrees about the importance of such enhanced output. Therefore, the steady rise in recent years in the volume of retail sales (up 9.4 percent in 1982 over 1981, and up more than 10 percent in 1983 over 1982)[38] must be considered a positive factor by all decision makers.

Over time, however, the state's proportion of this trade has been declining, and the percentage of *increase* in the value of trade that has been undertaken by the state sector has also been much lower than that for collective and individually run trade in the past few years.[39] Although collectively operated trade accounted for only some 16.1 percent of the total value of retail sales in 1982 (up from 14.5 percent the year before) and individual trade was just 2.9 percent of the total (an increase from 1981's 1.6 percent),[40] the creeping advance of these other two sectors may be seen as a danger signal to those of the bureaucratic persuasion.

Another dimension of the reform, the increase in sites for trading, has also been remarkable over the past five years. As of 1982, China had 1.47 million commercial, catering, and service centers and establishments, a 7.7-fold increase over 1978.[41] But here again, the state is in the process of being overtaken, if the amount of new sites and not their volume of business is taken as the measure:

only 210,000 of these are large state-owned shops (a 2.5-fold increase); 340,000 were collectively owned (a 5.9-fold increase), and 920,000 were individually run (an increase of 77.7-fold).

The number of trade fairs has also expanded significantly over the past few years. In 1979, the year after their initial relegitimization following the Cultural Revolution, there were around 36,000 of these across the country. By the end of 1983, the *People's Daily* reported that there then were "about more than 46,000." Besides their growth in numbers, trade volume in these marts went from a figure equivalent to 6.6 percent of total retail sales in 1978 to 11.4 percent in 1981 and 13 percent by late 1983.[42] Though none of the present leadership abhors these markets for their taint of "capitalistic" money, prices, and profits, as the radicals around Mao did, many current leaders do look askance at them when their patrons and peddlers engage in what the socialist Chinese see as "corruption" and "collusion"—shortweighting, price gouging, adulterating, reselling rationed goods, and the like. Since the time of their revival there have been repeated official directives calling for tightened control over them.

Other statistics describe the loosening of bureaucratic arrangements in the allocation of commodities to the populace, in the industrial sector, and in the realm of price-setting. As of 1978, 73 categories of commodities were supplied by coupon, by certificate, or via other forms of rationing. This number had declined to only 17 by 1982.[43] Of 256 materials under the state's unified allocation, all but thirty or forty had become available for market purchase by mid-1983; by that time also, state-owned industrial and commercial departments, instead of just price departments, had the power to set prices (which still meant state-fixed ones) for 160 small commodities of the "third category" (those goods viewed by the leadership as less vital to basic livelihood or not needed for export purposes).[44] And 170 of some 200 farm tools, machines, seeds, and other means of agricultural production, formerly allocated by state distribution agencies, had entered the market as commodities by late 1983.[45]

Moreover, by as early as 1981, direct factory sales already accounted for 9.2 percent of total retail sales, a proportion judged by one economist as representing a relatively large percentage of industrial consumer goods output, since, he reasoned, basic food products account for more than half of retail sales.[46] All of these changes spelled a reduced role for state suppliers, pricing bureaus, and commercial offices. Thus it is likely that, while their institution may be seen as positive by the more marketeer-inclined proponents of reform, they may well awaken defensive feelings and behaviors by the units whose duties have been diminished.

Another reason for caution in assessing the effects of commercial reform is the regime's own admission that "poor management" existed in "quite a number of [state] commercial enterprises." Examples included longer turnover periods for circulating funds in 1982 over 1981, expenses rising in commodity circulation, and a decrease in profits of 34.2 percent in 1982 over 1981 for enterprises under the Ministry of Commerce, and of 14.2 percent for enterprises under the All-China Federation of Supply and Marketing Cooperatives.[47] Thus, with the increase in the number of units now engaging in trade *outside* the state commercial sector, and with efficiency actually declining overall *within* that sector, over the long term the state may be losing out in the competition.

It seems clear that reform (not just reform in commerce, but the companion reforms in other sectors—the responsibility systems in agriculture and the various schemes of enterprise autonomy in industry) must be responsible for heightened sales activity in a range of forms throughout society. Still, these findings could be brewing danger over the long run for commercial reform as a sanctioned policy, at least in its most liberal guise. The presence of an incentives program, which draws unanimous elite support *only* for its ability to motivate output, seems to be weakening the sinews of the plan. Caught between two differing interpretations of what reform should do, and how far it should go, the socialist state may be stuck in a bind: its leaders want this heightened productivity that comes from permitting more flexible forms of trading. But, at the same time, a significant segment of this elite grows uneasy over the concomitant loosening of the plan, a loosening caused by the same incentives that created that productivity.

Now that producers have obtained permission to use extrabureaucratic channels for a portion of their trade, channels that promise higher prices, many are tempted to turn to those channels before their planned obligations to the state have been met. The more this process occurs, the more likely it is that eventually there will be a turn, at least for a time, to more bureaucratic modes of "reform." As we have seen, this genre of reform entails such activities as having SMCs "help" peasants find outlets for their goods and urging state trading organs to become more efficient, so that they can win out in the competition—that is, it aims at using the reform to serve the plan.

In the end, the intent of reform by and large has not amounted to—and will not amount to—any total abandonment of state-managed socialism. Instead, its aim is to serve as a supplement to socialism, as Academy of Social Science President Ma Hong's paraphrasing of Deng Xiaoping's *Selected Works* in late 1983 evinced:

> Every step and measure of reform must be beneficial to completing the various regulations and tasks of the state plan . . . and toward ensuring that the state's financial revenue shows rational increases year by year. . . . The aim of reform is to perfect, consolidate, and develop the basic system of socialism, to make its various concrete systems become healthier, to fully develop the superiority of the socialist system, and to promote the continuous development of the social productive forces.[48]

Thus, for the policy-making elite, it appears that the state guidance and plan of socialism still lie at the heart of the Chinese economy, where they impose an ultimate limit on full-fledged reform.

Notes

1. For a discussion of the concept of "tendency," see Franklyn Griffiths, "A Tendency Analysis of Soviet Policy-Making," in *Interest Groups in Soviet Politics*, ed. H. Gordon Skilling and Franklyn Griffiths (Princeton: Princeton University Press, 1971), pp. 335–77.

2. See my *Chinese Business under Socialism* (Berkeley: University of California Press, 1984), chap. 2.

3. *Renmin ribao* (People's daily) (hereafter *RMRB*). December 18, 1981, p. 5.

4. James T. C. Liu, *Reform in Sung China* (Cambridge: Harvard University Press, 1959), pp. 49–50.

5. Paul Cocks, "The Rationalization of Party Control," in *Change in Communist Systems,* ed. Chalmers Johnson (Stanford: Stanford University Press, 1970), p. 188. These two varieties of reform also roughly parallel what Burks has referred to as "Type A Reform" and "Type B Reform." See R. V. Burks, "Technology and Political Change in Eastern Europe," in ibid., pp. 289–91.

6. John F. Burns, "In Moscow, More Questions than Answers," *New York Times*, January 1, 1984, p. E5; and Burns, "Andropov Assails Economic Failings of Soviet Regime," ibid., December 29, 1983, p. 1.

7. See the quotation of Chen in *Da gong bao* (Impartial daily), November 26, 1956, p. 1, editorial. For the early 1960s, see Chen Yun, "Muqian caizheng jingji de qingkuang he kefu kunnan de rogan banfa" (The situation of financial and economic matters at present and certain methods for overcoming difficulties), in *Chen Yun tongzhi wengao xuanbian (1956–1962)* (Selected documents of Comrade Chen Yun [1956–1962]) (Sichuan: Renmin chubanshe, 1981) (Neibu faxing), pp. 157–63, 168.

8. *RMRB*, December 9 and 11, 1983, both on p. 2. The moral here is drawn from experience in one of the counties of Shanghai, an area where, if anywhere, one would think, the peasants should have learned to do marketing without the help of state-run business. That such an argument is made in discussing trade even in this sort of area serves only to illustrate the strength of the commitment of at least some of the leadership to socialist commercial organs.

9. For a report on the work conference and its outcomes, see Michael Parks, "China's Political, Economic Reformers Appear to Win Significant Victory," in the *Los Angeles Times*, April 5, 1984. The opening of fourteen coastal cities to foreign trade and investment, wholesaling reforms, and more powers for enterprise managers followed in its wake. I thank Stanley Rosen for sending me this article.

10. See *RMRB*, July 31, 1983, p. 5.

11. *Foreign Broadcast Information Service (FBIS)*, September 9, 1983, pp. K9–10; September 22, 1983, p. O8; September 8, 1983, pp. Q6–8; and October 7, 1983, p. K16.

12. *FBIS*, September 9, 1983, pp. K12–13, is only one example of many directives on strengthening market controls periodically appearing in the press in recent years. This one was issued by the State Administration of Industry and Commerce.

13. Ibid., November 11, 1983, p. K2.

14. Ibid., September 9, 1983, p. K13; and *RMRB,* December 18, 1981, p. 5.

15. *RMRB,* February 23, 1982, p. 2, describes a union between a county-level SMC in Sichuan and a production team; ibid., June 26, 1983, p. 5, presents an account of a Liaoning county-level SMC "linking up" with brigades.

16. This chapter touches only very lightly on the theme of the petty private sector—the small merchants, individual and collective enterprises, and free markets. For more on this subject, see my article, "Commerce: The Petty Private Sector and the Three Lines in

the Early 1980s," in *Three Visions of Chinese Socialism*, ed., Dorothy J. Solinger (Boulder: Westview Press, 1984). This is Chapter 10 of this volume.

17. *Hongqi* (Red flag) (hereafter *HQ*), no. 5 (1982): 29–30.

18. *FBIS*, February 17, 1983, p. O7.

19. *RMRB*, August 26, 1983, p. 5.

20. Barry Naughton, "The Profit System," *China Business Review* (November–December 1983): 16–17; *FBIS*, February 17, 1983, p. O6; September 23, 1983, p. K6; October 26, 1983, p. K6; September 16, 1983, p. K14.

21. *FBIS*, September 16, 1983, p. K14.

22. *RMRB*, March 23, 1983, p. 2; and Liu Yi (present minister of commerce), "Establish Our Country's New Commodity Circulation System," *HQ*, no. 8 (1983): 26.

23. See *RMRB*, August 26, 1983, p. 5.

24. Wan Dianwu, "Several Theoretical Questions on the Reform of the Commercial System," *Jingji guanli* (Economic management), no. 10: 37.

25. *RMRB*, December 5, 1981, p. 3, and August 26, 1983, p. 5.

26. *FBIS*, August 26, 1983, p. 5.

27. Ibid., November 23, 1983, p. K16.

28. *RMRB*, December 22, 1983, p. 2.

29. See note 16.

30. *RMRB*, September 24, 1982, p. 2, and July 25, 1983, p. 2.

31. *FBIS*, September 23, 1983, p. K8.

32. *RMRB*, March 20, 1982, p. 3, and January 15, 1983, p. 3.

33. *FBIS*, February 17, 1983, p. O7, translated from *Jeifang ribao* (Liberation daily), February 7, 1983, p. 2.

34. *FBIS*, March 10, 1983, p. K13.

35. Ibid., July 13, 1983, p. 07.

36. *RMRB*, January 11, 1983, p. 2. Similar stories are in ibid., December 11, 1983, p. 2, and December 19, 1983, p. 2.

37. Ibid., January 16, 1981, p. 2, December 15, 1981, p. 3, and February 27, 1982, p. 2.

38. *Beijing Review (BR)*, no. 19 (1983): viii, and *RMRB*, January 7, 1984, p. 1.

39. In 1982 trade by state organs was variously reported as having accounted for 84.5 percent (*FBIS*, February 24, 1983, p. K14) and 76.6 percent (*BR*, no. 19 (1983): viii) of the total volume of retail sales; for 1981 the same two sources cite 87.7 percent and 80 percent, respectively. The two sources also show state trade increasing by 3.9 percent or 4.7 percent in 1982, collective trade by 30 percent or 21.3 percent, and individual, by 80 percent or 99.5 percent, respectively. The discrepancies are not explained.

40. *BR*, no. 19 (1983): viii.

41. Ibid., no. 28 (1983): 19. It is not clear why this number is so different from one published about a year earlier, in *RMRB*, May 27, 1982, p. 1: 3,299,000 national commercial sites as of the end of 1981, representing various kinds of economic forms of commercial, catering, and service sites.

42. *RMRB*, January 6, 1984, p. 2, *FBIS*, March 24, 1983, and October 26, 1983, p. K9.

43. *FBIS*, January 11, 1983, p. K2.

44. Ibid., September 23, 1983, pp. K3 and K6.

45. Ibid., October 26, 1983, p. K9.

46. Naughton, "The Profit System," p. 17.

47. *BR*, no. 19 (1983): ix.

48. As summarized in Ma Hong, "Reform is also a Revolution: A Discussion on Studying 'Deng Xiaoping's Selected Works' on Economic System Reform," *HQ*, no. 20 (1983): 28.

4
China's New Economic Policies and
the Local Industrial Political Process:
The Case of Wuhan

A well-publicized program of economic reform has been under way in the People's Republic of China since 1979, involving, in schematic terms, decentralization of powers and the purse on a vertical dimension and redistribution of investment among sectors and regions on a horizontal one. In short, there have been some fairly significant alterations in the rights and moneys allocated to— and drifting into—the hands of lower-level officials and managers, while capital and material allocations have shifted among economic ministries, broad geographical areas, industrial sectors, provinces, and individual cities.

One might hypothesize that these new policies would bring in their wake certain political phenomena tending in the direction of democratization. Specifically, many of the behavioral effects of the policies seem to suggest that privatization may be appearing as the state withdraws and that pluralization could be accompanying intergroup clashes that have emerged in response to the state-led redistribution schemes. Indeed, the past few years have seen in China new forms of noncentrally directed marketing activity; the birth of urban and firm profit-retention

This chapter was originally delivered at the 1984 Annual Meeting of the American Political Science Association, Washington, DC, August 30–September 2, 1984. I wish to thank the City Foreign Affairs Bureau, the Municipal Planning and Economic Commissions, and the Textile and Machine-Building Bureaus of Wuhan for their assistance and cooperation in providing the interviews on which this chapter is based. The two trips to Wuhan for interviewing were both financed wholly by grants from the University of Pittsburgh (the Research Development Fund, the Asian Studies Program of the University Center for International Studies, and the Contemporary China Program).

and profit-seeking, an explosive growth of extrabudgetary funds in the hands of local leaders and enterprise managers and their use of these funds in unauthorized capital construction; regional interest articulation and advocacy in public arenas; and a sudden spurt of competition throughout the system.

This chapter tests the often accepted notion that economic liberalization lays the ground for or at least is closely correlated with political transformation of the same type. For the sake of simplicity, recent data from one Chinese city will be used to assess the extent to which, at the local level, two key modifications are taking place. First, has decentralization sparked privatization, as the state "sheds" its former functions, relegating these tasks to nonstate actors?[1] Second, has redistribution (termed "readjustment" in Chinese parlance) produced a process of pluralization, involving bargains, battles, negotiations, and lobbying among "multiple, voluntary, competitive, nonhierarchically ordered and self-determined" units, as they attempt to defend threatened policies and pork barrels that benefit them and as they fight against proposals harmful to their interests?[2]

The purported linkage between economic and political forms, and a related trend of homogenization between systems, has been suggested in the writings of a number of social scientists in recent years. Thus, J. L. Metcalfe has concluded that "neither an atomistic nor a unitary model adequately represents the structure and behavior of the modern economy. . . . In short, the economy is more accurately portrayed as a pluralistic political order rather than an atomistic or unitary system . . . characterized by the existence of a number of centers of power and decision making." He views all modern economies as being situated within functionally, if not formally, pluralistic systems, which are "geared to the competitive pursuit of sectional interests."[3] Moreover, he claims that the line between public and private is everywhere blurred and that the two realms are interdependent and overlapping in any system, so that "antithetical capitalist and socialist models polarize discussion towards unrealistically extreme portrayals of economy."

Following this same line of reasoning, Olson's "distributional coalitions that slow down the capacity to adopt technologies and to reallocate resources"[4] and Thurow's "zero-sum society," incapable of allocating loss in investment planning and beset with demands for protection and security from an array of lobbying groups,[5] need not be characterizations that delineate democratic societies alone. Moreover, even the "pluralistic stagnation" Beer identifies as having "paralyzed public choice" in Britain,[6] the fragmentation and dispersion of power in the United States that Krasner states has limited the ability of the American government to influence private groups,[7] and the resistance to restructuring the organization of production that Reich complains occurs here, as it threatens vested economic interests and established values,[8] all may be creatures and features of complex modern industrialized society. If this is in some general sense the case, then the competitive, self-protective responses of Chinese groups affected by economic transformation may be fitted into a mold familiar to students of the countries of the West.

Yet, interview material from fifty hours of discussions with economic policy officials in Wuhan, China, conducted in May 1983 and May 1984 shows that, despite the bestowal of a range of new opportunities and privileges on lower-level actors and regardless of redistribution, the fundamental features of the political process there had not changed. Instead, local actors have retained and merely adapted their wanted stances—toward their superiors and toward other regions—in order to respond to these new opportunities and investment shifts.

I chose Wuhan—the major industrial city of central China (ranking fourth in gross value of industrial output among the twenty-five most industrialized metropolises of the country as of the early 1980s), some 700 miles down the Yangtze from Shanghai and 800 miles to the south of Beijing—as the site of my study primarily because new management schemes for the sectors of industry in which it is strong have been at the heart of the decentralization and readjustment programs. In particular, machine-building and textiles are, with metallurgy, among the three leading trades of the city, and my interviews and thus this study focused specifically on their experiences.

As a prime component of heavy industry and as the foundation for the massive capital construction drives that have characterized Soviet-type systems, the machine-building trade in Wuhan, as throughout China, had been the recipient of much state investment over the years. But the post-Mao economic readjustment was undertaken to transfer resources from their previous lopsided allotment to heavy industry to the light industrial sector and to agriculture. Machinery enterprises, then, suffered severe cutbacks during 1979–81, forcing them to confront markets for their supplies and for the disposal of their end products, as the state ceased disbursing inputs and procuring the entire output of firms in this industry.

Machine-building was prominent among the trades in Wuhan but backward technologically by national and international standards. Therefore, such factories here had at once to cope with a sudden decentralization of their activity as the central government "shed" its former function of caring for all the firms' needs and also to deal with the need to compete in an environment challenging to their endowments.

In addition, readjustment entailed compelling machinery enterprises to switch their service orientation away from producing machine parts for the heavy industrial sector and toward turning out equipment to meet the needs of consumer production and agriculture. This dimension of the program also required these firms to operate independently and competitively, as they found it necessary to set up sales connections with firms with which they had not previously had exchanges. In this regard, the experience of Wuhan illustrates a national pattern in cities strong in the machine-building trade.

Textiles, as a key branch of the newly favored light industrial sector, got new investment and loan capital, along with a series of other preferential measures designed to boost their growth. Again, Wuhan, as one of the five leading textile centers in the nation, provides representative material on this department, one suddenly encouraged to use its new assistance as a foundation for an equally novel activity, profit-making. In the textile trade, as in machinery, Wuhan industry, though near the top of the list in terms of output value, is deficient in technique and quality. Thus, in this realm, too, a local trade had a head start in terms of its foundation, but a need to work harder than other leading regions in competing. Therefore, Wuhan seemed to be an apt case for testing the connection between economic reforms and their possible political concomitants.

In the discussion that follows, I begin by sketching the basic structural aspects of the prereform socialist political economy, drawing in particular on the work of Jerry Hough on Soviet local political organs and of Janos Kornai on the Hungarian economy (no similar work exists on China for the topics covered by these two authors). This will show the approximate starting point in the local industrial political economy in two key centrally planned economies.

In the next section I will detail many of the new economic policies in China, alluding to some of the more economically specific effects they have had. I will address my analysis particularly to several principal components of the new policies especially relevant to urban industrial policy and to the two sectors noted above. The issues I will concentrate on include shifts in investment among sectors, the closing and converting of plants in the heavy industrial sector, and the use of "economic levers," the Chinese label for market forces.

Finally, I will present my data from the Wuhan interviews to test for the presence of a link between economic liberalization and political processes— privatization and pluralization—tending toward democratization. My conclusion explains my reasons for rejecting the hypothesis of a necessary bond between liberal economic policy and democratic outcome, at least for this stage of the Chinese reforms.

Local Industrial Politics in Soviet-type Economics

To use my recent Chinese data to test the connection between economic liberalization and privatization/pluralization in centrally planned economies, it is necessary first to outline the nature of the local socialist political economy. Such an outline can then be used as a guide and benchmark in judging where China had gone by mid-1984. Probably the most comprehensive and widely cited treatments of the industrial political process at the municipal level in Soviet-type, centrally planned economies are Janos Kornai's *Economics of Shortage* and Jerry Hough's *The Soviet Prefects*.[9] Together, these two books, whose contents overlap a great deal, present a rather thorough portrait of the politics and economics of the local policy process in such systems, drawing on Hungarian and Soviet data, respectively.

The basic fact about these systems is state ownership of the overwhelming bulk of the economy. Several traits flow from this fundamental condition. First of all, there is a greater need for official coordination of economic activity because of the state's supervision of a wide range of disparate functions, for all of which it takes responsibility and pays. Then, the omnipresence of the plan and of state-designated prices means that there is no really effective market for organizing economic activities. And finally, most labor power, supplies, equipment, and materials come from and are allocated by one common source.

Closely linked to this dominance of the state sector is the inescapability of scarcity and shortage. With so many claimants on one pot, demands unavoidably surpass the amount of available funds, and a predictable set of behavioral patterns follows. First and most obviously is a pervasive competition, both among individual firms within functional hierarchies and among the various hierarchies themselves. Taut plans and "investment tension" accompany this competition, while they aggravate the shortages as well.

A third feature of Soviet-type systems pinpointed by both Hough and Kornai is the responsibility of each state-run unit—and, by extension, of its state-appointed official head—for fulfilling some centrally identified success indicator. Most typically through the course of the history of centrally planned economies the principal indicator has been plan fulfillment, and the part of the plan that has been crucial has been the economic growth of each unit in the system. Since every cadre in the state bureaucracy identifies closely with his job and so with his unit, and since both his current reputation and his future career prospects depend on his achieving the demands associated with the indicator in effect, localistic and departmentalist behavior is a natural outcome of such a system.

Such localism takes a number of forms. Alliances, even "complicity" according to Kornai, grow up between local officials, the enterprises in their regions, and the immediate industrial bureau (department) heads to whom they appeal for supplies, funding, and labor power. Such complicity can result in minor illegalities, in the service of seeing that success indicators are met (although only within limits, for local officials are aware that they will be audited and generally are cautious about grossly exceeding the bounds of the law). Another manifestation of this localism is, as one would expect, local advocacy, as officials at municipal (and higher) levels become spokespersons for the areas under their jurisdiction. Though these spokespersons—"allocators" in Kornai's terms—must become to a certain extent restrictive when they distribute supplies and investment to the units under their charge, when appealing to higher-level allocators they become expansive.

A fourth aspect of the usual Soviet-type economy is its centralization of decision making on investment issues. Associated with this is allocation of funds along the vertical lines of the various industrial branches. Such responsibility serves to strengthen these specialized hierarchies. Consequently, each individual plant, when requiring money, must direct its appeals to its immediate functional superior, the local bureau for its sector, which in turn pushes these requests up the hierarchy. Local advocacy pitted against branch power often causes the formation of local alliances that assert themselves in the face of the functional hierarchies. And, because of the often largely single-stranded distributional network, local officials must emerge as arbitrators, coordinators, and intermediaries (both within and among localities) in solving supply problems, setting priorities, and handling departmental disputes.

Last of all, but most important in Kornai's analysis of the workings of these systems, is the paternalistic role of the state under socialism. What he calls the "soft budget constraint" means that the state will always, ultimately, provide for plants in difficulty, thereby rendering failure impossible and erasing calculations of risk from the decision structure of the firm. In his account, the "expansion drives," "investment hunger," and "investment tension" that he finds in socialist economies are all traceable to this central condition. Moreover, these drives, hungers, and tension add to the pervasive competition and shortages in these systems.

Since neither state ownership, shortage, local officials' responsibility for success indicators, branch-type allocation, nor soft budgets have undergone alteration in any Soviet-type system, the behavioral correlates of these principles and conditions are likewise unlikely to shift. Both Hough and Kornai found only marginal changes over the years in the two countries they studied, even in the presence of several party reorganizations in the Soviet case and major economic reforms in Hungary.[10]

New Economic Policies, 1979–84

The Vertical Dimension: Decentralization

The Chinese state's difficulties in restraining local investment, though more a problem in some areas than in others, can be traced back to the 1950s, and some of the components of locally managed funds, such as retained depreciation allowances and a portion of fixed investment moneys, had been decentralized long before 1979.[11] Enterprises started to keep depreciation allowances in 1967 (though set at somewhat lower rates than today—then, the percentages were in the range of 2–3 percent; today they are from 5 to 7 percent of the equipment in question). And fixed investment capital came under lower-level organs' control (and so was not a part of the central budget) under the fourth five-year plan (1971–75), although this figure was reduced to 31 percent in 1978.

But in 1979–80 the fiscal relations between the center and the provinces were significantly restructured, and a host of autonomous behaviors have issued from the change. Interviews conducted by Donnithorne in 1980 uncovered a set of five new and distinct types of financial relationships among the twenty-nine provincial-level units. The majority of them (fifteen), however, were then being governed by a system labeled "apportion revenues and expenditures; give responsibilities to different levels" (*huafen shouzhi fenji baogan*). This arrangement permitted provinces and the authorities under them to keep all the profits earned from all enterprises housed in their area of jurisdiction for the enterprises that were not managed by the central government.

This new reform greatly increased the proportion of their own revenue kept by the lower-level authorities, in addition to bestowing on their leaders the power to determine how to spend the revenue retained. In addition, these provinces were entitled to retain all the proceeds of taxes (with the exception of the industrial and commercial tax, whose receipts were shared with the center according to negotiated rates) from firms in their area.

In 1982, despite a central-level promise that this set of practices would remain unaltered for five years, a new method was designed for allocating finances, one that favored the provinces even more. This new scheme allowed the majority of the provinces to retain 80 percent of the revenues generated in their own areas, on the average. The key change here was that most provinces were entitled to draw a larger percentage of the industrial and commercial tax, which in recent years has been a growing tax base, as it rises with the increase in total output. In exchange, the provincial-level governments gave Beijing a share in local tax revenues. But these revenues were actually in decline, as the enterprises from which they were derived have been allowed to keep more of the profits they generate and have been enjoined not to raise the prices of their products, despite rising costs.

Moreover, provincial officials were granted new authority to adjust the tax rates imposed at their levels of jurisdiction, and a set of "extrabudgetary funds," monies that local authorities can gather that do not enter into their budgets—and so escape Beijing's inspection—expanded drastically after 1979. These funds are drawn from industrial, agricultural, and commercial surtaxes, the profits of collective enterprises; and fees for administering free markets, among other sources. They existed from the early 1950s but never before had reached anywhere near present proportions. According to central-level reckoning, extrabudgetary revenues in recent years might have amounted to the equivalent of about half of total budgetary revenues, as against only about 17 percent in 1960.

In addition, relaxation of the controls on bank loans and the granting of new autonomy to the provincial branches of the Chinese People's Bank to issue loans for capital construction have also freed local decision makers from the hold of the centrally planned economy and its administrators' rulings.[12] Furthermore, regulations for enhanced enterprise autonomy issued in the period under review included the right of firms to retain portions of their profits and to grant bonuses to more productive workers (this later regulation, however, has generally been skirted by across-the-board hand-outs, in the interest of keeping peace within the plant). Naturally, such rules provided enterprise managers and their staffs with an added incentive to negotiate lower "base figures" for profit deliveries to the center and to attempt to conceal their actual profit levels.

Besides these new arrangements bolstering the financial position and powers of localities domestically, in the same period the central government adopted policies permitting provinces to engage in foreign trade through the local branches of the national foreign trade corporations, though at times it has attempted to recentralize these powers (as in early 1981 and March 1984). Different provinces have been allowed to keep different percentages of their earnings from this trade and to conduct different volumes of transactions on their own authority, but all may raise loans abroad and be partners to cooperation ventures with foreign governments and firms. The administrative level authorized to give permission for these forms of business has been lower at some times than at others.[13]

The search for a relationship between center and locality that satisfies central leaders, however, did not stop with these arrangements. Because much of the national elite has become concerned about the amount of funds now controlled by lower-level officials and plant managers, central decision makers have continued to tinker with the financial system. Deficit, overissuance of currency, inflation, and declining receipts in the national treasury as of late 1980 led the leadership to enforce provincial purchases of central treasury bonds, to freeze bank accounts, and to engineer a compulsory "loan" from the provincial governments to the center in early 1981, formalized in law in late 1982. Also, in 1983 the state set up regional quotas for total fixed investment, along with a 30 percent surcharge on all over-quota projects. These various efforts to regain central financial control have been relatively successful.

Moreover, in June 1983 the central government extended to all state-owned enterprises a system first pioneered in about 200 firms in 1980, entitled "change-profits-into-taxes" (*li gai shui*). This program substituted an income tax payment of 55 percent of enterprise profits (on the average) to the central government (and a tax of some 15 to 35 percent of profits to the firms' city governments, letting firms retain what was left) for the total profit deliveries of the pre-1979 years and for the retained-profit schemes of 1979–83.

In the first phases of reform (beginning in 1979), each enterprise and its supervisory body had negotiated a profit "base figure," which the enterprise had to deliver to the state, while the firms could keep somewhere between 50 and 100 percent of the profits above that base. The *li gai shui* "reform" was meant to introduce more standardization and reliability into the collection system, so that enterprises would have less opportunity to conceal profits and to retain what the central government considered excessive amounts of funds as a result of highly particularized negotiations. As a necessary corollary, the new reform was meant to ensure that the state recouped what the leadership believed to be its rightful share of national income. The new plan, *li gai shui*, however, also failed to satisfy completely the demands of national-level planners, and a second phase of this reform was instituted in October 1984. This effort is aimed at further specifying a range of eleven different taxes that must be paid to the central government and at using taxation as an economic lever to change the discrepancies in profits of a number of products that were rooted in their "irrationally" high prices.[14]

Thus, the principal sources of decentralized investment funds, as of the past five years, have been these: higher retained depreciation allowances; bank loans, increasingly substituted for the outright grants of capital that had been allocated from the central government through ministries down their hierarchies and ultimately to the firms for nearly three decades through 1978; retained enterprise profits; and the expanded "extrabudgetary funds" in the hands of provincial, municipal, and county governments.

These new or enlarged pots of locally controlled moneys, along with a reorganization of the materials supply system (whereby primary responsibility for supplemental materials allocation has been turned over to material supply companies based at the provincial level), have aggravated a characteristic "expansion drive" that has typically marked socialist states.[15] This is possible because firms now have more resources under their control and less supervision over their use. Local authorities, as always, welcome their enhanced opportunities to initiate construction projects in their areas, for such programs offer more local employment and a chance to obtain and manage more scarce materials, as well as provide the extra profits from new industry that will now accrue to their own localities' accounts.

Manifestations of the problems growing out of the new regulations appeared as early as late summer 1980. At that point central leaders discovered that profit deliveries to the state budget had declined by 17 percent, as many enterprises surpassed the base figures they had set for profit delivery and as the profits they held themselves steadily grew. According to calculations by Naughton, between 1978 and 1982 the portion of total fixed investment in state-owned units that was in the hands of local enterprises and governments increased from 31 to 58 percent.[16]

Yet one more sort of decentralization in the reform era has been a set of new rights in marketing for industrial units. Since 1979–80, factories may independently market products not purchased by state commercial organs, as well as the output they produce above what the state plan designates, and are able to collect both wholesale and retail mark-ups from this trading. For the above-plan production, they are responsible for securing their own inputs, rather than counting on state supplies, and they may negotiate over the prices charged, within limits prescribed by the government.

Although the amount of such free marketing varies widely among firms, direct factory sales already accounted for just over 9 percent of total retail sales by 1981. The brisk business and bartering resulting from this relaxation of the state commercial apparatus's controls, along with a burst of new locally initiated building activity, have drawn crucial raw materials such as coal, cement, iron, and steel away from central control. According to one account, the proportion of output of such materials that had come under local control as of 1983 was over 50 percent.[17]

Overall, the decentralizing reforms have made a rather significant impact on national-level income receipts. Thus, from 1979 to 1982, although the national income increased by 41 percent, state revenue dropped by 3.3 percent. Also, while the 1982 total output value of industrial and agricultural production was 8.7 percent higher than in 1981, state revenue increased only 2.3 percent in that period; the proportion of financial revenue in the national income declined from 37.2 percent in 1978 before the reforms began to 25.5 percent four years later; and extrabudgetary funds rose from 37.1 billion yuan in 1978 to 65 billion yuan in 1982, an increase of 75.2 percent in only four years.[18]

From the evidence presented above, it would certainly appear that the framework for financial control shifted markedly in the years after 1979. But before considering what impact this set of "reforms" has had on the local political process, I shall first consider another facet of economic policy that has been modified in this period, the one called "economic readjustment."

The Horizontal Dimension: Readjustment

In addition to the program of economic readjustment mentioned above, which is the focus of the present discussion, other economic reforms of the post-1978 era have also altered the relationship between geographical units of the same rank in the state administrative hierarchy and have heightened the salience of such units. These reforms have been discussed in part in a paper by Falkenheim on the politics surrounding the command to the various provinces to pursue their "strong points," a policy aimed at reorganizing production and exchange along the lines of regional comparative advantage.[19]

This package of interrelated reforms entails legalized interregional barter trade; exchange reoriented along "natural," historically followed trading routes (rather than being forced to flow along the administratively demarcated avenues formed by the hierarchies of the state planning system); several forms of cross-provincial technological cooperation, such as compensatory trade, joint ventures, technological transfers and consulting, and investments by the developed, industrialized coastal areas in the interior, more backward regions; and the creation of zones for regionally based growth (as against the vertically organized, ministerially directed development schemes of the planned economy). This last policy involves large-scale, multiprovince planning based around macroregions, along with the reestablishment of economic zones focused on "key" or "central" cities, metropolitan areas whose economic centrality in the early 1950s and before was largely obliterated by the imposition of the vertical structures and pathways associated with centralized planning.

Reactions to the policy of economic readjustment have been similar to but broader than the responses to these more geographically rooted reforms. For readjustment is a program that decreed a massive shifting of capital and resources among state ministries, economic sectors, firms, and, as a side effect, regions (since certain types of industries are located in particular areas of the country). Thus, readjustment, like the comparative-advantage-focused programs just noted, sharply delineates the economic interests of horizontally defined units.

The program of economic readjustment was first publicly announced at the second session of the Fifth National People's Congress in June 1979. It emerged as a critique of the economic policies pursued during most of the previous three decades in China. This critique pointed to excessively high production targets, an undue emphasis on heavy industry, a dependence on new capital construction for expanded reproduction rather than on the technical transformation of existing plant capacity, an overconcentration on the output of primary and intermediate products with a concomitant neglect of final consumer goods and services, and a bias toward high rates of "accumulation" (investment) instead of the allocation of funding to consumption needs.[20]

The new program was to reorient capital, supplies, equipment, energy, and transport capacity away from heavy industry, and to change the service orientation of the heavy-industrial firms so that they could aid in the production of commodities needed on the market. There was also a new focus on improving the quality of goods. In addition, the program was directed toward righting imbalances within sectors and raising the economic returns both to individual firms and to the national economy as a whole.

Along with readjustment went a policy of renovating plants whose equipment was outdated through "technical transformation," sometimes by supplying them with more modern parts, sometimes by granting them altogether new machinery, either domestically produced or, where necessary, imported. One more plan put forward in this era involved setting a target for quadrupling output on a national scale by the year 2000, announced at the Twelfth Party Congress in September 1982.

Thus, economic policies of recent years presented local municipal and industrial officials with a number of measures to which they have felt a need to respond. As early as September 1980, at the third session of the Fifth National People's Congress, representatives from a number of provinces spoke out for the industrial sectoral interests concentrated in their own areas. This happened again in the fall of 1981. At this time heavy industry was in serious decline, and the press of provinces in the northeast, where much heavy industry is located, complained about the plight of this branch. And once more at the fourth session of the congress, in December 1981, a number of deputies made claims for the industries in their regions.[21]

That such discussion also went on behind the scenes, not reported in the public media, is evident from several sources. Economic adviser Xue Muqiao, discussing the shifts in investment between sectors that took place in 1981 (first away from heavy, but eventually back toward heavy), revealed in a book in early 1982 that there had been "much debate about the abnormal state of the economy in 1981 ... [and] some thought readjustment was too extreme and believed the future of the economy would be affected."[22] Ma Hong, an economist who is currently the head of the Chinese Academy of Social Sciences, evidently attempting to specify the state's limited financial capacity in the face of excessive claims and claimants, wrote in a *People's Daily* article of October 1982 that it would be impossible to carry out technical transformation in all enterprises but that the process must be done "in stages and groups." He also explained that "not all departments, localities, and enterprises must quadruple output . . . [nor can] the output of all products . . . be quadrupled."[23]

At the same point, Lu Dong, then vice-minister of the State Economic Commission, advocated applying new technology, equipment, materials, and products to new and expanded factories, mines, and equipment.[24] But Ma Hong published a book around this same time saying that it was necessary to "rely mainly on tapping the potential of the existing enterprises."[25] In general, a variety of sources lend the distinct impression that cleavages between old and new enterprises, among large, small, and medium-sized firms, between coastal and interior provinces, between "key" and ordinary factories and construction projects, among regions, and in industrial sectors and branches housed in them were activated by the new policies for growth and reallocation.

But can one conclude from the fact of seeming autonomy and from indirect evidence of conduct that these various reforms have sparked a significant shift in the conduct of local industrial political processes? In this regard, the interviews from my case study offer a more fine-tuned interpretation of just how these economic changes actually affected politics, at least through mid-1984.

The Chinese Case in the Midst of Reform: Data from Wuhan

Wuhan, like other major industrial cities, experienced the various reforms detailed above beginning in the late 1970s. This municipality did take a sudden lurch forward when it was granted economic management powers equal to those of a province and received separate line-item status in the state plan in May 1984. But the general pattern of its reform process had been largely in sync with the nation as a whole during the preceding five years.[26]

To what extent does the Hough/Kornai model fit Wuhan as well? Interviews with urban economic bureaucrats (city officials and enterprise managers) in the spring of 1983 and 1984 revealed that the structural conditions described by these two authors have also characterized the Wuhan municipal political economy over the years, albeit with some differences in emphasis. To apply the framework to this Chinese situation as reflected in my talks, it makes most sense to collapse the five conditions noted above down to three: the roles of the state as owner, which in China encompass planning and approving (*pizhun*), providing and balancing (*pingheng*), and preying and pressuring; the responsibility of local officials for their units and for meeting the success indicators by which these units are assessed from above; and scarcity-induced competition.

These traits correspond rather neatly to the factors identified by Hough and Kornai. Thus, state ownership, branch-style allocation, and the soft budget parallel the functions of planning and providing, while the predatory dimension may be felt particularly in the relatively richer areas of the country, such as Wuhan. For example, in 1981 Hubei Province, of which Wuhan is the capital city, derived 41.4 percent of its total revenue from the city while allocating to Wuhan for expenditure only 12.6 percent of the province's total outlays.[27] I retain the Hough/Kornai condition of local officials' concern with their units' meeting norms, and I treat shortage in the context of the competitive forces it engenders. In general, then, Chinese urban bureaucrats operate in an environment which they define in terms quite close to those explicated by Hough and Kornai.

On the other hand, despite the fact that it is still the central government—and of course the Communist party and its leaders—that defines the rules of the game, many of these rules have been altered since 1979. As outlined above, enhanced autonomy for the lower levels of the administrative hierarchy and investment shifts among sectors, regions, and types of firms have introduced a new flux into the system. As a result, the planned priorities that continue to define economic activity have changed. The provisioning and balancing that characterized the prereform economy go on, but in a manner geared to serving redefined goals and in terms of new forms of largesse: pressure may be lightened but still is ultimately present. Success indicators assigned on a unit basis and concomitant responsibilities for reaching them have not disappeared but are only written differently. And rivalry for resources persists even if its focus has shifted, while its resolution must yet come from the top.

Because of state ownership, the central plan continues its job of structuring economic activity, and this came across in a number of policy areas. At least seven new policies in particular affected urban-managed enterprises in Wuhan up through mid-1984. These are an emphasis on the "technical transformation," or renovation, of old plants with their outdated equipment and technology; efforts to conserve energy; an increase in market activity among state-run firms; attempts to boost the output of the light, consumer-goods industries; the substitution of loans, with rather low rates of interest, for the outright grants of the past in financing investment; the introduction of profit-retention schemes for industrial firms instead of forcing the plants to remit their entire earnings to the central treasury and permission for local areas and even some enterprises to engage directly in foreign trade, sometimes only with central approval but also sometimes (usually for smaller deals below a fixed amount of money) on their own initiative.

In each of these policy areas, however, many of the prior parameters and procedures for proper behavior persist. There has been an increasing use of "economic levers" rather than the old administrative allocations and commands, in the style of the "indicative planning" and "industrial policy" practiced in and advocated for capitalist countries. But such similarities should not obscure the fact that state-designed and distributed incentives are fashioned at and furnished by the highest levels of the political system, with probably only the most marginal and minimal input from below. A closer look at the seven policies listed above will bear this out.

First of all, much state direction goes on, despite a switch to economic means of encouraging activity. For example, technical transformation projects are encouraged in a number of ways. The city government has been authorized to give low-interest or interest-free loans for such items, plus extended repayment periods. In the machine-building trade, 10 percent of investment still comes gratis, but this must be used for technical renewal. Firms managing several key projects in the machine-building trade have received the right to calculate their depreciation allowances at the rate of 6 and even up to 8 percent of valuation, while the ordinary rate is 5 percent. Textile firms may get interest-free loans for totally renewing their equipment. None of these benefits exists for other kinds of capital expenditures. Similarly, for energy-saving projects the rate of interest on loans is as low as 0.21 percent per month, about half the usual rate.

Though all firms are now permitted to market some percentage of their output (usually in the range of 5 to 20 percent), an interesting dimension of the new "market freedoms" appears in the case of two Wuhan firms. The first is a machine-building plant that turns out small (eight and twelve horsepower) diesel engines for agricultural machinery, the other a textile plant producing woolens. The engine factory sells on its own initiative a full 70 percent of its output, while the woolen one markets its entire output (in a sector where, prior to 1984, 98 percent of output was organized according to planned specifications and in which even in 1984, 85 percent was still so arranged). The explanation given to me for why the diesel engine plant was allowed to sell so much of its own output by itself was that it had been successful in doing so. But perhaps a more telling piece of information is the fact that each of these firms represents the only one of its kind in the city. Thus, the "markets" in which they operate are highly protected ones. Even with reforms, the amount of independent selling in which a given firm may engage is by no means a matter of the manager's choice. Rather, the permitted proportions are strictly spelled out (even if probably transgressed somewhat in practice).

Light industry has seen accelerated growth and has boosted its output in recent years in the main not because of some new competitive, market-type activity among its firms or because of contention between this sector and the heavy industrial one. Instead, it was the recipient of the "six priorities," mainly between 1979 and 1982: the state gave its enterprises superior treatment in the supply of energy, raw and semifinished materials, transport, investment, loans, and foreign exchange during these years. For instance, in the first nine months of 1979, power consumption in the textile industry in Hubei Province increased by 52.7 percent. In the same year, Hubei appropriated over 100 million yuan from the province's circulating capital (obtained from the central government expressly for this purpose) as a special loan for speeding up these industries' growth. The loans were closely earmarked for "tapping the potential" of the firms, increasing their output and varieties, technical innovation and reform, improving product quality, and developing products for export.[28]

Also, in 1980, 130 million yuan in loans was distributed to 123 enterprises in the light and textile sector in Hubei Province; in mid-1981, the Wuhan branch of the Chinese People's Bank reported having given 400 light and textile enterprises medium- and short-term loans totaling 74.29 million yuan for procuring and installing new equipment from the second half of 1979 through the first quarter of 1981.[29] Light industry quickly registered gains as a result of this favored treatment: in 1980, the output of light and textile industries in Wuhan rose from 45 percent of overall GVIO in 1979 to 48 percent; by 1981, it had reached 52.2 percent across the province. Moreover, while the overall growth rate of GVIO in 1981 was 9.8 percent in the province, output in light and textile firms increased by 20 percent.[30]

But the ultimate dependence of the light industries on this special nurturing became apparent after 1981. According to municipal planning officials, in that year its proportion of GVIO began to drop in Wuhan. While light industry accounted for 52.2 percent of GVIO in 1981, the figure fell to 51.3 percent in 1982 and 48.9 percent in 1983, as central decision makers shifted their attention to the recovery of heavy industry, and to large-scale infrastructural construction projects.

The disbursement of loan capital is similarly strictly kept within the purview of centrally set plans, at least formally. The central government distributes a set amount of loan capital to the provincial level for capital construction,[31] and this dollar amount is not to be surpassed, regardless of local economic conditions and any possibly existing extra, locally generated sources of funding. Municipal Economic Commission bureaucrats explained that the loan capital that the province bestows on the city in this fashion accounts for 70 percent of the investment capital in the city. The channel through which this allocation is made is the state-run People's Bank, which gives its lower-level branches the money so that the branch can then distribute the money down to the factories in need of it.

The criteria that guide (or are supposed to guide) the decision (aside, of course, from matters of connections and politicking that did not come under discussion in this set of interviews) are fixed by the government and include whether the project for which a loan is requested has a "good foundation" (which I take to refer to a standard whose approximation could be judged through a feasibility study), whether the plant has other requisite technology in place to make possible the absorption of the new machinery, whether its staff and workers possess the necessary technological talent to make proper use of what is to be installed, whether the raw materials, transport capacity, and energy needed to utilize the equipment are present or readily accessible, and whether there is a market for the end product.

For each construction or technical transformation project proposed by the firms, it is necessary to obtain a loan from the local bank branch (which "balances" the several requests before it at any time, both within and among trades) and to acquire approval from the firm's superior bureau (which similarly balances the request and then also must consult on the project with the urban economic and planning commissions and the city finance, tax, and banking offices, all of which must finally reach a consensual agreement on the project). Moreover, for larger loans, both the bank branch and the bureau must seek approval from their superior-level units. Thus, state bureaucracies retain their hierarchical controls and ultimate formal power over disbursements for much economic activity.

About half the loans in the textile trade come from the city government, for which the ultimate approval must be obtained from the mayor. For the other half, larger projects that might eventually serve national needs, the city textile corporation (formerly called the bureau) carries the request first to the provincial level, which then presents it to the textile ministry in Beijing, a process that usually takes about a quarter.[32] Thus, it is finally the state that sets standards for loans and the amounts that can be offered per locality. And it is also state cadres who explicitly approve the allocation of loans in particular cases.

In the realm of foreign trade, the machine-building sector works through two channels, both of which are to operate within the guidelines of state policy. The local branch of the central ministry of foreign economic relations and trade is one channel, and an import-export company under the central machine-building ministry has a local branch under the municipal machine-building bureau. In the case of agricultural machinery, I was told something that doubtless applies to other exports as well: that a state-run corporation for such products arranges which plant will export what items, in the interest of ensuring that the best varieties hit the international market.

Furthermore, firms are entitled to purchase equipment abroad with the foreign exchange they have earned from their own sales but must first obtain approval to do so from upper levels (their local bureau for most cases, probably even higher levels for large-scale items). Also the bureau in the city—and sometimes the bureau at the provincial level above it— "adjusts" foreign exchange among the enterprises under its jurisdiction, in line with bureau or provincial priorities. Textile corporation officials stated that provincial-level approval for importing is necessary for purchases up to U.S. $1 million; above that, central-level permission is required.

Finally, with regard to profits, the rate retained under the "change-profits-into-taxes" reform of June 1983 (in effect during my second set of interviews) varied from sector to sector, with machine-building plants keeping about 30 percent of their earnings, but textile plants getting only 15 to 25 percent. These moneys flow first to the bureau (corporation for textiles), which then allocates them to the individual plants not strictly in accord with what they have earned.

For instance, in textiles the output value in dyeing and finishing firms is relatively higher (mainly because of the state-set price structure), and they have fewer employees, so they acquire higher profits almost regardless of their efforts. Consequently, the state policy is to allow them to retain a comparatively lower percentage of these profits. Spinning and weaving plants, on the other hand, have higher costs and more employees, leading to lower profits, so they may retain relatively more of them. In addition, textile firms as a whole retain a lower percentage of their profits (since the profits are higher) than do machine-building firms. The diesel engine plant noted above, for example, retains 45 percent. Thus, while firms that are better placed to earn high profits may be better disposed to the reforms (but not necessarily, since they retain a smaller proportion), it is inaccurate to assume that the new policies release the enterprises from the control of the state and its plan.

Along with the continued presence of the state plan and the need for obtaining state approval for local economic activity that goes with it, the government is maintaining its position as the provisioner of last appeal for firms in trouble, even as it allegedly moves toward granting more and more enterprises the right to be "responsible for their own profits and losses" as "relatively independent accounting units." For instance, the urban finance bureau offers a form of subsidy that need not be returned for important and large-scale projects for which an enterprise would have difficulty repaying a loan. Then, there is no tax on the newly added output of technical transformation projects which enhance a firm's productivity, so that the firm can use the profit from the new output to repay the loan. When a textile firm is making no profit because of the poor quality of its output (a problem that is unfortunately rather common in Wuhan's textile trade), the corporation as a matter of policy allocates the firm new machinery or alters old parts, if it adjudges its products to be at all marketable.

Machine-building firms that have suffered losses or are in danger of doing so because of "irrational" state-set prices, or enterprises beginning to produce a new line of product and which therefore have high start-up costs, are permitted to hold on to quite high proportions of their profits, sometimes as much as 65 percent. Three stories of enterprises undergoing serious losses illustrate the fact that municipal industrial bureaus still stand ready to help plants fulfill centrally designated priorities. Whereas in the past Chinese firms, like those described by Hough and Kornai, were charged with meeting quantity-of-output targets, today a significant new demand is that they must turn loss into profit. In the first example, an electric-wire factory was losing money, according to machine-building officials responsible for it, not because its products were unsalable, but because of "management problems" and because its raw materials often arrived too late. The bureau in charge switched the leadership group in the plant and also appealed to the city government, which obtained the necessary raw materials from another city by working through connections possessed by the city bureau of metallurgy. In addition, the firm was accorded a special deal in its depreciation rate, along with two other enterprises in this trade. Second, an automobile plant whose losses were attributed to its inferior designing in 1983 has now improved its product quality after being integrated into the national Nanjing Automobile Company, set up in that year by combining seventeen enterprises from across the country. The new company helped the firm to redraw its design. And a third case, a lathe-producing plant, also had management problems (again solved by a shift in leadership arranged by the bureau) and improved its product structure by introducing new models with enhanced precision. In all of these instances, the chances of failure and risk that were formerly removed in the interest of reaching planned quotas are now similarly eliminated, but with a new goal—turning a profit—as prod.

The state's continued role in provisioning came across at the level of the city as well. In accord with the May 1984 decision mentioned above, Wuhan received the right to import up to U.S. $5 million worth of goods without seeking upper-level approval, as well as the power to determine its own management policies. But, ironically, the city remains largely dependent on investment from the central government for the port, waterway, and airport construction that are mandatory if it is to realize the full economic potential that these new powers promise. Local leaders, no doubt aware of the imminent growth in their rights, had been appealing for such investment over the year prior to obtaining these rights.[33]

Furthermore, inasmuch as the central state is still the dictator of the plan and the determiner of the priorities embodied in it, the state must continue to appear to some at times as the predator or the source of pressure, as well as the final provider. This continuing feature of the planned economy appears in several ways. The persistence of the policy of *pingheng* (balancing) at every administrative level and within each bureau means that better-off firms, higher-profit sectors, and wealthier regions under a common geographical superior (one pressure from which Wuhan has recently been exempted with the May 1984 decision) all must go on submitting to a certain amount of exploitation for the sake of the larger unit of which they are a part.

Thus, dyeing and printing firms sacrifice somewhat for spinning and weaving plants; textile firms under the control of the city surrender some of their market-derived profits, while machine-building plants get gratis allotments; and Wuhan up until 1984 gave up some of its earnings and foreign trade opportunities for the sake of smaller cities within Hubei. As officials in Wuhan mentioned, the Sichuanese city of Chongqing down the Yangtze has developed faster than Wuhan in the past year because the nation, not the province, has been doing its balancing. Presumably, redistribution within a province where only a few cities are industrially developed and where the city in question vastly outstrips the great majority even of these, drains a municipality's coffers more than nationally arranged redistribution does.

In a similar vein, when the central government reduced the proportion of the textile corporation's output that had to answer to the national plan in 1984 (from 98 down to 85 percent), it enjoined the trade at the same time to raise its profit rate (up to 6 percent, but I do not have the figure for what it had been before). A fair percentage of these profits (in the case of some firms as high as 85 percent) will go as taxes to the central and local governments under the tax system in effect at that time.

The second large structural condition identified above as common to socialist systems was the responsibility of officials for meeting regime-specified success indicators (and the self-identification of these officials with the units they manage). Here again the structural relationship shows continuity, even if the content of the indicator has changed. For now enterprises—and consequently the bureaus and regions that manage them and are responsible for their successes and failures—are no longer judged primarily by their ability to reach some preset quantity of output. However, their performance in making profits, especially in turning loss to profit, is at present the preeminent measure of their worth.[34]

Consequently, urban bureaucrats currently devote the same energy to helping firms secure the wherewithal for profit making that they once exerted in assisting the firms to produce more output and meet plan targets, and the activity is much the same, as the discussion above illustrated. This activity consists of finding supplies and raw materials, balancing resources among the firms under their control, and building exchange relationships with similarly placed urban cadres in other locales who can trade needed inputs.

Industrial officials and the units they manage are also supposed to eschew unplanned capital construction that is outside the state budget, for from the perspective of central politicians such ventures waste and divert capital, resources, and scarce fuel and transport capacity. However, much in the manner that Hough details for local officials in the Soviet Union, these cadres try to conceal unplanned construction, in the hope that such projects will yield resources, revenues, and jobs that will accrue to their area's economy. As one cogent analysis of this phenomenon put it:

> Though the state has promulgated documents and methods of control over self-collected capital construction funds, there have not been investigations into the economic and political responsibility of units that grossly exceed the norms for self-collected funds. *Because some units are secure in the knowledge that they have strong backing,* there are more and more of these projects, the norms are surpassed by higher and higher amounts, and the scale of such activity is bigger and bigger.[35]

Furthermore, the article reveals, the capital for building these projects initially comes entirely from the state, although the funds being used are moneys legally designated for other purposes. Examples are funds for repair, technical renovation of equipment, maintenance of the simple expanded reproduction of fixed assets, labor union expenses, and scientific and technological work, or else they are profits that ought properly to be handed over to the central treasury. And a last kind of interesting twist lies in the fact that enterprises engaged in this practice justify it by appealing to currently espoused state policies: they claim to be "developing their local economic superiorities" or "enlivening the economy."

Thus, this seeming exception to the argument in fact underscores the main point. For collusion with and protection from state officials, the availability of state funds, and the nominal adherence to state-sponsored policies all provide the necessary foundation for this only apparently private-like activity of the state-sector firms. Though putting a halt to such construction has been one of the thorniest problems in central-local relations in recent years, as local powers and finances have increased with the decentralization reforms, still, this activity itself is nothing novel. Nor is it essentially private or pluralistic. Indeed, it is quite akin to that associated with the wonted "expansion drive" of state-defined administrative and economic units that has cropped up for years in the more tightly planned economy that Kornai describes.

Shortage-induced competition is the third structural condition borrowed from the comparative literature that is also present in the current Chinese context. Both Hough and Kornai, looking at politics within individual localities in the countries they studied, stress the limited resources in the hands of regional officials and the need for setting priorities among the many demands on those funds and supplies.[36] Even though Hough repeatedly calls attention to the localism that comes from the hopes of district bureaucrats to further the general growth of their area as a whole, ultimately there is always a need for choice among rival requests within the region.

While such interlocal jostling and selecting undoubtedly still occurs in China today, the decentralization measures and the investment shifts of the early 1980s have heightened and made more blatant and explicit the contention *among* regions for recognition and allocations. Such agitation takes several different forms. As noted above, spokespersons for provinces in the northeastern section of the country pushed for the recovery of heavy industry and for the investment and resources that would make this possible in 1981, in the midst of the readjustment campaign; a bit earlier, in autumn 1980, places where agriculture was a more central component of the economy clamored at national meetings that, despite readjustment, no new investment had been directed away from heavy industry and toward the rural areas.[37]

Also, with new privileges for varying degrees of autonomy in attracting foreign investment (in four special economic zones in two provinces and, as of April 1984, in fourteen coastal cities), other, inland provinces have been pleading for similar powers for their areas. In Wuhan, where vast new rights have been granted, warnings were already necessary within a month of the bestowal of these rights that Wuhan was not to become a "province within a province" but should still recognize its place as just another point within a total national system.[38] And the encouragement given to localities across the country to develop their individual strong points (that is, to follow a strategy of comparative advantage) once they had been released a bit from the tight bonds of the vertically structured, highly centralized command economy of the past led to the large-scale erection of protectionist trade barriers and hoarding. For each region and province sought to guard its own treasures and use them for projects that would eventually boost its own separate development.[39]

In the face of this new-style protectionism, the regime has since 1980 tried to build regional economic zones that would force a noncompetitive cooperation among provinces or cities whose economies are so similar that they would otherwise engage in wasteful duplication of production and damaging price wars. It has also attempted to create joint ventures and domestic investment schemes between the more and less developed provinces, in a bid to lead the lower administrative levels to finance their own growth without the thoroughly dictated mandates and expensive capital grants of centrally organized plans. But the localistic forces unleashed by the reforms have often tended to thwart these projects, as each geographical segment of the country now angles for the wherewithal to make it on its own.

However, it is again important to recall that such competitive behavior means something different in the state-owned economy than it does under democratic, capitalistic conditions. What is described above is still a competition between state-defined and state-financed units and not a conflict between two essentially private groups such as business and labor, private business firms, or even private and public sectors, such as characterizes capitalist economies in structural transition.[40] Moreover, although geographical units, such as states in the United States, may also compete for capital investment, their rivalry has tended in recent years to be geared to attract private investment. In China, on the other hand, vying for more state investment (or for state-approved foreign investment) up through mid-1984 was still really the only game in town.

Moreover, when heavy industry, and in particular machine-building, did recover by early 1982, this was not simply the result of political clout and lobbying by representatives of the machinery interests. As pointed out in Wuhan interviews, central planners had concurrently set in motion a series of crucial policies in the economy as a whole. These in turn led to new demands on the machine builders. In the course of responding to these demands heavy industry almost automatically revived. These policies included the "agricultural responsibility system" in the countryside, whereby the large-scale commune has been broken down. For this process eventually created a huge market for vast quantities of smaller-sized farm machinery suitable for the family farms that now organize production over much of the landscape. Also, as light industry underwent renovation, its factories required new or rebuilt installations, which the machine-building firms had to supply. Third, as the nation gears up for a significant modernization drive in the next two decades, mammoth infrastructural projects—in transport, mining, oil exploration, and energy production—are getting under way, all of which again need the technology turned out by machinery-producing enterprises. And, fourth, higher income levels that have resulted from higher state purchase prices, the new rural system, and a set of wage increases in the cities have led to new consumer demands for such things as refrigerators and even air conditioners, whose parts must be turned out by the machine-building sector.

These kinds of examples of the forces that drive growth in heavy industry illustrate that China's economy remains essentially closely interdependent. Its direction of growth is very much the result of decisions at the top, and the effects on any one sector cannot be viewed in isolation from their overall systemic impact. Thus, despite the enhanced competitive activity that meets the observer's eye at first glance, this is still a contest fired by officials who fight for their units, within the bounds of a state-owned economy, governed by a centrally supervised and circumscribed planning mechanism.

Conclusion

In sum, there may be a superficial similarity between behaviors issuing from the new Chinese economic polities of the late 1970s and early 1980s and those in the decentralized and privatized polities of the industrialized West. But this is by no means an indication that true processes of privatization and pluralization were occurring in the PRC up through 1984.[41] For as the material recounted above suggests, this is still a state in which the central government retains the dominant power in economic resource allocation and responsible local officials work for the interests of the units under their control, units defined by the state ownership system. Moreover, it is still a system in which the politics of scarcity and poverty continue to structure the play of interest articulation and mediation. Reforms have not obviated the practices of applying to and receiving approval from the center in undertaking development ventures, and bureaucrats persist in orienting their conduct largely around centrally set standards, even if they do so by illicit means at times.

Neither is this yet a system that exhibits what is considered pluralistic activity in the West. For the units—and their leaders—who angle for place and assets are in no sense members of self-defined or voluntarily constituted groups. Instead, it is the key features of the Chinese socialist political economy that structure the local industrial political process—state ownership (with the state doing the planning, the final providing, and some redistributing that is sometimes experienced as preying); local officials responsible for ensuring that their regions (or other units defined by the state ownership system) satisfy the current regime-set criteria of achievement; and limited state resources in the face of massive state-set goals. And these properties, along with the bureaucratic hierarchies that embody them, still regulate the patterns of bargaining and authority that make up the urban industrial political process with its local advocacy, competing claims for state resources, ultimate reliance on the state for investment, expansion drives and investment hunger, and resultant absence of fear of failure or risk. Though the game may have changed slightly, it is still the center that defines its rules and could, presumably, change them once again.

Notes

1. For a good, if short, discussion of the concept of "privatization," see Richard P. Suttmeier, "Reforms in Science," paper prepared for the conference on "To Reform the Chinese Political Order," June 18–23, 1984, Harwichport, Massachusetts. Drawing on the work of E. S. Savas, *Privatizing the Public Sector* (Chatham: Chatham House, 1982), Suttmeier terms privatizing a reform that alters the relationship between state and society in a way that proscribes the role of the state, and thus increases the relative autonomy of groups in society. Such reforms, he goes on, "imply an expectation that the activities effected [*sic*] by these reforms will no longer require conscious state intervention for them to be carried out" (p. 4).

2. See Philippe C. Schmitter, "Still the Century of Corporatism?," in *Trends toward Corporatist Intermediation,* ed. Philippe C. Schmitter and Gerhard Lehmbruch (Beverly Hills: Sage, 1979), p. 13.

3. J. L. Metcalfe, "Government/Industry Relations in a Post-Keynesian Economy," ms., Civil Service College, June 1980, pp. 8, 10, 17.

4. Mancur Olson, *The Rise and Decline of Nations: Economic Growth, Stagflation, and Social Rigidities* (New Haven: Yale University Press, 1982).

5. Lester C. Thurow, *The Zero-Sum Society: Distribution and the Possibilities for Economic Change* (New York: Basic Books, 1980), pp. 10, 15–16, 22–23, 77.

6. Samuel H. Beer, *Britain Against Itself* (New York: W. W. Norton, 1982).

7. Stephen D. Krasner, *Defending the National Interest: Raw Materials Investments and U.S. Foreign Policy* (Princeton: Princeton University Press, 1978).

8. Robert Reich, *The New American Frontier* (New York: Times Books, 1983).

9. Janos Kornai, *Economics of Shortage* (Amsterdam: North Holland, 1980); and Jerry Hough, *The Soviet Prefects: The Local Party Organs in Industrial Decision Making* (Cambridge: Harvard University Press, 1969). The analysis that follows is derived from these two books.

10. Hough, *The Soviet Prefects*, p. 256; and Kornai, *Economics of Shortage*, pp. 206–10.

11. Unless otherwise indicated, the material in this section comes from three articles by Audrey Donnithorne, "Centre-Provincial Relations in China," Contemporary China Papers, no. 16, Department of Economics, RSPacS, The Australian National University, 1981; "Fiscal Relations," *China Business Review* (November/December 1983): 25–27; "The Chinese Economy Today," *Journal of Northeastern Asian Studies* 2 (1983): 3–21; Martin Weil, "The Sixth Five Year Plan," *China Business Review* (March/April 1983): 23–24; Robert F. Dernberger, "The Chinese Search for the Path of Self-Sustained Growth in the 1980s: An Assessment," in Joint Economic Committee, *China Under the Four Modernizations, Part 1* (Washington, DC: U.S. Government Printing Office, 1982), pp. 67–68; Thomas G. Rawski, "Productivity, Incentive and Reform in China's Industrial Sector," paper prepared for the Annual Conference of the Association for Asian Studies, Washington, DC, March 1984; and especially Barty Naughton, "State Investment in Post-Mao China: The Decline of Central Control," first draft paper presented at "Policy Implementation in Post-Mao China," Columbus, Ohio, June 1983; Barry Naughton, "The Profit System," *China Business Review* (November/December 1983): 14–18; and Victor

Falkenheim, "Distributive Politics and Regional Reform in Post Mao China," paper presented to the Annual Conference of the Association for Asian Studies, Washington, DC, March 1984. I have also summarized some of this material along with some other material in Dorothy J. Solinger, "Reform of the Structure of the Economic System: A Spatial Interpretation," paper prepared for the conference on "To Reform the Chinese Political Order," June 1984, Harwichport, Massachusetts, pp. 26–33. See Chapter 7 of this volume.

12. For information on banking reforms, see Katherine H. Y. Hsiao, "Money and Banking in the People's Republic of China: Recent Developments," *China Quarterly* (1982): 462–77; and William Byrd, *China's Financial System: The Changing Role of Banks* (Boulder: Westview Press, 1983).

13. Donnithorne, "Centre-Provincial Relations in China," pp. 24–30. See also Victor C. Falkenheim and Thomas G. Rawski, "China's Economic Reform: The International Dimension," paper prepared for the workshop on "Policy Implementation in Post-Mao China," June 1983, Columbus, Ohio. For an indication of the more concrete nature of the foreign trade and investment activities of one province, see Carolyn L. Brehm, "Shanghai Unleashed," *China Business Review* (September/October 1983): 12–14.

14. For the 1983 measure, see *Foreign Broadcast Information Service* (hereafter *FBIS*), March 3, 1983, p. K14; April 19, 1983, pp. K1–3; May 3, 1983, pp. K7–14. The second 1984 phase is outlined in *FBIS*, June 27, 1984, p. K10 (translated from *Renmin ribao*, June 22, 1984). See also *China Daily*, September 13, 1984.

15. See Kornai, *Economics of Shortage*.

16. See Naughton, "Policy Implementation," table 1. A Chinese source states that in 1982 in-budget investment represented 36.7 percent of total fixed assets while extrabudgetary investment was 63.3 percent, the highest since the founding of the People's Republic in 1949. See Zhang Guocai, "Kongzhi jiben jianshe guimo bixu jiaqiang zichou zijin guanli" (Controlling the scale of capital construction requires strengthening management over self-collected assets), *Jingji yanjiu* (Economic research) 3 (1984): 73.

17. Naughton, "The Profit System," p. 17. See also *FBIS*, July 7, 1983, p. K19, which carries a translated Xinhua report on the need to centralize financial and material resources. This source states that from 1965 to 1982 the amount of rolled steel distributed by the state under the unified plan dropped from 95 to 53 percent, of cement from 71 to 25 percent, and of timber from 63 to 57 percent. It goes on to comment that "Nothing can be accomplished and time will be wasted if forces are scattered, with each doing things his own way."

18. These various figures can be found in *FBIS*, February 22, 1983, p. K12; June 13, 1983, p. K9; June 23, 1983, pp. K11–12; and August 16, 1983, p. K5.

19. Falkenheim, "Distributive Politics." See also Solinger, "Reform."

20. For a discussion of the rationale behind the objectives and methods of readjustment, see Ma Hong, *New Strategy for China's Economy*, trans. Yang Lin (Beijing: New World Press, 1983), esp. pp. 24–28, 41–43, 71, and 79.

21. I document this in Dorothy J. Solinger, "The Fifth National People's Congress and the Process of Policy Making: Reform, Readjustment, and the Opposition," *Asian Survey* (December 1982): 1257–59, 1263–64, and 1266–67. See Chapter 2 in this volume.

22. Xue Muqiao, *Wo guo guomin jingji de tiaozheng he gaige* (The readjustment and reform of our country's national economy) (Beijing: People's Publishing House, 1982), pp. 93–97.

23. *Renmin ribao*, October 28, 1982, p. 5, translated in *FBIS*, November 3, 1982, pp. K3, K7.

24. Ibid., p. K18.

25. Ma, *New Strategy*, p. 28.

26. I have discussed the period 1978–84 in Barry Naughton and Dorothy J. Solinger, "Hubei and Wuhan: Shifting Strategies for Economic Development," paper prepared for the Economic Bureaucracy workshop held at the East-West Center, Honolulu, Hawaii, July 17–20, 1984. For a review of the post-May 1984 reforms, see Dorothy J. Solinger, "Wuhan: Inland City on the Move," *China Business Review* (March/April 1985): 27–30. For the decision of May 1984, see *Renmin ribao*, June 3, 1984; and *FBIS*, June 27, 1984, pp. P5–7, and July 3, 1984, pp. P1–2.

27. Guo Wuxin, "Wuhan: A Case Study in Chinese Urbanization," University of California, Berkeley, Institute of Urban and Regional Development, Working Paper no. 418, October 1983, p. 19.

28. *FBIS*, November 28, 1979, p. P8.

29. *FBIS*, March 24, 1981, p. P5, and June 23, 1981, p. P8.

30. *FBIS*, February 27, 1981, p. P3, and January 18, 1982, p. Pl.

31. Loan capital was to go to the city without filtering through the province after May 1984. But interviews in May 1985 indicated a continuing need for provincial-level approval for urban loans.

32. Again, as of May 1984 the level of the province is now omitted in the approval process for Wuhan (as well as for several other cities, but not for the average city).

33. See, for example, Li Chonghuai, "Pingjie 'liang-tong' qi fei, ba Wuhan jiancheng wei 'neilian Huazhong, waitong haiyang' de jingji zhongxin" (Rely on the two tongs to fly, build Wuhan into an economic center that internally links Central China, externally connects with the ocean). *Wuhan Daxue xuebao* (Wuhan University Journal) 6 (1983): 71–78.

34. This point comes across clearly in a State Council ruling of mid-1984. According to this regulation, the job of turning enterprises from losers into profit-earners is the responsibility of the official in charge, whether it be the factory manager, the city bureau chief, the mayor, or even the provincial governor. See *Zhonghua Renmin Gongheguo Guowuyuan gongbao* (Bulletin of the State Council of the People s Republic of China) 430 (May 20, 1984): 278–81. The document in question is 1984, no. 62, passed on May 3, 1984.

35. Zhang, "Kongzhi jiben jianshe," pp. 71–74 (emphasis added).

36. Kornai, *Economics of Shortage*, p. 191; Hough, *The Soviet Prefects*, pp. 213, 263–68.

37. See note 21 above.

38. *FBIS*, June 27, 1984, pp. P5–7.

39. This is graphically documented in Falkenheim, "Distributive Politics."

40. Reich, *New American Frontier*.

41. For an interesting and insightful discussion of the possible existence of interest groups in socialist systems which are neither lobbies nor reflections of pluralism, see Michael Waller, "Communist Politics and the Group Process: Some Comparative Conclusions," in *Groups and Politics in the People's Republic of China,* ed. David S. G. Goodman (Armonk: M. E. Sharpe, 1984), pp. 196–217, esp. pp. 196–201.

5
Urban Reform and Relational Contracting in Post-Mao China: An Interpretation of the Transition from Plan to Market

Urban economic reform in China has been geared toward effecting a transition from a centrally planned economy to one significantly driven by market relations. In fashioning this transition, China's reformist leaders have sought to create an economic system that matches, in many essential features, the ideal-typical model of market exchange presented in neoclassical economics textbooks. They believe that through market reform it will be possible to overcome a host of structural weaknesses that have led to recurrent inefficiencies and stagnation in the operation of China's socialist planned economy.[1]

In its bare outlines, the reformist argument neatly counterposes the administrative logic of state-determined prices and state-mandated coordination of exchange, on the one hand, to the market logic of supply-and-demand-responsive prices and voluntary contracting, on the other. Thus framed, the issue of systemic reform appears to be one of dichotomous choice, that is, a clear and simple "either/or" proposition.

This chapter takes as its main theme the idea that such a dichotomous conception, however elegant and parsimonious in theory, is profoundly misleading in

This chapter draws on material in an earlier paper on which comments by Peter Gourevitch, William Parish, and Susan Shirk were helpful. The final revision benefited immensely from the comments of Bernard Grofman, and from the skillful editing of Richard Baum. The original writing was done in late 1987.

©1989 by the Regents of the University of California. Reprinted from *Studies in Comparative Communism*, 22 2 and 3 (1989): 171–85. It also appeared in *Reform and Reaction in Post-Mao China: The Road to Tiananmen*, ed. Richard Baum (New York: Routledge Press, 1991), pp. 104–23. Reprinted with the permission of the Regents and Routledge Press.

practice. Specifically, I shall argue that the actual line between plan and market in China is not nearly so sharply drawn as neoclassical Western economists and Chinese reformers have averred. I shall further argue that certain operational features of China's prereform economy have clearly survived the demise of mandatory central planning, taking the form of hybridized, informal relations of exchange. One such hybrid, residual feature—"relational contracting"—provides the main empirical focus of this chapter.

In seeking to account for the actual economic behavior of Chinese enterprises in the period since comprehensive urban economic reform was first introduced in 1984, I have found that the most important operational distinctions do not concern the familiar conceptual dichotomy of plan vs. market, but rather depend on the presence or absence of certain infrastructural/developmental constraints that exist independently of both plan and market. Three such constraints are of particular relevance to the present study: (1) the *degree of shortage* of vital productive inputs and capital goods; (2) the *lack of design standardization* (and/or uniform quality control) in the manufacture of productive inputs/capital goods; and (3) the *weakness of existing channels of supply information* (and consequent high managerial uncertainty) concerning the availability and reliability of these inputs/goods.

Below, I shall demonstrate that, depending on the degree to which these three constraints are both present and salient, "relational contracting"—a highly-patterned, repetitive form of economic exchange—will tend to occur; and I shall further show that this will hold true regardless of whether the local economy is nominally driven by the plan or by the market.

The following key points derive from this finding. First of all, the planned economy, as it existed in China before the reform period, shared many features with the typical imperfect market. The three structural properties cited above conducing to these features continue to exist, making for considerable continuity in the current transitional era.

Second, some elements of the old, bureaucratic command economy have actually *eased* rather than thwarted the conversion of the system in this transitional period. In consequence, the ostensible "marketizing" of the Chinese economy has resulted in the creation of a "market system" wherein much economic exchange paradoxically continues to be structured along lines very similar to those that existed under a more centrally planned economy. In short, it is suggested here that structural continuities in the Chinese economy are disposing firms to choose to trade via tied partnerships even when they are no longer forced to do so.

The article begins with a brief sketch of the concept of relational contracting. I then go on to explain how in several crucial ways the planned economy in China before 1979 not only fit but also furthered the conditions for this type of trading, leaving lasting marks on the system—marks that are very much in evidence today. Next, I offer a brief overview of the main components of the urban economic reform program proposed in late 1984. The subsequent section presents empirical data pertaining to the points mentioned above. These data have been drawn from the large central China city of Wuhan, designated in 1984 as one of the key experimental centers of comprehensive urban reform. Sources include newspaper and journal articles for the three-year period 1984–1987, plus 35 hours of interviews conducted by the author in Wuhan in the summer of 1987. The conclusion brings out explicitly the relevant interconnections between the Chinese data and the various analytical observations and hypotheses presented in the body of the chapter.

The Concept of Relational Contracting

Following I. R. Macneil, Williamson discusses relational contracting as one of three generic transaction modes, the other two being classical and neoclassical contracting.[2] Drawing further on Macneil, he distinguishes this mode in the following manner: relational contracting entails contracts of relatively longer "duration and [enhanced] complexity" as compared with the other two modes. Moreover, this form of contracting requires "adjustment processes of a more thoroughly transaction-specific, ongoing administrative kind"[3] as opposed to the more standardized contracts that typically accompany impersonal marketized exchange. Thus, characterizing forms of contracts in terms of their relative frequency and their transaction specificity (or idiosyncrasy), relational contracting would be the form of contracting that "develops for transactions of a *recurring* and *nonstandardized* kind" [emphasis added]. By contrast, classical contracting would apply to all standardized transactions (whatever the frequency), and neoclassical contracting would be needed for occasional (as opposed to recurring), nonstandardized transactions.[4] Others have stressed more the omnipresence of varying *degrees* of this mode of exchange in a variety of trading contexts. Goldberg, for example, notes that "Much economic activity takes place within long-term, complex, perhaps multiparty contractual (or contract-like) relationships; behavior is, in varying degrees, sheltered from market forces."[5] Also, he explains, "the relational exchange approach . . . recognizes that [the] sheltering is inevitable and, moreover, that it can be functional."[6] Dore makes the related point that "All economies in practice, notwithstanding Adam Smith, contain a fair proportion of . . . trust relationships, as opposed to arm's-length contractual relationships. . . . 'Relational contracting versus spot contracting' [is one way of putting it]."[7]

On specific national economies, Goldberg tells us that "In modern Western economies a significant amount of economic activity is conducted within organizations or other relationships shielded in varying degrees from market forces," though Dore thinks that the Japanese economy, where "established customer relations ramify throughout the economy . . . moves a good deal further in that direction than most."

The propensity to build trading relationships that offer a premium in trust, predictability, and security of supply, and that cut down on information-search costs, is very likely universal; and the need for such values drives parties to exchanges in many contexts to adopt what Dore terms the "intermediate alternative" of relational contracting, whereby a user combines with a tied supplier in stably patterned "networks of preferential trading relations."[8] Stated differently, relational contracting builds upon the social dimension of marketing. That is, all markets are embedded in a social context, so that to varying degrees in different economies such personal, cultural, and political factors as trust, reputation, past dealings, habits, and institutions always have a bearing on the choice of trading partners.[9]

In addition, all transactions take place within a certain technological environment. The key technological factor is the stage of development, which affects the infrastructure for trade, such as in transport and communications. The developmental stage also influences the amount of supply (shortage versus plenty) and the degree of standardization of products within an industrial sector, with greater technological sophistication permitting higher levels of quality control. Through its impact on marketing framework and on quantity and quality of output, then, developmental stage determines, from a technological standpoint, the degree of certainty and predictability that pertain in a given market.

Growing out of these two contextual factors, the social and the technological, is another crucial element affecting the nature of exchange: the richness or impoverishment of information networks.[10] Where information is hardest to come by for social, political, or cultural reasons, and where shortage, nonstandardization, and hence uncertainty and unpredictability are greatest, one would expect relational contracting, with its reassuring recurrence and its catering to idiosyncrasy, to be the solution of choice.[11] Thus, in economies where shortage, nonstandardization, and weak information channels are pronounced, we would expect to find a prevalence of relational contracting. Such "mutually obligated trading relationships," as Dore calls them, sometimes involve the use of nonmarket prices that cause at least short-term economic loss to one or the other party.[12] And Goldberg's "sheltering" means, of course, that deals are not struck with "all comers without restriction." So in those cases where relational contracting is occurring, one could argue that administrative adjustment of some sort will act to disrupt the pure play of neoclassical market forces.

Relevant Properties of the Planned Economy

As the dominant force shaping the social foundation for trading in the prereform Chinese economy, the state plan itself promoted relational contracting. In fact, to understand the presence of our three structural properties—shortage, nonstandardization, and weak information channels—in China today, we need to consider how the Stalinist-style command system fed their growth for nearly three decades, embedding these properties deeply into the Chinese political economy. It should be noted at the outset that this was an economy generally characterized by oft-mandated, initially idiosyncratic—but with time, habitually recurrent—exchanges. And these exchanges were structurally similar to those in other economic systems wherein sunk costs lock buyer and seller into a relationship of bilateral monopoly.[13]

Kornai's famous study of the socialist planned economy explains the prominent role played by *shortage*.[14] According to Kornai, shortage occurs in the socialist economy's "atmosphere of growth at a forced rate," which leads to an "insatiable demand" for inputs on the part of firms, especially those in the heavy industrial sector, and to an "expansion drive" coupled with "investment hunger," as each firm is instructed by its superior planning authority that it "must grow." As total claims for funding always surpass prescribed investment quotas, competition for investment along with the accompanying tensions serve to exacerbate the general state of shortage.[15] Thus, for example, despite the massive amount of funds invested in the heavy industrial sector—mainly for metals and producer goods—over decades of Communist party rule in China and other socialist systems, shortage inevitably prevailed.

Hanson, writing principally about consumer goods, finds another reason for perennial shortage in these economies. He speaks of sellers' markets, whose presence he blames on controlled prices, which lead in turn to repressed inflation. Thus, at low, fixed prices there is excess demand and a consequent shortage of almost everything consumers want.[16] And, of course, the consumer goods sector generally suffers from an imbalanced pattern of investment in socialist systems, which regularly slight consumption in favor of investment in producer goods.

Kornai also has an explanation for the low level of standardization in centralized command economies. He describes how state-owned firms, charged with meeting specific output targets, engage in "forced substitution." That is, they are compelled to alter the input combination of their products as a result of shortage. If a necessary input is unavailable, firms often end up with a nonstandard product as they attempt to adjust to the shortage.[17]

Kornai also discusses information problems in command economies. He refers to the "imperfect information of the participants in the allocation process"; and he stresses the value of information in reducing costly searches and alleviating the need to make forced substitutions.[18] One structural reason for the existence of deficiencies in the information networks of command economies is the long-term relative neglect of sectors other than heavy industry. Because of the skewed investment patterns in these systems, the infrastructure of transportation and communications, so vital to the establishment of information channels, has long been ignored in all socialist systems, including the Chinese.[19]

Perhaps the most intractable problem in information networks in these systems, however, is the fact that state organs dominate the allocation of goods at each administrative level. The personnel of such organs—particularly, in the industrial sector, workers in the materials supplies departments and the planning commissions—are the agents best placed to receive and disseminate market information. True, there are also informal channels of information that grow out of but exist independently of the formal state-operated supply channels. But even here, the purchasing agents of the factories who scout for extra economic intelligence must depend upon state-sponsored meetings and "deals" made with other state-run units to locate and procure their required inputs.[20] As a result, state design severely circumscribes the scope and boundaries of economic behavior, and thus limits as well the flow of vital information.

Shortage, nonstandardization, and weak information channels, then, are endemic features of the command economy. Where these features are especially pronounced, relational contracting—recurrent exchanges with known partners—often becomes the most reliable form of exchange. Under the command economy the majority of recurrent exchanges are compulsory, that is, they result from couplings mandated by the state planning bureaucracy. In China under the regime of the state plan, with the exception of the largest and most important enterprises whose managers could at times negotiate and conclude their own supply and sales contracts, most legitimate transactions were arranged by administrative departments.[21] Recent interviews have confirmed that recurrently planners paired the same partners over many years.[22]

Failure properly to match input specifications to need was not uncommon under the reign of the plan. Indeed, such mismatches have attained great notoriety in critiques of the command economy. But the larger picture was one in which, most of the time, most firms got what they needed to produce what they were ordered to turn out, even if quality was wanting. This laid the foundation for a relatively satisfactory recurrent allocation of materials among enterprises, so that firms came to count on supplies from particular plants with which they were conjoined by the plan. On the other hand, another, unofficial type of relational contracting also commonly occurred. When maldistribution did occur, firms tended to engage in illicit or quasi-legal activities that made up what is known as the "second" or "gray" economy. They did this in order to overcome breakdowns in the formal supply system that threatened to prevent fulfillment of planned targets.[23]

In China in prereform days, gray-market dealings usually took one of two forms, both of which probably led to recurrent exchanges between the same enterprises. These were, first, trading in which raw materials were supplied by one enterprise to another which made goods for it; and second, bartering sometimes of inappropriate for appropriate parts, sometimes of such disparate items as chemicals traded for equipment or trucks for steel.[24] Once a procurement agent had identified his source, it seems likely that he would continue to build upon personal connections fostered by previous transactions thereby saving himself additional, unnecessary search behavior.

It is certainly true that relational contracting occurs in commodity transactions in all sorts of economies, especially where a relatively low developmental level renders such behavior optimal.[25] But structural properties peculiar to the socialist, command economy clearly reinforce the state plan's forced pairing of enterprises. The outcome, then, is to make this sort of transaction the overwhelmingly dominant one in centrally planned economies. The continuing strength of known connections built up over time in these systems, along with the persistence of several conducive features in the technological environment—*viz.*, shortage, nonstandardization, and inadequate information—have led many enterprises to continue doing business with their original, preform partners long after the advent of the "market." The upshot is that the transition from command to commerce has been smoother (i.e., involving minimal disruption or dislocation) than would have been predicted by a model that presumes a bold leap from pure planning to open markets.[26]

The Chinese Urban Reform Program

In China a process of economic reform has been under way since the much publicized Third Plenum of the Eleventh Central Committee, held in December 1978. At first, rural reform commanded center stage. Despite scattered experiments, urban/industrial reform did not really go forward in an energetic way until October 1984, when the party issued a major document on urban reform at the Twelfth Central Committee's Third Plenum.[27] A new definition of the Chinese economic system emerged from the latter meeting, a definition which, at the rhetorical level, subtly shifted the balance of regulatory forces away from the old, primarily planned framework. It was decreed that China was now "practicing a planned commodity economy on the basis of public ownership," a characterization that legitimized commodity production and exchange, and placed them at the heart of the system's operation. Such activities, with all they implied in terms of reliance on market forces, had for decades been viewed in China as lacking in socialist legitimacy.

The 1984 document, which was more a statement of intent than a plan of immediate action, contained four major points, coinciding with the four main arenas of reform—the planning system, management, prices, and wage policy. In planning, central commands (the equivalent of what are called "imperative plans" in developed economies) were to give way to "guidance"-type directives (similar to what is known as "indicative" planning in Japan and the West) and to market forces, with obligatory norms applying only to major products having a significant bearing on the national economy. In management, state control over enterprises was to be relaxed, with firms thenceforth to be responsible for organizing more and more of their own supply procurement and sales. Enterprise managers, taking on new authority, were to be responsible for their own profits and losses. "Irrational" prices, set according to political objectives and largely unchanged since the 1950s, were to be readjusted with the proviso that real incomes should not be disturbed. Finally, wages were to be linked to an individual's actual work output, with differentials between wage grades correspondingly widened. Since 1984, an effort has been made to implement these general principles. Enterprises have been granted the power to trade materials not procured by the central government; and lower-level administrations have been given the authority to allocate and manage significant proportions of key supplies. The number of commodities handled by the state's distribution system has also declined precipitously in recent years, from 256 in 1978 to only 20 in 1986. By the summer of 1987, a new mode of management had been introduced in 75 percent of China's 12,398 larger state-owned industrial enterprises. Known as the "contract responsibility system," it was to give managers added control over their enterprises' operations. A new profit retention scheme was also pioneered, under which profits retained by enterprises rose to 39 percent of total profits, a threefold increase over what they kept at the beginning of the reform era, in 1979.

With respect to the reform of prices, the proportion of items with prices fixed by the state decreased dramatically: from 98 percent in 1978 to only 20 percent in 1986.[28] Based on the above statistics, it would appear that a number of nontrivial alterations have taken place in the form of inter-enterprise trade in China since 1978. Yet, certain data from the city of Wuhan suggests that despite such alterations, there are definite continuities in firms' choices of trading partners— continuities that belie any assumption of radical, market-oriented change.

Relational Contracting and Reform in Wuhan

In June 1984, four and a half months before the seminal October urban reform document was issued, the central Chinese city of Wuhan, whose gross value of industrial output then ranked fourth nationwide, was chosen as the second city to be granted separate line-item status in the central plan. Through this move, Wuhan secured economic management powers equal to those of a province; and the city was expected to lead an experiment in comprehensive urban reform for provincial capitals.[29]

Both historically and under the People's Republic, Wuhan has occupied a place of special importance as a transport hub and a transshipment center. Sitting astride both the Yangtze River and the Guangzhou–Beijing Railway, almost equidistant from Chongqing, Shanghai, Guangzhou, and the national capital, Wuhan's traditional role has been that of "thoroughfare of nine provinces." But this role was to a large extent thwarted under the rule of vertical (that is, provincial and central-level) bureaucracies, with their planned, compulsorily conducted commerce and their transport coordinated by separate, enclosed, political authorities along administratively demarcated boundaries.[30] With the advent of urban reform, it was hoped that Wuhan, with its new independent powers, would be able to reenact its historical role as a center of foreign trade, finance, banking, and information, even as it reinforced its post-1949 position as a base of industry, higher education, and research.[31] In short, Wuhan's new powers would underline the overall national economic reform's dramatic shift toward market-oriented commerce and economically based, decentralized decision making. It was undoubtedly for this reason that Wuhan was selected as a reform model.

In the remainder of this chapter, I will examine in detail one particular aspect of the "model" urban reforms undertaken in Wuhan—the way in which enterprises select their transaction partners. As the material below will illustrate, firms often elect to trade via relational contracting. That is, they frequently pick tested associates, in most cases, the very same supply sources and sales outlets that were once written into their plans. The outcome has been to replace prescriptive relational contracting with relational contracting by preference, thereby preserving the essence, if not the form, of the old state plan. The persistence of various traditional structural properties of centrally planned economies mentioned above—namely, shortage, nonstandardization, and inadequate information channels—can be shown to play a significant role in shaping this outcome.

Persistence of Structural Properties

Shortage

Kornai's "insatiable demand" has not disappeared with the diminution of demands from central planners. Indeed, the urge of urban officials and enterprise managers to expand their operations has if anything increased in recent years. For beginning in 1980, financial reforms permitted firms and localities to retain a portion of the profits they generated, instead of having to turn over all receipts to higher-level offices.[32]

Under the new economic regime, not only do firms compete among themselves for supplies and investment as they once did in the old planned economy,[33] but they strive to obtain and hold on to resources that official regulations regard as belonging to the central government. An indication of this loss of central control over resource allocation is the estimate from the first half of 1987 that, nationwide, 47 percent of rolled steel, 48 percent of coal, and 84 percent of cement were at that point no longer distributed by the state.[34] Another effect of the reforms has been to permit the free trading of materials left over after delivery quotas to the state have been met. This has created a dual price structure, with market prices of goods on the second (supply-and-demand governed) track often at least twice as high as those set by the state. The high market prices clearly indicate continuing materials shortages.[35] Another piece of evidence of the persistence of shortage is the central government's frequent issuance of bulletins bemoaning its inability to carry through with national construction projects. The crux of the problem reportedly lies in the state's loss of control over raw materials.[36]

Yet another indication of shortage is contained in a 1985 report which describes the operation of new wholesale materials "trade centers." The report claims that these marts, authorized in 1984 for selling supplies that flow outside the plan's networks, operate in what are essentially sellers' markets. It holds that,

> Now when motor vehicles and steel products are in unusually short supply, if the materials departments sponsor some trade centers, they are only going through the form of a "center," concentrating all the extra-plan trade in one place, to prevent speculation and stop improprieties. Strictly speaking, this isn't what was originally meant by a trade center, [so] calling it a sales center is probably more appropriate.[37]

Continuing materials shortage is further revealed in a decision made by the Wuhan Heavy Machinery Plant (Wuzhong). This huge plant was supposedly placed under Wuhan's municipal control under the 1984 urban reform program. However, at a meeting at the Ministry of Machine-Building in Beijing in 1985, plant managers were given a choice: thenceforth, they could depend upon either the Ministry, the province (which previously had controlled it), or the city to procure the basic allotment of material supplies guaranteed under the state plan. Because plant officials believed that there was a greater certainty of supplies coming from the central level, they picked the Ministry of Metallurgy as the firm's source of stocks. Even so, the amount of supplies they were able to obtain from the ministry decreased each year after this arrangement was instituted. Where 40 percent of the plant's total needs had been met through the state plan in 1983, successively lesser amounts were delivered to it thereafter, varying in accord with the amount of supplies the ministry had on hand at any time.[38] This example shows the continued presence of shortages in two respects: first, in the firm's perception of a shortage of supplies at the local governmental level—this despite the grant of increased management powers to that level; and second, the story underlines the steady decline of steel supplies under central control and thus the diminishing amount available for use in accord with national objectives.

Non-standardization

Non-standardization—specifically in the form of uneven quality—further predisposes economic agents to opt for relational contracting. One telling piece of evidence for the continued salience of this problem is an exhibit of "shoddy products" that was to be held by the Ministry of Light Industry in Beijing in August 1987. The purpose of the show was to shame (and to fine) factories into improving the quality of their products. Substandard goods were collected from consumers, who were compensated or given replacements, while the negligent producers were required to buy back their products. For about a week following the announcement of the show, the ministry was "bombarded with telephone complaints from consumers."[39] Ultimately, pressure from affected factories led to a cancellation of the exhibit. A 1987 report in the Chinese press acknowledged the severity of this problem. Due to poor management decisions, "there were cases where different types of equipment bought by one factory were not compatible with each other.... In one chemical fibre company, for example, five production lines were imported from five different countries, leading to poor quality products and small production capacity because of the different characteristics of the equipment."[40]

Reports of uneven quality also appear frequently in my Wuhan data. One incident involved a large department store which invested a sum of 100,000 yuan in a particular bicycle plant in a distant eastern Chinese city (one with which they had had dealings in prereform days). The store buyers' motive in striking this deal rested on their belief that this one plant would produce high-quality bikes, while most other factories would not.[41] Another case concerned Wuzhong, which signed a contract pledging the plant to invest three million yuan in a factory in Hunan, in exchange for a three-year supply of iron at the low, state-controlled price. The supply relationship between the two plants had its foundation in the prereform days of the plan, when their respective staffs made frequent mutual visits (*lailaiwangwang de guanxi*). Those earlier shared experiences taught Wuzhong's buyers that only the iron from this particular firm in Hunan could meet their specific quality requirements.[42]

Information

Problems of quality and uncertainty are found in markets of many kinds.[43] But where quality is particularly variable and thus questionable, such as in the still rather undeveloped Chinese industrial system (and thus in the incipient domestic market), its link with uncertainty is closest. In such a context, the need for reliable information must be most crucial, the more so if shortage is present as well. And yet information networks today remain relatively impoverished despite the commitment to developing markets, while at the same time they continue to be state-dominated.[44] One press account makes the extreme claim that Chinese information and consulting services are still so weak that firms cannot even locate partners for exchange.[45] A less drastic appraisal is simply that, "because of the absence of a regular feedback system, enterprises normally obtain information through personal connections or just by chance. Thus, many of them have reached cooperation agreements with others without being guided."[46] This latter characteristic of the Chinese market system today resonates with the analysis in this chapter.

The state's recent, heavy investment in information management and control is glaringly apparent in the section on "Information and Consulting" in the 1986 Wuhan Yearbook.[47] That section describes the functions of a dozen networks, committees, and centers created in recent years to disseminate internal bulletins to and promote economic intelligence exchanges among Wuhan and similar official, state-managed agencies at city and provincial levels across the country; the new agencies are also expected to engage in economic forecasting. The dozen networks and bodies mentioned in the yearbook include the Wuhan City Economic Information Forecasting Center, the Wuhan City Industrial Economic Information Center, and the Wuhan Commercial Information Network. That all of these are state-sponsored and managed underlines the persisting dominance of the public sector in this field, and suggests a generalized poverty of market avenues outside its control.

Perhaps the most efficacious information channels of all are those, carried over from the days of state planning, manned directly by personnel in state organs. One such organ is the local materials supply bureau, which for decades allocated supplies for industrial production in accord with the plan's directives. The bureau now plays a strong role in managing market information in the new reform environment. Its cadres have long-standing ties with factory managers across the country, many of whom have been on the job for years. Another set of key actors is composed of the old factory purchasing agents *(caigouyuan)* who have served their firms over decades whenever the plan proved inadequate. All industrial enterprises have a half dozen to a dozen such personnel. Each agent specializes in one to several materials about which he has built up a stock of knowledge over the years with respect to what can be obtained where and how. Most of these people are still in place. They operate by linking into the pervasive enterprise information networks *(qiye xinxi wangluo)* that have long stretched across China, of which there are two main types. The major network, or *da wang,* tells what can be found in particular cities; the minor one, the *xiao wang,* is more specific and pertains to the materials held by individual factories. By continuing to communicate through these networks, factories are able to locate much of what they ostensibly buy "on the market."[48]

In sum, abiding shortages, problems of standardization, and limited information channels all incline firms to continue to rely on those enterprises with which they have long-standing, well-tested and trusted trading ties. Transaction cost efficiencies of such relational contracting certainly facilitate the smooth implementation of the "market" reforms currently being pushed in China. For this type of commerce obviates the need to spend precious time and resources locating new partners; consequently, more business can be contracted more expeditiously than could be done through a sudden leap to spot markets. It is ironic that such exchanges, which serve to reduce transaction costs, stand in the way of what many critics have presumed to be the most economically rational marketing arrangements in the purest neoclassical sense. A few examples drawn from my interviews in Wuhan will demonstrate this general point.

Relational Contracting in Wuhan

Several of the new reforms are explicitly geared toward encouraging cities and firms to break out of the boundaries previously imposed by the bureaucratic strictures of the state plan, and to join together for what are presumed to be more economically rational purposes. One example is the program for "lateral (as opposed to hierarchical) exchange," *hengxiang lianxi,* which is being advocated to connect supply sources directly with consumer demand, and to demolish the "blockades" between districts imposed by administrative orders. In conception, lateral exchange entails the coordination among several enterprises of capital, technology, materials, and sometimes even personnel across administrative and geographical boundaries. Other relevant innovations include trade centers, markets for the means of production, capital markets, and "enterprise groups" (also called "socialist trusts").[49]

Apparently in violation of the spirit underlying these schemes, many relational contracting configurations remain exclusively within local boundaries, maintaining intact linkages first forged under the plan. The 1986 Wuhan Yearbook, for instance, reveals a total of 255 offices registered in the city for the purpose of fostering exchange, representing outside administrative units from the county level on up. These agencies were staffed by a total of 4,994 personnel. Yet, less than 5 percent of these offices were set up by higher- (province or city) level units, and only 2.5 percent of the personnel working in them were delegated by province or city governments.[50] This indicates that the overwhelming bulk of the business was being conducted with smaller, localized units very near Wuhan. This also suggests a continuing reliance on known partners. The remarks of a local economist back up this inference of an unbroken relationship between localism and the state plan: "In the past we were sealed up (*fengbi*), so we managed work according to administrative [planned] relations. As a result, relations with Hubei [the province of which Wuhan is the capital city] and Wuhan are the main part of our present exchanges."[51]

Indeed, localism shows up in much of the implementation of reform. When the city government in Wuhan designated the Wuhan Bazaar (a major department store) as a "keypoint" for reform, extending it permission to draw up a share group (*gufen jituan*) in late 1986, the store picked seven investors.[52] All were city-based firms, including the mammoth Wuhan Iron and Steel Works, an insurance company, and the Wuhan branches of the People's and Agricultural Banks. Since, as its managers explained, the risk would be smaller with local partners whose business acumen was well known to the store, these managers intentionally invited only units from Wuhan to join. This strategy was also meant to contribute to the growth of the local economy, thus boosting consumer purchasing power in the city.

Another case in point was a capital market centered in Hubei Province. This particular market was one of five such interbank networks for which Wuhan constitutes the hub. But a researcher from the local branch of the People's Bank admitted that this provincial market was the most active. Within the province, he said, communications were easiest (no doubt for both social and technological reasons) and transactions were frequent, if not in large denominations. This was true despite the fact that one of the other capital networks was composed of the cities like Wuhan that have separate status in the state plan, plus several of the special economic-zone cities; one might have expected that network to have comparatively more autonomy than usual and thus the clout to form a lively market for funds.[53]

The story was not substantially different for Wuhan's department stores. Much of their stock came from factories whose staff the stores' managers had met over the years at state-run semiannual national supply meets. These meets, which each present a particular type of commodity, were formerly run by the relevant wholesale companies within the state commercial system. In the past, under the regime of the plan, factories, whose total output was automatically purchased and allocated to retailers, participated merely to learn about the stores' demands; now they come to do business. Today, the *guanxi* (personal connections) built up over years of attending the same meets stand these stores in good stead. At the Central-South Large Commercial Building, a sizable department store that opened in Wuchang (one of Wuhan's three component towns) in early 1985, almost all of the staff had previously worked in one of Wuhan's two other big stores. Spokesmen estimated that as much as 40 percent of the store's stock came from factories known to their co-workers from the past. Though this figure may not seem high at first glance, one might well have expected the percentage of old suppliers to be much smaller, given the institution of several new modes of locating stock, such as via ads, or by becoming a sales outlet for new industrial enterprise groups.[54]

In the lateral exchanges, too, previous connections have smoothed the transition from the mandatory plan to the market. For instance, of the eighteen units in the Wuhan Cement Machinery Complete-Set Company *(Jixie Chengtao Gongsi)*, a new firm organized around the Wuhan General Machinery Factory, eleven are from Hubei Province and five others are from Wuhan. The other two, a design institute in Anhui and a factory in Jiangsu, were both units with which this machinery factory had previous business ties *(yewu guanxi)* based on meetings, "exchange of experience," and mutual visits under the plan.[55]

Examples of this sort figured prominently in my interviews.[56] The picture suggested by the data is this: in implementing the new reforms, firms have employed a number of specific practices, many of which share certain common features. Most outstanding among these is the general principle of relational contracting, which often works where it does because "the plan" and its patterns have paved the way. That is, a significant portion of the trading of today takes place through the reinstitution on a voluntary basis of relational contracting, which makes use of previously established channels and ties, and which relies on personnel with inside knowledge of the availability and whereabouts of goods.

Conclusion

Once the argument is laid out, its gist appears commonsensical. We have seen that trading in any context tends to depend upon trust and so is socially embedded; we have also seen that the technological and informational environments of socialist economies such as the Chinese may enhance existing social propensities for engaging in patterns of recurring, idiosyncratic exchange. Apparently, in this era of reform, exchanges established on this basis are forming the springboard for the leap toward more marketized activity. Transaction cost analysis suggests that such behavior is economically rational; indeed, it is arguably much more rational at this stage of the Chinese reform process than would be the installation of a neoclassical textbook model of a free market, wherein firms search out the optimal partner for each new exchange de novo on a nationwide scale.

All told, it seems clear that once the state plan's formal commands were lifted—commands that in the past joined firms by fiat in relational, bilaterally monopolistic contracts—the pathways they left behind would in many instances persist, at least for a time. And so the networks composed of those pathways continue to bring the old partners together, this time, however, as a matter of choice. The overall effect of such behavior on the reform process is positive. This is because relational contracting forms a foundation for market trading, and thereby enhances the sheer quantity of market-based economic activity. This it does by lowering transaction costs, at least in the short run.

Since the socialist economic system in its heyday itself furthered relational contracting in China, these findings should hold in any environment where socialist planning systems institute market reforms. There are a few caveats here, however. These would include the possibilities that (1) the historically less tightly planned Chinese economy may have better preserved preexisting marketing ties over the years than was the case in other socialist systems;[57] (2) the relatively greater degree of technological backwardness of the Chinese economy may mean that information channels are less well developed there than elsewhere; and (3) the state and economic system are so much larger in China than in most other socialist nations that localized marketing—where partners know each other well—must more often be the case there.

Despite the manifest nature of the case made here, the overlap of plan and market, with the one tending to merge into the other, has been heretofore completely ignored by theorists of the reform of socialist systems. Instead, commentators have tended to focus their critiques on widespread bureaucratic obstruction of enterprise autonomy, or on the ways in which pricing-system rigidities have stymied the institution of perfect neoclassical markets. From the opposite vantage point, other observers have seen in the gradual elimination of compulsory targets over the past decade, and in the flourishing of urban produce markets, the birth of a totally new free market phenomenon in the People's Republic. This too is overly facile. In this chapter I have deconstructed both of these models. In their place, I have presented an analysis grounded in the empirical observation that in practice the operational distinction between plan and market is much more blurred than neoclassical theory would suggest. The concept of relational contracting has helped to highlight the fact that in the world of social experience there is no clear or necessary dividing line distinguishing the pattern of enterprise transactions under the plan from that under a certain type of market.

Notes

1. For instance, the journal *Jingji guanli* (Economic management) (hereafter *JJGL*), no. 8, 1987, carries an article entitled, "The Aim and Direction of the Reform of the System of Capital Goods Circulation," translated in *Foreign Broadcast Information Service* (hereafter *FBIS*), October 6, 1987, pp. 16–20. Page 17 in the translation states that "The final target of a means of production market is that through competition on terms of freedom and equality the renewed combination of the important factors of production is realized."

2. Oliver E. Williamson, "Transaction-Cost Economics: The Governance of Contractual Relations," *Journal of Law and Economics* 22 (October 1979): 248.

3. Ibid., p. 238.

4. Ibid., pp. 248, 250.

5. Victor P. Goldberg, "Relational Exchange: Economics and Complex Contracts," *American Behavioral Scientist* 23, 3 (1980): 338.

6. Ibid., p. 342.

7. Ronald Dore, *Flexible Rigidities: Industrial Policy and Structural Adjustment in the Japanese Economy, 1970–80* (Stanford: Stanford University Press, 1986), p. 2.

8. See Goldberg, "Relational Exchange: Economics and Complex Contracts," p. 351; and Dore, *Flexible Rigidities*, pp. 2, 3, 77, 80.

9. On this, see the seminal article by Mark Granovetter, "Economic Action and Social Structure: The Problem of Embeddedness," *American Journal of Sociology*, 91, 3 (November 1985): 481–510.

10. This draws, but also expands upon Oliver E. Williamson, *Economic Organization: Firms, Markets and Policy Control* (Brighton, Sussex: Wheatsheaf, 1986), p. 55.

11. Dore notes that the Japanese system of relational contracting was "created out of shortage." See Dore, *Flexible Rigidities*, p. 162. Also, Williamson (1979), p. 260, points out that, "As generic demand grows and the number of supply sources increases, exchange that was once transaction-specific loses this characteristic and greater reliance on market-mediated governance is feasible."

12. Dore, *Flexible Rigidities*, pp. 70, 162.

13. Williamson (1979) identifies idiosyncrasy of investments as the crucial factor distinguishing relational from other types of contracting: "Idiosyncratic goods and services are ones . . . where investments of transaction-specific human and physical capital are made [and] . . . the relationship between buyer and supplier is quickly thereafter transformed into one of bilateral monopoly—on account of the transaction-specific costs." See p. 241.

14. Janos Kornai, *The Economics of Shortage* (Amsterdam: North Holland, 1980), 2 vols.

15. Ibid., pp. 27, 29, 193, 200, 201.

16. Philip Hanson, *Advertising and Socialism: The Nature and Extent of Consumer*

Advertising in the Soviet Union, Poland, Hungary and Yugoslavia (White Plains, NY: International Arts and Sciences Press, Inc., 1974), pp. 10–13, 20.

17. Kornai, *The Economics of Shortage*, pp. 37, 39.

18. Ibid., pp. 171–72.

19. On this, see Ma Hong, *New Strategy for China's Economy,* trans. Yang Lin (Beijing: New World Press, 1983), p. 38.

20. Barry Richman, *Industrial Society in Communist China* (New York: Random House, 1969), p. 714, speaks of the large ordering conferences which disseminate information in the industrial sector; Jean C. Oi, in "Commercializing China's Rural Cadres," *Problems of Communism* (September–October 1986): 10, makes this point for the agricultural sector.

21. Richman, *Industrial Society,* pp. 710–20.

22. More on this will appear in the next section.

23. For example, see Hedrick Smith, *The Russians* (New York: Ballantine Books, 1977), p. 132; Benjamin N. Ward, *The Socialist Economy* (New York: Random House, 1967), p. 179; Gregory Grossman, "The 'Second Economy' of the USSR," *Problems of Communism* (hereafter *POC*) (September–October 1977), p. 29; Marshall I. Goldman, *Soviet Marketing: Distribution in a Controlled Economy* (New York: Free Press of Glencoe, 1963), p. 62; and Charles Lindblom, *Politics and Markets* (New York: Basic Books, 1977), chap. 5.

24. See Richman, *Industrial Society,* pp. 389–90; and Audrey Donnithorne, *China's Economic System* (New York: Praeger, 1967), pp. 175, 290, 291.

25. To bolster this point, a reviewer has pointed out that shortage and shoddy work of uneven quality characterize all underdeveloped economies (of which China is one), socialist or not.

26. An important difference, however, that is not addressed in this paper is the greatly heightened incidence in corrupt behavior as strict, state imposed and supervised controls and prices have diminished and a two-track pricing system has evolved.

27. I analyzed this document itself and the politics surrounding its issuance in "Economic Reform," in *China Briefing, 1984 ed. Steven M. Goldstein* (Boulder: Westview Press, 1985), pp. 87–107. The reform document is in Renmin ribao (People's daily) (hereafter *RMRB*), October 21, 1984, translated in *China Daily* (hereafter *CD*), October 22, 1984.

28. *Far Eastern Economic Review* (hereafter *FEER*), July 16, 1987, pp. 69–71; *Beijing Review* (hereafter *BR*), no. 34, August 24, 1987, p. 4; *FBIS*, September 11, 1987, p. 25; and *BR,* no. 37, September 14, 1987, p. 15.

29. Within a year, five other cities got this status in the central plan (Chongqing, not a capital, was so designated in early 1983): Guangzhou, Xi'an, Shenyang, and Harbin, all of which are also provincial capitals, and Dalian, which is not a capital. *RMRB*, July 18, 1987, p.1, lists two new cities in this category, neither of which is a provincial capital: Ningbo and Qingdao.

30. See speech by Zhou Taihe, *FBIS*, July 3, 1984, p. P1.

31. Xu Rongan, "The Central China Economic Region Must Be Built," *Jianghan luntan* (Jianghan forum) (Wuhan) (hereafter *JHLT*), no. 3, 1986: 8.

32. See Christine Wong, "Material Allocation and Decentralization: Impact of the Local Sector on Industrial Reform," and Barry Naughton, "False Starts and Second Wind: Financial Reforms in China's Industrial System," in *The Political Economy of Reform in Post-Mao China,* ed. Elizabeth J. Perry and Christine Wong (Cambridge, MA: Council on East Asian Studies, Harvard University, 1985), pp. 253–78 and 223–52, respectively.

33. Kornai, *The Economics of Shortage,* chap. 9, outlines this competition among what he terms "claimants."

34. *FEER*, June 18, 1987, p. 76. See also *BR*, no. 9, March 2, 1987, p. 24.

35. As one analyst put it succinctly, "many production materials are in short supply; and their prices keep rising." This is in *FBIS*, December 18, 1987, p. 24. Also, economist Zhou Shoulian, writing in the *People's Daily* on February 20, 1987, p. 5, explained that the formation of a normal means of production market requires that supply and demand are basically balanced. But at present, the phenomenon that the supply of some major means of production falls short of demand is still a serious one in our country.

36. E.g., already in 1983 the central media decried the "scattering" of resources that has been accompanying the decentralizing reforms. *FBIS*, July 7, 1983, p. K19, carried a translated Xinhua report that stated that from 1965 to 1982 the amount of rolled steel distributed by the state under the unified plan dropped from 95 to 53 percent; of cement, from 71 to 25 percent; and of timber, from 63 to 57 percent.

37. Deng Shaoying, "The Conditions for Development of Trade Centers and Their Functions," *JHLT*, no. 11 (1985): 14.

38. Information from interview at the plant on June 29, 1987.

39. In *FBIS*, August 20, 1987, p. 7.

40. In *CD*, December 18, 1987, p. 2.

41. Interview at this store, June 23, 1987.

42. Interview at Wuzhong on June 29, 1987.

43. On this issue, see George A. Akerlof, "The Market For 'Lemons': Quality Uncertainty and the Market Mechanism," in *An Economic Theorist's Book of Tales* (Cambridge: Cambridge University Press, 1984), pp. 7–22.

44. See Oi, "Commercializing China's Rural Cadres," pp. 9–10. She stresses that Chinese peasants are experiencing difficulties in the new rural markets because of their lack of information about demand and prices; thus, they remain heavily dependent on their local cadres.

45. This is in Wang Ding and Lu Yang, "Several Problems Needing Solution in Horizontal Economic Exchange," *JJGL*, no. 6 (1987): 13.

46. This is from *RMRB*, April 10, 1987, p. 5, translated in *FBIS*, April 22, 1987, p. K14.

47. *Wuhan nianjian 1986* (Wuhan yearbook 1986) (Hankow: Wuhan Nianjian Bianzuan Weiyuanhui Bianji [Wuhan Yearbook Compilation Committee], 1986), pp. 356–59 outlines and describes the functions of the massive local information network created by government organs in recent years in Wuhan and nationally.

48. This information on information flows, the *caigouyuan,* and the *xinxiwang* came from an interview at the Wuhan Chemical Machinery Factory on June 25, 1987.

49. The new enterprise groups (*qiye jituan*) are discussed in *RMRB*, on July 21, 1987, p. 2, translated in *FBIS*, July 29, 1987, p. K14. According to *RMRB*, August 10, 1987, p. 2, there were then over 1,000 of such groups registered nationwide.

50. *Wuhan nianjian*, p. 359.

51. July 1, 1987, interview with a local economist.

52. Interview at the store on June 23, 1987. The group offers a 15 percent dividend on shares (twice the rate of bank interest) and had already collected 10 million yuan in shares by mid-1987, all drawn from the partners picked by the store.

53. Interview on June 24, 1987, with representative of the Financial Research Institute of the Wuhan branch of the People's Bank.

54. Information obtained from an interview at the Central-South Large Commercial Building on June 29, 1987.

55. Interview at the factory, June 24, 1987.

56. I was unable to obtain the sort of data that would indicate the prevalence of such exchanges or the proportion of the total of voluntarily selected transactions that they

represent, and available published statistics do not provide a clear answer, either. In early 1985 Xinhua (New China News Agency) reported that 20,000 interprovincial economic and technical cooperation contracts had been signed in 1984, an amount that was two times the figure in 1983 (Xinhua, March 11, 1985, in Joint Publications Research Service—China East Asia–85–034 (April 5, 1985), p. 72). And by the end of 1986, over 32,000 organizations composed via lateral economic ties had formed into twenty-four lateral economic liaison networks (*RMRB*, May 8, 1987, p. 5, in *FBIS*, May 20, 1987, p. K14). But this gives us no idea as to the nature of these unions. Nor does it indicate the degree to which combinations form within provinces and more local areas—thus, continuing to respect the old administrative boundaries—as opposed to those of a cross-provincial nature. Wuhan, for example, reported in 1985 that enterprises there had built up 517 economic associations and cooperative organs with partners in the city's suburban counties, and had signed over 300 cooperation projects with more than 20 counties and cities of Hubei—but without telling how many ties it had established outside the area (in *FBIS*, February 5, 1986, p. K7). Yet another source states that in 1986, 1,140 enterprises in the city engaged in such cooperation (there termed *lianhe xiezuo*, or united cooperation) with a total of 2,593 firms and units in 28 provinces and municipalities, signing 3,324 cooperative projects involving 251 million yuan, but this time without saying the number of local projects in that year (See Qi Caozu, "Wuhan jingji tizhi zonghe gaige di huigu yu sikao" (Looking back and reflections on the comprehensive reform of Wuhan's economic system), *Wuhan jingji yanjiu* (Wuhan economic research), no. 3 (1987): 8.

57. On the less thorough planning in China as compared with Eastern Europe, see David Granick, "The Industrial Environment in China and the CMEA Countries," in *China's Industrial Reform*, ed. Gene Tidrick and Chen Jiyuan (New York: Oxford University Press, 1987), pp. 103–31.

6
Capitalist Measures with Chinese Characteristics

China's experiment in economic reform caught the world's eye a decade ago. Observers were shocked at the sudden shift away from doctrinaire Maoism, when the nation's massive communes started to split apart at their seams, its sidewalks became the arenas for petty peddlers' stalls, and a few of its factories first achieved the right to retain a portion of their profits and to market a measure of their output, after they had fulfilled mandatory deliveries to the state.

By the mid-1980s some seemingly far more drastic measures appeared to forebode a much more startling reshaping of the structure of the urban economy: industrial firms began selling off their state-owned assets as shares; bigger, more successful enterprises were taking over failing ones, in a manner suggestive of mergers in the West; and a tiny handful of hapless plants even went bankrupt, a nearly unprecedented phenomenon in a socialist country.[1]

But a paradox lurks behind this drama. These apparently most capitalistic practices of all have in reality not been sanctioned out of an urge to reorient the economy away from state ownership, toward privatization. In fact, the impulse behind this second stage of reform is state-centered, in two senses. In fiscal terms, the new reforms are inspired by an effort to recoup for the central budget losses that it sustained when the first, heady stage simply went too far. In October 1988, the progressive Shanghai *World Economic Herald* noted the problems and tied their solution to a genuine revolution in property rights: "the

I wish to thank the Wuhan Foreign Affairs Office and the U.S. Consulate in Shenyang for their very great assistance in arranging interviews for me during the summers of 1987 and 1988.

This chapter originally appeared in *Problems of Communism* 38, 1 (January/February 1989): 19–33. Reprinted with permission of *Problems of Communism*.

serious problems resulting from the pursuit of this policy [the policy of "decentralization and the concession of profits" to lower administrative levels and enterprises] are making more and more people realize that China must make some real and thorough structural changes in the economic field."[2] The political leadership, however, while ready to borrow the *idea* of a change in property rights, is far from prepared to take the concept to its logical conclusion, as will be seen below.

The reforms are, in a related vein, meant to contribute to the creation of an increasingly elusive stability in the national economy. All these reforms, in the eyes of the politicians, amount to means of managing the state's macro finances, and they are to do so while preserving state/public ownership. The Chinese state at present stands in what its leadership perceives to be a fiscal crisis. Indeed, at this writing (early 1989), though a variety of interpretations abound over just where the roots of crisis lie, Chinese analysts nearly unanimously trace them one way or another to some aspect of the first stage of reform. Most crucially, the first set of reforms decentralized to local administrations control over profits and taxes and over many industrial raw materials, along with granting new management powers to local governments and enterprises. Already by the end of 1986, the proportion of funds in the national income that were controlled by localities, departments and enterprises outside the state budget had jumped from 1979's 13.5 percent up to 21.4 percent; as a result, the proportion of state revenues in the national income dropped from the 31.9 percent of 1979 down to only 25 percent.[3]

Another component of the reforms added to central governmental financial commitments even as the money under its direct control was slipping away. State purchase prices for agricultural products for farmers and wages (plus bonuses) for workers were increased beginning in 1979, as incentives to enhance productivity. Subsidies extended by the state accompanied these payments: the draft state budget for 1987 had to allow for over a quarter of state expenditures for enterprise losses (in part a function of new expenses for the firms as their wage bill expanded and the prices of their inputs rose) and to compensate consumers for price rises.[4] As of mid-1988, state enterprise subsidies for the year were expected to amount to more than 40 billion yuan (U.S. $11 billion), equalling almost half of total industrial profit nationwide.[5]

Accordingly, the measures pioneered in the current second round of reform, begun in an attempt to rationalize the national industrial structure and more efficiently utilize its assets, are now turning out to be handy solutions to urgent problems. If successful, these ostensibly capitalist-like programs are to lift burdens from the state budget, by Chinese standards currently experiencing a serious deficit;[6] to sop up some of the excess currency that has been issued in recent years[7] to which many have attributed the uncharacteristic double-digit inflation now plaguing the country;[8] and to direct the at present relatively massive funds in consumers' hands into accumulation for state concerns.[9] The need to save state funds and check inflation, then, are crucial spurs driving the new programs.

The second dimension of this state-centeredness is managerial. Official agents have been inserted into the new markets as middlemen, to direct their activities. Indeed, in the case of virtually every innovation a corresponding office has been reassigned or a new one created within the state bureaucracy to act as a sort of broker. As a consequence, the preexisting power of state bureaucratic organs and their cadres is readily being translated into market power. According to the analysis in the *World Economic Herald* cited above, "the government organs' administrative functions have turned into the monopolization of the market."

Such power rests on control over key supplies and large facilities and especially on *guanxi,* or personal relationships, formed over many years of maneuvering within the state-planned economy. A key question for the future in this regard is whether, by multiplying the amount of exchange going on within the economy, the activities of the bureaucrats will eventually promote genuine marketization;[10] or, alternatively, whether the cadres will simply utilize the opportunities presented by the new environment to perpetuate their own power.

The material below considers these arguments and questions, illustrating them with reference to the present-day Chinese version of stock markets and shareholding; enterprise mergers and takeovers; bankruptcies; "horizontal exchange" (which redirects commerce and investment from the vertical pathways designed by bureaucratic planning to exchanges that cross administrative borders); markets for the means of production (replacing the administrative allocation of supplies that obtained under the regime of the state plan); and economic cooperation regions, which encourage division of labor and specialization among areas across the country, instead of the localized self-sufficiency enforced in the days of Mao Zedong.

All of these efforts at breaking down the hegemony of the command-driven economy appear at first glance to be borrowed from capitalist, market-style economies. But behind each of them, I will show, lies a statist rationale and a statist organization. In short, what can easily be mistaken for a Chinese lurch toward capitalism is actually the fleshing out of that vague concept of "socialism with Chinese characteristics" that Deng Xiaoping has been using to justify his reforms for the past several years: a bureaucratically arranged regrouping of state-owned assets.

Saving the State Budget by Capitalist Measures

"The lack of funds is the biggest problem facing China's economic development," the New China News Agency announced in mid-1988, quoting an economist's article in the *World Economic Herald*.[11] The adoption in still socialist China of a set of measures widely practiced in capitalist contexts— namely, enterprise bankruptcy, enterprise takeovers, and shareholding and stock markets—must be understood as a response to this urgent constraint. For later on in the year when rapidly rising inflation and a new sense of crisis about the deficit forced leaders to halt experiments in price reform, these other reforms were allowed nonetheless to go forward.[12] In effect, these more recent reforms are to solve a very basic problem hobbling the efficiency and thus the growth of the Chinese economy, and, therefore, threatening to cripple the central government's treasury: "backward" firms waste equipment, energy, capital, land, personnel, and material supplies. Meanwhile, many well-managed enterprises capable of turning out marketable products are starved for these very same resources.[13] Precious and scarce state assets, in short, are seriously misallocated in the Chinese industrial economy. Party General Secretary Zhao Ziyang, one of the chief initiators of the industrial reform program in 1978, placed his late 1988 justification of the continuation of these particular policies squarely within the framework of saving and even building up the store of capital for the state when he delivered his speech to the Third Plenary Session of the party's Thirteenth Central Committee:

> The public sale in a planned way, and under organized leadership, of the property rights of small state-owned enterprises and encouragement given to large and medium-sized state-owned enterprises to issue their own stocks will turn a portion of consumption funds into accumulation funds, curtail the rise in market commodity prices, promote the flow of productive factors toward areas with better economic results, and optimize the allocation of resources. . . .These reforms will never pose a threat to the dominant role of public ownership. On the contrary, they will enable us to make good use of idle funds in society to reduce the state's financial burden.[14]

Clearly, in spite of an enormous mass of journalistic and academic comment in China over more than a year, in which publicists toyed with the notion of revamping the Chinese ownership system, the bottom line in the official promotion of this group of reforms is an intention to shift around state assets, in the interest of eliminating state subsidies to failing firms and, at the same time, earning new profits from expanding the holdings of the winners. For the time being, there is no privatization of any significance going on. A brief look at the content of these measures will bear this out.

Bankruptcy

Allowing firms to go bankrupt goes against the grain of several of the most fundamental assumptions of existing socialist societies: state ownership of productive assets and thus state responsibility for their management and maintenance; and the right of all workers to employment, plus provision for their welfare. And yet, beginning with a 1983 study prepared by the Technology and Economics Research Center of the State Council, some economists in China concluded that a bankruptcy law would nevertheless be necessary, to purge the economy of technologically obsolete enterprises in order for modernization to get under way.[15] In the next year Cao Siyuan, later made chairman of a bankruptcy law drafting task force, published a draft of a law on enterprise bankruptcy in the Chinese journal *Democracy and Legal System*.

Early in 1985 the northeastern industrial capital of Shenyang issued the first bankruptcy law in post-1949 China, in the form of trial provisions for collectively (as opposed to state-) owned enterprises, to apply within this one municipality. Over the next two years two national-level drafts followed, accompanied by opinion polls, conferences, and propaganda seminars until, in December 1986, the members of Standing Committee of the National Peoples' Congress (China's parliament) were able after months of inconclusive debates and disagreements finally to hammer out a law entitled the "Enterprise Bankruptcy Law of the People's Republic of China (Tentative)." The law went into effect on November 1, 1988, although by that time some thirty firms had already been issued yellow warning cards over a three-year period, but only a trifling few had actually gone bankrupt.[16] The law defines an enterprise as bankrupt if "because of a deficit caused by mismanagement, [it] cannot repay debts which are due."[17] This is different, of course, from bankruptcy in capitalist economies, where companies simply fail when their owners run out of funds. For in China, the state generally subsidizes deficit-ridden firms; the new law, then, essays to differentiate enterprises suffering losses because of poor management from ones whose losses have resulted from state actions, such as state pricing or procurement policies or state allocation to the firm of inferior equipment or insufficient supplies.[18] Indeed, some of the literature discussing the measure viewed the aim of the law to be to compel enterprises in danger to shape up and avoid bankruptcy, rather than to cause them to fall prey to it.[19]

Another special feature of this socialist bankruptcy procedure, one that underlines the continuing dependent status of state-owned firms, is the heavy responsibility bestowed on the official department (industrial bureau) that is in charge of managing the firm. The law decrees that the officials in that department (in addition to the enterprise's own management) must submit to administrative sanctions if it can be shown that, through departmental interference in enterprise affairs, these officials have had primary responsibility for the firm's losses. In addition, it is the department's leaders that must petition for the right to initiate the two-year reconciliation and reorganization program that the court permits failing firms to undertake; they are also charged with carrying out this program. A third provision of the law that, again, stamps it as socialist is its attention to the fate of the employees of the terminated firm. The fourth article demands that the government arrange new jobs for them and ensure that their basic livelihood needs are met during their time of unemployment. To fulfill these promises, the State Council passed two sets of regulations: one, the "Temporary Regulations on the Adoption of a Contractual Employment System for State-Owned Enterprises"; the other, the "Temporary Regulations on Security Provided for Unemployed Former Employees of State-Owned Enterprises."

By mid-1988, in spite of these several twists in standard bankruptcy practice to accommodate socialist sensitivities, the effort clearly was not working as intended. One report at that point referred to a group of over 7,000 firms, which it said amounted to 20 percent of the total firms within the state budget, that were experiencing losses and sustaining a combined debt of 2.6 billion yuan a year.[20] Another mentioned 6,364 state firms that had suffered from economic losses totaling 3.637 billion yuan, an alarming 27 percent increase over the same period in 1987.[21] Yet a third counted over 400,000 enterprises running in the red, of which, it considered, three quarters should be annexed by other firms or declared bankrupt.[22]

One of the problems in relying solely on bankruptcy to solve these financial problems was clearly that sufficient funds could not be gathered to provide for the social welfare of all the employees who would then have been dismissed. In Shenyang, for example, the city government ordered the 5,000 collective firms under the jurisdiction of its district administrations to pay 5 percent of their workers' standard wages as relief funds to compensate the retired and jobless workers of bankrupt enterprises. But the city was able to collect only 100,000 yuan a month, just enough to help out a thousand people. Thus, if any more enterprises had gone bankrupt, there would be no way to handle insurance for them.[23] On a national basis, the staff and workers in losing enterprises were estimated to number in the several millions. If their firms were all permitted to go under, the housing, rations, social security, and social services for these people, not to mention the work of finding them new jobs, would surely overwhelm the state.[24]

A second issue grew out of the law's concern to pin responsibility on administrative departments. One famous case was that of the Shenyang Explosion Plant, the first to fall nationally. It had possessed fixed assets worth 300,000 yuan and debts of 500,000 yuan when it went bankrupt in August 1986. But it died only after eating up more than 200,000 yuan worth of assistance arranged for it by its departmental supervisor during its probation period.[25] Knowing that such aid—in the form of tax reduction and exemption, low-interest loans, and temporary forgiveness from debt repayment—would be forthcoming if a firm were declared to be on the brink; the supposedly ominous yellow warning card has become a coveted item.[26]

Thus, the effort to devise a bankruptcy law that met socialist expectations foundered on its own internal contradictions. Obviously, under such conditions instituting bankruptcy on a large scale would eventually mean more not fewer state budgetary losses. That the experiment seems to be in the midst of quietly being shelved bears out the point that bankruptcy was undertaken primarily for the sake of bolstering the government's treasury, and not for enhancing enterprise autonomy.

Enterprise Takeovers

One answer to this dilemma that, it is hoped, should enable the state to slough off the load of losing firms without having at the same time to sustain their staff and workers is the experiment in enterprise takeover, sometimes translated by the Chinese as annexing or merging enterprises. In Wuhan, for instance, in thirty-two firms that were taken over by others, 9,803 workers and 3,719 retired persons found a healthy payroll in the new plant to care for them. In one case work in an electrical machinery equipment factory had been suspended for nearly four years, rendering the plant unable to issue wages to its employees for a full two years. Not surprisingly, during this time the staff and workers there frequently appeared at the offices of the city government appealing for help. After being absorbed by a solvent firm, they could count on their monthly pay.[27] Another story comes from Shenyang where two collective firms recently went bankrupt. There merging, rather than implementing bankruptcy procedures, "achieved a better result," from the perspective of the official Chinese press. For when the twenty-six employees of one of these, a chemical plant, threatened a sit-in strike if their plant were declared bankrupt, the city agreed to let a profitable carpentry machinery firm that needed extra workshops assume responsibility for it, employees, debts, and all.[28]

In the Chinese context, mergers of state enterprises amount to the transfer of management power and right to benefit away from firms in trouble to firms better suited to use their assets. By the end of 1988, more than 1,800 factories had been merged to form a total of 1,779 new ones.[29] According to the press, this innovation should resolve the dilemma, noted above, that is posed by bankruptcy under conditions of state ownership and socialist principles, while at the same time securing the state treasury.

Thus, "economists believe that mergers will help avoid the social shocks that would follow bankruptcies," one commentary holds. At the same time, mergers should "also pave the way for the further development of profitable enterprises."[30] Vice-Minister of the State Commission for Restructuring the Economy Zhang Yanning put it rather more bluntly. He admitted that merging enterprises which might otherwise face bankruptcy with profitable firms would avoid social unrest, the threat of which has always terrorized the Chinese leadership.[31]

The other claim, this one for the economic gains to be realized from promoting mergers, echoes the same statist bias. Its promoters point to the more than 200 billion yuan of fixed assets in the Chinese industrial economy that were lying idle as of late 1988.[32] Thus, the noted economist Dong Furen, head of the Institute of Economics at the Chinese Academy of Social Sciences, advanced the startlingly bold estimate that mergers could help China save in its total investment an amount equivalent to that scheduled for the Seventh Five-Year Plan. For, he reasoned, mergers encourage the more effective use of existing fixed assets.[33] Figures to show he may be correct are hard to come by to date, at least on a national scale.[34] But in Baoding city's thirteen mergers a balance of 10.3 million yuan was recovered after offsetting the total deficits of merged enterprises with the profits made by the mergers.[35]

Aside from making possible the more effective deployment of assets, there are other ways that mergers are to help shore up the state budget: by directing the flow of state investment into more marketable, even internationally competitive products and industries, thereby raising the returns on investment; by allowing stronger concerns to expand production while lowering their costs; by furthering an industrial structural arrangement in accord with economies of scale and macroeconomic industrial policy; and, ideally, by slowing down the essentially duplicative investment that separate localities have been fostering.[36] On a smaller but by no means insignificant scale, the responsibility for buying new equipment and reinvestment in a merged firm is shifted from the central financial departments to the more successful enterprise that has swallowed up that firm.[37]

One telling piece of evidence that state treasury gains should accrue from mergers is the appreciation state banks show for this measure. This is because, finally, loans are being repaid upon which enterprises suffering losses had defaulted in the past.[38] That the government is heavily involved in this reform is clear in the frequent reports of city leaders "proposing" the mergers;[39] or even of their "forcibly ordering" profit-making enterprises to absorb others incurring losses.[40] Critics charge that in extreme cases merging—supposedly part of a "revolution in property rights"—actually amounts to the state's using old and tried administrative means to allocate the property of one enterprise to another. This, ironically, is a feat only possible of course, precisely because there has been no change in the overall system of ownership.[41]

It is at the city level especially that there is strong interest in enterprise takeovers. As an article on Baoding explains, the city is responsible for maintaining and adding to the value of the state's assets represented by firms based there, so it is up to the local government to guide and coordinate the mergers.[42] Such guidance in Wuhan entails combining firms to encourage the growth of particular trades through favorable tax and credit policies and by showering concerned parties with relevant information on the potential partners with which they should connect.[43]

The city's role in this area became even more crucial after 1984. Then many large-scale firms were delegated to urban management. Thus, much of the job of subsidizing their losses has fallen to these local budgets. In Wuhan, for instance, in 1986 this particular load on the city's financial administration amounted to 4,440,000 yuan; in 1987 it shot up to 20,000,000 yuan.[44] So, obviously, when losing firms are annexed this can save a city millions of yuan in subsidies.[45] Zhao Baojiang, Mayor of Wuhan, reportedly expressed his delight with the program in these words: "Enterprise annexation has benefited enterprises, the bank and the mayor. It will help boost production, pay back debts and rationalize our social production structure."[46]

Sometimes the rewards to the municipality can be such that city leaders struggle against the central government on behalf of particularly mammoth mergers. In Shenyang, local officials permitted a takeover of three smaller firms by a cable works plant. They courted this plant—already the biggest contributor of taxes and profits in the city—with special "economic levers" to encourage the merger, in the hope of even greater returns to local coffers. People in the central government, according to the plant's manager, had complained that his firm was already too large;[47] probably their qualm was a reflection of the battle between administrative levels over the skyrocketing funds being accumulated in recent years by localities, outside the reach of central control.

Shareholding

Despite the evident success of this experiment in saving investment and generating new revenue for the state—at both national and local levels—commentators have nevertheless indicated that it involves an important potential political pitfall. As a consequence, shareholding and stock markets have been receiving more and more attention as the ideal way to collect capital while at the same time avoiding possible worker discontent.

Shareholding began in post-1949 China in Shenyang in 1982. But the purchase of shares beyond the internal sales within firms did not get under way until 1984, when equity markets first opened up.[48] The real breaking point occurred in August 1986, when the Shenyang Trust Investment Company sponsored a securities exchange with a national reach. Following this, Shanghai, Beijing, Harbin, and other cities set up fixed sites for the transfer of shares and bonds.[49] By the fall of 1988, nearly eighty cities were said to be engaged in the business of negotiable securities transfer.[50]

Economists favoring the system hoped that it could, in the words of one of them, "provide the necessary conditions for enterprises to truly operate independently, to assume sole responsibility for their profits and losses, and to exercise self-control."[51] Others saw it as capable of facilitating the flow of funds, absorbing idle capital, distributing risk, and promoting the rational movement of production factors.

Given the current fiscal crisis in China, top politicians have seized on this particular reform as the safest way of stabilizing the economy (without upsetting the workers) while still maintaining some sense of momentum behind the reform program. For they do hope to return to the reforms in a more all-around manner, once stability has been achieved. The rationale behind the preference for shareholding over other efforts at easing the state's fiscal crisis comes across clearly in the following quotation from an essay by three economists printed in the party organ, the *People's Daily*, in summer 1988:

> In terms of the needs for reorganizing production elements and improving the structure, asset unification [i.e., via takeovers] is superior to management

unification [via contracting out or leasing firms], but considering people's current mentality and ability to withstand strains, it is not necessary to insist on striving for the unification of assets and it may be more practical to regard the unification of management as a transitional step. . . . Ideologically, only when we admit that some enterprises will "survive" and others "die" or some enterprises will develop and others perish can we support superior enterprises in "swallowing up" inferior ones.[52]

Soliciting investment through the sale of shares to employees or even to the public, or by permitting firms with surplus funds to buy into other firms is inherently less threatening to employees than a merger would be. For joint stockholding, unlike enterprise merging, does not entail the transfer of asset rights. Thus, shareholding should maintain the original structure of the enterprise intact and so, presumably, protect the jobs of the staff and workers in the original, inferior enterprise. At the same time, shareholding is an efficacious way of staving off the state's fiscal crisis: according to the president of the People's Bank, Li Guixian, "We can sell a number of enterprises or the stocks of some large, state enterprises to reduce state investment and loans and lessen the burdens of the state and the enterprises."[53]

Published figures suggest that shareholding may be changing the shape of the Chinese industrial structure: the total volume of bonds and shares issued had reached 90 billion yuan by September 1988. But of this total, shares account for a mere 2.2 percent, and enterprise bonds that require repayment of the principle amount to 22 percent.[54] Indeed, the majority of the firms selling their shares still offer them internally, to their own employees, rather than putting them on the market.[55] The other types of securities involved include state treasury bonds and keypoint project construction bonds, both of which are not voluntarily purchased but, rather, are apportioned by fiat by the state.[56] Furthermore, while more than 6,000 medium-sized and small enterprises had offered shares to the public, only a dozen large enterprises had done so, as of late 1988.[57]

The use of securities has two primary purposes: first, they are to accumulate funds for the construction projects designated by the central government and to relieve the state financial organs and the banks from their burden of finding investment funds for all the firms demanding it. And second, taking on heightened significance as inflation mounts, they should sop up the excess currency in the hands of the populace. That is, as people invest in enterprise shares, they will "shift social consumption capital to social accumulation capital."[58]

Regardless of the novelty of selling state assets, the primacy of state needs is always underlined: as an account in the proreform *Economic Daily* assures, "China's state enterprises must not be privatized and the adoption of a shareholding system with the predominance of public ownership is by no means privatization."[59] One mechanism to guarantee this is a governmental stipulation that stocks issued by a state enterprise cannot exceed 30 percent of its total capital stock.[60] Also reflecting this commitment is an analysis, cast in the mode of supply-side economics theory, in the journal *Economic Management*. Its author states that the share system is being implemented in order to invigorate the enterprises, and, he reasons, as this occurs the state will be able to collect more financial receipts from them.[61]

In a number of crucial ways shareholding in socialist, state-owned China can be distinguished from the institution that goes by that name in capitalist economies, just as "bankruptcy" also can, as seen above. Most fundamentally, the Chinese concept of the "enterprise share" does not exist outside the socialist system. Linked to this concept, the effort to define just what portion of the firm's assets separately belong to the (state-owned) firm as distinguished from that amorphous entity, the state itself, has aroused endless debate.[62]

Another serious point of difference is that even for stocks dividend rates are determined in advance and the interest on dividends is covered in the firm's production costs. As a result, the shareholder bears no risk. Moreover, the claim in the press that shareholders' selection of a board of directors to manage the enterprise eliminates governmental interference in the affairs of the firm[63] is often betrayed in practice. For instance, one candid report admits that local financial departments are entrusted with representing the state's shares in the firm. But these organs go on to delegate this task to the enterprise's own management bureau. This practice, in effect, serves to reinstate the old management system, despite the fact that the firm is now drawing investment funds from new sources.[64]

At this point the effort at creating a stock system in China is still very preliminary. One example of this came across in an interview last summer in Shenyang, where the whole experiment began. Members of the city's Commission for Restructuring the Economic System frankly acknowledged that there was no change in the old relationship between enterprises employing the share system and their original management departments.[65] Even at the famous Jinbei [Gold Cup] Automobile Share Limited Company, the first large industrial enterprise in the country to turn its entire assets into shares for sale to the public,[66] an official explained that the company's production was still dictated by a three-year contract with the City Economic and Planning Commission. Indeed, the content of this contract closely resembles the company's old state plan, replete as it is with unchanging targets for varieties and product quality.[67]

It has been noted in China that many of the preconditions for a genuine stock market are still absent. These include an ability for enterprises to operate truly independently, a stable taxation system, and a well-developed financial market. Belying the publicized statistics, Chinese sources have acknowledged that of the thirty-six enterprises selected in Sichuan Province in early 1988 to try out the joint-stock system, seven withdrew from the experiment by the end of the year, another dozen were still engaged in "marathon" negotiations with the city government a year later, and yet another dozen had just had their plans for implementation approved at year's end.[68] One last, but very common, problem is that many firms use the share system as a means of providing extra welfare supplements or bonuses to their own workers. As economist Dong Furen explained, "They underrate state-owned assets and fix the dividends and bonuses. After that, they distribute the shares among workers and staff members."[69] In effect, then, selling shares only enhances the very pressure of consumption funds on the market that this same reform was installed expressly to alleviate.[70]

In the main, then, much skepticism must attend the analysis of capitalist-like reforms in the Chinese urban economy. Nonetheless, isolated data do indicate that in some ways they may be initiating a certain, if incipient and as yet still minuscule, alteration in the shape of the Chinese economy. In the city of Qingdao, for instance, some sort of bankruptcy caused 10,800 workers to lose their jobs after 500 of the municipality's firms were reorganized; in Shanghai, 30,000 workers were "made redundant" in 1988 and were said to be living on social security. There are similar, scattered reports from other places.[71]

As for mergers, some may be occurring without any pressure from the bureaucracy. In Wuhan, officials from the Municipal Commission for the Restructuring of the Economic System claimed that "There are some mergers we don't even know about until they are done."[72] And, in the case of the share system, enterprise bonds sold to staff and corporate investors can be freely traded,[73] even if conditions are not yet ripe for the creation of companies specializing in the transfer of stock ownership.[74] Besides, the tiny stock market of Shanghai actually bears a stock index that fluctuates.[75]

The important point, however, is the intention behind the current promotion of these reforms at the level of top leadership. The justifications that are being offered for their use as well as the effort to contain their application all bespeak a continuing statist orientation.

Mediation of Marketing Through State Bureaucracies

We have seen above how the operation of "capitalistic measures" is netting new income for the state treasury—through the larger profits and extra sales of better products that mergers and stock solicitation make possible—and how these measures also permit savings for the state treasury (at both central and local levels), as bankruptcies and mergers make it possible for governmental budgets to cut back on the dispersal of subsidies for failing firms. These same measures add to the assets under the control of, and thus strengthen the economic power of, the large, successful, already well-endowed state enterprises that take over the weaker ones and that absorb new funds as they turn their assets into shares.[76]

These and related market-like reforms are also enhancing the power of the state-run economy in yet another way: by bestowing on its old bureaucracies new functions, and by designing new public agencies to stand as intermediaries and expediters between and for the firms as the firms venture into new arenas. Like local brokers in seventeenth-century China, the middlemen working in state agencies manage the novel modes of exchange and the regrouping that make up the reforms, by providing information, advice, and emergency assistance; by locating customers; by guaranteeing credit; and by reducing risk.[77] Since organizational restructuring is being built on the foundations of prior bureaucratic power, those who suppose bureaucratic opposition to reform may not have analyzed the situation closely enough.[78]

This second section expands on these points first by showing how certain bureaucracies, namely, the materials supplies departments and industrial companies, have taken on new roles in the changing environment; and second by enumerating the array of state-directed agencies recently established to enforce the various reforms: property transfer markets for arranging mergers; city offices for overseeing enterprises under threat of bankruptcy; management stations for bidding on construction projects; trade associations; trust investment companies; and vast and intricate networks of local bureaucracies to shape the new horizontally articulated economic cooperation regions.

Material Supply Bureaus

Official statistics revealed in late 1988 that in the first three quarters of the year 73 percent of the sales volume in the goods and materials system had been contributed by sources not included in the plan.[79] This indicates not just that a great deal of marketing is going on outside the scope of the planning system. It also shows that the materials supply bureaucracy, formerly located at the hub of the command economy, remains heavily involved in transactions in the industrial sector, even if these transactions are not laid out in advance in the central government's plans.

Scattered reports tell of individual cities that have been installing officially approved materials exchange markets.[80] These markets can corner or at least heavily influence the conduct of trade in raw materials that goes on outside the state plan.[81] Interviewing in Wuhan revealed that the steel market in that city operates under the supervision of the city Materials Supply Bureau. The bureau has set up a new company to do this job[82]—which earns commissions for its work—and thus should in no way be undermined by the market reforms; presumably the same situation obtains elsewhere.[83]

In Changchun in the northeast the materials supplies departments are actually *supposed to* "pull strings" for the firms to guarantee the stable economic development of their corporate manager, the city government. There the departments enjoy expanded profits from their heightened sales activity: in 1987, the increase was over 20 percent. The bureau's brokering saves the firms from searches: "If only the materials supply departments find sources for supplies, we needn't go outside [the city] to procure," a local paper quotes "many enterprise" personnel as avowing.[84]

In the past few years more and more accounts in the press have charged the materials departments with using their control over increasingly scarce supplies to engage in profiteering.[85] The year 1988 saw repeated, apparently vain, official efforts to counter this burgeoning business.[86] The various regulations pointed to arbitrary fee collections, to the practice of raising the price again and again at every level up the administrative hierarchy, and to the habit work personnel in this field exhibit of forming "relationship networks" to benefit relatives and acquaintances with whom they can trade favors. A colorful article in the *People's Daily* in the fall alleged that "The worst offenders in the illegal sales of the means of production are the various levels of state materials departments and the work units underneath them."[87]

Thus, materials supply departments, through their long-term participation in well-established exchange networks under the reign of the state plan—with all the information and personal connections that that participation afforded—and through their command over supplies, are excellently situated to profit from the reforms. This obviously means that this arm of the bureaucracy has nothing to object to in the new measures.

Industrial Companies

The industrial bureaus that manage production and sales in particular trades in the urban economies are subdivided into specialized industrial companies that, in turn, are responsible for directing the individual firms. Like the materials departments, rather than losing power in the reforms, many of these agencies are benefiting handsomely. As instructed by the tenets of the reform program, they are now operating as business enterprises, instead of as administrative offices.

Accordingly, their officials interpose themselves between their own firms and "the market." By relying on their original suppliers and procurers, they are becoming wholesale salesmen and sources of market information. Since they have long played a similar role in the days when the commonly inaccurate state plans left firms wanting extra scouting, the companies' cadres can utilize long-standing relationships and buy cheaply in large quantity. Then, drawing profits from price differentials and taking fees in exchange for information, cadres in the companies can garner incomes that are greater than ever before. It is the small firms (ironically enough, those often labeled most lively in the reform era) who become their captives, with fewer personnel to spare, more frequently shifting product structures, and need for smaller and less fixed quantities of supplies.[88]

New Bureaucratic Organs

In the two examples above, it is clear that materials supply departments and industrial companies have simply widened the arena of their wonted activities and, because of new policies, have earned new recompense in the reform era.

But for other reforms the old offices have been regrouped, or, in some instances, brand new ones fashioned, in an effort to guide the course of the experiments.

Property Rights Markets

For instance, Wuhan was the first city to create a property rights market in early 1988. But that "market" seems in reality to be more like a substation of the city government. In March the city government formulated the policies that were to guide that market's activities. In the next month it issued a document entitled "Provisional Ideas of the City Government on Realizing the Rational Transfer of Property Rights Through Encouraging Enterprise Mergers," along with an "Implementation Program for the Wuhan City Enterprise Merger Market." These rulings spelled out the principles of exchange and the organs that would guide the market.[89] The city government's involvement was said to lead to "greater initiatives in and an obvious strengthening of the mergers." Also, in a third of the cases, both of the firms in the pair being merged were managed by the same industrial bureau; in these cases the bureau served as the intermediary, encouraging the merger.[90]

In other cities, where special markets had not yet been established, enterprise takeovers were "mostly organized [directly] through the competent government departments acting as a go-between." The purpose has often been to ensure that the localities fulfill their urban *guihua*, a kind of long-range direction for development, a mini-, municipal industrial policy. Thus mergers serve to focus urban investment on high-priority industries and products and to help cities readjust their productive forces to suit their own natural resource endowments.[91]

Enterprise Bankruptcy Offices

In the cities that have experimented with enterprise bankruptcies, such as Shenyang, the city government installed a new office expressly to handle the bankruptcies. Its function is to arrange tax reduction and exemption, and low-interest loans from banks and insurance companies, and to permit the temporary suspension of debt payments for firms warned of imminent failure.[92] A high official from the Enterprise Bankruptcy Office of the city government proudly recounted how his office worked to rescue the nationally notorious Hardware Casting Factory, tagged as on the brink of bankruptcy in August 1985 but fully recovered two years later.[93]

In addition to the kinds of assistance noted in the press, this agency provided a wide array of other sorts of services: He and his staff drew on a special "bankruptcy fund" to provide a temporary loan. They arranged for publicity for the firm, which ultimately led a research and design academy in Beijing to develop new products for the plant to produce. Then they helped the factory's management in obtaining permits for new product development, forestalling likely interference and opposition from the tax and industry and commercial management departments; and, perhaps most crucially, were able, as an office just under the city government, to procure for the factory key raw materials that it would have been impossible for the people from the plant to acquire on their own from the producers or suppliers.

Most of this behind-the-scenes relief extended by the bankruptcy office received no press, allowing the case to stand as an example of the self-reliance that a firm could muster to revive itself just by "breaking the iron rice bowl," as its manager claimed. In this case the phrase referred to her forcing individual workers to bear the responsibility—in deductions from or bonuses added on to their own wages—for the profits and losses of their workshops.[94] The intention behind this new office's creation—but also behind keeping its work out of the limelight—fits the purpose of experimenting with bankruptcy in the first place; as one analyst of the bankruptcy law noted, "the original idea, as illustrated in the many press articles on warned enterprises that have returned miraculously to profit, seemed to have been that the warning would so galvanize the workers of the enterprise that they would be able to reverse the losses within one year."[95]

Bidding Market Management Offices

Another market reform aimed at breaking down the rigidity of the command economy is the use of bidding in construction 'work, instead of having specific bureaucratic units assigned to supply equipment to specific projects. Here too in Shenyang, where the first construction projects bidding market nationwide has been set up, the city government instituted a "bidding market management office." This body, conveniently placed within the old bureaucracy, is under the city's bureau of construction work. It is responsible for managing the bidding, which all capital construction and renovation projects in the city that were written into state plans (at any level), and having a scale surpassing 2,000 square meters and a price-tag above 300,000 yuan, must enter.[96] Again, an innovation is brought within the purview of state control.

Trade Associations

Trade associations have been organized in many cities, supposedly as a "bridge between the people and the government," in the words of a local economic planner in Wuhan, where there were some twenty to thirty of these new associations in mid-1988.[97] Their job is to provide the enterprises in a given trade with information and help. But their chief function is to see to it that each of the various firms in their particular line of industry plays its part in helping to realize the city government's *guihua*. In effect, in most cases the urban administration hopes to use these associations to push a trade to develop along the lines its planners have worked out. For particularly important trades, the associations can actually have some clout, according to the head of the national association for cable-manufacturing enterprises;[98] on the other hand, disgruntled members of the undoubtedly less powerful Wuhan Lamps and Lanterns Association did not even bother to pay their fees for a year.[99]

Trust Investment Companies

Yet another state-managed innovation that, like the bidding office, was meant to shore up the old command economy, is the Shenyang Trust Investment Company, established in 1985. Most big cities now also have this kind of organ. The industrial bureaus of the city commission this body to invest their surplus capital and, in turn, to provide them with capital when they need it to complete technical transformation projects provided for within the city's annual economic plan. The company's purpose, as outlined by one of its officials, is to help to realize the city's plan.[100]

Economic and Technical Cooperation Committees

Probably the most fascinating of the bureaucratic arrangements devised to monitor and encourage the new markets revolves around the work of the Economic and Technical Cooperation Committees that most municipalities now maintain. These organs, established in the mid-1980s, are to sponsor and further economic and technological exchanges among firms across the administrative and geographical boundaries that delineated the flow of goods, services, and materials under the state planning system. Not only the city itself, but every administrative unit down to the county level houses an agency of this sort. Their job is to guarantee that the transactions of local firms work to execute that area's *guihua*. This they do by using the usual preferential policies—loans, taxes, subsidies—to coordinate particular exchanges; by bringing firms together to negotiate over terms; and by supplying them with relevant market information once their union is achieved.[101]

Especially interesting is the background of the thirty-some personnel who staff this committee in Wuhan. All of them previously worked in the area of materials exchange, and so they are quite familiar with the situations and products of the enterprises in the city. Some were employees of the city's Materials Supply Bureau in the past; others were agents delegated by the city government (planning or economic commissions, or the city government's office) to get market information to supplement planned supplies.

The organ at the city level is enmeshed in a complicated set of networks at least as bureaucratic as the one that supported the command economy it is meant to replace. First of all, its members report on their work to Hubei Province, where a similar committee presides over exchanges at that level.[102] Then, along with Jiangxi and Hunan provinces, Hubei forms an economic cooperation region centered on Wuhan, and the mayors of the ten major cities of the three provinces join periodically in a liaison committee. There is also a working committee composed of the economic and technological cooperation committees of these ten cities and those of the seven districts in the region, and their staff comes together once a quarter, while an office under that committee performs the daily work of the liaison and the working committees. Another working network consists of the chairmen of the economic commissions in each of the seventeen member areas; each of the seventeen areas also delegates the heads of its science and technology committee, its industrial bureaus, its agricultural commission, its commercial commission, its branch of the state bank, and its propaganda and news system to combine to form work and informational networks.[103]

As each of these networks passes along information on the projects and the production structure in its area, it essays to satisfy the needs of its own *guihua* through what is called "horizontal"—as opposed to the hierarchically ordered vertical—exchange of the planned economy. "Help from the leadership can't be avoided," explained a Wuhan economist. For, "information is hard to come by," he went on, "and the enterprises don't know where the supplies are, or where there is technical ability."[104] In the midst of so much new bureaucracy, the state is holding its own.

Thus, the Chinese approach to economic reform has a strong statist, organizational component. In the leadership's effort to keep a grip on unplanned transactions, it is relying on old organs whose cadres know the market, and it is designing new offices that often emerge without significant metamorphosis from the units that made up the original state-run bureaucracy and that directed the planned economy. In the process, they are further empowering the public side of business, rather than as they proclaim to wish to do, "separating the government from the enterprise."

Conclusion

A recently cited statement by economist Dong Furen neatly conveys a key message of this chapter:

> There is an old Chinese saying, [he recalled]: "Things turn out differently in different localities or surroundings." While transplanting the successful foreign market experience, we should avoid losing the shape of our reform. Apart from considering the practical conditions of China, we must also pay attention to the soil needed in the transplantation, so that the plant we are transplanting can take root in proper soil.[105]

Dong's point, as one of the strands of my argument here has also been, is that the capitalistic measures being injected into or, perhaps more accurately, overlaid atop of the administratively planned, state-owned economy in China are more apt at this stage to take on the features of that old system than to remold it, more likely to be forced to adapt to the state's own fiscal needs and purposes—and to be installed and supervised by its offices—than to retain their own usual form.

To recapitulate the argument, three central aspects of the post-1978 economic reforms—the connection with the world economy, with the demands for foreign exchange that this ushered in; the consumer revolution initiated to right injustices from Maoist days and to offer incentives for greater individual productivity; and programs of decentralizing decision-making power, funds, and supplies in the hope of stimulating growth—by the end of a decade had cost the state dearly, pumping up prices and delivering deficits to the central treasury. In response, by late 1988 the top leadership had decided to promote a set of market-style innovations (most of which had been under way at least since 1985)—stock markets and shareholding, enterprise bankruptcies, mergers, raw materials markets, horizontal exchange—not for the sake of privatization, but in a stab for budgetary savings and economic stability. Ironically, "capitalistic" practices are being resorted to in the hope of recouping central-level, macro controls. Moreover, in a further irony, as the central state budget sheds responsibilities—as, by encouraging firms to invest in each other or buy each other out—state assets and "market" power are becoming even more concentrated than ever in the best and the biggest state enterprises, through the operation of policies that intentionally favor the fittest. Additional increments of power are also flowing to state-run bureaucratic offices, such as the materials departments, as their personnel are charged with supervising the disposal of the surplus supplies being traded outside the plan's pathways.

Thus, even as bureaucratic brokers take advantage of their location at the crucial middle links in the transactions channels to gain from corruption, and even as the clout of local administrations may be eclipsing that of the center, it is still "the state" that wins. In large part this is possible because the real prices that would truly reflect cost and scarcity do not obtain in the Chinese "market"; in addition, information is still hard to come by and tends to be a monopoly of state cadres at this point. Until these two conditions have radically altered, and until—if ever—the political leadership at the top can make a genuine commitment to revamp property relations in the industrial system, the reforms may continue to permit a flourishing of exchange. But they certainly will not drastically restructure the Chinese economy.

Notes

1. China was the second socialist country, after Hungary, to pass a bankruptcy law.
2. Translated in U.S. *Foreign Broadcast Information Service* (hereafter *FBIS*), November 16, 1988, p. 40.
3. In *FBIS*, July 30, 1987, p. K2.

4. Out of a 245.946 billion yuan of expenditures projected in the budget, 35.972 billion were to go for subsidizing enterprises for losses and 33.723 billion to consumers for price hikes; together these two categories amounted to 28.34 percent of the state budget. This is in *FBIS*, April 15, 1987, p. K14.

5. Ibid., August 18, 1988, p. 39.

6. Between 1977 and 1987, China accumulated a 59.2 billion yuan financial deficit. This figure appeared in *Liaowang Overseas Edition*, no. 48 (November 28, 1988), translated in *FBIS*, December 6, 1988, p. 36.

7. In 1987 an additional 20 billion yuan in banknotes were issued to cope with rising demands for bank loans for construction projects and for wage and bonus funds in the enterprises. *FBIS*, December 16, 1988, p. 26. Also, though the volume of paper money issued in 1983 already had increased more than 30 billion yuan over 1978, growing about 150 percent in five years, compared with 1983, the paper money issued in 1987 again increased over 900 billion yuan, or 170 percent in four more years. Another report predicted tht the amount of currency in circulation could rise by 35 percent in 1988; and stated that the purchasing power generated by the currency increase had exceeded the supply capacity by more than 20 percent. *Renmin ribao* (People's daily) (hereafter *RMRB*), December 8, 1988, translated in *FBIS*, December 20, 1988, p. 32.

8. As of the end of November 1988 the officially recorded inflation rate had reached 17 percent, shockingly high by the norms by which the Chinese population had been living for most of the preceding four decades. *FBIS*, December 27, 1988, p. 38. According to the *Far Eastern Economic Review*, January 5, 1989, p. 54, throughout the months July through September 1988 there was an average monthly increase of three percent in the consumer price index, which, by October, had reached 27.1 percent on a year-on-year basis. The year-end figure was estimated at 17 to 18 percent on a year-to-year basis, compared to 7.3 percent for 1987.

9. Since the implementation of reform the per capita income for living expenses of both uban and rural residents has doubled; the ratio of urban residents' income in gross domestic product expanded from 38.3 percent in 1978 to 58.6 percent in 1987. As of the end of 1988, workers' total wages increased 22 percent over the same period a year earlier, and their bonuses had risen 31.5 percent in the same time. Moreover, in 1987 funds under the control of state factories and local governments that were not a part of the state budget amounted approximately to a wallopping 200 billion yuan. *FBIS*, December 20, 1988, p. 34, translated from *Liaowang Overseas Edition*, no. 50 (December 12, 1988); and *FBIS*, December 20, 1988, p. 31.

10. Mark Granovetter, in "The Strength of Weak Ties: A Network Theory Revisited," in *Social Support and Network Analysis,* ed. Peter V. Marsden and Nan Lin (Beverly Hills: SAGE Publications, 1982), pp. 105–30, implies that the multiplication of connections in a social system spawns yet more connections. For instance, on p. 113, he states that "the number of weak ties is increased by the development of the communications system, bureaucratization, population density, and the spread of market mechanisms."

11. Translated in *FBIS*, July 18, 1988, p. 40.

12. *FBIS*, December 27, 1988, p. 39.

13. See, for instance, two articles of the many making this argument in *FBIS*, January 25, 1988, p. 27, and *FBIS*, September 2, 1988, p. 40.

14. Translated in *FBIS*, November 17, 1988, p. 27.

15. The following chronology is drawn from Ta-kuang Chang, "The Making of the Chinese Bankruptcy Law: A Study in the Chinese Legislative Process," *Harvard International Law Journal* (hereafter *HILJ*) 28, 2 (Spring 1987): 333–72.

16. As of November 1987, in the six cities of Shenyang, Wuhan, Chongqing, Taiyuan, Nanchang, and Xi'an, twenty-eight enterprises had been made "trial points" for the reform, of

which fifteen were state-operated firms and thirteen were collectives. Only two of these had been declared bankrupt, twenty-two had already revived after being warned and four were still undergoing "readjustment" at that point. See *RMRB*, November 6, 1987. *FBIS*, November 4, 1988, p. 44, states that Shenyang city had recently closed down two more unredeemable enterprises.

17. As translated in Peng Xiaohua, "Characteristics of China's First Bankruptcy Law," in the same issue of *HILJ*, p. 377.

18. See Chang, "Chinese Bankruptcy Law," p. 357.

19. *Guangming ribao* (Bright daily), May 2, 1987.

20. *FBIS*, July 27, 1988, p. 38.

21. *FBIS*, October 25, 1988, p. 35.

22. *FBIS*, August 18, 1988, p. 39.

23. *FBIS*, November 4, 1988, p. 44.

24. *FBIS*, September 2, 1988, p. 40.

25. See *Survey of World Broadcasts*, FE/8331/BII/6 (August 7, 1986), for the value of the firm's assets and debts; the figure on assistance is in *FBIS*, November 4, 1988, p. 44.

26. *FBIS*, November 4, 1988, p. 44.

27. This is in Liu Xuede, Fan Rubing, and Jiang Aiying, "Enterprise Mergers—A New Road in the Development of Industrial and Commercial Enterprises," *Zhongguo jingji tizhi gaige* (Chinese economic system reform), no. 11 (1988): 47.

28. *FBIS*, November 16, 1988, p. 69.

29. *FBIS*, December 7, 1988, p. 36.

30. Ibid., p. 37.

31. *FBIS*, November 30, 1988, p. 37.

32. *FBIS*, October 25, 1988, p. 35.

33. *FBIS*, January 28, 1988, p. 13.

34. A survey of eight provinces and cities revealed, simply, that of 557 merged enterprises, 405 of the 470 losing enterprises had "already begun making money." *FBIS*, October 25, 1988, p. 35.

35. Ibid.

36. *FBIS*, March 25, 1988, p. 56; April 7, 1988, p. 27; June 23, 1988, p. 38; and September 29, 1988, p. 55; and *RMRB*, October 18, 1988, p. 1.

37. This is the situation at the Shenyang Cable Works, the city's largest tax and profit contributor, which was urged by the municipal government to take over three failing firms. Interview with manager there, July 10, 1988.

38. Interview with Wuhan University Economics Department Professor Wu Xinmu, June 30, 1988.

39. The report notes that in Baoding city, all of the mergers were proposed by the city's leaders. *FBIS*, April 6, 1988, p. 46.

40. *FBIS*, March 25, 1988, p. 58.

41. *FBIS*, February 29, 1988, p. 31.

42. Wang Bingyi and Shi Zhishun, "Reflections on Baoding City's Enterprise Mergers," *Jingji guanli* (Economic management) (hereafter *JJGL*), no. 7 (1988), p. 43.

43. Interview with the Municipal Commission for Restructuring the Economic System, June 30, 1988.

44. This data comes from Liu, Fan, and Jiang, "Economic Mergers," p. 47. The authors note that these sums are increased by the several million yuan in "loans" that the city's financial administration has had to hand out to the firms at new year's time in recent years to issue as wages.

45. *Beijing Review* (hereafter *BR*), October 17–23, 1988, p. 9.

46. *FBIS*, September 30, 1988, p. 34.

47. Interview at the Shenyang Cable Works, July 10, 1988.

48. Interview with the Shenyang City Commission for Restructuring the Economic System, July 5, 1988; and *FBIS*, September 16, 1988, p. 50.

49. *RMRB*, September 14, 1988, p. 2.

50. *FBIS*, September 16, 1988, p. 50.

51. These are the words of Zhou Shulian, director of the Institute of Industrial Economy of the Chinese Academy of Social Sciences, as reported in *FBIS*, January 3, 1989, p. 53.

52. *RMRB*, August 12, 1988, p. 5, translated in *FBIS*, August 23, 1988. These sections are on pp. 29 and 30.

53. *FBIS*, August 30, 1988, p. 36.

54. *RMRB*, September 14, 1988, p. 2.

55. *RMRB*, November 3, 1988, p. 2.

56. According to a report published in *FBIS* on January 15, 1988, p. 15, the value of these two types of securities constituted 63 percent of the total value of stocks and bonds issued nationally in recent years, as of that date.

57. *FBIS*, October 21, 1988, p. 26.

58. These arguments can be found in *RMRB*, July 3, 1988, p. 2; September 14, 1988, p. 2; and September 26, 1988, p. 1; and in *FBIS*, August 30, 1988, p. 36; and October 21, 1988, p. 26.

59. In *Jingji ribao*, October 19, 1988, translated in *FBIS*, October 21, 1988, p. 26.

60. As reported in *BR*, no. 40 (1987): 22.

61. Xiang Dong, "Smooth out Distribution and Relationships in the Assets of Share-System Enterprises," *JJGL*, no. 7 (1988): 34.

62. See, for instance, *FBIS*, June 23, 1988, p. 42, and *BR*, no. 40 (1987): 22.

63. This claim appears, for example, in *RMRB*, August 23, 1988, p. 1; October 24, 1988, p. 2; and November 3, 1988, p. 2.

64. *BR*, no. 40 (1987): 22.

65. Interview, July 5, 1988.

66. *RMRB*, August 5, 1988, p. 1.

67. Interview, July 11, 1988.

68. Translated from the November 30, 1988, issue of *Economic   Daily* in *FBIS*, January 6, 1989, p. 32.

69. In *RMRB*, December 12, 1988, p. 5, translated in *FBIS*, December 30, 1988, p. 32.

70. This is reminiscent of the dilemma noted above in which caring for workers dismissed from bankrupt firms only increases, instead of lessening the state's financial burden, thereby achieving just the opposite of what the reform was intended to accomplish.

71. *FBIS*, September 14, 1988, p. 36; and September 28, 1988, pp. 52–53.

72. Interview, June 30, 1988. On the other hand, it's quite possible that those mergers were arranged by the firms' industrial bureau and not by the enterprises on their own.

73. *FBIS*, January 15, 1988, p. 15.

74. *FBIS*, August 19, 1988, p. 15.

75. Nicholas D. Kristof, "Selling China on a 'Public' Privatization," *New York Times*, January 8, 1989, p. 8F.

76. Large enterprises have been favored over the years and especially recently in that they have been granted the right to import equipment and technology at or near internationally progressive levels. For instance, the 153 large and medium-sized enterprises in Wuhan, whose fixed assets equal 73.6 percent of the assets in the more than 3,000 industrial firms in the city, had a total of 537 computers in early 1987; and many of them work with automatic production lines. In these firms in the city, for every 100 staff

members and workers there are seven engineers and other specialists, while in the small plants there are only two per 100 on the average. This is in Zhang Dingfang, "A Preliminary Analysis of the Technical Progress in Wuhan City's Large and Medium-Scale Industrial Enterprises," *Zhongnan caijing daxue xuebao* (Central-South Finance and Economics University Journal) (hereafter *ZCDX*), May 1987, p. 83.

77. See Susan Mann, *Local Merchants and the Chinese Bureaucracy, 1750–1950*, (Stanford: Stanford University Press, 1987), p. 63; and Mann, "Brokers as Entrepreneurs in Presocialist China," *Comparative Studies in Society and History* 26, 4 (1984): 626, for a description of the roles brokers played in pre-1949 China.

78. For instance, see Marshall I. Goldman and Merle Goldman, "Soviet and Chinese Economic Reform," *Foreign Affairs* 66, 3 (1988): 558, which states that "China's urban and industrial reforms have encountered more ideological and bureaucratic resistance than the rural reforms. As opposed to the party cadres in the countryside, who benefited from the reforms ... the party cadres in the urban industries gain little. If anything, they are likely to lose power." Also, "party resistance in China today comes more from inertia and opposition at the individual enterprise and local levels" (p. 559).

79. As reported in *RMRB*, December 1, 1988, p. 2, translated in *FBIS*, December 8, 1988, p. 55.

80. For the background on the Shanghai municipal materials exchange market and its mode of operation, see William Byrd, "The Shanghai Market for the Means of Production: A Case Study of Reform in China's Material Supply System," *Comparative Economic Studies* 27, 4 (1985): 1–29. Byrd states that the first such markets appeared in 1979; by 1981 there were already sixty-four of these across the nation, dealing in a range of materials.

81. Suzhou's was reportedly handling 40 percent of the extra-plan trade as of mid-1988, according to *RMRB*, August 30, 1988, p. 2; Beijing's was charged with locating materials for firms in need, and with buying up their unwanted stocks and finding outlets for them, and it also was allowed to engage in commission business for township enterprises outside the city. *RMRB*, January 3, 1989, p. 2. In Shenyang, a nationally famous materials trade center is directing massive and complicated barter deals among large firms in major industrial cities. For example, in exchange for a loan of funds, the Anyang Steel Company sells its surplus steel to the center, which trades it to Hubei's No. Two Automobile Company, in exchange for cars not procured by the planners. Interview at the trade center, July 8, 1988. There is a report on this center in *Shenyang ribao* (Shenyang daily) (hereafter *SYRB*), June 8, 1988, p. 1. The manager, Dong Shijie, also published an article on his center entitled, "Seek Results in Union," in *JJGL*, no. 6 (1987): 42–44.

82. Interview with City Commission for Restructuring the Economic System, June 22, 1987, and June 30, 1988, and at the Wuhan General Machinery Plant, June 24, 1987.

83. Such markets are especially active in serving the smaller firms; the larger ones continue to deal directly with the same stable supplier with which they trafficked under the state plan. Interview with Wuhan's Commission for Restructuring the Economic System, June 30, 1988, and with the No. 3 Machine Tools Factory of Shenyang, July 9, 1988. According to management at the machines tools plant, the same small firms that used to go to the materials supply department now go to the materials trade center in the city, underlining the continuity between organs.

84. *Dongbei jingjibao* (Northeast economic news) (hereafter *DBJJB*), March 22, 1988, p. 1.

85. Party Politburo member Yao Yilin advocated strict measures for dealing with "excessive intermediate links and profiteering in materials circulation." "The problem is not caused by small businessmen and traders, not by speculators," he averred. "It is linked to corrupt phenomenon (*sic*) inside the party and [obviously referring to the materials

supply departments] to the many enterprises which are essentially the production and commercial organs of the party and government raw organs." Translated in *FBIS*, June 9, 1988, p. 33.

86. The *Guowuyuan gongbao* (State Council bulletin), no. 554 (or, no. 1, 1988), January 30, 1988, contained "Temporary Management Methods for the National Unified Highest Price Limit for Extra-Plan Means of Production," on pp. 10–12. November 2, 1988's *RMRB*, p. 1, carried the news that the State Council had decided to strengthen the management over the trade in steel products; and the issue of the same paper on November 5, 1988, p. 1, reported that the Ministry of Materials Supply had promulgated ten measures to clean up its work.

87. *RMRB*, October 8, 1988, p. 1. One of the examples in the article explains how vehicles costing 115,000 yuan (about U.S. $32,200), which should have had a fixed price, finally sold for 152,000 yuan apiece after passing through four different materials service companies and trade centers. In another case, a certain factory in Wuhan colluded with the Hubei provincial metal materials company and, by falsifyig accounts, netted over 220,000 yuan in illegal income.

88. Interview, July 1, 1988.

89. *FBIS*, October 6, 1988, p. 26.

90. *FBIS*, December 7, 1988, p. 37.

91. See *RMRB*, August 12, 1988, translated in *FBIS*, August 23, 1988, p. 27; and *RMRB*, June 6, 1988, p. 5, translated in *FBIS*, June 23, 1988, p. 38. Fuxin city encouraged its more progressive firms to take over failing firms by using favorable credit and tax policies, as reported in *DBJJB*, May 10, 1988, p. 1; the same paper on April 19, 1988, p. 1, stated that Dalian city's government was acting as a go-between to get the mergers to contribute to a rearrangement of the city's industrial structure. In Shanghai, according to *FBIS*, September 29, 1988, p. 55, the leading organ for economic restructuring was studying the city's economy and planning future mergers; and Nanjing's municipal administration was urging its firms to link their own short-term interest to the city's long-term development interest, under the guidance of the leading departments in the city, as recounted in *RMRB*, October 18, 1988, p. 1. The article on Nanjing mentions the city's *guihua*, as did a number of interviewees in Wuhan in June and July 1988.

92. *FBIS*, November 4, 1988, p. 44.

93. Interview, July 12, 1988.

94. In an interview at the plant itself, on July 12, 1988, the manager accounted for her successes mainly by reference to the use of implementing a contracting system "down to the individual level." In fact, a total of only two people were fired in the process! Upon inquiry, she did admit to some of the forms of assistance mentioned by the city bankruptcy office official, but in less detail.

95. Chang, "Chinese Bankruptcy Law," p. 358.

96. *SYRB*, June 23, 1988, p. 2.

97. Interview, July 1, 1988.

98. The manager of the Shenyang Cable Works revealed that his association's remonstrations to the State Economic Commission were able to force an increase in their product's price so that it met the costs of their raw materials. Interview, July 10, 1988.

99. Wang Haisu, "Preliminary Exploration of Wuhan's Industrial System's Reform and Improvement of its Structure," *ZCDX*, no. 2 (1987): 46.

100. Interview, July 7, 1988.

101. Information supplied by member of the Mayor's Consultative Committee, July 1, 1987.

102. Interview with the City Commission on the Reform of the Economic System, June 22, 1987.

103. Information supplied by the Wuhan City Economic and Technological Cooperation Committee, June 28, 1988.

104. Interview, July 2, 1988.

105. *RMRB*, December 12, 1988, p. 5, translated in *FBIS*, December 30, 1988, p. 33.

Part III

Reforms in Restructuring Regions

7
Uncertain Paternalism: Tensions in Recent Regional Restructuring in China

Reform of the regional structure of the Chinese economy since the late 1970s is, most broadly interpreted, directed against the highly bureaucratized and over-centralized systems of the command economy. More closely considered, the program is twofold. One part, a decentralization program, has gone beyond central schemes in its implementation. The second part, which often clashes with the first, stresses specialization, division of labor, building on regional "strong points," interdependence, and cooperation, in short, comparative advantage. Its enforcement is often obstructed. Comparative advantage has emerged in a range of guises and not without a measure of accomplishment, but it frequently seems stymied by local habits of relative self-sufficiency. Those habits can be traced to historical patterns in China, as well as to the modern planned socialist economy.

The seeming paradox between too much success of one part of the program and pitfalls encountered by the other is resolved by a key principle of the Chinese political economy: the endemic local particularism and economic localism that delimit the link between periphery and center. This localism, which has a recurring and cyclical nature,[1] fosters the first facet of reform while frequently vitiating the second. A phenomenon common to two types of states, the Chinese state in history and socialist states today, undergirds this localism; it can be termed uncertain paternalism. Lower-level economic entities suffer under uncertain paternalism in both contexts. That is, regional administrations can count on what Kornai termed the "paternalistic relation-ship between state and firm" whereby the "state considers the firm its 'own child.' "[2] (The word *region* could be inserted in the place of *firm* for the purposes of this

This chapter originally appeared in *International Regional Science Review* 11, 1 (1987): 23–42. Reprinted with permission of the journal. It was first presented, in a longer version, at the conference "To Reform the Chinese Political Order," Harwichport, Massachusetts, June 18–23, 1984.

chapter.)[3] Localities know that the paternal care is qualified. In the socialist planned economy, it is most obviously qualified by the deficiencies of the supply system. In the imperial era it was limited by the circumscribed reach of the official bureaucracy[4] and temporal variation over the dynastic cycle. Stability and economic opportunity permitted perfection of the revenue system and social overhead investment, but with dynastic decline came depression and instability.[5] Thus, Chinese local systems and local bureaucracies are oriented toward the state—the motherland or fatherland, the nation-family (*guojia*)—and are comfortable with dependence on the center when the center can provide parenting. These local institutions, however, are also long-schooled in the tactics of encapsulation and self-reliance when the need arises.

Uncertain paternalism, then, governs the behavior of localities in China today, much as it always has. This chapter examines the circumstances under which the dialectic between dependence and encapsulation tends to shift toward the latter. It then discusses four classes of spatial economic reforms over the past several years and their respective progress and problems, and, finally, speculates about the potential contribution of these reforms to the overarching aim of modernizing the Chinese economy.

Analytical Framework: The Central-Local Link

Historical Patterns

The central dilemma of the present reforms is this: The paternalistic state apparatus derives its power and maintains its place as crucial legitimating symbol only to the extent that it continues to fulfill paternalistic functions. These functions are to provide and uphold a shared ideology, to appoint and discipline elites at all levels, and ultimately to guarantee economic security for the populace (as well as to defend the state and uphold internal order, which are not germane here). Historically, insofar as the state could fulfill these tasks, the political elite and at least the educated among the masses accepted and embraced the concept of the central state and often oriented their activities to its institutions.

When these institutions faltered, whether because of foreign incursions, internal weakness or disorder, or certain types of reform effort, lower-level actors and entities have tended to encyst. This tendency reinforces what have been called regionally significant "latent factors,"[6] including differences in topography and climate and other features that have long fed regionalism in China, such as its large size and internal natural barriers, its poor communications and inadequate transport, its disparate dialects, specific identities, and loyalties, and the separate historic traditions in many parts of the land.

Similar Dynamic under Socialism

Added to the historical habits of encystation and local self-reliance is a new form of localism under socialism. Again there is a paradox. On the one hand, the grand concept of the state that universal cosmopolitan Confucianism helped uphold appears in a new guise under socialism; indeed, the annual national economic plan is prepared and promoted for the sake of actualizing the concept of the state as the interest of the whole (or of the people). Party leaders after 1949 used the plan to forge, as Lardy put it, "a politically unified and economically integrated nation-state." They meant for the centralized mode of arranging economic activity to fulfill distributional goals and to guarantee an allocation of services to the various regions independent of their resource bases.[7]

Yet, the paternalism that the plan was designed to realize is undermined in the plan's implementation, because the plan creates new incentives for lower-echelon officials oriented around plan fulfillment. Subordinates in the localities become attached to the institutions relied upon in their own regions to enforce their little part in the national plan. Also, the structure of security and opportunity for localities and their leaders requires a measure of dependence on the national supply network and the national budget. The provision of needs bolsters a certain compliance with that structure on the part of local elites.

Given the well-known deficiencies of the planned economy, a fair degree of uncertainty attends localities' material receipts. Thus, that structure also dictates that skillful lower-level elites learn how to scrounge for themselves by barter, concealment, or hoarding whenever centrally run systems slacken, whether in the course of daily business, as a longer-term secular trend, or as the result of intentional devolution from the capital.

Most conducive to the spawning of localism is a conjuncture of all three factors: the normal irregularities of the plan, the unhinging of the long-term integrating links (whether ideological, bureaucratic, or financial) in the system, and the country's purposive initiation of decentralizing reforms. Then, localities and their elites fall back upon their customs of encystment, and localism (in which a demanding but unreliable provider has unwittingly trained them and their forebears) becomes exacerbated. In addition to localities' inclination to turn inward, both to fulfill state-set tasks and to protect themselves against want, the command economy also provides local cadres with the power to aggrandize their own domains. For, as Donnithorne has pointed out, "Socialism reinforces the significance of local administrative boundaries because the authority which runs the administration also runs the economy."[8] The same local government controls both local commercial distribution and local industry.[9] Thus, the plan, fashioned around the commitments of local units to the nation, founders on a dilemma cited by Nove, who quotes a Hungarian emigrant: "It is [localities'] duty to give priority to the interests of the state, but it is not the task for which they are directly responsible."[10]

In other socialist states, as in China, when the parentlike center lets go its hold, local bodies leap from their limits.[11] Whether such reforms are a positive response to changed incentives or whether local leaders intensify a defensive scramble that they were already involved in need not be resolved here. Probably the motives contain a mix of the two. In any event, the effect is the same:

decentralizing reforms often weaken the fiscal strength of the central government and threaten the state's overall direction of the economy.

In sum, the imperial Chinese state and the centralized socialist regime are neatly comparable to each other in terms of "uncertain paternalism." This mode of integration, which is never complete and easily falters, provides a useful framework with which to interpret the current efforts to reform the spatial arrangement of the economic structure.

An Emerging Regional Program, 1977–84

Beginning in the late 1970s, the Chinese leadership set out to reform the structures of productive and transactional activities. This effort has proceeded haltingly and has not always followed the course set forth by the original proposers. The tangled web of cause and effect behind the difficulties, once unraveled, points to economic localism as the source.[12] Policy evolved gradually after Mao's death, but around 1979 it settled into four major programs, all loosening vertical links in allocation and exchange processes. One changes the locus of decision-making authority through devolutionary schemes. The other three, through more marketlike measures, shift the boundaries within which economic activities occur from administrative to "natural" contours.

These reforms have been staged in a period in which all three historically significant integrating links—ideology, bureaucracy, and financial control—have become loosened and when socialism's localism has taken priority over obedience to and dependence on a now less venerable and reliable patriarch. This weakened integration and its concomitant enhanced localism have worked to block interregional exchange and strengthen decentralism.

The Cultural Revolution of 1966–76 served as a crucial watershed. It had several effects: a pervasive cynicism toward state ideology engulfed society, the central government's ability to command local officialdom was vitiated by factionalism and divided loyalties, and the financial control that had shored up local areas' sense of subservience was challenged. Fast on the heels of the initial recovery from that disorder came a slew of decentralizing experiments. These, it seems, only spurred on the self-seeking and self-supplying in which the regions were already well schooled.

The first public mention of a decision to think in regional terms occurred at the National Conference on Learning from Daqing in Industry held in May 1977.[13] There, Yu Quili, head of the State Planning Commission, described regional development as the second step in a two-step plan following the creation of a "nationwide, independent, and relatively comprehensive industrial and economic system." He envisaged regions that would house "economic systems which vary as regards standards and coordination and which function self-reliantly while working in close coordination and have a fairly harmonious development of agriculture, light and heavy industry." As in previous periods (1949–54,

1961–66), such regions would be groups of three to six provinces each. The principle of self-reliance honored here was coupled with a strong emphasis on vertical hierarchies, discipline, and central planning and supply. Such a program was clearly at variance with the schemes of comparative advantage and decentralization that became policy later on.

In early 1978, Premier Hua Guofeng in an authoritative address referred to a strategy of regional self-sufficiency: "a regional economic system in each of the six major regions."[14] Within a few months, however, the leadership began to shift its conception of how to organize space. On June 2, 1978, an article in the *Renmin ribao* revealed that some had begun to consider a strategy of regional specialization, as the piece referred to "efforts to build various regions along the coast into large, strong industrial areas."

Another sign of movement away from complete, self-reliant regional systems is suggested by the Academy of Social Science forums in the spring of 1978 in each of the six major regions. Discussions focused on a different set of specific keypoints for development in each of them.[15]

The great dividing line came with a speech entitled "Observe Economic Laws," first delivered at a secret session of the State Council in July 1978 and published openly in October. Its author contended that "because the various provinces are vastly different from one another in resources, if, by disregarding local conditions, each province strives to be self-contained and self-sufficient, it is bound to cause a tremendous waste of manpower and material resources and delay the four modernizations." "Proportionate development of a planned national economy," he maintained, "calls for effective specialization and coordination."[16]

The speech proved to be highly influential. It provided the theoretical framework for the many innovations associated with the seminal reforms of late 1978, but at first it by no means commanded full support. More than a year later a discussion of centralization and decentralization in the *Renmin ribao* exposed continuing disagreements (November 9, 1979).

After the crucial Eleventh Party Central Committee's Third Plenum in December 1978, however, those ready to implement the "economic laws" prescription had carried the day. Judging from a 1980 interview with economist Xue Muqiao, the regional development strategy still in place as of mid-1986 was already being put into effect by 1979.[17] He described the following reforms, all borrowed from Yugoslavia and Hungary: Some Shanghai factories had started to manage joint enterprises with factories in other provinces by sharing funds, technical personnel, and raw materials; large, economically developed industrial cities were permitted to play roles as economic centers; and geographic areas were allowed to invest in other regions. "We must," he urged, "make use of the strong points of the advanced regions and encourage them to help develop the backward regions." Overall, his words were a plea for regional specialization and division of labor.

By the spring of 1982, the then president of the Academy of Social Sciences, Ma Hong, wrote of mapping out "regional economic zones" and establishing "a rational regional economic structure to give full play to the relative advantages of different regions."[18] This vision, couched within the context of overall planning, was of a commodity (exchange-oriented) economy in each region with regions supplying each other's needs. The plan he spelled out was to be contingent on the demarcation of zones drawn on the basis of the location of natural resources, the level of industrial and agricultural production, the condition of communications and transportation, and the nature of historical economic linkages among regions. Moreover, each region was to put its manpower and other resources into "those spheres of production which will ensure high economic results and produce goods with the lowest costs."

The Sixth Five-Year Plan (adopted in December 1982) was yet more specific.[19] The coastal areas would draw on their advanced capabilities of various kinds including research, technology, management, and efficient transportation to develop export industries and reap foreign exchange earnings while also stimulating development in the interior. In April 1984, special powers were granted to fourteen coastal cities (an extension of the creation of four "special economic zones" in 1980), positioning them to attract foreign investment.[20] Meanwhile, the inland areas were to concentrate on the speedier development of their energy, communications, and raw materials industries so as to back up the coast logistically while reorganizing their often outdated machine-building industry. The plan's main gist was to implement nationwide coordination ultimately directed toward maximal overall national efficiency.

Since then, past proposals in the direction of "balanced growth" have been shelved even more explicitly. One article interpreted Deng Xiaoping's "Selected Works" as permitting some regions, as well as some enterprises and individuals, to "get rich first of all."[21] A commentary in the *Renmin ribao* provided an economic rationale for the relative neglect of modernization in poorer areas:

> More investment and consumption are required in the development of new and outlying backward regions and economic results are poorer, whereas because of the better technical and economic foundation in the old regions, economic results are better. Therefore, the development of new and outlying backward regions on too large a scale will also, for a certain period, retard the increase of the national income.... Within this century, the focus of our economic regions is in the East, but at the same time, we must make proper preparation for the large-scale development of regions in the West.[22]

Thus, the new central leadership slowly discarded the earlier effort at a more equitable development for all regions. That earlier effort sometimes attempted to negate differences between regions in demanding autarkic development in each of them, but it also skewed central investment toward the needier areas. For instance, the backward inland regions, the source of only one-third of industrial output, received about half of all investment during the First Five-Year Plan, and through at least 1974 the center continued to redistribute substantial revenues from rich to poor provinces.[23] The Sixth Five-Year Plan does state that the state will "continue to give financial, material, and technological support to the minority and other economically underdeveloped regions through a 10 percent annual increase in financial subsidies as well as disbursing 500 million yuan a year to help develop the economies in these places."[24] Chinese national paternalism, however, has become more uncertain than usual for its component units as regions, provinces, and even enterprises are expected to create wealth for themselves on their own through new schemes of regionally coordinated growth.

Four Kinds of Reform

The spatial reform program is analogous to a parent sending children out to work for their survival rather than giving them a free allowance. It has generated self-serving and often greedy coping mechanisms as both local (subprovincial) and provincial leaders have adapted, frequently with gusto, to the shift in incentives associated with new modes for security and opportunity. The approach is centered around self-help and localized incentives much more than any previous plan. In theory it ought to be cheaper for the center by devolving some investment responsibilities and by permitting producers and exchange partners to work from their own profits. On the other hand, locally controlled revenues have grown, at times threatening the accumulation at the center.

These reforms are perhaps better termed reorganized formats to avoid the usual connotation for the word reform that something has necessarily improved. They can be divided into four sorts: (1) the decentralization of some autonomy and financial power, (2) organizational changes in commercial activity, (3) measures to increase technical specialization and cooperation, and (4) geographical blueprints for regionally based growth. Of these four, the first, which changes the locus of economic decision making, has provided the impetus for a heightened economic localism that frequently works to counteract the other three. The last three all depend on furthering the comparative advantage of the country's regions and on basing economic activity more on natural and less on administrative units.

Decentralization

Probably the most significant dimension of decentralization was a restructuring of fiscal relations. In 1980, five new types of financial relationships were created to govern the apportionment of revenues and expenditures between center and provinces.[25] In this system, fifteen of the twenty-nine provinces were to follow a plan that permitted provinces and their local authorities to keep all the profits earned from enterprises that were housed within them (except those enterprises under central control). In the previous system, local units retained a share that coincided with the expenditures in their district. This reform greatly increased the revenue kept and spent by the lower-level authorities.[26] According to one calculation, it increased the funds in the hands of local leaders from about one-fifth of the state revenues to one-half of them.[27]

In 1982, a new method to allocate finances favored the provinces even more. It applied to the majority of the provinces and allowed them to retain an average of 80 percent of the revenues generated in their area. The key change here was that most provinces were allowed to obtain a larger percentage of the industrial and commercial tax, which has been a growing tax base because it rises with total output. Provinces had to give Beijing a share of local tax revenues in exchange, but these revenues were in decline as enterprises were permitted to keep more of their profits.

Moreover, provincial officials were granted new authority to adjust the tax rates in their jurisdiction.[28] Also, a set of "extrabudgetary funds" expanded drastically after 1979; local authorities can gather these funds, but they do not enter into their budgets, thereby escaping Beijing's inspection. (According to Naughton, in Chinese parlance, the term "extrabudgetary funds" includes profits and depreciation funds.)[29] By central-level reckoning, extrabudgetary revenues in recent years might have amounted to the equivalent of about half of total budgetary revenues, up from about 17 percent in 1960.[30]

In addition, relaxation of the controls on bank loans and the granting of new autonomy to provincial bank branches to lend for capital construction have also worked to give more freedom to local decision makers. Localities depend far less on central grants and central approval for their projects than they once did.[31]

In the same period, the central government permitted provinces to engage in foreign trade through local branches of the national foreign trade corporations (though at times it has attempted to recentralize these powers, as in early 1981 and March 1984). The share that may be kept from this trade varies from province to province, but all may be partners in ventures with foreign governments and firms and raise loans abroad (which must be guaranteed by the Bank of China, however). The administrative level authorized to permit these forms of business has varied over time.[32]

In 1984, six major industrial cities received special powers akin to those that had been granted to Chongqing in April 1983. The cities—Wuhan, Xian, Guangzhou, Dalian, Shenyang, and Harbin—have economic management powers equivalent to those of a province, hold separate line-item status in the state plan, and may conclude deals with foreign firms, generally up to the amount of U.S.$5 million. County authorities also got greater power in the early 1980s to permit them to create horizontally integrated systems of management and incentives. All these reforms are meant to break through hierarchical, vertical controls and to spur local initiative.[33]

What have been the effects of these various regulations? Heightened powers, more funds, and an uncertainty about central-level provisioning (an uncertainty which is not entirely new but has become far more pronounced) have all refashioned the incentives to which local elites respond. Yet the central plan, although less totalistic and specific than in the past, still structures the overall contours of the economy. Provincial and other lower-echelon leaders may have funds and rights, but, mainly because of a failure to implement a price reform, they lack the genuinely open-market environment that truly encourages and rewards a judicious exercise in capital and other factor mobility. The planned economy sets up barriers to such mobility, and actors' defensive actions to cope with the barriers add to the barriers' force. As Rawski put it: "An interactive cycle with subordinate autarky also comes into play. The existence of trade barriers promotes vertical integration, and once self-supply becomes feasible, protectionist motives generate further restrictions, which lead to more integration, etc."[34]

The forms of defensive behavior that have grown up within this milieu have enjoyed a wider scope for action over the past several years, but again, they are not novel. They include protectionism in its various guises—pushing the sales of local products, refusing to permit the export of local materials or the import of commodities produced elsewhere, and hoarding local products such as cement and steel. Localities have used the hoarded supplies to construct new local enterprises, including small, duplicative, inefficient, outdated factories known in some quarters as "local money trees" or "little treasuries."[35]

Local governments, aware that their profits will rise under the recent rulings, have exercised a heightened despotism over their own districts' enterprises and projects, thereby thwarting other reform efforts to increase enterprise autonomy.[36] In those areas not yet able to fend profitably for themselves, leaders engage in special pleading. On occasion they have even done so vociferously enough to attract attention in the national press and at National People's Congresses.[37]

At various times, the central leadership took steps to redefine the recently set up relationships and rights, hoping to curb some of these practices. In December 1982, the State Council called attention to "defects" in the financial management system first laid out in 1980. "To concentrate necessary capital," it decreed that all provinces (except for Guangdong and Fujian) would obtain their revenues according to a fixed proportion of the total amount of revenues generated in their areas. This notice also institutionalized the provincial "loans" to the center (to the tune of 8 billion yuan), first assessed on an ad hoc basis in 1981.[38]

A 1984 measure, which based taxation on a calculation of the price of products, on economic activities, and on assets or total income, rather than on the administrative level to which a given enterprise belongs, was at first aimed at recentralization: a commentary on this regulation stressed that intention, stating, "It is imperative for the central government to strengthen macroscopic control over local government."[39]

In addition to draining the central budget, the decentralizing reforms have become roadblocks for other major components of spatial change. They often work to stymie flows of commodities, capital, and information that are essential to exchange and development based on comparative advantage, the concept on which the remaining three parts of the overall program depend.

Organizational Changes in Commercial Activities

The organizational changes in commercial activities are not unprecedented in the People's Republic. Both barter (if not usually legally sanctioned) and attempts to reorient exchange along natural, historical trading routes existed in the past,[40] but they have never before been promoted with such energy and enthusiasm.

As early as 1980, Xue Muqiao lamented the elimination of an interurban network of economic flows after 1956, said that he would like to see it rebuilt, and enunciated a scheme by which cities would have "direct contact with one another and help supply each other's needs [though still] under the guidance of state plans, instead of going through commercial departments at various levels."[41] This design began to be realized in the years following, picking up momentum after 1983.

Nonetheless, barter trade among regions that totally bypasses central-level cognizance has aroused concern in Beijing when it has diverted vitally needed materials from state-sponsored projects at prices above the official ones. For this reason, central elites have at times suggested ways to impose an official structure on it, as is evidenced in the continuing commitment to an overarching state-run rubric for economic activity. Xue also suggested in mid-1982 that in addition to the customary top-to-bottom unified plan, future state plans would also incorporate supplemental base-to-top interregional coordination plans.[42] Thus, the new tactics are still a rather large step away from the truly spontaneous interchange of a free market.

At the same time that the state hopes to hold on to a measure of control, localities have obstructed the new, unplanned trade by creating "blockades." Their new taxation and revenue-sharing powers have encouraged them to do so. Some districts have even set up what amount to internal customs points. According to a State Council regulation of mid-1982 aimed at abolishing such practices, some districts have established organs to examine and approve the merchandise destined to cross regional boundaries. Others have forced the banks to refuse credit for contracts governing sales outside their own areas—even for contracts already signed by local customers.

In summary, some organizational and structural changes in commercial activity have been implemented. But concurrently, there have been some efforts to encompass such trading within the scope of state-designed plans and procedures, though such administrative interference seems less cumbersome and intrusive than in the past. It is clear as well that old modes of localism have been reinforced by the decentralization decisions and stand in the way of freely flowing movements of goods.

Technical Specialization and Cooperation

The second facet of the market arm of reform is a program of domestic technological "cooperation," including compensatory trade, joint ventures, technology
transfer, consulting, and investment by the industrialized coastal areas in the
more backward regions. All these arrangements rest on the fact that the coastal
regions in the east are rich in technological equipment and facilities, have skilled
labor and management, and are able to contribute funding. The less developed
west can provide raw materials, such as bone glue, soldering tin, timber, and
coal, that the coast generally lacks. According to incomplete statistics, by the end
of 1983, 8,549 items of interprovincial cooperation had been concluded, and
materially based forms of cooperation that could be quantified amounted to 4.9
billion yuan.[43] In 1984, provincial officials signed another 17,000 interprovince
contracts of cooperation.[44] By urging each region to satisfy its demands through
bilateral agreements, the central leadership hopes to reduce the burden on state
bureaucracy and central-level investment. Another motive, however, lurks in the
minds of at least some of the leadership. This reform is also meant to overcome
the contradictions of competition among localities. As Xue Muqiao explained,
when processing enterprises cooperate with firms in the raw material producing
areas, their mutual vying over materials, energy, and markets should dissipate.[45]

Cross-regional cooperation can sometimes create conflict with the requirements of the plan, such as when some local units use resources and transport
facilities or court customers that ought to be handled under the plan's guidelines.
In response to this problem, an article in *Economic Daily* in late 1983 suggested:
"Regional cooperation should be included in the regional plan and comprehensive balancing undertaken. . . . [A]t present, much of it is scattered . . . [having] a
certain blindness."[46]

Not all of the collaboration is voluntary and, therefore, not truly market based.
For example, one report revealed, "Shanghai was designated last year (1983) by
the central government as one of the four major partners to work with the [Tibet
Autonomous] Region to help speed up its economic development."[47] Thus, the
state has been ready to guide as well as to limit the direction of cooperation.

Often regional elites would rather not participate in these exchanges at all.
The problem here should be a familiar one by now. Both the assessment and the
statistical systems are grounded at governmental levels, and the offices at each
such level are judged according to their respective output, profits, and growth.
This situation in itself discourages the more developed regions from investing in
or joining with other places, and the regime has yet to work out a way to divide
profits, output value, and quantities produced that will keep both participating
units from feeling cheated.[48] As things stand now, most regions feel safer building grass-roots industries at home rather than risking being bested by their partner, losing needed resources, or forfeiting revenues.

As with the other aspects of the reform program, here, too, the leadership is trying to create wealth through state withdrawal, while at the same time being unwilling to cede entirely central plans and the controls over supplies and assets that are part of these plans. Caught in the trap of uncertain paternalism, most provinces have hesitated to risk their newly won surplus holdings in cooperative schemes from which they might not benefit.

Zones for Regionally Based Growth

The zones for regionally based growth are probably the most far-ranging element in the strategy stressing comparative advantage. They encompass two sorts of reform. The first entails large-scale, national planning based around macro regions composed of several provinces or parts of provinces. The second is the creation (or re-creation, since such systems existed before 1956) of economic zones focused on "key" or "central cities." This second reform is closely tied to a new arrangement called "counties led by cities." Each reform is discussed in turn below.

  Macro Regions. The new macro regions are supposed to be formed through the operation of "economic levers." Their boundaries are to be drawn in accord with economic costs and results; "these zones and networks are open ... [and] form a jagged and interlocking pattern in between and among various administrative zones of cities."[49]

  Nonetheless, often the state steps in to steer the process, carrying on a centuries-old tradition of regrouping territory to achieve control over power centers at lower levels.[50] With this brand of reform, as with all others, there is intraelite disagreement (or at least ambivalence) as to whether genuinely new institutions, embodying new incentives, ought to be spontaneously and voluntarily created by their constituent units, or whether Beijing bureaucrats should contain that experimentation a bit and fashion mergers that compel the sharing of material interests according to central plans. In the latter case, some central leaders hope it would become possible to reduce the competition among areas spurred by the decentralization reforms in order to minimize what they view as the negative effects of such competition.

  Not surprisingly, this division of the nation into regions for economic growth has activated the same sorts of sibling rivalry and self-serving behavior as with provinces (although on a rather grander scale). For instance, in operating region-wide power grids, the energy-rich northwest has been loath to spare its resources for fuel-short neighboring regions.[51] No doubt springing from a similar urge to take care of one's own, spokespersons in northeast, northwest, and southwest China regions have all laid claims to the special features and (as they see it) the deserved prominence of their own areas. Understandably, the leaders do not wish to watch their regions get left behind.[52]

  Thus, the macro regions development program is viewed by regional elites as both opportunity and threat. Which it is depends upon the state investment their region can hope to receive and its capability for surviving without the central support it could count on in the past.

Central Cities. One seemingly brand-new economic reform in 1983 was "to maximize the role of the more economically developed cities." In fact, this idea was already in the air for at least two or three years at that time.[53] Although the policy spoke of extending urban economic activities "to towns, small cities, and the vast rural areas . . . to form a flexible network type of economic structure," here again the leadership did not have the goal of nurturing the pure spontaneity of an untrammeled free market. The strategy was meant to break down those barriers between regions that were rooted in traditional localism, which first the plan and then the decentralization decisions had worked to aggravate. Economic associations centered on the key cities were meant to merge economic interests between the areas so joined. The hope was that the high-growth areas would subsidize the poorer through shared profits; regions with similar resources would no longer set up their own duplicative ventures; and areas would cease waging price wars that either underbid state purchasers or enabled foreign firms to benefit at the expense of domestic sellers.[54]

Through specializing and cooperating, central cities are to solve problems of blockages and duplications by organizing economic unions that transcend the bureaucratic departments and administrative districts that have organized China's economy for three decades. As of February 1984, the national media claimed that one-quarter of China's more than 2,000 counties were being administered by nearby cities in accord with this reform and that 121 of the country's 286 cities were exercising jurisdiction over 541 neighboring counties.[55]

The kinds of obstacles this particular program is encountering are by now familiar. In defiance of the centrally sponsored design to encourage a less bureaucratized arrangement of bailiwicks, officials in these cities are quickly turning their areas into new little systems with the city as the exploiting nucleus. Thus, "responsible persons" in key cities have used their expanded areas of jurisdiction to place cadres, have forced the urban hinterland to perform more services for the cities, and have garnered more land or raw materials from the countryside to solve the problems of urban plants.

Meanwhile, some cities' cadres refuse to link up with other places and demand that the factories in their areas break off cooperative relationships already under way. They also order local firms to process in the central city any items and parts purchased in other areas and forbid enterprises at home from buying parts from other places. Such practices have led the national press to enjoin city governments from seeing these new spheres as territories for them to rule in their own interests.

Thus, the experiment in comparative advantage based on activities among "natural" economic units—in commercial activity, in technical cooperation, and in zonal development schemes of various scales—has definitely undergone some testing as of this writing. Mired as they are in the midst of murky market signals mixed with a largely unchanged structure of security and opportunity, however, many of the officials involved in these schemes seem to be as prone to the same sort of self-protective strategies as their counterparts within the more traditional borders that delineate the provinces.

Conclusion: Reform and Modernization

In mid-1983, an article appeared in *Hongqi*, the party's theoretical journal, that touched on the linkage of reform to growth. It made the point that the purpose of the decentralization policies of recent years had been to stir up the initiative of the localities, departments, enterprises, and the masses in order to promote the national economy, and that the purpose was not to inspire profit seeking that interfered with the state plan. This view raises many interrelated questions that are crucial to an assessment of the reforms in the spatial structure of the economy. Can reform and modernization be carried out simultaneously? Can the institution of marketlike reforms, seemingly a strategy in itself more modern, more pragmatic (as many claim, both in China and outside) than the growth by fiat of the command economy, result in modernizing the economy? The task is complicated by the distorted signals bearing "hybrid, contradictory, and misleading information"[56] of China's current "compromise economic model," which is part central plan and part incentives borrowed from capitalist systems.

Short of throwing out the socialist planned economy altogether, is there at least some hope that the measures of market exchange being tested in China today might finally yield central revenue that can be invested into national economic growth? Might the regions formed around individual provinces, counties, or cities in time merge into at least a quasi market capable of generating the capital (and other kinds of factor) mobility requisite for development? From a somewhat different angle, is reform destroying the reforming government?

These questions are posed in light of a consensus about modernization in a surprisingly wide range of commentators' conceptions. Analysts and political and social actors as diverse as Mancur Olson, the commercial bourgeoisie in China on the eve of the 1911 Revolution, Josip Broz Tito, and Alec Nove, and, on occasion, present-day Chinese economists and politicians, have all spoken on behalf of the importance for economic growth of strong central management and control, if for rather different reasons and from somewhat varying perspectives.[57]

They come at the problem of development from diverse sets of assumptions. Olson, for one, has coined a term, *jurisdictional integration,* a condition he deems essential to growth, referring to free trade within domestic borders, free movement of the factors of production (labor, capital, and firms), and the ability to make at least some important decisions about economic policy at an all-nation level. He points out that the achievement of a centralized government (which in turn was able to bring about economic unification and improvement in internal transport) occurred early in England, which was also the first nation to establish a nationwide market relatively free of local trade restrictions. This market, he suggests, spawned the commercial revolution and ultimately the Industrial Revolution.

Following the same line of reasoning, the Chinese commercial bourgeoisie of the early twentieth century, according to Bergère's account, lobbied for a national market to facilitate commercial expansion, one based upon reforms of currency and weights and measures and on the abolition of the internal customs system, all of which required an effective national government.

From a socialist perspective, Nove has pointed to the importance of centralized planning for the potential control it affords over externalities, for its implementers' opportunity to obtain an overview of the whole economy, and for the focus the planners must direct on probable future needs of the nation. In his concern for narrowing interregional income gaps but also for the promotion of some form of capital mobility, he refers to Tito's critique of the "little protected markets" that grew up in Yugoslavia with the increase in local autonomy given to the regions there. Nove charges that this autonomy has actually hampered economic performance in that country.

Turning to China itself a quarter of a century ago in the wake of the Great Leap Forward's dispersal of key materials, Chen Yun supported centralized assemblage of the nation's limited resources in the interest of a speedier and more focused developmental effort, and at different points since 1980, social scientist Ma Hong, economist Xue Muqiao, and Premier Zhao Ziyang have each made reference to the necessity for an overall plan and a national viewpoint, which they have claimed is needed for properly "giving play to local strong points," for creating a regionally structured but comprehensive state-run development scheme, and even for carrying out reform. All of these leaders, despite their association with the incentives programs of the last few years, recognize a need for mobilizing scattered but essential resources, such as energy, steel, lumber, cement, and coal,[58] and concentrating them for what the state has decided should be "key construction projects." They also are aware that such projects—rail lines, ports, mineral exploration and mines, power-generating stations and petroleum refineries, and highways—require investments provinces cannot afford, as well as gestation periods that they are unlikely to sustain and a selfless shepherding of capital for enterprises whose benefits, being shared with other provinces, will not accrue to themselves alone.

The decentralization of economic decision making and the material incentive-based mode of motivating productivity that has marked the total economic reform package since 1978 has led to a boom and made possible unprecedented improvements in income for much of the population. Whether such advances might be at the expense of long-term directed national economic growth, however, is a question central leaders have been seriously concerned about in the last few years. Though the situation had improved as of early 1986, the national media had reported, for example, that from 1979 to 1982, when the national income increased by 41 percent, state revenue dropped by 3.3 percent.[59] Although the 1982 total output value of industrial and agricultural production was 8.7 percent higher than in 1981, state revenue increased only 2.3 percent in that period.[60] The proportion of financial revenue in the national income declined from 37.2 percent in 1978, before the reforms began, to 25.5 percent four years later.[61] Finally, extrabudgetary funds (funds under the management of provincial leadership and outside the control of the central government) rose from 37.1 billion yuan in 1978 to 65 billion yuan in 1982, an increase of 75.2 percent in only four years' time.[62]

Such a loss of central revenue could be compatible with economic growth, if a complex modern economy were already in place. For, if China operated its national economy completely through the institution of a market model, with fully free prices and with customers and suppliers (along with widespread knowledge of their whereabouts and their needs) readily available to producers nationwide, investors could concentrate and rationally allocate their own capital for developmental ventures that would lead to modern growth.[63] Yet, as Vice-Premier Yao Yilin instructed his audience at the Sixth National People's Congress in June 1983, "Though there have been great changes in the past thirty years, there is still no unified and sensitive market based on a comprehensive information network." Thus, "each district, department, or enterprise quite naturally pays more attention to its own needs . . . [and] pays little heed to arranging production, circulation, and consumption to suit the national economy."[64]

The outcome Yao documents is exacerbated, as this chapter has shown, by a less-than-total free market and a planning system that leaves localities ultimately uncertain and self-protective. The power of central efforts to reverse such tendencies, when these efforts are made by a center whose integrative mechanisms are weakened, cannot match the strength of economic localism, once activated. Often unprotected by the imperfect plan that is socialism's version of China's age-old "uncertain paternalism," and not having available a real market in which exchange can be guaranteed to be reciprocally satisfactory, local administrations, which were carved out over centuries of history and are reinforced by the plan's bureaucracy, duplicate, waste, hoard, and blockade within their own safe borders. The words of Rusinow depict the situation in China; describing the partial decentralization within Yugoslavian socialism, he noted, "The power [is] nowhere and everywhere."[65]

Notes

1. G. W. Skinner, "Chinese Peasants and the Closed Community: An Open and Shut Case," *Comparative Studies in Society and History* 13, 3 (1971): 270–81.

2. J. Kornai, "Adjustment to Price and Quantity Signals in a Socialist Economy," *Economic Appliqué* 35, 3 (1982): 503–24.

3. See N. R. Lardy, *Economic Growth and Distribution in China* (Cambridge: Cambridge University Press, 1978), for an analysis of the state's commitment to the viability

of less endowed regions through the mid-1970s. That the Chinese dynastic order had a similar commitment is asserted, by among other people, M. C. Wright, *The Last Stand of Chinese Conservatism* (Stanford: Stanford University Press, 1957), pp. 126, 133, 135. The socialist states in Yugoslavia and Czechoslovakia also wrestled with the problem of regional redistribution; see D. Rusinow, *The Yugoslav Experiment, 1948–1974* (Berkeley: University of California Press, 1977); B. Pleskovic, "Regional Development in a Socialist, Developing, and Multinational Country: The Case of Yugoslavia," *International Regional Science Review* 7, 1 (1982): 1–24; and B. Jancar, *Czechoslovakia and the Absolute Monopoly of Power* (New York: Praeger 1971).

4. G. Rozman, ed., *The Modernization of China* (New York: Free Press, 1981), refers to the history of "restricted state economic involvement and the resultant use and distribution of resources within local communities, especially given the high levels of local self-sufficiency" (p. 211) and the "high degree of decentralization customary in premodern times" (p. 148). J. E. Sheridan, *China in Disintegration: The Republican Era in Chinese History* (New York: Free Press, 1975), p. 13, notes the "economic self-containment of loyalties and regions." Others, however, question this view of local self-sufficiency.

5. Skinner, "Chinese Peasants."

6. C. M. Wilbur, "Military Separatism and the Process of Reunification under the Nationalist Regime, 1922–1937," in *China in Crisis*, ed. P. Ho and T. Tsou, pp. 203–76 (Chicago: University of Chicago Press, 1968).

7. Lardy, *Economic Growth*, pp. 10–14.

8. A. Donnithorne, "The Chinese Economy Today," *Journal of Northeastern Asian Studies* 2, 3 (1983): 9.

9. T. G. Rawski, "Chinese Management Capabilities," manuscript, 1983, p. 62; C. P. W. Wong, "Rural Industrialization in the People's Republic of China: Lessons from the Cultural Revolution Decade," in *China Under the Four Modernizations, Part 1*, U.S. Congress, Joint Economic Committee (Washington, DC: Government Printing Office, 1982), p. 408.

10. A. Nove, *The Economics of Feasible Socialism* (London: George Allen & Unwin, 1983), p. 78.

11. H. Schwartz, *The Soviet Economy Since Stalin* (New York: J. P. Lippincott, 1965), pp. 87–93.

12. *Foreign Broadcast Information Service (FBIS)*, September 23, 1983, pp. K8–9.

13. *Renmin ribao* (People's daily), May 8, 1977.

14. *Peking Review*, no. 10 (1978): 19.

15. D. J. Solinger, "The Shadowy Second Stage of China's Ten-Year Plan: Building Up Regional Systems, 1976–1985," *Pacific Affairs* 52, 2 (1979): 241–64.

16. *FBIS*, October 11, 1978, pp. E1–22.

17. *Beijing Review (BR)*, no. 36 (1980): 20–23.

18. H. Ma, *New Strategy for China's Economy* (Beijing: New World Press, 1983), pp. 64–66.

19. *BR*, no. 22 (1983): 6–8.

20. *BR*, no. 27 (1984): 7–8; no. 31 (1984): 7–8.

21. *FBIS*, December 16, 1983, p. K7.

22. *FBIS*, February 8, 1984, p. K20.

23. Lardy, *Economic Growth*, pp. 88, 136–37.

24. *BR*, no. 22 (1983): 7.

25. A. Donnithorne, *Centre-Provincial Relations in China* (Canberra: Australian National University, Department of Economics, Contemporary China Papers 16, 1981); Donnithorne, "The Chinese Economy Today"; Donnithorne, "Fiscal Relations," *China Business Review* 10, 6 (1983): 25–27.

26. R. F. Dernberger, "The Chinese Search for the Path of Self-Sustained Growth in the 1980s: An Assessment," in *China under the Four Modernizations, Part 1*, U.S. Congress, Joint Economic Committee (Washington, DC: Government Printing Office, 1982): pp. 67–68; N. Chen, "China's Capital Construction: Current Retrenchment and Prospects for Foreign Participation," in *China under the Four Modernizations, Part 2*, U.S. Congress, Joint Economic Committee (Washington, DC: Government Printing Office, 1982): p. 56.

27. M. Weil, "The Sixth Five-Year Plan," *China Business Review* 10, 2 (1983): 23.

28. Dernberger, "The Chinese Search," p. 68.

29. B. Naughton, "The Decline of Central Control over Investment in Post-Mao China," in *Policy Implementation in Post-Mao China*, ed. D. M. Lampton, pp. 51–80 (Berkeley: University of California Press, 1987).

30. See Donnithorne, "The Chinese Economy Today," p. 6; and "Fiscal Relations," p. 27.

31. Donnithorne, "The Chinese Economy Today," p. 7; "Fiscal Relations," pp. 15, 17; V. C. Falkenheim, "Distributive Politics and Regional Reform in Post-Mao China," paper delivered at the Annual Conference of the Association for Asian Studies, Washington, DC, 1984; K. H. Y. Hsiao, "Money and Banking in the People's Republic of China: Recent Developments," *China Quarterly* 91 (1982): 462–77; and W. Byrd, *China's Financial System: The Changing Role of Banks* (Boulder: Westview Press, 1983).

32. Donnithorne, *Centre-Provincial Relations*, pp. 24–30; V. C. Falkenheim and T. G. Rawski, "China's Economic Reform: The International Dimension," paper delivered at the Workshop on Policy Implementation in Post-Mao China, Columbus, Ohio, 1983; and C. L. Brehm, "Shanghai Unleashed," *China Business Review* 10, 5 (1983): 12–14.

33. D. J. Solinger, "Wuhan: Inland City on the Move," *China Business Review* 12, 2 (1985): 27–30; and Y. Y. Kueh, "Economic Reform in China at the 'Xian' Level," *China Quarterly* 96 (1983): 665–88.

34. Rawski, "Chinese Management Capabilities," p. 61.

35. *FBIS*, July 15, 1983, p. K19.

36. Naughton, "The Decline of Central Control," p. 15.

37. Falkenheim, "Distributive Politics."

38. Donnithorne, "Fiscal Relations," p. 27.

39. *FBIS*, February 17, 1984, pp. K23–25.

40. D. J. Solinger, *Chinese Business under Socialism* (Berkeley: University of California Press, 1984).

41. *BR*, no. 36 (1980): 22–23.

42. *Hongqi* (Red flag), no. 8 (1982): 31.

43. *FBIS*, November 9, 1983, p. K1.

44. *BR*, no. 10 (1985): 17.

45. *BR*, no. 36 (1980): 20.

46. *FBIS*, November 9, 1983, p. K13.

47. *FBIS*, March 26, 1984, p. K14.

48. *Renmin ribao*, October 21, 1983, p. 5.

49. *Hongqi*, no. 18 (1983): 24; *Renmin ribao*, November 7, 1983, p. 5; *FBIS*, July 20, 1983, p. K12.

50. D. J. Solinger, *Regional Government and Political Integration in Southwest China, 1949–1954* (Berkeley: University of California Press, 1977), p. 20.

51. *FBIS*, March 20, 1984, pp. K5–8.

52. *FBIS*, February 10, 1984, pp. S2–3; June 29, 1982, pp. K9–11; February 9, 1984, pp. K9–10.

53. *BR*, no. 3 (1983): 4; *FBIS*, April 1, 1981, pp. K3–5; *BR*, no. 36 (1980): 20.

54. *Renmin ribao*, June 3, 1983, p. 5; *Hongqi*, no. 16 (1983): 13–17; *Renmin ribao*, October 21, 1983, p. 5.

55. *FBIS*, March 2, 1984, p. K2.

56. D. Rusinow, *The Yugoslav Expreiment, 1948–1974* (Berkeley: University of California Press, 1977), p. 345.

57. M. Olson, *The Rise and Decline of Nations: Economic Growth, Stagnation, and Social Rigidities* (New Haven: Yale University Press, 1982), pp. 119–37; M. Bergere, "The Role of the Bourgeoisie," in *China in Revolution*, ed. M. Wright, pp. 229–95 (New Haven: Yale University Press, 1968), pp. 275–79; Nove, *The Economics of Feasible Socialism*, pp. 95–97, 138–40; Chen Yun, *Hongqi*, no. 5 (1959): 1–16; Ma Hong, *New Strategy*, p. 65; Xue Muqiao, *BR*, no. 36 (1980): 20; Xue Muqiao, *Renmin ribao*, June 3, 1983, p. 5; Zhao Ziyang, *FBIS*, June 23, 1983, p. K16.

58. Such resources have become "scattered" with the decentralizing reforms outlined above. FBIS, July 7, 1983, p. K19, carries a report on the need to centralize financial and material resources, which states that from 1965 to 1982 the amount of rolled steel distributed by the state under the unified plan dropped from 95 to 53 percent; of cement, from 71 to 25 percent; and of timber, from 63 to 57 percent.

59. *FBIS*, February 22, 1983, p. K12.

60. *FBIS*, June 13, 1983, p. K9.

61. *FBIS*, June 23, 1983, pp. K1–12.

62. *FBIS*, August 16, 1983, p. K5.

63. Nove, *The Economics of Feasible Socialism*, p. 139.

64. *FBIS*, July 20, 1983, p. K16.

65. Rusinow, *The Yugoslav Experiment*, p. 253.

8
City, Province, and Region: The Case of Wuhan

Regarding the positive role that the old economic system played in the country's socialist construction in the past, its positive aspects, and our positive experience in our past work, we must not adopt a nihilist attitude and negate everything. Thus, in designing target patterns for reforms, we are required to take into consideration the problem of replacing one pattern by another, the need to keep the economy running, and the problem of continuity between patterns.

—Liu Guoguang, *Renmin ribao*, July 31, 1987

This quotation by one of the country's leading theoretical economists captures very succinctly what has been the (often unintended) experience in Wuhan's economic reform. Right at the heart of the process of economic reform lies the issue of replacing that "old economic system's" vertical, bureaucratically organized channels of command and coordination with lateral, market-style linkages. The idea behind this move is that, given some freedom, lower-level entities should choose horizontal bonds, since these are more economically rational than the old, planned ones. But to what extent can a command to reform, to alter old economic patterns into drastically different designs, really be obeyed in a short stretch of time? If, instead, there are crucial continuities, just what form do they take?

This chapter, based in part on newspaper and journal articles from the past three years, but mainly on thirty-five hours of interviews conducted in Wuhan in June 1987, talks to this topic. In addition to the big question just posed, it raises these correlative queries as well: Is decentralizing and reorienting reform really occurring in and around Wuhan, and if so, is it empowering the city in important ways? Is a rearrangement of responsibilites in fact breaking down vertical, administrative bureaucratic patterns of investment, management, and exchange? And are these new relationships then allowing and inducing economic agents freely to opt for horizontally based connections?

The usual line of argumentation in analyzing the recent Chinese reform process has gone like this, for the most part: reform is blocked by bureaucratic interference, whether by "conservative" politicians and commissions in the capital, or by local departments and their cadres. For, so commentators hold, such forces fear the loss of their funds, powers, and ultimate control over economic and financial activity. Such descriptions pit plan against market.

Actually, the picture is a lot more complex. For those in charge of reform have been able in some cases to turn the old structure to advantage. By a complicated combination of removing but also relying upon planks from the plan, reformers can do a great deal to bring about changes that appear to be market-based, in the spirit of the state's propaganda on reform. But rather than junking the plan altogether, reform has in many cases been possible simply through adaptation of old (plan days') offices, channels, personnel, and relationships.

There is a second way in which the previous system facilitates reform. Those promoting and implementing reform are sometimes doing so just by expanding, legalizing, formalizing, in short, by making explicit the formerly semilicit and even illicit coping strategies used for years whenever the plan had proved inadequate.

And third, reform-minded powerholders in Beijing (as well as those in cities such as Wuhan, probably through the connections such city political leaders manage to fashion with reformers at the top) can in many cases throw the considerable weight of the state behind local models or test points (*shidian*) in order to promote particular projects they sanction. At the urban level, politicians may help models succeed in order to win a name for their city as a pioneer in reform. Political facilitation, called *youhui tiaojian* (preferential conditions) in the more economically slanted jargon of today, thus pushes along pet reform designs. At the same time it provides a model of what the reformers hope to realize on a much larger scale later on, when the political climate has been more fully prepared.

These three state-sponsored reform strategies at the policy level—remolding old organs and their connections for new purposes, bringing coping modes out of the shadows, and providing political facilitation for models—when put into play, evoke further efforts in the direction of reform from the cities and enterprises that benefit from them. The result is a still inchoate, but potentially developing set of new relationships among five key layers of the central-local economic hierarchy: center, province, city, bureau, and enterprise. But before one can ask to what extent this process is leading to the substitution of vertical chains by horizontal rings, it is necessary to take note of another trend, often in opposition to the reforming one. That one is also state-centered, as it seeks to place an overlay of state management atop the burgeoning business brought forth by the facilitation and encouragement described above.

As always, with liberalization in the economic realm in China, state control and management offices are springing up in tandem, in an effort to ensure that altered modes of transaction do not lead to economic instability, transgress state mores, or result in the shortchanging of prime state construction projects.

The two trends come together at times as well: there can be a thin line between promotion and prevention, when commissions composed to prod on the new relationships try to channel their initiatives, or when planning bureaucracies seek to compete with the new forms or to control the commodities and funds flowing through them. The effect of this is that a double image is emerging: there are flourishing free-wheeling ventures, not just protected but even urged on and coddled.[1] But those ventures play to an accompaniment of state-sponsored super-vision.

This is not to say that reform is being seriously stymied. In fact, many changes have occurred or are occurring right within the state-run bureaucratic economy. But to a large extent they must be understood not as the birth of purely free markets in China, but, on the positive side, within a context of adaptation and remolding within the bureaucracy and against a backdrop of specific politi-cal support; and on the negative side, at times against a countervailing regimen of restraints.

More concretely, at the lower echelons, the reform movement appears in a mixture of modes. Cities such as Wuhan have received some release from their provincial overseers, as have enterprises from their management departments (bureaus). But in finding their way in the new, unfamiliar "marketplace," in many cases firms and municipalities draw on the very supply sources and sales outlets that were once written into their plans, rather than seeking some reorien-tation according to new, supposedly economically rational principles of associa-tion.

Another form of this search for certainty and security is localism, whereby factories and stores pick exchange and investment partners close at hand. Simi-larly, "departmentalism" crops up in a new guise, as firms in the same area and trade choose to associate in what are mergers or even oligopolies to boost local economies and to rationalize the product structures of municipal or provincial trades for better competitive advantage.

The remainder of this chapter will first say something about Wuhan and its significance in the urban reform experiments. It will then review four of the most progressive types of urban reforms under way in Wuhan (many of them being pilot-tested there) from 1984–87 (the period during which Wuhan has had the status of a trial point for comprehensive urban reform). In doing so, it will assess the contribution of these reforms to an altered pattern of relationships among state, province, city, bureau, and firm.

These four reforms are Wuhan's designation in June 1984 as a separate line-item in the state plan (*jihua danlie*) and the concomitant decentralization (*xiafang*) of some fifty central and provincially managed enterprises to the city from Autumn 1984; the schemes to separate management from ownership of firms through such measures as bankruptcy, leasing, and manager responsibility systems; new investment sources—stocks, bonds, share systems, and short-term capital markets and networks; and new circulation methods that are to shift the vertical supply and sales channels in use before reform to ones based on lateral exchange. Also in this fourth category are enterprise groups, bidding for component parts, markets for the means of production, and trade centers. The conclusion will comment on the connection between market and plan and the functions and dysfunctions of continuity between systems in this transitional era.

Wuhan as a Pilot City for Reform

Wuhan was selected to pioneer an experiment in granting provincial capitals separate line-item status in the central plan in June 1984.[2] By then a year had already passed since Wuhan University Professor Li Chong-huai coined the phrase *liangtong* (the two *tongs*, *liutong* and *jiaotong*, or, in English, the two C's—circulation and communications) to serve as the focus for this city's reform.[3]

This slogan was meant to express the particular strengths of the city, which sits astride both the Yangtze River and the Guangzhou–Beijing Railway, almost equidistant from Chongqing, Shanghai, Guangzhou, and the national capital. Both historically and under the People's Republic it has had a place of special importance as a transport hub and a transshipment center. But its traditional role as the "thoroughfare of nine provinces" was to a large degree thwarted under the rule of vertical bureaucracies, with their planned, compulsorily conducted commerce and their transport coordinated by separate, enclosed, political authorities along administratively demarcated boundaries.[4]

The city's mission, once it was singled out as an experimental point for "comprehensive urban reform," was to use its new powers, supposedly equal to those of a province in economic affairs, to form the core of an economic region in central China. It could then go on to stimulate commodity production in all the surrounding hinterland and in nearby cities.[5] Moreover, it was hoped, with its new independent powers, Wuhan should be able to reenact its historical role as a center of foreign trade, finance, banking, and information, as it reinforced its newer, post-1949 position as a base of industry and of higher education and research.[6]

All in all, the purpose of the *jihua danlie* initiative was "to enhance Wuhan's economic position in the country and bring into more extensive play its role in establishing economic ties throughout the province and the nation."[7] In short, Wuhan's new powers would underline the overall national economic reform's dramatic shift in emphasis in the running of the Chinese economy, toward commerce and economically based, decentralized decision making.

Under Wu Guanzheng, mayor of the city from March 1983 until the fall of 1986, the city became noted for "opening wide the gates" of its three joined cities (Hankow, Wuchang, and Hanyang) to outside competition. Its progress even caught the attention—and the praise—of Premier Zhao Ziyang, who announced in 1984 that he had "placed his hopes in Wuhan," and came to see for himself in April 1985, when Wuhan was "marching at the head of the urban reform."[8]

Immediately upon gaining its new status for their city, municipal leaders set about organizing trade centers, forming a wholesale network, introducing bidding on a nationwide basis for parts in light industrial production (instead of relying solely on allocations from local factories), inviting peasants from the countryside and residents of other cities to open shops and manage factories, and relaxing price controls and rationing, all of this before most—and in the case of some of these measures before any—other cities in the country. Other steps were taken to improve transport management and to revive the financial sector.

Three years after that heady first taste of autonomy, Wuhan continued to stand in the forefront of the urban reforms, being picked, for instance, as one of the pilot cities for financial reform in early 1986[9] and as the site for one of seven national steel markets in the beginning of 1987. But to what extent have all of these reforms really led to a divorce of Wuhan from the vertical bonds that bound its business, and in what sense is this leading to the creation of a presumably more rational routing of economic relationships?

Four Kinds of Reforms

Jihua Danlie

Financial and Behavioral Outcomes. According to one Wuhan scholar, the *jihua danlie* reform must be viewed as an interlinked set of three component parts: getting separate standing in the state plan, obtaining economic powers equal to those of a province, and gaining control over the four dozen or so large industrial enterprises decentralized (*xiafang*) to city management in and after autumn 1984.[10] Not surprisingly, this measure has not rested easily with Hubei Province, which felt threatened by each dimension of these changes. Indeed, during the period surrounding the granting of this new status to Wuhan, it was clear from press material that there were tensions here between province and city.[11]

But we need to assess the concrete outcomes of the reform, both financially and behaviorally, in order to understand the extent to which and the manner in which this step has enabled Wuhan actually to gain new power. That is, we need to know whether Wuhan does in fact now have more autonomy, what sort of autonomy it is, and what are the costs and benefits such autonomy brings at this point. For the purpose of *jihua danlie* was to "make central cities step out of the small world created by administrative demarcations,"[12] and, particularly in the case of Wuhan, to give that city "fuller scope to play its role as a major city."[13]

First of all, it seems that the reforms have not really done all that much to give Wuhan the capital base it needs for larger-scale change.[14] Despite a shift in the direction of the flow of funds between Wuhan and Hubei beginning in 1985, the amounts of monies going between these two levels and the central government has really changed very little. Though Wuhan can now retain about 20 percent of its local revenue, which is a figure a little higher than before, this retention rate is the lowest of all the cities that now have provincial status in the state plan.[15]

Moreover, the center now subsidizes Hubei for the approximately 100 million yuan it lost as a result of the *xiafang*, while Wuhan now gives the center about 100 million yuan more than Hubei used to give to the center, when it was Hubei that benefited from the profit and tax collection coming from the enterprises now *xiafang*ed. It seems that financially the principal advantage to Wuhan is that, since its fixed ratio for retention is now a little higher than before, and since it is now the collection point for the revenue from the decentralized factories, its incentives have increased. And correspondingly, Hubei's loss is more in this gray area of potential reward for enhanced activity.

The argument those in the city made, both on the eve of reform[16] and in the midst of its implementation[17] was that, as the city's economy becomes stimulated, this will go on to invigorate the entire provincial economy. This could happen, local proponents held, given Wuhan's superior transport and commercial advantages and the possibilities for these systems to set a chain reaction in motion.

Still, it appears, Hubei feels cheated by the reform. Consequently, the always ambivalent relationship between the province and its premier city—one marked from the start by paternalistic protection but also by pressures on Wuhan—has now become even more complicated. Most blatantly, as recently as early 1987, Hubei withheld resources over which it still has control from Wuhan enterprises, acting on the premise that the province no longer stood to gain from their successes.

The items involved were cotton, the great bulk of which (95 percent according to a spokesman at the No. 1 Textile Mill in Wuhan) is still directly allocated by the plan, and electricity, allegedly now under the control of a newly organized Central China Electricity Network. With the creation of this network, Wuhan's electrical power should in theory come from that organ's administrators directly. But, according to a local economist, "Whether we can realize this change depends on the relations between Hubei and the Network."[18] The interesting point here is that Hubei's power is evidently still so much greater than Wuhan's own that if Hubei's *guanxi* (personal relations) with the Network's management is good enough, and if it chooses to apply pressure, it could work to override Wuhan's rights under a new allocation system specifically designed to ensure Wuhan's allotment.

The opening of all sorts of new circulation channels with the reforms means that Wuhan can now go outside the province for the materials withheld by Hubei, but at a cost: cotton obtained further away, for instance, means higher transport charges. And true, steel, petroleum products, and home appliances from Wuhan can be bartered. But that puts a drain on these valuable local barter chips that the city could otherwise be using for items the center never allocated to it in the first place.

And one final area where Hubei still can hold sway is industrial deployment. It seems that Hubei is resisting placing new firms in Wuhan, and that arguments over this occurred in Beijing in the first half of 1987. Though feasibility studies could presumably settle the issue, personal factors can influence such studies, just as they affect every other aspect of economic life in China.[19]

As for the nature of working relations that now obtain between the two echelons, there appears to be some confusion as well. According to the tenets of the *jihua danlie* arrangement, Hubei no longer has an economic, but only an administrative connection with Wuhan in hierarchical terms. Economically, the two get together simply on a business (*jingying*) basis, but not as superior and subordinate. That is, since investment is no longer allocated through the province for Wuhan, but comes directly from Beijing, Hubei's formal means of exercising financial control over the city have terminated. But administrative powers still in Hubei's hands include the crucial one of personnel control, and, as one now highly prominent city factory manager admitted, "Economic and administrative affairs are hard to separate."[20]

Indeed, though Hubei now no longer approves the projects Wuhan undertakes, and though the city does not report on its activities to the province anymore, the expectation that Hubei will provide support of various sorts continues to obtain. There are still occasions on which Hubei's offices provide suggestions, market information, and even grain, nonstaple crops, and raw materials, and offer help in dealing with such matters as the disposition of economic criminals.[21]

The fuzziness of the relationship came through in a discussion with a man from the Financial Research Institute of the People's Bank's local branch office on June 24, 1987. At different moments in the space of one interview he agreed that the province supports an eight-city intraprovincial financial network centered on Wuhan, still exercising a lot of "leadership" over it, but then later explaining that capital outside the state plan is not under Hubei's control, and that, since such capital is what is used in the short-term capital markets in this network, Hubei has no power over it.

Taking together all of these factors—the continuing capital shortage, the persistent control by Hubei over some really crucial resources, and the combination of support and control that the province still extends over the city—it is fair to conclude that Wuhan is not yet a truly autonomous center of economic activity.

Decentralized Enterprises. Probably the most significant dimension of *jihua danlie* should be the decentralization of enterprises from provincial to city management that began in the fall of 1984. About fifty firms fell into this category. The motive behind the *xiafang* was to enable cities to unify the management and organization of the production and circulation activities occurring within their borders, and ultimately to permit urban centers to encourage more specialization among their firms.[22]

The process of decentralizing has not proved easy. One source held that, as of late June 1987, not all of the firms had been decentralized yet;[23] a city economist revealed that the *xiafang* was not a thorough one in all cases;[24] and cadres at the Wuhan Heavy Machinery Plant (Wuzhong) explained on June 29, 1987 how the process in their plant, begun in January 1985, was not completed until August 1986. The sticking point, apparently, involved settling the division of finances between levels.

Interestingly, the three *xiafang* firms that I was able to visit each exhibited a different pattern of decentralization in their management and thus a different relationship to the city. One (Wuzhong) chose to remain within its old, tried planned relationship; one (the Wuhan Steam Turbine & Generator Plant) is branching out, so its manager says, entirely on its own, to become the head of several "socialist trusts," one nationwide (the Yangtze Energy Corporation) and one within the Central China Region; and one (the Wuhan Iron and Steel Works, Wugang) is too huge for Wuhan to administer, but is now more available for forging the sort of barter relationships with city firms that once took place on a more ad hoc basis but which have now become formalized.

In the case of Wuzhong, the plant attended a meeting at the Ministry of Machine-Building in Beijing in 1985 at which it was given a choice: thenceforth, it could depend upon the ministry, the province, or the city to procure for it the raw materials that constituted its base, guaranteed amount under the state plan. Because of the greater certainty of supplies coming from the center, the firm picked the Ministry of Metallurgy, whose office in Wuhan (which has no connection with the city government or its local Machine-Building Bureau) thereafter sent the plant its allocation. In this case, thus, the only real difference from before in its *source* of supplies was that the plant ended up drawing them from the center through its own choice, and not as the result of a compulsory plan.[25]

The original Wuhan Steam Turbine & Generator Plant had expanded itself into a trust called the Yangtze Energy Corporation by the time of my visit, as well as creating several smaller such groups.[26] This company, established in January 1986 after the *xiafang,* had recruited member firms nationwide on a competitive basis, to a total of fifty-nine by the time I arrived. The corporation had factories responsible for every phase of production, from design to installations.

For this as well as his other trusts, Manager Yu Zhi'an claimed there had been neither economic help nor interference from either Hubei or Wuhan. However, he did admit to a vague "support" from top city government officials, and in China political facilitation can go a long way. As a Wuda professor put it, "In China political support is economic support."[27] Nonetheless, the upshot is that the city has not really enhanced its management powers over this firm and its activities.

Of the three, it was only in the case of Wugang that the city truly changed its situation with regard to one of these decentralized plants. Of course, everyone queried quickly commented, Wugang was far too massive for the city to handle. As the City Planning Commission's officials explained, the province couldn't manage it, and so Wuhan can't either. For only the center is competent to dispose of its sales and guarantee its material supplies.[28]

But an exchange has been arranged between the city and the plant, by which Wuhan agreed to provide services to the firm's employees, such as in housing, schools, and shops. In return, the plant ensures the city of 1 percent of its output, which is sold to the city at state prices. In addition, Wugang has formed a merger with a number of small city steel factories that had been operating at a loss. According to this deal, these small plants process parts for Wugang, and the plants can count on a guaranteed source of steel.[29]

In forming this merger with twenty-one plants manufacturing such items as rolled steel, steel sheets, strip steel, coke and refractory materials, Wugang took over the direct control and unified management of these firms, which previously belonged to a city metallurgy company and a local mining area. In this way, Wugang was at once able to expand its own capacity, help out small factories that lacked raw materials and the funding to modernize themselves, and solve a portion of the city's deficit-enterprise problem. In this one instance specialized production did result from the *xiafang* even though Wugang remained essentially under ministry management.[30] Such exchanges as Wugang's occurred in the past in Wuhan. Notably, in recent times, during the readjustment period of 1979–82 local heavy machine-building plants were desperately short of supplies and bartered such products as valves for Wugang's steel.[31] But unlike the valve deal, which had been more covert, this new one was approved by the city's Party Committee and the urban government.[32] So in this case too what seems to be innovation when it goes under the name of "reform" is actually an adaptation and formalization of a type of relationship that grew up first outside of official channels in a previous period.

Overall, then, *jihua danlie* and the accompanying *xiafang* of local enterprises present a complicated picture. Though there is some financial return to the city, it falls far short of providing for the sort of major transport and communications construction the city desperately needs in order really to realize its autonomy.[33] And then on some occasions it seems that all this has only aggravated Wuhan's relations with Hubei. Perhaps at such times the city finds that the old superior/subordinate bond may in some ways have been a more convenient one than today's more purely business ties. The degree of ambivalence local people feel toward the changes was evident in one remark made to me by a local economist in particular: "*jihua danlie* has good points . . . you can't say that it is without any good points at all."

And certainly the enterprise decentralization remains a long way from the point where Wuhan can truly organize the enterprises within its borders for purposes of its own. Looking just at my material on this one theme, Wuhan's powers still remain circumscribed, if in different ways from in the past. Thus, all in all, there is at best only an incipient basis for the city to form the core of a regional economy building on the enterprises newly supposedly under its jurisdiction.

Enterprise Autonomy: Bankruptcy, Leasing,
Manager Responsibility Systems, and the Bureaus

The much publicized movement to give enterprises power over their own productive processes and responsibility for their profits and losses—as the Chinese put it, to separate ownership power from management power—finds its expression in an extremely limited experiment with bankruptcy, a larger-scale program of leasing small state-owned firms (mostly in the commercial system) to their staff and workers, and an array of factory and store manager responsibility systems.

Often it turns out that in the model cases where these reforms are going on, old arrangements are being recast so that management and workers get new incentives, while the essential relationships between firm and bureau have not been grossly altered. Success seems dependent on political facilitation for these firms in particular, where management bureaus seem to have been explicitly forbidden from intervening, even though such intervention is still rife in ordinary, non-trial-point enterprises.[34]

Bankruptcy. The bankruptcy experiment is at this stage still nothing more than a demonstration, and apparently is heavily laden with political elements. As of early 1987, only eleven state- and collectively owned firms in four test cities (Wuhan, Chongqing, Shenyang, and Taiyuan) had been targeted nationwide for trying out this system and given yellow warning cards indicating imminent bankruptcy. Of these, only one, in Shenyang, actually went under in August 1986. These firms were warned that unless they reduced losses within one year, they would be declared bankrupt.[35]

But the draft law passed by the National People's Congress Standing Committee in December 1986 shows the heavy role still reserved for the failing firm's management bureau. For it is the bureau that makes the application for bankruptcy; whose agreement the creditor must secure before it can appeal its claims; which has three months to find a way to straighten up management (*zhengdun*) within the firm and two years to carry out this adjustment; and whose personnel are subject to administrative penalty should the enterprise fail.[36]

In Wuhan, the No. 3 Radio Factory was the first to recover of the three ailing factories in the city picked for liquidation if they did not reduce their debts within a year. Press material gave the credit for its revival to a change to new management, plus heightened effort by the workers in response to the threat of closing down.[37]

But when an official from the city planning commission was pressed in an interview on June 23, 1987, he agreed that any manager requires support, help, and cooperation in order to make a turnaround, and that can only come from bureau leadership in the form of capital, loans, and raw materials. So at this early stage, enterprises are selected to "go bankrupt," and it seems that whether they in fact do so is still a matter of political choice.[38]

But there are a number of other options from which political decision makers and local firms can draw to deal with the pervasive problem of deficit.[39] One of these other possibilities for a failing firm is to form a merger with a large, successful plant, such as in the case of Wugang's arrangement with the twenty-one little local factories noted above.

Another, smaller-scale version of this was reported in the city paper in June 1987: a state-owned towel factory signed a one-year lease contract with a street-managed thread enterprise which was losing so much money that no wages had been paid for three months prior to the takeover. Management powers went to the towel factory, while the thread firm paid it monthly rental fees.[40]

This public, formalized union is apparently being copied spontaneously in other firms. For instance, I witnessed this happening just by chance in the midst of one of my interviews, on June 25, 1987, at a national model factory. A staff member interrupted to inform the manager with whom I was speaking that a nearby firm under the same industrial bureau, about to go bankrupt, had come to appeal to be bought out. These other solutions indicate the flexibility and innovation now present in the system, but also serve to underline the disinclination to allow bankruptcy to become a reality.

Leasing and Manager Responsibility Systems. Leasing, which requires official sanction, is yet another possibility.[41] By mid-1987, over 10,000 small-scale industrial and commercial enterprises had been leased nationwide;[42] in Wuhan, 120 small-scale state-owned industrial firms were leased by summer 1987, constituting half of the total number of such firms in the city, while more than 300 (about 44 percent of the total) of the commercial enterprises in the city were leased, including both state- and collectively owned ones.[43]

This reform entails the lessees—usually the manager and a group of top staff personnel—putting down personal property or cash as collateral and losing it or getting it back plus a bonus depending on how well the contract (which stipulates a profit target) is fulfilled. Alternatively, staff and workers' wages can be supplemented by bonuses or diminished in accord with the amount by which the firm fails to meet its target.[44]

Though the staff and workers who lease their firms do obtain the right to operate state property according to decisions they freely make, they are enjoined from dismissing the original workers "at will." Besides, these firms in the final instance remain under the charge of their old administrative departments.[45] Telling is a report from a forum on invigorating small state enterprises in Wuhan held in late April 1987. It notes that in some, "administrative interference still exists; . . . we need to 'open the bird cage and release the sparrow.' "[46]

In distinction from these solutions for failing firms, the new manager responsibility systems[47] tend to be placed in larger enterprises and stores and in ones where the management has been successful.[48] Where management may be switched in bankrupt-prone plants, this probably will not happen in these firms. Even where elaborate bidding and examination schemes were installed to select new leadership, the previous assistant party secretary of a large department store can emerge as the new manager from a competition of over forty applicants.[49] This system is also distinguished from leasing in that enterprise income, not mortgaged personal property (as in leasing) is forfeited when there is loss.[50]

In most cases, the contract—whether for leasing or for manager responsibility—is meant to replace the old state plan for the firm.[51] Though it holds for three to five years, not one as the plan did, its specifications are some of the same targets as those that were once the contents of the firm's plan. These include profit, gross value of output, quality, and growth of fixed assets, or sales volume, in the case of stores. These contracts are signed by the firm and its management bureau, which acts as the representative of the owner (the state), after the bureau has formulated the contract with the city economic commission, the bank, and the tax and finance bureaus.[52]

True, there are fewer overall stipulations than the plan had, and there is more leeway on some matters—such as in new product development, finding supply sources, and choosing sales outlets. But one informant made the interesting point that his plant's four-year contract actually firmed up and stabilized its old production targets, which used to shift a lot even within the space of a year, and thus used to lead to confusion.[53] And another admitted that the city's Finance Bureau supervises the contract's implementation on a monthly basis to make sure the factory is operating within the scope of state regulations.[54] Moreover, another factory's personnel hinted at disagreements with its bureau over the selection of new product development, even though this power now belongs to the firm, decisions in this sphere not having been written into the contract. But in this case the interviewees maintained that in such cases of dispute the bureau usually lets the firm do what it wants.[55] Often enough, though, according to the press, as of summer 1987 departments in charge of enterprises were "still focusing on requiring enterprises to fulfill the main economic targets," despite the institution of contracts.[56]

If they do not interfere as much as before in these now contracted-out firms, the bureaus can still ensure that their firms do well, thereby facilitating the success of these experiments. For despite the manager's new responsibilities under these contracts, it seems that the firms go on resting rather heavily on market information supplied them by the bureaus, which have access to far wider networks than does the typical enterprise itself. And depending upon the principal raw materials that the firm requires, the bureau can continue to be a crucial supplier.[57]

But where no special experiment is under way, the bureau has definite incentives to continue to intervene. For, in the first place, the statistical system has not kept up with the management reforms, so that the bureau is still held responsible for the enterprises' financial achievements. Each year it must report to the city government on the taxes and profits all of its firms have earned. In addition, the bureaus remain dependent for some of their expenses on the management fees (*guanli fei*) the firms yet must pay them. This important source of their funding reinforces the tie of interest between the bureau and the enterprise's success. Until these bonds are broken, the new reforms can only hope to bear fruit at selected, showcase sites.[58]

In sum, the reforms in enterprise autonomy, while certainly a step toward cutting the controls the administrative system has historically clamped on the firms, cannot succeed on a large scale at the present. This is not to say that there has been no reform, nor that there cannot be more of it. Its strengths so far lie in using but loosening old arrangements—in this case the state plan—for new ends, as contracts with fewer but some of the same, stipulations now guide enterprise behavior.

In addition, those who produce the plant's economic results in the trial firms—*if* their bureaus let it happen—will have to suffer financially if their firm does, but may benefit as it thrives. This "if," however, is central to the scheme at this phase in which political support is being used to demonstrate possibilities. Where there are those possibilities, as will be seen below, exchanges are taking place that supersede the old administrative arrangements and the territorial boundaries within which they were confined.

New Investment Sources: Shares, Stocks, Bonds; Capital Markets and Networks

The creation of new sources of investment in the last few years, to supplement if not to supplant the prereform planned pooling of funds through banks and financial departments, is crucial for invigorating enterprises. In Wuhan, the problem of capital was considered an outstanding issue in economic construction in late 1985. Causes lay in a slowdown in the circulation of capital because of the readjustment of the early 1980s that suspended, merged, or converted many firms; in backward technology and outdated equipment; and in a batch of new enterprises desperately awaiting funds before they could develop their productive potential.

It was estimated that as of 1985 some 300 million yuan was needed in the city for the renovation of fixed assets, while another 230 million was required for technical transformation. But, according to one source, only a portion of all this was then available through the usual channels. Meanwhile, rising income in enterprises, other units, and among the working population in both city and countryside was leading to an accumulation of idle funds that had no outlet other than the purchase of consumer goods.[59]

To deal with this problem, a nationwide one, new forms of fund-raising have been endorsed and are under experimentation. These include raising funds by issuing shares (usually by selling stock in a firm to its own staff and workers), bonds issued by banks, and, most recently, opening stock markets in a few trial-point cities. Other methods are through joint operations, as when enterprises invest in each other, or when they exchange scarce raw materials or products for capital from the other party.[60]

Yet one more channel is the short-term interbank lending beginning since 1986 that constitutes the first step in the formation of capital markets. That program was launched in five cities including Wuhan and then was extended to others. By early 1987 interbank loans amounted to 30 billion yuan nationally.[61] The other four initial cities were Shenyang, Changzhou, Chongqing, and Guangzhou.

Here is a type of reform that really has no precedent in the old system. But it is one which, though proceeding haltingly, is still stymied to some extent by the *tiaotiao* (roughly, vertical lines of authority) of the bureaucratically organized banking of the old administrative system. Too, its operations scope at this point is still largely quite localized. To play their intended role, capital markets must eventually really cut across city and provincial borders, and be open to economic and not just administrative regulation.

Shares, Stocks, Bonds. In Wuhan, a city Financial Trust Company *(Jinrong Xintuo Gongsi),* set up in 1981, constituted the spearhead for reforms in the financial sector. Its job from its initiation was to raise funds for local economic construction. This it does by acting as a broker for companies and factories in the city. Its list of subscribers includes academic and research institutions, factories, organizations, and even individuals.[62] But mainly it brings together capital-short firms with others that have idle funds they can use to subscribe shares in the former. It also helps to direct such funds into urban construction projects, public facilities, and public transport.

By the end of 1984, the company had raised 101,600,000 yuan mainly by issuing shares, and had granted 66,980,000 in loans. And in 1985, savings in the city increased by more than 400 million yuan over the year before. In that year the city organized enterprises to issue stocks and bonds to the general population and to staff and workers in the enterprises, collecting over 100 million yuan by doing so.[63] As of mid-1987, only four enterprises were directly issuing their own shares, while nearly 1,000 firms were issuing bonds. At that point, "society" held 400 million yuan worth of bonds and shares, with the overwhelming majority of bondholders being firms and individuals resident in the city.[64]

As early as 1985 problems had already surfaced in Wuhan's money market. Illustrative of these were cases of firms using dividends as disguised bonuses, thus evading taxes on the bonuses; seeking funding without first doing feasibility studies, with the result that very few people bought the shares put up for sale; collecting funds that never got used; only soliciting funds for investment, but neglecting to consider production costs; and setting the dividends too high. As of autumn of that year, Wuhan had already established a management group to control the issuance of these shares.[65]

In spring 1987, in the midst of a period of nationwide retrenchment of economic reform, the State Council published regulations to control the sale of bonds by enterprises.[66] The purpose was to try to ensure that the collection of funds would serve state goals and guarantee the construction of key state projects.

The ruling placed the People's Bank in charge of issuing all enterprise bonds. And thenceforth any effort to raise funds for investment in fixed assets would require approval by departments concerned and incorporation into the funds under state control explicitly set aside for this purpose. Moreover, state-owned firms were enjoined against selling shares, and collective firms could only issue shares among themselves but could not sell shares to the public. Criticisms of extortion and of blind construction accompanied this call for strict supervision.[67]

Wuhan took advantage of the continued permission to offer bonds even if under strict bank control in late May 1987. At that time the Hankow Branch of the People's Bank put up for sale bonds with a time limit of one year at a 9 percent interest rate.[68] Then, at the end of June, Wuhan became the third city in the country to open what it is calling a "stock market," after Shenyang in August 1986 and Shanghai in September 1986.[69]

The Wuhan Trust Investment Company under the Industrial and Commercial Bank was given the task of managing this market.[70] By then the city had issued various kinds of long-term bonds, stocks, and a large amount of certificates of deposit, including various large and middle-sized enterprises' stocks and bonds, altogether reaching a value of more than 800 million yuan.[71]

But the continuing controls, both administrative and economic, that the People's Bank still exercises over its specialized component[72] limit the new stock market's ability to function as a genuine site of exchange.[73] And, oddly for a stock market, local observers admit it does not promise soon to be a place where the actual transferal of stocks will occur. Moreover, the paucity of capital in the city seems likely for the present to confine the activity there to local buyers and sellers. As a local economist told me on July 1, 1987, "If you don't have any real strength, it won't do to go outside [the city]."

Two other forms of funding are coming into wider use in recent years, and these also aim to break out of the restrictions imposed by the old system of administrative hierarchy. One of these is illustrated by the Wuhan Bazaar Share Group's investment in the Yangtze Aluminum Products Factory's pressure cookers. According to the agreement, the factory will give the store 100,000 cookers over a three-year period at a preferential price, regardless of demand. In exchange, the store has invested two million yuan in the factory as a kind of interest-free loan.[74] As in other instances, political facilitation sparked this reform. The city made this store (the Wuhan Bazaar) a keypoint for reform, when it extended permission to it to draw up the share group, the only one of its type in Wuhan. Set up in late 1986, the group, which offers a 15 percent dividend on shares (i.e., twice the rate of bank interest) had already collected 10 million yuan in shares by mid-1987, all drawn from partners picked by the store.

Its seven investors include Wugang, an insurance company, and the local branches of the People's Bank and the Agricultural Bank. Since the risk was smaller with local partners whose business acumen was known to the store, and in the interest of developing the local economy and thereby boosting purchasing power there, the store intentionally invited only units from Wuhan to join.

And the last type of nonadministrative funding is foreign exchange, the dispersal of which, however, in most cases still is tightly controlled by the People's Bank and secondarily by the management bureaus of the firms. In the tiny handful of privileged experimental reform firms, though, as I was told in an interview at Wuhan's No. 2 Bicycle Factory on June 25, 1987, managers get full authority over their own imports of foreign technology in return for having successfully exported.

Offering stocks, shares, and bonds is a valuable means for reorienting the structure of funding in Chinese enterprises. To some extent these practices are already under way. But many elements of the old system continue to keep the scale of such business small and the scope localized. These elements include capital deficiencies at the urban level; the state's concern to supervise the use to which funds are put; ongoing management by the People's Bank and its branches; and the tendency of even experimental units given freedom to pick partners to stay within the confines of the local economy. Here, then, we see that even political facilitation does not yet necessarily override the persistent presence of features and organs from the previous era.

Capital Markets and Networks. Wuhan historically had played the role of financial center in the middle Yangtze region. At one time Hankow boasted some 230 traditional and modern banks, and was one of the nation's three large capital markets. Its interest rate, foreign exchange rate, and gold and silver prices influenced the neighboring districts.[75] And its geographic position, convenient transportation and developed communications, scale of commercial exchange, and economic strength in industrial growth all make it a favorable site for the development of a financial center again in this period of reform.[76]

Indeed, in commercial credit, regional banking, and short-term interbank loans the results are promising, according to a local economist.[77] And by the end of 1986, nearly eight billion yuan had been traded in four different capital market networks and four special capital markets, all centered on Wuhan.[78]

In April 1987 a fifth short-term capital network based in Wuhan formed.[79] This fifth one comprises fifty-five cities that form a "financial cross" in the Yangtze Valley and along the Beijing–Guangzhou Railway, and the Construction Bank acts as its agent. Its particular mission is to collect loans to support national keypoint construction.

The first of these five networks to be established was one of seven cities within Hubei Province; the second involves eleven cities (the first seven *jihua danlie* cities, plus Shenzhen, Zhuhai, Changzhou, and Haikou); the third is of twenty-seven cities along the Yangtze, including Shanghai, Nanjing, and Chongqing; and the fourth has thirty-three central-south cities that are not along the Yangtze, and is managed by the Industrial and Commercial Bank.[80] These networks offer loans usually about a half year in duration, to be used for circulating capital rather than for fixed asset purchases. They also provide for the exchange of economic information.

Although the cities in the eleven-member network have the most economic strength and are subject to the least administrative interference, in fact it is the web within Hubei that sees the most action. For there communications are easiest and exchange is frequent if not in large amounts. But, as noted above, the research official from the People's Bank who discussed these networks was ambivalent about the extent of Hubei's control over this market. This suggests that some administrative interference from the Hubei branch of the People's Bank is probably present, which would limit the market's ability to respond freely to economic forces.

This inference derives support from the comments of a local economist that Wuhan cannot really be counted yet as a financial center in the true sense of the term. For, he pointed out, the banks located and doing business there are not yet enterprises, and so, as the bank's researcher admitted, they lack the necessary independence for economically based decision making. And in the same light, the participants in the various capital networks are branches of the People's Bank and of the specialized banks linked to it, all of which must answer to their administrative superiors in the banking bureaucracy.[81]

New Circulation Methods

Lateral Exchange. Lateral exchange (*hengxiang lianxi*) is the name for the new, supposedly economically based transactions developing in China since the reforms began. Its purpose, just as with all the reforms, is better to connect supply sources with demand, and to demolish the blockades between districts imposed by the plan and its administratively structured marketing. In the urban environment in particular, the aim has been to create economic liaisons between enterprises and between regions centered on cities as the financial and economic management powers of cities grew.[82]

These new partnerships serve a myriad of disparate functions, depending on the specific needs of the firms that form them.[83] Some enterprises join them to gain a guaranteed source of supplies and parts. Thus, Wuzhong obtains a fixed supply of iron from a Hunan factory; the Wuhan No. 3 Printing and Dyeing Factory gets some of its cotton from such cooperative arrangements. The Wuhan General Machinery Factory and the Wuhan No. 2 Bike Factory both placed themselves at the center of "enterprise groups" (*qiye jituan*)[84] that ensure each of them needed parts: the former gained expanded capacity by pulling together failing firms under its own aegis; the latter, after bidding, formed a liaison with the nation's premier bike firms in Shanghai which send it components.

Others draw on these deals for locating work or making sales. The Wuhan Chemical Machinery Factory, which mainly is in the business of processing steel, uses these unions for finding jobs. Another similar case is Wuzhong, which is linked to a company that sends it equipment to repair. And the No. 2 Bike Factory has an arrangement with commercial bureaus in several major cities that in essence give it three-year interest-free loans in exchange for a shipment of bicycles. Both sides profit, since the plan's old intervening wholesaling companies are cut out of the picture.

The Yangtze Energy Corporation has formed several enterprise groups, as noted above. These "socialist trusts," as their manager calls them, pool investment funds from their members which are donated to the central firm in the group in exchange for equipment, electrical power, and activities such as building a reservoir. And a union made up of the wool-producing firms of Wuhan constituted itself as a company. These textile plants hope to enhance specialization and improve their organizational structure and to allocate more rationally capital and raw materials within the local trade.[85]

In the course of implementing this reform over the past several years, to what extent and in what ways has the initial intention taken shape? That is, has free exchange arranged according to comparative advantage really begun to replace the plan? Or are prohibitive obstructions from administrative organs stopping it up? Or is there yet another way to understand what is occurring?

Available statistics do not provide a clear answer. In early 1985 Xinhua reported that 20,000 interprovincial economic and technical cooperation contracts had been signed in 1984, an amount that was two times the figure in 1983.[86] And by the end of 1986, over 32,000 integrated organizations with lateral economic ties had formed into twenty-four lateral economic liaison networks.[87] But this gives us no idea as to the nature of these unions. Nor does it indicate the degree to which combinations form within provinces and more local areas—thus, continuing to respect the old administrative boundaries—as opposed to those of a cross-provincial nature. Wuhan, for example, reported in

1985 that enterprises there had built up 517 economic associations and cooperative organs with its suburban counties and had signed over 300 cooperation projects with more than 20 counties and cities of Hubei—but without telling how many ties it had established outside the area.[88]

Yet another source states that in 1986, 1,140 enterprises in the city engaged in such cooperation (there termed *lianhe xiezuo*, or united cooperation), with a total of 2,593 firms and units in twenty-eight provinces and municipalities signing 3,324 cooperative projects involving 251 million yuan, but this time without saying the number of local projects in that year.[89] While these figures give the impression that the bulk of these exchanges are national in scope, qualitative data from interviews with Wuhan firms, governmental departments, and economists would suggest the opposite.

But is this because of resistance from administrative units? In many cases it is. A Wuhan University economics professor, Wu Xinmu, explained in an interview on June 29, 1987, that in the last few years these exchanges have developed quickly, and pointed out that both academic economists and governmental bureaucracies agree on the policy. But, he also noted, the State Planning Commission wants to put some 500 of the largest enterprise groups under its own control, and a lot of the unions of all sizes are suffering from administrative interference. The press seconds his views, as in this example: "If state planning departments can grasp about 100 very large industrial groups, that will help in promoting the organic combination of plan and market."[90] And the press from the outset has been bemoaning the "conflicts" that "always arise between planning and cooperation." One analysis among many that are similar explains how cooperative undertakings, not provided for in the state plans, are eschewed by many units, since the fruits of their investment will not accrue to their mandatory target fulfillment.[91]

There are also many stories of horizontal (as opposed to vertical, administratively arranged) contacts being forbidden by management departments (bureaus) who resist the outflow of funds and raw materials under their control and the transfer of key technology that might cause them to lose their competitive edge.[92] In Wuhan by 1984, thirty-five enterprises were already reported to be getting their spare parts through bidding. But when the scheme was just beginning in 1982, some former parts suppliers of the washing machine company involved tried to prevent the switch.[93]

But there are also cases where political facilitation and the plan's bonds themselves are permitting the exchanges to go forward. In such cases the bureaucracy is no impediment but is in fact promoter and expediter, if not always intentionally. Where the promotion is purposive, it may take the form of assistance from top local party and government officials who are creating showcase models.

Thus, the manager of the Yangtze Energy Corporation, for instance, claimed to have no interference in his activities, and no economic support from the state, as mentioned earlier. But, being the party secretary of a major, once centrally managed state enterprise, his personal connections with the mayor and the city's party secretary are strong enough that the "interest" he admitted that they have shown in his firm must have translated into having his way smoothed in the face of any opposition. Similarly, the No. 2 Bicycle Factory, a national model in bidding for parts, was selected for this project by the city Economic Commission; the decision to carry it out was announced (i.e., at least endorsed, probably backed) by the still-powerful ex-Mayor Li Zhi.

On a more explicit level, the city has set up two crucial committees to further exchanges of which it approves. One is an Economic Levers Adjustment Committee (*jingji ganggan tiaojiehui*), composed of representatives from the city's tax and finance bureaus, the People's Bank, and the Price Commission. This unit is empowered to give favorable treatment in pricing, taxes, and bank loans. For example, it ensures that there will be no income tax on the parts supplied by the minor partners of the enterprise groups, which become workshops of the larger firm. That larger firm alone pays a value-added tax.[94]

The second, equally significant body is the Wuhan Economic and Technology Cooperation Committee, set up in June 1985.[95] This organ is designed specially to promote lateral exchange and to help solve any problems that may arise in the process. When feasible, it encourages firms in the same trade to combine, brings them together to negotiate over terms, and supplies them with relevant market information once their union is achieved.[96]

But the existence of these committees has a double edge, sometimes supportive but also at times restrictive. They clearly entail a state-sponsored effort to keep a grip on the growing trade. For instance, the primary job of the second organ is to make out a program (*guihua*) for the projects city enterprises join and for the surrounding region. Moreover, it reports to Hubei Province, where a similar committee presides over exchanges at that level, and Hubei maintains a relationship of business leadership (*yewu lingdao guanxi*) over the city in this regard.[97]

Especially interesting is the background of the thirty-some personnel who staff this committee. All of them previously worked in the area of materials exchange, and so are quite familiar with the situations and products of the enterprises in the city. Some were employees of the Materials Supply Bureau in the past; others were agents delegated by the city government (planning or economic commissions, or the city government's office) to get market information to supplement planned supplies. Yan Qingfu, now the head of the committee, had been deputy secretary general of the city government before the formation of this body.[98] Here then people and bureaucracies held over from the past are in a position to facilitate at least as much as to obstruct reform.

The Materials Supply Bureau also aids firms in need of raw materials whose planned allocation was cut drastically with the advent of "guidance planning." One beneficiary is the Wuhan Chemical Machinery Plant, which now receives less than 10 percent of the steel it needs from the state plan.[99]

Similarly, Wuzhong's extra-plan activity depends on a company directly derived from the former Second Ministry of Machine-Building, now entitled the Chinese Machine Tools General Company. This body was established in 1982 as an economic, not an administrative entity. It manages the sales of its member firms, all of which are factories originally subordinate administratively to the Ministry.

Wuzhong also gets repair jobs as a result of its membership in the Wuhan Machine Tools Repair Associated Company, which is a subunit under the larger company. Its leading staff were all employed by the Second Machine-Building Ministry, so they know what equipment every factory, nationwide, has and what it might need in the way of repairs.[100]

Turning these administrative agencies into business firms helps to coopt them into the reform process. It is clear that they have been given crucial new responsibilities that virtually set much of the "market" activity in motion. In fact, the Materials Supply Department's personnel now receive an economic payoff, in the form of commissions, for doing so.[101] Some have been able to go even further, turning this new business mode to illicit advantage, rerouting materials that could be exchanged without their assistance and extorting "management fees" from the process.[102]

Information flows, still heavily dominated by state-run organs, are also expedited by those in the know from the past.[103] Here again the local Materials Supply Bureau plays a role, for its cadres have relationships with factory managers across the country, many of whom have been on the job for years.

But the most significant actors are the old factory purchasing agents (caigouyuan) who served their firms where the plan proved inadequate. All industrial enterprises have some half dozen to a dozen of such personnel. Each agent specializes in one to several materials about which they have built up a stock of knowledge over the years as to what can be obtained where. Most of these people are still in place.

They go to work by linking into the pervasive enterprise information networks (qiye xinxi wangluo) that stretch across China, of which there are two main types. The major net or da wang tells what can be found in particular cities; the little one, the xiao wang is more specific, pertaining to the materials held by individual factories. By continuing to communicate through these networks factories find much of what they ostensibly buy "on the market."

For department stores the story is not too different. Much of their stock comes from factories whose staff they met over the years at semi-annual national supply meets. These meets, which each present a particular type of commodity, were formerly run by the relevant wholesale station. Under the regime of the plan, factories, all of whose output was automatically purchased and allocated to the retailers, participated just to learn about the stores' demands; today they come to do business. The guanxi built up over years of attending the same meets stands the stores in good stead today.

Spokesmen from the Central-South Large Commercial Building, a sizable department store that opened in Wuchang in early 1985 (almost all of whose staff worked in one of Wuhan's two other big stores previously), estimated that as much as 40 percent of its supplying factories were known to their coworkers from the past. Though the remaining 60 percent of purchasing done with strangers may seem a lot, one might have expected the percent of old suppliers to be rather smaller, given the institution of several new forms of forging stocking relationships, such as through ads, or through becoming a sales outlet for the new industrial enterprise groups.[104]

In the lateral exchanges too, previous connections smooth the transition. Of the 18 units in the Wuhan Cement Machinery Complete-Set Company *(Jixie Chengtao Gongsi)* organized around the Wuhan General Machinery Factory, eleven are from Hubei Province and five more are from Wuhan. The other two, a design institute in Anhui and a factory in Jiangsu, were both units with which this machinery factory had business ties *(yewu guanxi)* from meetings, the "exchange of experience," and mutual visits under the plan.[105]

The Wuhan Bazaar's enterprise group invested 100,000 in a bicycle plant in Changzhou, one with which they had *laiwang* (dealings) in the prereform era, so they know their products are high quality.[106] And Wuzhong signed a contract with a Hunanese factory by which it invested three million yuan in exchange for a three-year supply of iron at the state-set price. Their supply relationship had a foundation in the days of the plan, where they had frequent comings and goings *(lailaiwangwang de guanxi)*. Those shared experiences before taught the plant that the Hunan firm's iron's quality met their specific demand.[107]

Perhaps the key point about all of these relationships is that the heavy hand of the plan still lingers over the world of exchange in China. As a Wuhan economist explained the situation, "In the past we were sealed up *(fengbi)*, so we managed work according to administrative relations. As a result, relations with Hubei and Wuhan are the main part of our present exchanges."

When asked what proportion of Wuhan's extra-plan exchange now is localized within Hubei Province, he replied that it was hard to say, given the large number of paths now open for establishing ties. But he made the only estimate he felt he could in saying that probably 30 percent of the goods produced in Wuhan were sold there, another 40 percent were sold in the province, and the remaining 30 percent traveled to destinations nationwide. Of those, he speculated that the majority of such outside destinations were still in the middle Yangtze region.[108] This material, added together, suggests the following: because of the adaptability of old organs, networks, and personnel, the distinction between plan and market is far less sharp than theorists might presume. For the same reason, although reform is often enough attended by bureaucratic recalcitrance, where bureaucracies can develop a new vested interest by capitalizing on old skills, they need not resist reform in every instance. But in this transitional era, when such adjustments ease a fair portion of the conversion of systems, the bulk of exchange will probably only gradually seep out of its wonted seines.

Materials Markets. As early as 1979, the state permitted firms to sell on the open market production machinery and raw materials left over after they had met their delivery quotas to the state. Soon a dual-price structure emerged—a state-set price for materials allocated by the plan and a sometimes far higher one for those exchanged privately "on the market"—accompanied by inflation and speculation. In July 1984 a State Council directive authorized special urban materials markets in part to try to curb these dysfunctions.[109]

Their purpose is to centralize and regulate the trade in scarce supplies, stabilize prices, promote the output of short-supply items, and urge investment goods out of the warehouses where firms had accumulated stockpiles purchased in a panic. At these markets the parties to the exchanges can negotiate over prices, but at least the presence of the markets brought some regularity to pricing. The centers offer business information, consulting, advertising, communications, food, and accommodations.[110]

But this trade occurs within what is still really a sellers' market. As one source put it,

> Now when motor vehicles and steel products are unusually tense, if the materials departments sponsor some trade centers, it's only going through the form of a "center," concentrating all that trade outside the plan into one place, to prevent speculation and stop up improprieties. Strictly speaking, this isn't what's originally meant by a trade center, [so] calling it a sales center is probably more appropriate.[111]

During the Sixth Five-Year Plan period, one source states that materials worth 223.9 billion yuan were bought on these markets. The traded materials included 99 million tons of steel, 837 million tons of coal, 100 million cubic meters of timber, and 137 million tons of cement. Collected statistics according to this source indicated that these represented one-half the country's total consumption volume.[112] A study published in *Economic Management* made a more conservative estimate, concluding that the amount of the means of production traded outside the plan in 1985 represented "not less than 30 percent" of the total amount of the means of production nationwide.[113]

In Wuhan in July 1984 trade centers and warehouses opened for such things as metals, construction materials, motor vehicles, timber, electrical products, and chemical and light industrial products, comprising 29 categories of over 2,000 kinds of means of production.[114] Nationwide, by early 1985 there were said to be 130 large trade centers across China buying and selling materials above the state quota.[115]

A study of the Wuhan materials markets judged that the amounts of various categories of goods supplied by the plan and the amounts traded on the markets in 1986 each represented about one half of the total.[116] More specifically, the City Planning Commission calculated in mid-1987 that the city requires about 400,000–500,000 tons of steel a year, and obtains about 130,000 tons from the plan's allocations. Enterprises then get the rest on their own. About 50 to 60 percent of the steel used in the city is purchased outside the plan, commissioners believe, and at least half of that goes through the official steel market set up in January 1987.[117]

Despite the liberalization implied by permitting surplus materials to be traded as commodities for the first time in three decades, by early 1987 the state acted to impose a tighter measure of control over this commerce. At this time, the government opened seven state-controlled markets for steel circulating outside the plan in major industrial centers—in Shanghai, Tianjin, Shenyang, Wuhan, Chongqing, Xi'an, and Shijiazhuang.[118]

An interesting footnote here is a small notice in the August 11, 1987, *People's Daily* announcing that Hubei opened a steel market of its own a few days before "to develop fully Hubei's steel superiority in central China." This would seem to be another instance of the province's continuing jealous oversight of the city.

These new markets came equipped with special incentives designed to draw all the steel that is outside the plan into their arena: enterprises using steel would be exempt from taxes on added value if they sold their products at these marts, and firms exchanging surplus products there for raw materials for use in state-approved projects could get their materials at government-set or negotiated prices.

At the same time, in Wuhan, the city began to run monthly "materials adjust-ment markets" (*wuze tiaoji shichang*) where all sorts of raw materials could be exchanged between enterprises at prices close to state-set ones. The city govern-ment adds materials from its stocks to keep prices stable there.[119] And the city also created a market for idle equipment and parts, where enterprises could mutually adjust their excesses and deficiencies.[120] In the case of all these various markets the very concept of trading means of production is innovation and reform, but it is qualified by state attempts to keep it within bounds.

Another theme these markets share with other elements of urban reform is the use of old bureaucracies for purposes of management. Wuhan's 1987 steel mar-ket is, in effect, under the supervision of the city's Materials Supply Bureau, increasing further the responsibilities of that bureau in the new reformed eco-nomic system.[121] For the Wuhan Metals Materials Company, under the bureau, is in direct charge of this trade. This company had existed in the past to handle supplies inside the plan, but this new role means it has now taken on an added function: it manages the materials outside the plan as well. The main difference from before, however, seems to be that the company only supplied Wuhan in the past, whereas it now draws steel from and offers steel to outside places too.

Trade Centers. More broadly, aside from the special markets set up to handle the means of production, wholesale centers for all sorts of commodities are also meant to be changing the pattern of Chinese commerce. As one analysis of their role described them: "An important economic means of smashing blockades is to establish circulation networks with extensive connections with cities as centers, ...

forming extensive sales networks in accordance with economic rationalization."[122]

At first, Wuhan proudly publicized its promotion of 90 different such centers.[123] But after expanding to a total of 102 in 1985, they were consolidated down to about 30 according to product.[124] The centers were presumably planned to rectify the ills of a rigidly bureaucratic commercial apparatus, which, in Wuhan in late 1984, was composed of some 68 different specialized companies.

These companies were said to lead to an artificial severing of commodity production's intrinsic horizontal linkages, and to create irrational flows and blockades, as each constituted its own separate system, limiting the city's function as an economic center. For the companies split the economy into departmental and local ownership systems.[125]

In contradistinction to wholesalers within that old system, these centers within the new one were to be open to everyone, private or public, and to goods from all parts of the country, using many forms of sales operations, allowing the producers and sellers to meet, and working with flexible prices. In short, it was to be a new circulation system, open in form, many-channeled, and with few links. The new centers, besides, are enterprises, not administrative units, and work according to market-made prices, not state commands.[126]

In fact, even though the centers do handle trade outside the plan, and are much more open as to participants and wares than the old system was, here again there is continuity.[127] For most of the centers are run by the old wholesale companies, with the self-same personnel. To quote a local analyst: "[With one exception] all the other trade centers are old wholesale departments (*pifabu*) with changed nameplates (*paidz*)."[128] Moreover, the centers are managed at the city level by the Commercial Administrative Commission, an organ formed in 1984 as a semi-independent company from the former First and Second Bureaus of Commerce and the city's Food Grains Bureau.

But their goods come from factories from many places, with only half or less (40 to 50 percent) of the varieties in them produced in Wuhan itself.[129] In the same vein, already in mid-1985, the *Beijing Review* reported that only 25.5 percent of the centers' clients came from Wuhan, another 21.2 percent were residents of other parts of Hubei, and as many as 53.4 percent were from various parts of China.[130]

While this report gives no clue as to where exactly the marketers hail from, a piece in the local press in April 1987 claimed that one third of the firms on Wuhan's famous small commodities market street, Hanzheng Street, come from outside, with most of them traveling from East China and the middle Yangtze.[131] Though this does not indicate that Wuhan has become the commercial center for a Central China region, it does suggest that its markets draw traders from a wide surrounding area.

All of these reforms aimed at reorienting the bureaucratic organization of business so that its stuff flows laterally instead of vertically, activated by prices rather than by power, share some common features. Most outstanding is the general principle behind much of this marketing: it often works where it does, because "the plan" and its patterns have prepared the way. That is, much of the marketing of today takes place through the adaptation of bureaucratic organs, the use of tried channels and ties, and the reliance on personnel with inside knowledge of the whereabouts of goods.

And added to this unintentional "help" from the old system, the force of the state is intentionally brought into play at times as well—first to facilitate the success of models, but also to control what are judged adverse consequences when marketers' success outsteps what politicians had in mind.

Conclusion

This study of Wuhan's comprehensive urban economic reform has covered a large array of topics: the *jihua danlie* measure of 1984, the decentralization of enterprises, leasing, bankruptcy, manager responsibility, stocks, bonds, and capital markets and networks, lateral exchange, and materials markets and trade centers.

If there is one dominant theme, it is this: the state plan is still present, more as a grid than as a governor. It is present not just in the sense usually pointed to—that the purveyors of its orders fight to retain their powers. Its existence is manifest in its old offices (even if they now hang out a new nameplate), in the habits it shaped, the patterns of association it fostered, and the *guanxi* developed between those who have lived by those habits and patterns. And so the plan—through that grid of relationships—works both for and against reform. Indeed, in this human sense, there is no clear or necessary opposition or dividing line between plan and market.

In the case of the movement for urban independence and in the several experiments in enterprise autonomy, the form for change is there—in *jihua danlie*, in the *xiafang* of firms, in leasing—but Hubei and the bureaus still have the means to make an impact on what sort of content fills up those forms. And in new forms of investment and circulation, things work best where the old state system intervenes, if in a positive sense, through political facilitation and the use of old organs to serve new functions. But here too there has been some obstruction, as in regulations limiting stocks and bonds in April 1987, in banks' continuing vertical control over capital circulation, and in the new state-run steel markets.

The trick, one already being turned, is to shift the economic interest of all the units involved. So Hubei Province has been subsidized for its loss of the decentralized factories, and the bureaus will soon receive compensation when their firms stop handing them management fees.[132] Meanwhile, Wuhan City and the management and workers in the experimental firms are all gaining a stake in the new arrangements as the state offers them the incentive to do better on their own.

In all this, though, there is a paradox. For drawing on old information networks, organs, and personnel cannot help but influence the formation of enterprise groups, lateral exchange and associations, and extra-plan materials procurement; cannot but shape the business in the materials and capital markets and at the trade centers. Thus, many reform experiments will work better because plan ties, still potent, can facilitate these movements.

But those same ties can also prevent the emergence of totally new formations on a large scale and in all instances at this stage—fully autonomous cities and enterprises (working with neither interference nor support), genuine capital and stock markets. For all of these bodies and processes are still somewhat enmeshed in old power systems. And yet it is just such units and markets that must be the building blocks of a new economic system.

Notes

1. Here as throughout I am dealing with endorsed, legitimated forms of exchange. There is of course also a vast and expanding world of corruption in China in recent years that takes off from these opportunities for marketeering.

2. Within a year, five other cities got this status (Chongqing was so designated in early 1983): Guangzhou, Xi'an, Shenyang, and Harbin, all of which are also provincial capitals, and Dalian, which is not a capital. Chongqing also is not a capital. *RMRB*, July 18, 1987, p.1, lists two new cities in this category, neither of which are provincial capitals: Ningbo and Qingdao.

3. *Chiangjiang ribao* (Yangtze daily) (Wuhan) (hereafter *CJRB*), August 10, 1983; also see *CJRB*, May 26, 1983.

4. See speech by Zhou Taihe, *FBIS*, July 3, 1984, p. P1.

5. Li Chong-huai,*"Liang tong" qi fei* (Take off on the "two tong's") (Wuhan: Wuhan University Press, 1986), pp. 47–48.

6. Xu Rongan, "The Central China Economic Region Must Be Built," *Jianghan luntan* (Jianghan forum) (Wuhan) (hereafter *JHLT*), no. 3, 1986, p. 8.

7. Zhou Taihe, *FBIS*, p. P2.

8. *FBIS*, February 5, 1986, p. K7.

9. Wang Mingquan, "Review and Prospects for Financial Reform," *Xuexi yu shijian* (Study and practice) (Wuhan) (hereafter *XXYSJ*), no. 1 (1986): 6; and *CJRB*, December 22, 1986, in *FBIS*, January 7, 1987, p. K22. These include setting up capital markets and experimenting with different forms of banking. Some of this is explained in a later section.

10. Interview with local economist, July 1, 1987.

11. The *People's Daily* warned of contradictions between the *jihua danlie* cities and their provinces on April 4, 1985, p. 5. As the vice-minister of the State Commission for Reform of the Economic System, Zhou Taihe, admonished, "Separate listing in the state plan for Wuhan does not mean creating a province within a province . . . organs at the two levels (i.e., provincial and municipal) should not sing their own tune or a tune different from that of Beijing."

12. *RMRB*, September 21, 1985, p. 1.

13. *FBIS*, October 17, 1984, p. K18.

14. A statement that the big contradiction between the supply of and demand for capital had not yet been resolved appears in Wang Mingquan, "Review and Prospects," p. 6.

15. Professor Wu Xinmu of the Economics Department of Wuhan University on June

29, 1987, and an official local economist on July 1 explained the new financial arrangements to me. Wuhan, Professor Wu said, has a formal retention rate of 14 percent, but it may keep some extra funds for such things as wage adjustment, flood control, and other emergencies, bringing Wuhan's actual retention up to 20 percent of its receipts. Other cities' formal rates, again drawing on my interview with Professor Wu, are as follows: Shanghai, 18 percent, Tianjin, 21, Guangzhou, 24, and Shenyang, 23. According to the Municipal Planning Commission (June 23 interview), about 38 percent of Wuhan's income now goes to Hubei, whereas about 41 percent did in the early 1980s.

16. See the article on the reform in *Shehui kexue dongtai* (Social science trends) (Wuhan) (hereafter *SKDT*), no. 17 (June 10, 1984): 18; also, Li Chong-huai, *"Liang tong" qi fei*, p. 47.

17. Interview on July 1, 1987, with urban economist.

18. Ibid.

19. Interview with Professor Wu Xinmu, June 29, 1987.

20. Interview with Yu Zhi'an at the Yangtze Energy Corporation, June 21, 1987. This supposed differentiation between economic and administrative powers was also alluded to by speakers from the city Planning Commission on June 23 and from the Wuhan branch of the People's Bank on June 24.

21. Interview, Municipal Planning Commission (hereafter MPC), June 23, 1987; Interview, July 1, 1987, with official from Mayor's Consultative Committee; and Interview, June 22, 1987, with city office of the Industrial and Commercial Administrative Management Bureau.

22. *Joint Publications Research Service–China East Asia* (hereafter JPRS–CEA)–85–051 (June 5, 1985), p. 45, translated from *Jingji guanli* (Economic management) (hereafter *JJGL*), no. 2 (1985).

23. Interview with officials from the City Commission Reform of the Economic System, June 22, 1987.

24. Interview, July 1, 1987. From what he said, it seems that the main problem now is that the city is unable to guarantee all the material supplies for the firms, so that some retain their ties to upper levels, whether province or, more often, the central ministry in ultimate charge of them.

25. Interview, June 29, 1987. The *amount* of supplies it obtained through the plan also decreased each year after this arrangement was installed—40 percent of total needs was met in 1983, but less thereafter, in accord with the amount of supplies the ministry had on hand at any time. Despite about an hour of questioning on this point, I could not clarify to my satisfaction just what the "base, guaranteed amount" really signified, given this decrease in amount supplied over time. But the important point for our purpose at this stage is that the plant's connection with Wuhan underwent no change with regard to its official supply source, despite the *xiafang*. Its revenues went entirely to Wuhan, but, as explained above, Wuhan had to turn over to the center the great bulk of these.

26. Interview there on June 21, 1987.

27. Wu Xinmu, June 29, 1987.

28. Interview, June 23, 1987; and interview with local economist, July 1, 1987.

29. *China Daily* (hereafter *CD*), December 2, 1985, p. 1; "Record of Major Events in Wuhan's 1985 Economic System Reform," *XXYSJ*, no. 1 (1986): 71; and interview with MPC, June 23 and with local economist, July 1.

30. City economist, July 1, 1987.

31. Interview on November 30, 1984, at the Wuhan Valve Works.

32. *XXYSJ*, no. 1 (1986): 71.

33. Li Chong-huai, "Prospects for Wuhan's Economic System Reform," *XXYSJ*, no. 1 (1986): 4.

34. The national press is constantly replete with admonitions to bureaus not to interfere with the new management powers for the firms. This has been going on since the initiation of the reforms.

35. *RMRB*, overseas edition, November 6, 1986, p. 1. Also see Ta-kuang Chang, "The East is Red," *China Business Review* (March–April 1987): 42–45; and article by Nina MacPherson in *South China Morning Post*, December 12, 1986, p. 1, reprinted in *FBIS*, December 12, 1986, pp. P3–4.

36. The law appears in *Guowuyuan gongbao* (State Council bulletin), no. 521 (December 20, 1986, no. 33, 1986), pp. 979–985, under the name "Enterprise Bankruptcy Law of the People's Republic of China" (Draft).

37. *FBIS*, December 12, 1986, p. P4.

38. As Yangtze Energy Corporation Manager Yu explained, the whole point of bankruptcy regulations is to motivate staff and workers to mobilize themselves to work harder under threat of failure. Consequently, it is to be expected that propaganda surrounding the radio plant's recovery would stress the role of the independent efforts of those working at the firm.

39. Reportedly, "For a long time, one third of the small state-owned enterprises in Wuhan have been running in the red or just breaking even." See *FBIS*, November 26, 1986, p. P7.

40. *CJRB*, June 9, 1987, p. 1. See also *RMRB*, July 7, 1987, p. 2 in *FBIS*, July 17, 1987, p. K6, which discusses "big fish taking care of little fish," and advanced enterprises contracting for the management of backward enterprises, both examples of one plant rescuing another one.

41. The state-owned Wuhan Automobile Engine Plant, with 1,500 workers, was leased to twenty-one of its workers to manage in late 1986, "as the plant was on the brink of bankruptcy," according to the press release. This was reported in *Zhongguo xinwen she* (Chinese news) (Hong Kong), November 20, 1986, and translated in *FBIS*, November 26, 1986, p. P7.

42. *RMRB*, May 24, 1987, p. 2.

43. Interview with the City Commission on Reform of the Economic System, June 22, 1987.

44. A clear discussion of the various forms of the leasing system is by Zheng Li, Liu Zhao, and Xiao Wentong, "Different Forms of Rental Management," in *Hongqi* (Red flag) (hereafter *HQ*), no. 12 (1987): 17–18.

45. *RMRB*, February 6, 1987, p. 5, translated in *FBIS*, February 10, 1987, p. K7.

46. *CJRB*, April 27, 1987, p. 1.

47. Discussion of the various forms of this system are recounted in Lu Dong, "Contract Management Is an Effective Avenue for Invigorating Large and Medium-Sized Enterprises," *HQ*, no. 9 (1987): 21–24; and Feng Baoxing, "Exploration of Some Questions about the Contract Management Responsibility System," *HQ*, no. 10, 1987, p. 25.

48. Wuhan had forty-four experimental keypoints practicing this system as of mid-1987, and intended to expand this to another fifty-six soon thereafter. This information was given to me at the Wuhan General Machinery Plant on June 24.

49. This was the case at the Central-South Large Commercial Building, as explained at an interview on June 29.

50. *Guangming ribao* (Bright daily), July 18, 1987, p. 3, in *FBIS*, July 31, 1987, p. K9.

51. A *Beijing Review* (hereafter *BR*) article on the contract responsibility system in issue no. 34 (August 24, 1987), p. 5, states that, "No longer does the enterprise carry out production in accord with the state's mandatory plan."

52. Interview at Wuzhong, June 29, 1987.

53. This was from the interview at Wuzhong, June 29. Other interviews on leasing and on the management responsibility system were conducted at the Wuhan General Machinery Plant (June 24), the Wuhan Chemical Machinery Factory (June 25), the No. 1 Textile Mill (June 26), and the Central-South Large Commercial Building (June 29).

54. Interview at Wuhan General Machinery Plant, June 24, 1987.

55. Interview at Wuhan Chemical Machinery Plant, June 25, 1987.

56. *RMRB*, July 24, 1987, p. 2, in *FBIS*, July 31, 1987, p. K5.

57. The Wuhan General Machinery Plant still gets more than half its steel from the Machine-Building Bureau; the Wuhan No. 1 Textile Plant gets 95 percent of its cotton from administrative channels, and the Wuhan No. 3 Printing and Dyeing Plant depends on its bureau for half of its cloth, but for more when supplies are tense, since the bureau knows just which textile mills under its control can fill the gap. The bureau also helps this plant develop connections with the departments supplying electricity, "because we don't have direct relations with them." For a more thorough treatment of these issues of bureau assistance to and interference in the affairs of the firms in the reform period, see Andrew G. Walder, "The Informal Dimension of Enterprise Financial Reforms," in U.S. Congress, Joint Economic Committee, *China's Economy Looks Toward the Year 2000: Volume 1. The Four Modernizations* (Washington, DC: Government Printing Office, 1986), pp. 630–45.

58. This information was supplied by a member of the Mayor's Consultative Committee on July 1. On that day, the companies that stand between the bureaus and the firms were no longer to receive the management fees. And at some point in the near future these fees will no longer go to the bureaus either. At that point, the Ministry of Finance will have to give larger financial allocations to the bureaus, since that will then become the bureaus' sole source of funding. The reasoning in reform circles on this point goes that once bureaus stop intervening, production will increase as firm incentives increase, and as a result the Finance Ministry will take in more taxes, giving it more funds to disburse to the bureaus.

59. Hu Jizhi, "Some Issues in Opening Wuhan's Financial Markets," *JHLT*, no. 10, 1985, p. 14.

60. Li Chong-huai, *"Liang tong" qi fei*, p. 62; JPRS-CEA–85–008 (January 26, 1985), pp. 68–69.

61. *FBIS*, March 26, 1987, p. K40.

62. *FBIS*, July 23, 1984, p. P3; and Hu Jizhi, "Opening Wuhan's Financial Markets," p. 17.

63. Wang Mingquan, "Review and Prospects," p. 6.

64. Interview with the People's Bank, June 24, 1987.

65. Hu Jizhi, "Opening Wuhan's Financial Markets," p. 17.

66. *RMRB*, April 5, 1987, p. 3, in *FBIS*, April 7, 1987, pp. K29–33.

67. *RMRB*, April 7, 1987, p. 3.

68. *CJRB*, May 25, 1987, p. 1.

69. For Shenyang, see Hao Yanni, "Investigation into Strengthening Control Over the Bonds Market," *JJGL*, no. 12 (1986): 30. For Shanghai's, see *Los Angeles Times*, April 27, 1987.

70. The *Changjiang Daily* used the term *Wuhan Trust Investment Company* (*xintuo touzi gongsi*) in the article cited here. Is this the same organ as the Financial Trust Company referred to above and also mentioned in my June 24 interview with a representative of the research office of the Wuhan branch of the People's Bank? I did not think to ask when I had the chance, but it seems that it must be.

71. *CJRB*, June 27, 1987, p.1.

72. Specialized banks such as the Industrial and Commercial Bank by all accounts have little independence yet from the central, People's Bank.

73. For instance, Susan Shirk related to me that the prices at which given stocks can be sold are limited by regulations.

74. *CJRB*, April 6, 1987, p. 1; and also interview at the Wuhan Bazaar, June 23, 1987.

75. Hu Jizhi, "Opening Wuhan's Financial Markets," p. 15.

76. As explained by the Financial Research Institute of the Wuhan branch of the People's Bank, June 24, 1987.

77. Conversation on July 1, 1987.

78. Qi Caozu, "Wuhan jingji tizhi zonghe gaige di huigu yu sikao" (Looking back and reflections on the comprehensive reform of Wuhan's economic system) *Wuhan jingji yanjiu* (Wuhan economic research), no. 3 (1987): 8.

79. *CJRB*, April 11, 1987.

80. From bank interview, June 24. On the twenty-seven-city network, see *RMRB* Overseas Edition, October 11, 1986, p. 1; on the fifty-five-city one, see *FBIS*, April 20, 1987, p. P3, and *CJRB*, April 11, 1987, p. 1.

81. Interviews on July 1 and June 24, 1987. This data is consistent with a report in *Liaowang* from July 1985 translated in *FBIS*, August 1, 1985, which states that "finance is still vertically and rigidly controlled by the higher levels. As capital is not circulating, it is very difficult to invigorate enterprises and cities."

82. *RMRB*, June 3, 1987, p. 2.

83. All of the following information comes from interviews with the firms cited.

84. Enterprise groups are discussed in a commentator's article in the *People's Daily* on July 21, 1987, p. 2, translated in *FBIS*, July 29, 1987, p. K14. According to the *People's Daily* of August 10, 1987, p. 2, there were then over 1,000 such groups registered.

85. This comes from *CJRB*, April 10, 1987, p. 1.

86. Xinhua, March 11, 1985, in JPRS-CEA–85–034 (April 5, 1985), p. 72.

87. *RMRB*, May 8, 1987, p. 5, in *FBIS*, May 20, 1987, p. K14.

88. *FBIS*, February 5, 1986, p. K7.

89. Qi Caozu, "Wuhan jingji tizhi zonghe gaige," p. 8.

90. *RMRB*, August 10, 1987, p. 2.

91. JPRS-CEA–85–035 (April 15, 1985), pp. 40–46.

92. *CD*, May 12, 1986; see also *FBIS*, July 29, 1987, p. K15.

93. *BR*, no. 29 (July 22, 1985): 27.

94. Interviews with local economist and with member of Mayor's Consultative Committee, July 1, 1987.

95. *XXYSJ*, no. 1 (1986): 70.

96. Interview on July 1, 1987, with member of the Mayor's Consultative Committee.

97. Interview with the City Commission on the Reform of the Economic System, June 22, 1987.

98. Information supplied by member of the Mayor's Consultative Committee, July 1, 1987.

99. Interview at the plant, June 25, 1987.

100. Interview at Wuzhong, June 29, 1987.

101. On the increased role of the materials bureaus at all administrative levels under the reforms, an unpublished article by Christine P. W. Wong contains information from a pamphlet published in 1984 by the State Materials Bureau. Wong's article is entitled "Problems of Regionalization in Post-Mao Reforms," presented at the Third International Congress of Professors of World Peace Academy, Manila, the Philippines, August 24–29, 1987.

102. *RMRB*, August 31, 1987, p. 2.

103. The following data on information flows, the *caigouyuan,* and the *xinxiwang* come from an interview at the Wuhan Chemical Machinery Factory on June 25, 1987. It

fits with the analysis by Jean C. Oi, "Commercializing China's Rural Cadres," *Problems of Communism* (September–October 1986): 1–15, especially pp. 9–10, in which she speaks of Chinese peasants' difficulties in the new rural markets because of their lack of information about market demand and prices, and their heavy dependence on their local cadres for this. Also, *Wuhan nianjian 1986* (Hankow: Wuhan Nianjian Bianzuan Weiyuanhui Bianji [Wuhan Yearbook Compilation Committee], 1986), pp. 356–59, outlines and describes the functions of the massive local information network created by government organs in recent years in Wuhan and indeed throughout the country.

104. Information obtained from interview at the Central-South Large Commercial Building on June 29, 1987.

105. Interview at the factory, June 24, 1987.

106. Interview at this store, June 23, 1987.

107. Interview on June 29, 1987.

108. Interview on July 1, 1987.

109. Carl Riskin, *China's Political Economy: The Quest for Development Since 1949* (New York: Oxford University Press, 1987), p. 358. The first of these opened in Chongqing in 1984, according to *RMRB*, August 9, 1987, p. 2.

110. JPRS-CEA–85–037 (April 17, 1985), p. 47; and *CD*, January 20, 1986, p. 1.

111. Deng Shaoying, "The Conditions for Development of Trade Centers and Their Functions," *JHLT*, no. 11 (1985): 14.

112. *CD*, March 3, 1986, p. 2. Barry Naughton, however, informed me that for all these materials except steel, these figures probably represent closer to one-third of those in use.

113. Zhang Baohua, Dai Guanlai, and Li Jiqing, "Countermeasures to Solve the Large Degree of Inflation in Prices of the Means of Production Outside the Plan," *JJGL*, no. 1 (1986). Yet another source states that in 1985, "Less than 20 percent of the steel products in the country circulated among enterprises and on the market." This is from Zhou Shoulian, "On the Means of Production Market," in *RMRB*, February 20, 1987, p. 5, translated in *FBIS*, February 27, 1987, p. K33.

114. *RMRB*, May 21, 1985, p. 1.

115. JPRS-CEA–85–038 (April 22, 1985), p. 31. It's not clear what's being counted here or how. For *CD*, March 3, 1986, p. 2, states that "China now has 32,000 trading centers engaged in materials sales, 6,800 more than in 1980." If that's so these larger figures must pertain to markets of all sizes, the 130 noted above being only the most major ones. And *RMRB*, August 9, 1987, p. 2, cites 930 "urban industrial products trade centers."

116. Qi Caozu, "Wuhan jingji tizhi zonghe gaige," p. 7.

117. Interview on June 23, 1987, with the commission.

118. *FBIS*, January 9, 1987, p. K41. Wuhan's was actually set up on February 20, according to *CJRB*, May 12, 1987, p. 1.

119. Interview at Wuzhong, June 29, 1987.

120. *RMRB*, May 9, 1987, p. 2.

121. Interview with City Commission for Economic System Reform, June 22, 1987, and at the Wuhan General Machinery Plant, June 24, 1987.

122. Lin Ling, "Give Play to the Central Role of Cities, Develop Horizontal Economic Links," *JJGL*, no. 2 (1985): 3–7, in JPRS-CEA–85–051 (June 5, 1985), p. 47.

123. As in JPRS-CEA–85–032 (April 1, 1985), p. 63.

124. I was told that the consolidation was done to eliminate those without experience, with insufficient capital and equipment, or without skill in business. Probably some were also operating in illicit ways. Interview with the City Commission on Reform of the Economic System, June 22, 1987.

125. This analysis, a very common one, comes from Liu Guangjie, "Discussing the Position of 'Invigorating Circulation' in the Comprehensive Reform of the Urban Economic System," *JHLT*, no. 11 (1984): 7.

126. Deng Shaoying, "Trade Centers," p. 12; and interview at the City Commission on Reform of the Economic System.

127. The following information comes from Deng Shaoying, "Trade Centers," pp. 14–17, and interview with the City Commission on Reform of the Economic System.

128. This was the remark of a management cadre at the Central-South Large Commercial Building on June 29, 1987. This is especially the case for the "specialized" centers that deal in one or several related products. The other type of center is "comprehensive."

129. This was the figure supplied by the City Commission on Reform of the Economic System, June 22, 1987.

130. *BR*, no. 28 (July 15, 1985): 24.

131. The story, in April 30's *CJRB*, p. 1, says that the traders are from Zhejiang, Jiangsu, Guangzhou, Hunan, and Henan, as well as other Hubei cities and counties. A cadre from the city's Industrial and Commercial Administrative Management Bureau said in an interview on June 22 that individual firms from all over the country (twenty-eight provinces) come to Hanzheng to get goods which they take home and sell, and that the market has influence throughout the whole country.

132. See note 58 above.

9
The Place of the Central City
in China's Economic Reform:
From Hierarchy to Network?

A good way to approach the shifts in the position and role of large, key cities in China since the urban component of economic reform began is to draw on perspectives offered by scholars from various disciplines who have written on cities. The insights of several analysts, among them urban anthropologists, help to highlight the differences between pre-1949 and post-1949 urban policy; between prereform era plans for cities and the designs of the reformers; and between what has been intended by reformers, on the one hand, and the often convoluted offshoots of those intentions, on the other.

The literature to be drawn upon here differentiates cities by type and function: the commercial city as opposed to the industrial city;[1] the city as organizer of production as against the city as a "unit of collective consumption";[2] the "official" city as the heart of field administration versus the city as a "natural" settlement centered around marketing and trading, the hub of economic transactions.[3]

In some cases these distinctions apply more in some historical periods than in others, or, put differently, reflect varying stages of development: Hoselitz (drawing on Pirenne) has made the point, for instance, that while the medieval city tended to have either primarily commercial and financial functions or mainly an industrial role—as do municipalities in many underdeveloped countries—the truly modern city is more usually a multifunctional one.[4]

This chapter was originally presented at the First International Urban Anthropology–Ethnology Conference in China, Beijing, December 27, 1989, to January 2, 1990. The meeting was organized by Aidan Southall, Gregory Guldin, and Ruan Xihu.

But historical juncture need not unduly constrain the shaping of urban activity. The distinctions may also be consciously imposed on human settlements by outside forces. This was the case, of course, in the imperialistic creation of the Chinese treaty ports after the mid-nineteenth century, which emerged as nodes of economic growth along the coast and on the Yangtze, directed toward export trade. Or, alternatively, these differences may be the result of deliberate policy choice by indigenous rulers, as when post-1949 leaders sought to redirect city development toward interior cities through a targeted, planned investment strategy, which would emphasize the industrial production function of cities instead of the consumerism that had been celebrated in the treaty ports.[5]

Yet another way of accounting for the appearance of variation among urban areas is to consider the interaction between the forces of geographical location and resource endowment, on one side, and the effort of political will, on the other. Thus, as in late traditional China, sites along waterways served as nodes in the movement of economic goods, while officialdom placed its own centers in a manner to benefit from or at least to control the flow of commercial transactions. Following this logic, the city is far from a static or determined entity; it is, clearly, within variable limits a malleable one.

These distinctions among city type and function have implications for the form and pattern of the networks into which any particular city fits. Most importantly, they have a strong bearing upon the nature of the relationships and connections between the city and, to use the language of Leeds, other "localities." Localities, in Leeds's definition, are "highly organized segments of the total population, characterized by varying degrees of control over certain resources, . . . highly organized in a multifold, flexible, complex structure, . . . which act as 'loci of power.' " The distinctions also help explain the ties between a specific locality and the "supralocal structures and institutions" (essentially, bodies that supersede localities and treat localities in uniform ways) within the world of that locality. As Leeds points out, such relationships may be "cooperative, hostile, competitive, autonomous or several of these at once"; while the interactions among localities and supralocal structures may be "oppositional, cooperative, or complementary."[6]

Thus, cities focused on commercial interchange aimed at filling consumption needs should find their spheres of activity best articulated within what are principally horizontally interconnected webs with other similar localities or with supralocal institutions, while industrially geared, production-oriented municipalities would rest relatively more easily within vertically constructed supplier and procurer hierarchies of power. Elites bent on the close and detailed management of economic activity would be prone to lay heavy administrative structures atop entities engaged in this activity, at the extreme stifling the life and energy that is the very hallmark of the activity, by turning natural centers into official ones. In short, planned economies are most compatible with the industrial, producing, administrative city; in economies that honor market principles, commercial and consumption nodes thrive.

For the purposes of this analysis and for the case of China, relevant loci of power are the administrative superiors of the city (province, central government), the surrounding hinterland, and the larger economic region. In the administratively managed type of economy, the city is tied to other loci of power in a distinctive fashion: it is subject overwhelmingly to vertical bonds as it sits at once under the protection but also the domination of its immediately superior bureaucratic level, the province. The province, in its turn, lies as well under the custody but also the control of the central government. The exceptions to this generalization are the wealthier provinces and cities of provincial status (Shanghai in particular) whose "surplus" (so defined by the central government) funds and resources were siphoned off and redistributed to the more needy areas during most of the period of the People's Republic. In this case domination far outweighs or, better yet, replaces protection.

Horizontal linkages, as with firms in the city's rural hinterland and with loci of power (such as other cities and counties) that are part of the larger economic region to which the city "naturally" (geographically) belongs, are severely truncated in this model. Any interchange between such units must be mediated by supralocal institutions—functionally specific higher-level organs having national-scale jurisdiction over all similar lower-echelon loci of power. But no interchange may take place directly between such loci. Hierarchy, then, is the chief organizing principle.

To borrow Leeds's characterizations, cooperative (where support and protection obtains) but also hostile (in response to domination) interactions would commonly brand the dealings between units located at these different administrative levels. Since there were no direct, administratively sanctioned, licit dealings among units at the same administrative level or between a city and its hinterland, I will not define these relationships in Leeds's interactional terms.

In the ideal-typical market economy, conversely, localities are atomistic entities, thrust into the realm of exchange unshielded—but at the same time unobstructed—by administrative supervisors. They are free to operate in accord with tenets of competition and comparative advantage, as their behavior ramifies into networks of connections. Consequently, the city as economic actor under this model is at liberty to develop economically based relationships with any unit in its environment, whether it be the province or the central government acting as economic actors, firms in the countryside surrounding it, or other nearby cities, again in their role as economic actors. Network is the chief organizing principle in this model.

Using Leeds's notions, autonomous but often competitive interactions would mark the intercourse both among cities and between cities and their rural environs (power loci at the same administrative level), as well as between cities and supralocal institutions in this model. These conceptions will serve as the framework within which to understand the urban economic reforms that have been taking place in China during the past decade.

The Prereform Chinese City and
Its Intended Transformation

For most of the thirty years preceding the current economic reforms in China, cities were locked into a plan of urban growth dictated by the productive city model, as noted above. Especially after the installation of state planning in 1952, and even more so with the completion of "socialist transformation" (by which the great bulk of industrial and commercial enterprises were nationalized), the larger cities were charged primarily simply with expanding their own productive capacity.

To reach that goal, the economic activity of actors within and among cities was managed by administrative orders and bureaucratic agencies that supplied materials and goods and procured output according to plan. State-run commercial agencies monopolized trade in the urban sector and were not permitted directly to exchange with units in the surrounding countryside, where only the state supply and marketing cooperatives were allowed to do business through their own "commercial" hierarchy. The result was that, as commentators saw it by the early 1980s, "The central city's proper role was limited; . . . it could not fulfill its role in [coordinating the activity of] the whole city. Even more, it could not connect with the cities surrounding it or with its rural hinterland. . . . There was no way to develop specialization and coordination.[7] Instead, "the provinces tended to develop an economy closed to each other, resulting in needless duplication and unreasonable deployment of industries," complained a piece from 1988.[8]

The urban economic reform that got its start after 1979 was motivated by the aim of switching the defining principle of urbanism away from hierarchy and toward network, and toward transforming the production city into the commercial city. This has particularly been the case for what the Chinese label "central" or "key" cities. The notion of empowering these more economically developed, multifaceted, and (within their own geographical regions) centrally located cities came fast on the heels of the initial industrial enterprise–autonomy experiments of 1979.

Already in 1980 then-Premier Zhao Ziyang put forward the need to do research on the question of developing the role of central cities.[9] In that same year, official economist Xue Muqiao was lamenting the elimination in China of an interurban network of economic flows after 1956. He advocated rebuilding such a web, and he laid out a scheme by which cities would have "direct contact with one another and help supply each other's needs under the guidance of state plans, instead of going through commercial departments at various levels."[10] In that period the press outlined the formation of "a flexible network type of economic structure."[11] By 1982, at the fifth session of the Fifth National People's Congress (China's putative state parliament), Zhao listed as one of his "ten great principles for the development of the economy" a reliance on the big cities and the creation of economic centers at every level. This suggestion amounted to, as Kirkby labeled it, "a central city-based regional planning strategy."[12]

Around this time the former director of the Industrial Economics Institute under the Academy of Social Sciences, Jiang Yiwei, published material that laid out the notion that economic regions are properly viewed as "spheres" which "spread out from a central point," not regions defined by administrative boundaries. Rather than being bounded areas, they are instead districts where economic ties cluster.[13] Ties of all sorts could be much better fostered, he reported, by undoing the bureaucratic, hierarchical cords that had long restrained the free flow of funds, materials, and personnel among areas.

In the early 1980s and increasingly in 1983 and 1984 as the focus of reform shifted from the countryside to the cities, journalists and academics bemoaned that economic linkages between urban centers had been cut asunder by rigidly demarcated bureaucratic boundaries.[14] There was, for instance, a mid-1981 campaign to expand the influence of regional metropolitan centers within their respective regions, including Shanghai in East China, Tianjin in the north, and Guangzhou (Canton) in the south. Also, already by 1981, 15 cities had been labeled "keypoint cities"; with the end of 1982 another two had been added to this list.[15]

Bolstering the role of what had been major entrepôts in former times by breaking through such barriers was meant to stimulate growth—both within the city itself and in its surrounding region—through the pull of a commercially driven, open-ended, and unrestricted demand. In short, cities were to play out their role as centers of circulation, as horizontal linkages between enterprises, cities, and regions, and between city and countryside were to replace vertical ties.[16]

Thus, cities were to act as crucial building blocks in the formation of economic regions. As one author explained it, "The key for developing the role of the central city lies in establishing economic regions: the developed city within the region will lead the rural areas in a unified organization of production and circulation."[17] In that capacity, the city would, ideally, go on to create a division of labor and cooperation within the region, avoiding duplicated construction and excessive, unnecessary productive enterprises, as the city established connections with smaller cities in its vicinity.

The result would be an economic network, growing out of rings of concentric circles, as each increasingly lesser satellite city further and further down the hierarchy of central places worked as the center of its own smaller and smaller economic district. These smaller districts were to become a sort of colony around the one major regional central city, which was to coordinate the economic work of the area. In addition, the central cities of the various big economic regions across China were envisioned at first as being capable of promoting an interregional division of labor among these regions.[18]

The final step in the official validation of this strategy occurred in October 1984. Then the Twelfth Party Central Committee promulgated a landmark decision on urban economic system reform. This statement reaffirmed the notion that the economic functions of the large, central cities should be drawn upon to break up the contradictions between local (horizontal) and central (vertical) authority systems that had been hamstringing economic life in China for over three decades by that point. They were to do so by serving as props for networklike economic regions, rather than, as they had long done, acting merely as the receptors and implementers of orders about industrial production.

In sum, in the reform era conception of cities, a handful of central cities nationwide would lie, as economic centers, at the nuclei of several large economic regional networks and markets across the nation. Circulation, then, would replace hierarchically ordered productive activity as the organizing principle for the national economy.

Specific Innovations

Many of my examples in this and the following sections will be drawn from the large industrial city of Wuhan, the capital city of Hubei Province. This city is the ideal "central city," as it is located on the Yangtze River at the point where it is crossed by China's major north–south rail line, which runs from Beijing to Guangzhou. Wuhan's strategic location had made it a national center of trade and transport in the century before 1949, and one of the leading centers of foreign trade as well. This city was the second to be granted status as a separate line item in the national state budget in June 1984, and has been a major center for experimentation in the urban reform. I visited Wuhan and did interviewing and library research there on six occasions: May 1983, May 1984, September–December 1984, May 1985, June–July 1987, and June–July 1988.

A set of innovations for the cities has aimed to realize this vision. These entail, principally, the granting of provincial-type economic powers to a group of major cities; the formation of various types of networks centered around these cities and a warrant to the cities' leaders to strengthen these networks by building up economic cooperation regions with their own cities as the axis; and arrangements to facilitate interchange between cities and their hinterlands.

Preceding the implementation of this group of measures, the central government began in 1980 to allow local (first provincial, later city) administrations to retain a larger portion of their own revenues than they had in the past, and to receive all or a fixed portion of the profits and taxes from firms under their jurisdiction. With the devolution of management over a substantial number of the larger enterprises based within their territory to urban control, cities had more funds in their power. Another windfall for urban administrations was a significant increase in the material supplies falling under their control, as the central government ceased its tightly planned allocation of large numbers of raw materials and equipment.

Moreover, "extrabudgetary funds" expanded drastically after 1979. The major portion of these consisted of monies set aside to compensate for the depreciation of enterprises' equipment, which were turned over to the enterprises (and not to higher-level financial offices) to keep in larger quantities than before. Local authorities can gather these funds outside the state budget and use them more or less as they please. In addition, relaxation of the controls on bank loans and the granting of new autonomy to provincial bank branches to lend for capital construction have also worked to give more freedom to local decision makers. Overall, local governments, at both provincial and urban levels, have greater financial powers relative to the center than they ever have.[19]

Jihua Danlie

It was against this backdrop of heightened financial clout and autonomy at the local levels that reforms expressly intended to reorient the structure of economic activity took place. Although the concept of urban-cum-industrial reform had received attention from 1979 onward, it was not really until about 1983 and 1984 that concrete, focused work began in a few experimental points. In February 1983 the city of Chongqing in Sichuan Province was the first to be granted economic powers equal to those of a province and listed separately within the state plan, rather than, as it had been for decades, treated as just one component part in a hierarchical system under the province's jurisdiction.

This reform is called in Chinese *jihua danlie*, meaning, literally, listed separately in the plan. Wuhan followed a little over a year later. This was the beginning of a concerted effort to enhance the circulation activities radiating out from cities that had historically served as transport and commercial hubs, and, concomitantly, to free these cities from the sometimes protective, but often domineering, rule of their provincial supervisors.

Originally, explained one scholar, the province exercised great power and direct control over the city, supplying funds and electricity to the city, managing its financial income, and allocating its industry's main raw materials. But along with these grants, the province had the job of collecting the major portion of the wealth accumulated from the city's production and redistributing it to other cities throughout the province. The city itself was often stuck with deteriorating urban utilities for whose upkeep it had quite minimal or even no funds of its own.[20] Neither could the city work out any comprehensive urban plan, since its management powers were far too restricted by the myriad of vertical bureaucracies among which the arrangement of its activities was divided.[21] The *jihua danlie* reform was meant to free the city from these restrictions by allowing it to escape from the province's patronage and power.

A 1985 article in the *People's Daily* described the cities given this power as all being "cities that, historically, naturally formed economic centers, and whose economic role far surpasses the administrative demarcation scope of the province in which it is situated. *Jihua danlie* will make central cities leap out of the small world of the administrative district and energetically promote urban reform."[22] In each case, an agreement was reached between the central government, the province in which the given city was located, and the city itself stipulating the ratio of revenue that would thenceforth be retained in the city and the portion that would be paid to the central government. The center then allocated some agreed-upon percentage of its receipts from the city back to the relevant province. This altered the former procedure, in which cities' receipts were collected by their provinces. The provinces then held onto some previously defined amount, returned some smaller amount, and paid the bulk to the center. For each province–city pair, a separate deal was struck, generally on the basis of the given city's expenditure in the previous few years. In general, the retention rates for these cities ranged anywhere between 16 percent and 30 percent or so.[23]

By September 1985 there were seven such cities nationwide: Chongqing, Wuhan, Shenyang, Dalian, Guangzhou, Harbin, and Xi'an. Within another four years, seven more were added: Qingdao and Ningbo got this rank in 1987, Xiamen and Shenzhen in 1988, and Nanjing, Chengdu, and Changchun in early 1989.[24] A brief review of the experiments (most of which were probably encouraged and protected by leaders at the central governmental/party level who were trying to see economic reform succeed) that one of these cities, Wuhan, undertook upon obtaining this special status will indicate the kind of hopes placed in this reform measure.

Network Formation

By late 1984, less than six months after receiving the *jihua danlie* privileges, Wuhan was well on its way toward reactivating commercial connections that had withered away from decades of disuse. Its leaders rapidly restored a total of 78 trade centers, 17 wholesale markets for agricultural products, 177 trading warehouses, and 10 markets for the sale of small industrial products; they also revived trade fairs, an institution that had enlivened the business of pre-1949 China.[25]

Thus, in the space of only half a year, the city was already surrounding itself with a wholesaling network, easing if not yet supplanting the restrictiveness of the planned procurement system. It was claimed that more than 10,000 production units and sales firms nationwide entered the Wuhan market in the spring and summer of 1984, just after the city opened its once locked-up doors, almost doubling the sales volume of the city over what it had been the summer before.[26]

Its productive and management operations also expanded beyond the bounds of the city itself: A few "model" firms, one manufacturing washing machines and one producing bicycles, began to tender bids for superior-quality parts from enterprises around the country, rather than being subjected to making use of whatever parts were allocated in the state plan. In addition, peasants from the nearby rural areas and residents of other cities were permitted to open shops and manage factories in Wuhan, something that had been out of the question when administrative regulations had blocked off each city as a world unto itself.[27]

Other networks besides the commercial one evolved in this environment. In autumn 1984, the city set up a Yangtze River Joint Transportation Company with thirteen other cities along the river, including Chongqing, Nanjing, and Hangzhou, among others.[28] Joint shipping along the Yangtze was organized by the communications departments from the cities of Wuhan, Chongqing, and Nanjing along with eleven provincial governments in July 1984.[29] This was done in the interest of creating a waterway network that would invigorate the economies of the surrounding county seats and small market towns and even lead to the growth of new small towns, while enhancing the role of Wuhan itself as a transport node. By late 1988, it could be said that a comprehensive shipping network was forming along the Yangtze, which was promoting the economic prosperity of the whole Yangtze region.[30]

By the following year, the city government was busy bringing into being various types of networks in the fields of commerce, materials supply, transport, and finance, which, by mid-1987, had reached a grand total of sixty-four.[31] Their members were the municipal administrations of seventeen cities in the provinces of Hubei, Hunan, and Jiangxi, all placed along the middle reaches of the Yangtze. And in early 1986, Wuhan, along with another twelve localities (referring to both provinces and cities) along the Yangtze, set up a transport and market information network.[32]

The city also began to take part in financial exchanges outside its own borders, rather than relying for funds upon allocations from its hierarchical superior, the provincial-level government and its bank branch, as it had before reforms began. By summer 1987, Wuhan stood at the core of five different capital markets. One of these, created in late 1986, was sponsored by the state's Industrial and Commercial Bank (one of the five specialized banks that supplement the central People's Bank). Its job was to act as a short-term interbank market for the Central China region of which Wuhan is the central city. Its member banks grew from thirty-three at first to forty-six by mid-June 1987.[33]

Such a capital market was well positioned to finance the burgeoning "lateral exchange" and horizontal economic combinations (in Chinese, *hengxiang lianxi*, referring to transactions, joint ventures, and other common projects that occur outside of the geographical and administrative limits of the old, prereform bureaucratic system) occurring among firms, cities, and rural economic units (townships, counties) beginning in the early and mid-1980s. One source noted that this exchange had been progressing well among the cities along the river as of mid-1986.[34] Over the year 1988, twenty-three cities along the Yangtze drew up 1,035 economic and technical projects, and established more than 100 enterprise combinations and enterprise groups; and 1,538 new telephone lines were installed in the area.[35]

Economic Regions

Finally, in May 1987, these various developments were brought to a head by the formation of a Wuhan Economic Cooperation Region, composed of seventeen cities mainly from the central China provinces of Hubei, Hunan, and Jiangxi. The Wuhan branch of the Communications Bank (another of the five specialized banks) was to serve the region, with half of its share capital being donated directly by "the government," a term that probably refers to the central government.[36] Here then, was the institutional framework seemingly solidly in place to make a reality of the grand intentions that had informed the concept of the central city in the first place.

New Urban-Rural Ties

Another set of reforms erased the jurisdictional lines that had kept central cities isolated from their hinterlands. In 1983 a number of the larger cities each incorporated about a half dozen counties in their environs, sometimes increasing their populations as much as severalfold as they did so. Within the new borders, the city can now deploy the resources of the entire area under its jurisdiction, and thereby create yet more new economic linkages.[37] Here again, the notion of a network was employed in discussing the goals of this measure: it was to "promote an overall urban network [while] urbanizing the villages." This, its authors expected, would overcome the flaws of the original administrative system which, after 1949, "caused a split, so that cities only managed industrial development and rural areas only worked on agricultural development. . . . This separation . . . was bad for the development of a commodity economy." By contrast, this substitute system was to facilitate combining cities with the countryside, overall planning, rational deployment, the redistribution of resources, and a generalized readjustment of the industrial structure.[38]

In practical terms, for the most part this erasure of boundaries encouraged a spate of subcontracting, product diffusion, and joint investment schemes intended to spur rural development while enabling urban firms to use less sophisticated factories in the countryside to turn out their small parts. The reform also offered cramped or capital- and material-short city plants a chance to expand their operations and to engage cheaper, less-skilled labor from the country, while giving jobs to surplus workers from the fields and sending equipment and technical personnel into the rural areas.[39] It should be noted here that similar, if less sophisticated, practices went on at the end of the Cultural Revolution in the early 1970s, under the name of "local industry" or the "five small industries." Such industries were situated in the countryside and often involved subcontracting arrangements with urban enterprises.[40]

A set of urban reforms put into effect beginning in the early 1980s was designed to realize the principles spelled out above: they were meant to invigorate the economy and stimulate the development of larger regions by basing growth on urban nodes to be freed from the bureaucratic restrictions of the past. This the reforms were to do by forming the centers for wholesale, transport, financial, and information networks; by encouraging cities to join in exchange relationships on their own initiative with other power loci at their own administrative level but beyond their own administrative borders; and by permitting municipalities to build unions with units in their hinterlands.

To what extent did these measures reach their goals? This can be determined by evaluating the effects the measures have had on transforming hierarchies into networks and on shifting the nature of the relationships between power loci.

Paradoxes in the Dynamics of Urban Reform:
The Network Caught in a Hierarchy

As noted above, the intended switch from hierarchy to network ought to have resulted in a conversion of relationships among economic actors—central government, province, city, region, and hinterland. Essentially the alteration was to have been from a system marked only by ties between higher and lower levels, ties that were characterized by cooperation mixed with some hostility, to dealings marked by competition and autonomy among all of these actors.

In actuality, however, this transformation has not fully occurred. Instead, because of a still heavy presence of administrative control in the economic system and a concomitant slew of market imperfections, antagonisms have probably intensified between most central cities and their provinces as the reforms have caused the protective element to drop away while leaving a continuing realm for domination.

And following from that, relations between cities and the rural areas within their environs have been more strained than expected, and economic regions of the sort imagined have been difficult to construct. The overall result has been, despite the introduction of many new sorts of network, to retain a significant hierarchical element in the system, with the city tied to a higher-order superior, the central government, more tightly than before and still unavoidably dependent on the province in certain respects.

Continuing Administrative Controls and
Market Imperfections

The most fundamental problem with the purported decentralization of what are called *economic* powers—supposedly the right to engage autonomously in marketlike behavior without being limited by the bureaucratic authority of superior agencies—to the central (or *jihua danlie*) cities is that the "reform" retained very significant and restrictive *administrative* powers in the hands of provincial authorities. Therefore, since the economy is still overwhelmingly state-owned, and, accordingly, since the government still manages the economy, as one source explained, "Administrative power is still with the province and economic power rests on administrative power."[41]

This effort to use what are still basically administrative means in an effort supposedly to free the cities has led to much confusion about ultimate authority, since it is essentially nearly impossible to differentiate the one type of power from the other. Certainly administrative power entails power over personnel appointments, salaries, and dismissals, and often over final approval of supposedly "economic" decisions taken at lower levels. Relatedly, none of the new economic powers granted to the cities is backed by any binding legal guarantees, so what economic powers cities have been given are held in quite an uncertain fashion.[42]

As for market imperfections, the essential difficulty lies in the fact that there have still not been requisite reforms in the systems of investment, finance, taxation, and banking that must accompany the devolution of economic power in order for that power to take full effect. Therefore, the work of government administrators at the various echelons must substitute for market forces: it is still frequently up to officials to coordinate the allocation of materials and resources to firms and to set up exchanges between economic actors within "the market," to fix some prices, and to arrange tax rates and loans for firms in difficulty.[43] Cities that have not received the *jihua danlie* privileges do not even possess these powers to adjust taxes, prices, or credit for their own firms, but must still rely on the province to do so.[44]

A host of other, related problems abound from the perspective of urban bureaucrats anxious to claim their new management rights. For one thing, enterprises themselves are still partially bound to their management departments and to the ministries up the hierarchy above them, stretching ultimately to the capital. This limits the city's ability to organize its own, much less any larger regional, economy.[45]

Moreover, it is still in the province's sphere of authority to make such significant decisions as the placement of new industrial plant within the province, the allocation of certain scarce materials and electricity, the management of land use, and the examination and endorsement of new medical products. While there is certainly a logical case that can be made for locating these powers at the provincial level, the diminution in municipal autonomy that this implies grates on city officials.

In addition, many cities still lack the ability to approve capital construction projects costing more than a million yuan.[46] And yet one more, crucial issue in this general area is that localities—both cities themselves and their provinces as well—continue to be assessed and rated in an administrative fashion by the central government in terms of their economic activity.[47]

New Strains Between Provinces and Cities

The basic dynamic of the new, resulting strains rests on the fact that the large industrial cities that recieved separate economic powers with the *jihua danlie* reform were often the principal sources of income for their provinces in the prereform days. Once they were "pulled out" from the jurisdictional realm of their provinces, the provinces have defined the interests of the two levels as being sharply competitive, even hostile. The two sides now battle over the right to use resources and develop projects yielding high revenue, while both sides try to slough off the responsibility for any low-profit ventures or obligations.[48]

Where previously the province treated the central city as the cornerstone of its own system and supplied the city's industry with essential inputs, now the two have become rivals for electricity, raw materials, and sales volume.[49] For instance, nearly one-third of Wuhan's textile productive capacity is idle mainly because of lack of cotton, even as the textile industry in the cotton producing districts elsewhere in the province have been thriving in recent years.[50] Moreover, since each party gains in circulation, product, and value-added taxes for any output and sales that occur under its own jurisdiction, trade barriers have shot up between the two administrative levels.

Provincial leaders in Hubei reason, for instance, that Wuhan's taxes now go directly to the central government and not to the province, so that if Wuhan's industry or trade is more profitable Hubei won't benefit from it any longer. A July 1, 1988, interview in Wuhan revealed that Hubei has therefore forbade lesser cities in the province that are still under its immediate control to order goods—such as shoes or tape recorders—from Wuhan. Exchange in raw materials and manufactured products once active has become blocked; resultant scarcities have even aggravated the blockages, as each power locus essays to ensure its own complete, autonomous little economy. The unpleasant outcome is that the old duplication of investment and construction that once obtained among provinces now holds within the province itself.[51]

One more important aspect of the new tension between the levels is that, despite being nominally granted new economic powers, most of the central, *jihua danlie* cities were left with too few funds genuinely to realize the potential promised by the reform.[52] This is the result of the initial recalcitrance of most of the provinces in surrendering economic power to their cities; Hubei especially struck a hard bargain in the negotiations over revenue retention that took place among the central government, Wuhan, and itself when the terms of that city's *jihua danlie* were first arranged. These various conflicts of economic interest have seriously interfered with the realization of the reform's stated aims of altering China's economic pattern from hierarchy to network.

Tensions Between Cities and Rural Areas and Between Cities and Regions

It is true that subcontracting deals and product diffusion are extensive between some cities and their hinterlands. The two examples I have are, alas, not from central, *jihua danlie* cities: it has been reported that one-third of the 9,000 rural industrial enterprises in the vicinity of Wuxi city in east China had formed "cooperative linkages" with larger urban factories or research units by mid-1986,[53] and that in Shanghai's hinterland, township enterprises had taken on 70 percent of the city's clothing industry and were supplying most bicycles and handicraft products, along with various types of machinery and equipment parts in the area by early 1986.[54]

But there are definite negative payoffs for the central city. One scholar summed these up by explaining that "The rural villages are becoming invigorated while the cities are [stuck in] what is basically the same old pattern," especially in the suburban areas surrounding major cities.[55] The cities, therefore, are suddenly lagging behind in a competition.

Another severe disadvantage for the big, old industrial cities is that rural areas endowed with raw materials have been free to process those materials themselves since economic reforms began around 1980. These areas are no longer the storehouses of rich, cheap resources that the provincial government could once command to supply the nearby major urban centers.[56] The problem for cities such as Wuhan was well summarized in the following quotation:

> The sudden appearance of rural industries and the development of small and medium towns is turning the traditional resource-supply areas into resource-processing ones, causing a change in the basic pattern of industry that has long been kept centralized in large cities and making a serious threat to the processing industry in those cities with resource shortages. . . . How to survive and develop in the face of ever-increasing competition is a stern test for Wuhan's industry.[57]

Obviously, Hubei's withholding those materials over which it still has control only compounds the problem.

A related set of problems also calls into question the extent to which the sort of internally coordinated regions focused around a central city envisioned by reformers can really be brought into being. According to a member of the Wuhan Municipal Economic Planning Commission, parties involved in efforts to create a Middle Yangtze economic cooperation region based on Wuhan struggled through three whole years of discussion and negotiation, since apparently provinces and localities housing important resources could not always easily be persuaded to relinquish their newly won powers over these supplies.[58]

Moreover, it is evident that Wuhan must have difficulty commanding the allegiance and cooperation of other key cities within Hubei, given the fact that Hubei retains all of its old controls over these places and is hoarding their riches expressly to deny Wuhan. These considerations make it difficult for the economic structure fully to undergo the transition from hierarchy to network that the reform plan envisioned for it.

Conclusion: Return to Hierarchy and
Industry as Organizing Principles

Undeniably, central cities are now freer than in prereform days to enter into economic liaisons with other localities that result in the formation of new networks of various sorts. But as their ability fully to exploit the potential inherent in their new *jihua danlie* status is restricted by provincial jealousy, cities have at the same time become more oriented toward and dependent upon the central government. For it is now officials at that echelon that have a large hand in deciding the fate of the city's economic growth, since it is they, not the province, who now directly determine the scale of investment and the supply of energy and raw materials that the city receives.[59]

And since the city no longer gets provincial protection, its representatives must appeal instead to the leadership in central government departments for solving problems in their economic work, for preferential treatment in credit and taxation policy, for extra investment, and for raising their revenue retention rates.[60] The upshot is that Wuhan's networks are still caught in hierarchies, in two ways: first because the sense of rivalry experienced in the provincial government leads its officials to limit the city's ability to become an economic center in the fullest sense; and second because the yet powerful administrative elements in the economic system force the city to turn to a yet higher level for succor.

The other paradox in this urban reform that began with a notion of nurturing growth through emphasizing commercial nodes is that major cities like Wuhan are now turning back to industry as their primary basis for development. Local economists there have noted that the industrial growth rates of all large cities have dropped lower than that of the provinces in which these cities are located and below the average annual growth rate of the country at large. One source states, for instance, that the industrial growth rate nationally between 1983 and 1986 was 15.77 percent, but that in the nineteen largest cities it was only 12.12 percent, except where the city could include the output of village and township industries under its jurisdiction in its total.[61]

Too much concentration on marketing (network building) in the period after Wuhan obtained *jihua danlie* status, scholars now believe, was responsible for a neglect of industry: light industry fell there 2.7 percent in the year between 1985 and 1986, for example. Some of them quickly became anxious that if the city's industry were not stressed once again, it would atrophy, influencing other kinds of economic activity.[62] Where from 1983 through 1986 circulation was touted for its ability to invigorate the entire economy, writers in the academic journals by 1987 were pointing out that "Commerce and transportation cannot substitute for industry; . . . only industry can create use value [so that] it is industry that is necessary for the development of the 'two C's' [circulation and communications]."[63]

The conclusion a number of local economists in Wuhan have now drawn is that a large industrial base such as Wuhan ought to focus its energies on designing and then fulfilling its own urban industrial policy. Under the guidance of such a policy, the city must develop a set of new, strategic industries while renovating its traditional trades.[64] Such an outcome, if practiced in every large city, will only complicate the tasks of creating regional markets and of avoiding duplicative investment, tasks that the reform had been aimed at achieving.

Thus, the reform based on central cities, with their capabilities to energize regional economies through demand-side stimulation, has reached an impasse a half decade or so after it took off. Cities granted special status within the state plan and a measure of economic autonomy that should have helped them to realize that program have found their way to doing so only partially cleared.

These "central cities" are now at the node of networks still enmeshed in hierarchies rather than becoming fully independent economic actors. Going back to Leeds's conceptualization, it is by now clear that the at least partly cooperative relations that once obtained between cities and other power loci in their immediate environment—other cities within their own provinces, their own hinterlands—and with their superiors at the provincial level have now turned out to be not autonomous as was intended, but, at the same time competitive and hostile.

Notes

1. Bert F. Hoselitz, "The Role of Cities in the Economic Growth of Underdeveloped Countries," *The City in Newly Developing Countries: Readings on Urbanism and Urbanization*, ed. Gerald Breese, pp. 232–45 (Englewood Cliffs, NJ: Prentice-Hall, 1969).

2. Peter Saunders, *Social Theory and the Urban Question*, 2d ed. (London: Hutchinson Education, 1981).

3. G. William Skinner, "Cities and the Hierarchy of Local Systems," in *The City in Late Imperial China*, ed. G. William Skinner, pp. 275–351 (Stanford: Stanford University Press, 1977).

4. Hoselitz, "The Role of Cities," pp. 237, 239, 240.

5. Clifton W. Pannell, "Recent Growth and Change in China's Urban System," in *Urban Development in Modern China*, ed. Laurence J. C. Ma and Edward W. Hanten, pp. 91–113 (Boulder: Westview Press, 1981), pp. 92, 109; and Rhoads Murphey, "Urbanization in Asia," *Ekistics* 21, 22 (1966): 8–17.

6. Anthony Leeds, *Locality Power in Relation to Supralocal Power Institutions*, in *Urban Anthropology: Cross-Cultural Studies of Urbanization*, ed. Aidan Southall, pp. 15–41 (New York: Oxford University Press, 1973), pp. 26, 27, 36.

7. Peng Xiangyuan, "Fully Develop the Role of the Central City," *Jianghan luntan (Jianghan forum)* (hereafter *JHLT*), 9 (1983):6–11.

8. *Foreign Broadcast Information Service* (hereafter *FBIS*), November 16, 1988: 37.

9. Chiu Jingjin and Chen Jiagui, "The Success and Experience of the Comprehensive Reform of the Central City's Economic System," *Jingji guanli* (Economic management) (*JJGL*) (Beijing) 12 (1987): 17–20.

10. *Beijing Review* (hereafter *BR*), no. 36 (1980): 22–23.

11. Ibid.; *FBIS*, April 1, 1981, pp. K3–5.

12. R. J. R. Kirkby, *Urbanisation in China: Town and Country in a Developing Economy 1949–2000 A.D.* (London: Croom Helm, 1985), pp. 223, 230.

13. Kojima Reeitsu *Urbanization and Urban Problems in China* (Tokyo: Institute of Developing Economies, 1987), pp. 91, 176.

14. *Renmin ribao* (hereafter *RMRB*), June 18, 1983.

15. Kirkby, *Urbanization in China*, p. 222.

16. *Ban yue tan* (Semimonthly talks) (Beijing) April 10, 1985, pp. 18–20, translated in Joint Publications Research Service–China Economic Affairs (hereafter JPRS–CEA) July 30, 1985, pp. 1–4.

17. Peng, "Fully Develop the Role of the Central City," p. 7.

18. Ibid., p. 7–8, 10.

19. William Byrd, *China's Financial System: The Changing Role of Banks* (Boulder: Westview Press, 1983); Audrey Donnithorne, *Centre-Provincial Relations in China* (Canberra: Australian National University, Department of Economics, Contemporary China Papers no. 16, 1981); "Fiscal Relations," *China Business Review* 10, 6 (1983): 25–27; "The Chinese Economy Today," *Journal of Northeastern Asian Studies,* 2, 3 (1983): 3–21; Barry Naughton, "The Decline of Central Control Over Investment in Post-Mao China," in *Policy Implementation in Post-Mao China,* ed. David M. Lampton, pp. 51–80 (Berkeley: University of California Press, 1987); and Christine Wong, "Material Allocation and Decentralization: Impact of the Local Sector on Industrial Reform," in *The Political Economy of Reform in Post-Mao China,* ed. Elizabeth J. Perry and Christine Wong, pp. 253–78. (Cambridge: Harvard University, Council on East Asian Studies, 1985).

20. Mao Zhenhua, "The Predicament and Future of Urban *Jihua Danlie*," *JHLT* 1 (1988): 42–44.

21. Wang Xinhui, Cui Deyuan, and Zhang Qin, "A Consideration and Assessment of the *Jihua Danlie* Reform in Central Cities," *JHLT* 10 (1987): 33.

22. *RMRB*, September 21, 1985.

23. Wuhan interviews, summer 1988.

24. *RMRB*, October 22, 1987, p. 4; June 13, 1988, p. 2; and February 19, 1989, p. 1; *FBIS*, October 20, 1988, p. 27.

25. Dorothy J. Solinger, "Wuhan: Inland City on the Move," *China Business Review* (March–April) (1985): 27–30.

26. Ibid.

27. Ibid.

28. Ibid.

29. JPRS-CEA, 85–028:69; *BR*, no. 29 (1985): 25.

30. *RMRB*, November 26, 1988, p. 2.

31. *Changjiang ribao* (hereafter *CJRB*) (Yangtze daily) (Wuhan), May 23 and 28, 1987, both on p. 1; *RMRB*, May 28, 1987, p. 1.

32. *RMRB*, April 7, 1986, p. 3.

33. *CJRB*, June 10, 1987, p. 1.

34. "Summary of the Second Theoretical Forum on the Comprehensive Development of Hubei Province's Cities Along the Yangtze River," *Xuexi yu shijian* (Study and practice) (Wuhan) 9 (1986): 26.

35. *RMRB*, November 26, 1988, p. 2.

36. *CJRB*, May 28, 1987, p. 1.

37. Kojima, *Urbanization and Urban Problems*, p. 100ff; Ke Meicheng, "Certain Reflections on Deepening the Reform of the City Leading the County," *JJGL* 9 (1988): 9–11.

38. Ke, "Certain Reflections."

39. Lu Wen, "On Developing New-Style Urban-Rural Relations," *JHLT* 2 (1987): 20.

40. American Rural Small-Scale Industry Delegation, *Rural Small-Scale Industry in*

the People's Republic of China (Berkeley: University of California Press, 1977).

41. Chen Shengli and Chen Hongbo, "Review of *Jihua Danlie* and Thinking It Over," *JHLT* (Wuhan) 8 (1987): 8; Wang, Cui, and Zhang, "A Consideration," p. 35.

42. Wang, Cui and Zhang, "A Consideration," p. 35.

43. *FBIS*, November 13, 1987, pp. 44–45.

44. Zeng Haorong, "Suggestions on Expanding the Autonomy of Central Cities," *JJGL* 11 (1987): 15.

45. Wang, Cui, and Zhang, "A Consideration," p. 35.

46. *RMRB*, April 4, 1987, p. 5; *FBIS*, November 13, 1987, pp. 44–45; Wang, Cui, and Zhang, "A Consideration," pp. 35–36; and Zeng, "Suggestions on Expanding the Autonomy," pp. 15–16.

47. Chen and Chen, "Review of *Jihua Danlie*," pp. 8, 11.

48. Ibid.; Mao, "The Predicament and Future of Urban *Jihua Danlie*," pp. 42, 44.

49. Ye Jinsheng et. al., "A Sketch of the Central City's *Jihua Danlie*," *JHLT* 11 (1987): 22.

50. Mao, "The Predicament and Future of Urban *Jihua Danlie*," p. 44.

51. *FBIS* , November 16, 1988, p. 37; Mao, "The Predicament and Future of Urban *Jihua Danlie*," p. 44; Chen and Chen, "Review of *Jihua Danlie*," pp. 8–9.

52. Wang, Cui, and Zhang, "A Consideration," p. 35.

53. JPRS-CEA–86–078, p. 32.

54. JPRS-CEA–86–050, p. 18.

55. Lu, "On Developing New-Style Urban-Rural Relations," p. 18.

56. Wuhan Economic Research Institute Industrial Development Strategic Task Group, "Conception and Measures for Wuhan Industrial Development Strategy," *Zhongnan Caijing Daxue xuebao* (Central-South Finance and Economics University Bulletin) (Wuhan), no. 6 (1987): 65.

57. Chen Mengnong, "Development of Industrial Structure of Wuhan," paper prepared for Seminar on Regional Structural Change in International Perspective, Pittsburgh, October 1988.

58. Interview, June 23, 1987.

59. Chen and Chen, "Review of Jihua Dahlie," p. 9.

60. Wang, Cui, and Zhang, "A Consideration," p. 36.

61. Chen, "Development of Industrial Structure of Wuhan," p. 14.

62. Zhu Yanshan, "A Reconsideration of the Question of the Strategic Keypoint for Wuhan's Economic Development," *JHLT* 2 (1987): 32.

63. Ibid., p. 31.

64. Chen, "Development of Industrial Structure of Wuhan," p. 19; Ye et al., "A Sketch of the Central City's *Jihua Danlie*," p. 23.

Part IV

State Cadres and Urban Entrepreneurs

10
The Petty Private Sector and
the Three Lines in the Early 1980s

"The time's not been long since the individual economy once again took up its legitimate place in the arena of our country's economic life. Since the Third Plenum of the party's Eleventh Central Committee [December 1978], the majority of people have enthusiastically welcomed it, some people examine it with a suspicious eye, [and] part of the people reject it with disgust in their hearts."[1]

These lead lines come from an early 1983 *People's Daily* editorial. They alerted their readers to the fact that, some four years after China's top party leaders had unequivocally endorsed the petty private sector—with its open-air fairs and its sidewalk stalls—a range of opinions still sliced up the popular stance toward this business. Happily for our purposes here, the author points to three main sorts of attitudes adopted with respect to the trade that falls outside the state-run economy. I will allude to these attitudes in this chapter, respectively, as the marketeer, bureaucratic, and radical lines.[2]

One objective of this chapter is to draw on press material on the petty private sector[3] from the early 1980s to illustrate the efficacy of the three-line model in representing Chinese social reality. Another, closely linked purpose is to use that model to illuminate certain social features of fairs and small selling that are obscured by adherence to the time-worn two-line approach to Chinese politics. The claim here is that, following the quotation above, reports about this activity reveal three methods of viewing and handling it at the policy-making level; as well as three ways of dealing with it on the part of economic actors (a term that will include peasants and petty merchants, as well as workers in state-run enterprises, and cadres in government economic departments).

Reprinted from *Three Visions of Chinese Socialism*, ed. Dorothy J. Solinger (Boulder: Westview Press, 1984), by permission of the publisher.

The three-line model sensitizes the analyst to the ideological bases, social interests, power resources, incentives, and motivations of the concerned parties in a manner that the old left-right formula misses. It does so by beginning the investigation from a presumption of the presence in Chinese society of three "tendencies of articulation," to borrow the terminology of a scholar of Soviet politics,[4] and by rooting each line in one key value that informs its advocates' judgments, policy preferences, and behavior.

Most simply put, politicians pushing marketeer policies—in the case here, approval for largely untrammeled dealings at fairs and minimal interference with sidewalk salesmen—along with the practitioners of this trading, value above all wealth, prosperity, and strategies likely to further the creation of these goods. Marketeer-prone economic actors build their success in the marketplace on the power lent them by their riches. Policy makers with this preference support the fairs; well-placed peasants and peddlers take part in them and take advantage of them; and some local cadres collude with the traders in them.

The bureaucrat line or tendency above all prizes order, the regularity that is meant to arise from controls imposed on firms in the state sector, by the state plan, and by the bureaucracy that organizes and brings life to that plan. Statesmen supporting bureaucratic policies (who may or may not be the same set of individuals over time, as leaders' official positions, the prevailing political climate, and shifting economic circumstances skew their stands) and many local cadres stress economic stability relatively more than they do economic growth, and they find any competition with state sector-led exchange to be a serious threat. The principal constituency for the bureaucratic stance at the level of daily economic life is the group of cadres who staff lower-echelon economic departments and state-run enterprises. Such individuals draw on the power of the state and its offices to limit, "squeeze," or incorporate within the state sector the petty business of the private sellers.

Third, the radical line encompasses those who still, years after the dramatic deposition of Mao Zedong's most left-wing allies in autumn 1976 (a period marked by nearly continuous official denunciation of this group's philosophy), base their politics on what they consider to be the primacy of issues of social class. It may be the case that, as one article from the summer of 1980 put it, "no one has openly opposed keeping the [urban] farm product markets open."[5] Nonetheless, the press in the early 1980s practically never printed news about the private sector without alluding to and censuring those whose "lingering leftism," sometimes alternatively labeled "ossified, conservative thinking" led them to "misunderstand," call into question, or criticize the liberalization of economic policy of the post-1978 years.

Treasuring egalitarianism over economic well-being or financial equilibrium, "some people" apparently wish to see the private sector abolished, as they find free markets, penny capitalism, and the income polarization such institutions tend to produce to be inimical to socialist society. However, those holding this penchant for leveling stand in a weak position in China today, as their power in the past has peaked only in periods when ideology commanded respect. Thus, they may not now speak in the press in their own voices. We know of their views just through attacks on them; but the very frequency of these attacks indicates at the least that their adherents attract official attention. One can do no more than guess at the prevalence within society of those with these beliefs, or at the extent of their power at the local levels.

In contradistinction to this tendency/line model of three positions, each based on its own distinct values, and each of whose proponents draws on different sorts of power, the left-right dichotomy simply posits a "socialist road" in opposition to a "capitalist one" in policy circles, to use the Chinese's own terms; or else pinpoints a group of "ideologues" or "revolutionaries" set against the "pragmatists" or "moderates," as many outside observers have labeled them. For the analysis of policies toward and practices in the petty private sector, that left-right model is particularly unsatisfactory. For it indicates merely whether "leftists" are restricting or closing down fairs and stalls on the one hand, or if "rightists" are letting them live, on the other.

In fact, there are (and have been over the years) lively fairs and tamed fairs (those of 1956 versus those of 1961–62), where the purposes for holding them and the forces of control over them have varied considerably; cases of "pragmatists" banning fairs;[6] and, as the present chapter will reveal, efforts to check their scope that have little to do with what is usually referred to as "ideological" or "leftist" motives.

In short, the three-line model helps the observer to sort out the roots of support, conflict, and opposition that attend the practice of private sector business in socialist China. It also does a better job of uncovering the complicated interplay of opinions, values, and strategies that accompanies policy making and policy change than does the two-line approach. As an example of the type of insights afforded by the use of this scheme, bureaucrats (in the sense of those personifying the bureaucrat line) may look like marketeers when they support fairs. But when such generalized support is disaggregated by the model, their distinctive reasons for holding fairs emerge, and, as a consequence, one can then comprehend more easily why bureaucrats also at times restrain the development of the private sector.

Similarly, bureaucrats look radical when they interfere in markets. But, having different interests and power bases from radicals, they have their own motives for limiting the private sector, motives that are revealed by the three-line analysis. Thus, restrictions on fairs may have several causes, only one of which is "leftist" thinking; and holding them is not always "liberal" (or "rightist"), either in inspiration or in method.

The focus of this chapter will be on the period of the early 1980s for a couple of reasons. Most simply, I have already examined the data for and published work on commercial policy and practice for the years up to 1980, in a work that for the most part halted at the edge of the post-Mao loosening of economic controls.[7] This chapter will bring that study's findings more nearly up to date. But, in addition, in-depth treatment of a period presented to and viewed by the outside world as being largely liberal economically should afford some new insights about where support for and opposition to these more lenient policies lies within Chinese society. It will also show the effects at the local levels of society of the coexistence of different lines or tendencies within a given period, while at the same time highlighting the clashes between central leaders and the supposed implementors of their policies, the local cadres.

The chapter will also draw attention to very short-term pulsations in policy, as if the central elite entertains persistent ambivalence as to how unqualifiedly it ought to promote an active small trade sector (or, as if more bureaucratically biased politicians among the elite find occasions to convince the others to pull back the degree of permissiveness from time to time). The aim here, however, is not to document leadership splits on this issue as much as it is to demonstrate the presence of varying stances and behaviors and policies throughout society toward commercial activity during a "liberal" phase. The finding of all three lines operating in tandem with regard to a "liberal" policy during a "liberal" period is especially apt for demonstrating the methodology of the three-line model.

After presenting a brief overview of the recent policies toward and the scope of the phenomenon under study, the argument will expand upon the material presented above to show more fully the kinds of analyses, justifications, and action programs advanced toward the petty private sector by each of the three lines at the policy-making echelon. It will then go on to identify the economic actors or social groups whose behavior or whose thinking seems to place them in one of the three camps or the other. That section will consider the interests, opportunities, resources, motivations, power, incentives, threats, and positions that work to shape the stances taken by groups and individuals in their daily economic activity.

With these two sections as the backdrop, the chapter will then sketch the sorts of conflict—within and among administrative levels and between private and public sectors—that this liberal policy has brought into play. It will also address the tendency for various affected parties to over-respond (from the perspective of the elite) to central-level orders they find favorable to their interests. Last, I will draw on the analysis in all of these earlier sections to suggest how policy changes may result from the interaction among several forces—the presence of differing tendencies among the elite; conflicts and overreactions among affected administrative levels and social groups; and the consequences for the economy and society of these conflicts and over-reactions. All of these factors, I will maintain, are handily analyzed through the spectrum of the three-line model.

The Early-Eighties Petty Private Sector: Policies and Size

Policies

Advocates of liberal policies toward the private sector controlled policy councils and put their principles into practice on two previous occasions in the People's Republic, after socialization had already occurred. These times were in 1956–57 and in the early 1960s. But the ten-year period of Cultural Revolution saw the sweeping away of this sector, as even the relatively open rural fairs were castigated and controlled by the state, individual peddlers and shops were brought within the state economy, and merchants were often forced to engage in productive, not commercial, activity.

In early 1978, that is, a little over a year after the death of Mao and the arrest of the radical "Gang of Four," initial official reendorsement of the private sector allowed it to emerge once more. Then-Premier Hua Guofeng's report to the first session of the Fifth National People's Congress in February labeled limited private economic activity a part of the party's rural economic policy, and the state constitution promulgated at that point stipulated the same thing.[8]

But it was the Third Plenum of the Eleventh Party Central Committee at the end of the year that gave the real spurt to privately operated business. Whereas the earliest approval of fairs listed limitations upon them, a reflection of continuing bureaucratic sentiment in the period before the Third Plenum, by early 1979, freer markets were clearly permitted. Thus, at first no "pass-hands" (*zhuan shou*) trade, or reselling, was allowed; only second- and third-category goods, but no grain, oil, or cotton (those key "first-category" agricultural commodities) could be exchanged; and long-distance trading was still illegal. As 1979 and 1980 wore on, however, all of these caveats were taken away (except that selling cotton privately was never allowed, at least not through 1983).[9]

For the sidewalk sellers also, the Third Plenum was the critical turning point. This meeting redefined the overwhelming majority of the bourgeoisie, both large and small, as having been transformed into people who live by their own labor. Also, it accepted the small traders as socialist, and official policy dictated that Cultural Revolution era discrimination against them as "the tail of capitalism" be terminated.[10]

Throughout 1979 and into 1980 those participating in private-sector activity received from the leadership an increasingly free hand. Although some concern about inflation produced a State Council directive on price control and market management in April 1980, that document was less stringent in its regulations than one issued at the end of the year. However, in December 1980 a unified national-level elite, meeting at a Central Party Work Conference, clamped down on all extra-plan economic activity, in the wake of a discovery of a large deficit and an inflation rate higher than expected.[11]

An early 1981 article by the organ charged with managing markets (the Central Bureau of Industrial and Commercial Administrative Control) exemplified the new restrictiveness, as it authorized only trade that the individual could do by him or herself without hiring laborers or using mechanized transport vehicles (only what the individual could carry by pole or hand, or what he or she could pull by cart or tote on a bicycle constituted a proper volume of produce for legitimate selling). Also, the article placed some confines on long-distance trade, banned all first-category products from the realm of privately conducted sales, and allowed private vendors to engage only in retail but not wholesale trade.[12]

A few months later, in the summer of 1981, the State Council passed regulations in support of individual traders and workers, stressing that they are independent laborers (not capitalists or speculators), and a necessary supplement to the state and collective economies. But this directive still reined in the entrepreneurs in a few regards. For example, they were still to use only nonmechanized transport and to do only retail trade, and, for the most part, could hire only one or two "helpers." Even those who wished to pass special technical skills on to apprentices were allowed to have two or three but never more than five apprentices. At just about the same time, the State Council passed a set of "Provisional Regulations on the Prices of Agricultural and Sideline Products in Negotiated Purchase and Selling" that limited the types of foods for which "negotiated prices" could apply, and that referred to punishments for driving up above state-set ceilings negotiated prices where they were allowed.[13]

Subsequent national-scale commercial work conferences in November 1981 and November 1982 once again liberalized some of these policies.[14] The first of these allowed every self-employed person to hire up to seven employees, a decision of the party's Central Committee and the State Council that in effect authorized private retail firms to operate legally on a scale not seen in China in at least two decades.

The second, in 1982, reduced the number of varieties of rural produce under state control from 46 to 22; legitimated bargaining and using negotiated prices that can rise and fall with supply and demand (such prices had no doubt been in effect in practice in the markets, but they had been frozen officially since December 1980) for the less-essential third-category rural products; and let peasant producers as well as itinerant merchants carry out long-distance trade (either individually or in groups and caravans), whether retail or wholesale. It also aimed to lower the state's proportion of dealings in industrial products from 73 to 70 percent, to lower the proportion of rural sideline products purchased by state organs from 80 to 70 percent, and to change the percentage of total retail sales managed by the state and basic-level supply and marketing cooperatives from what was then 80 percent down to 60.

In the weeks following this late 1982 decision, the *People's Daily* printed a series of articles supporting liberalization that was reminiscent of the summer of 1980, the last time restrictions had been especially loose.[15] These pieces underlined the authorization of long-distance trade that could be undertaken by the peasants themselves; the right of peasants to pool capital to do trade; and the legitimacy of doing commercial work to get rich, even if that entailed abandoning agriculture for trading (a departure once considered corrupt and treated as illegal). No longer were mileage covered, amount carried, and form of transport utilized to be the objects of regulation. State Council notices on urban individual and cooperative laborers in mid-April 1983 held to this theme of leniency, as they specified that restrictions should be relaxed, motor vehicles could be used, long-distance peddling was legitimate, and wholesale business could be handled by firms outside the state sector.[16]

Curiously, though, almost immediately thereafter, the State Council issued a circular in May 1983 ordering far tighter regulation of the free markets: no enterprise or unit could "adjust" prices such that they surpassed the authorized limits; no enterprise or unit could "wantonly" do business in a field other than that approved by the industrial and commercial control departments; firm controls were to be exercised over wholesalers; and those working without licenses were to be strictly banned, among other commands.[17] While different from the very liberal tone of the press earlier in the year, this new directive struck a common chord with a new Food Sanitation Law passed in April, which was directed against food pollution and harmful particles found in the eatables in the free markets.[18]

In the wake of these two new sets of directives, municipal authorities started to crack down on malpractices in the markets. Stories in the press tell how they began to fine unlicensed peddlers and confiscate illegal earnings; suspend or withdraw the licenses for those who practiced reselling for profit; and send the public security organs to investigate and "attack" market overlords and bullies.[19] This quick review of the shifts and varieties of emphasis in commercial policy toward the private individual trading sector in the aftermath of the Third Plenum is not meant to trace in great detail every minor alteration. Nor does it expose any relentless trend of development. Rather, its purpose is to indicate the range of possible policy options that exist in policy makers' minds in China, even within a broad framework permitting private economic activity. The discussion below will shed some light on the forces, both ideological and social, that lie behind these switches. First, though, a look at the scope of the activity under consideration will set the scene.

Size of the Private Sector

It should be noted that, even in the midst of these comparatively frequent redefinitions of the realm of the legal, the total volume of transactions at produce fairs is reported to have grown rather rapidly in recent years—at a rate of about 5 billion yuan per year between 1979 and 1981, reaching 32.8 billion yuan in 1982, of which 28.7 billion was in the countryside and 4.1 billion was in urban fairs. Urban and rural free markets went from amounting to the equivalent of 6.6

percent of total retail sales in 1978 to 11.4 percent in 1981. The number of fairs was said to have risen from "more than 36,000" at the end of 1979 to 44,775 three years later.[20]

Over the same period, the number of individual laborers in the cities purportedly increased from 150,000 in 1978 to 1.36 million people at the end of 1982. By that later date, if such laborers in the countryside are counted as well, the figure was claimed to have reached 3.2 million people, and their total annual business volume, as counted by state offices, was a little over 10 billion yuan. In 1982 state-owned commercial enterprises furnished 84.5 percent of the nation's total volume of retail sales, down from 87.7 percent just the year before.[21]

But although the number of people engaged in such activity in 1982 was said to be thirty-one times the number in 1979, it represented only 1.3 percent of the total number of the workers and staff in state and collective enterprises, and less than 1 percent of the total urban population. Given this rapid growth, it seems likely that the numbers involved could be far greater yet, if the central-level marketeer policy makers who support a liberalized economy could enforce their will in society at large. It is to that story that I now turn.

Three Lines in Policy Making

As noted above, proponents of the radical line have not had access to the media in recent years. All of the commentary on the private sector, then, has been written from the viewpoint of those expressing either the marketeer or the bureaucrat tendency. Attacks on the "misunderstanding" of current policy shown by people who believe in radical standpoints, however, indicate for the researcher the continuing presence of this position within society. Without attempting to attach any particular individual leaders to any of these positions, and without pinpointing closely at what exact juncture the various positions below were advanced, this section will simply present the sorts of analyses, apologies, justifications, fears, interests, and philosophies that have informed these positions, and will note the separate action programs advocated by those of each persuasion over the years 1980–83 (see Table 10.1).

Marketeer

Basing their support for free markets and small independent trading on the purported efficacy of each in stimulating economic growth, marketeers' analyses typically emphasize the positive functions of such operations. These include their ability to respond to the "pressing need for an outlet for the growing rural commodity production" that developed in the wake of the Third Plenum's permission for readjusting crop acreage, its promotion of the production responsibility system, and its approval of "specialized" and "keypoint" households. For all of these measures increased the commercialization rate in the countryside beyond

Table 10.1
The Three Tendencies and Disagreements Over the Effects of Freer Trade

Tendency	Radical	Marketeer	Bureaucrat
Capitalism (Does free trade cause it?)	Yes*	No	It might*, if not properly managed by state organs
Inflation (Does free trade cause it?)	Yes*	No, not in the long run	Probably*, if not properly managed by state organs
Productivity/ Circulation (Does free trade increase productivity?)	No	Yes!*	Maybe*, but often not
State Purchase/ Plan Fulfillment (Does free trade increase state purchase?)	No*	Yes	Usually no!*
Income and Class Polarization (Does free trade cause polarization?)	Yes!	Not in any significant way, since everyone is getting richer*	Possibly, but not necessarily*

Note: I have used underlines and exclamation marks to indicate the key value for each tendency, the issue that shapes that tendency's overall appraisal of the fairs.

*indicates agreement between any two tendencies on a given issue.

the ability of the state-run supply and marketing cooperatives to cope. Articles written from the marketeer viewpoint insist that private trade activity promotes production, enlivens exchange, makes the overall economy prosper, and provides convenience to the daily lives of the masses. Under such circumstances, marketeers maintain that letting peasants enter the sphere of circulation should not even be a subject for debate; it is instead a "necessary trend."[22]

Having established this "necessity" for the private sector, marketeers also find ways to whitewash it before the scrutiny of those less well disposed.[23] For one thing, they offer a set of standards for distinguishing what is legal transporting of goods for sale, on the one hand, from speculation and reselling for exorbitant profits, on the other, thereby exhibiting for doubters that a legitimate form of free trade is indeed possible. They go on to build a case for the *socialist* essence of those who engage in this trade, a claim hotly contested by radicals. For instance, they draw attention to the fact that traders do their work by means of their own physical activity, and that this work is an integral part of the production process itself.

They go on to establish the legality of the private sector, presumably again for the benefit of doubters, by pointing to the small amount of capital and generally slight profits involved; and by noting that those few who may have a higher income have obtained it properly through possessing special skills, working extra hours, and participating in long-distance trade.[24] Moreover, marketeer arguments often allude to the facts that, even should private entrepreneurs attempt to strike out beyond the confines of what policy permits, they must rely on state-run enterprises for their materials and goods supply; and that the scope and methods of their business are allegedly delimited by government policies and state laws.[25]

As distinct from bureaucrats, who resent the rivalry presented by these traders, a marketeer writer views among the strengths of the private sector the competition it introduces into the Chinese economy. For, he holds, such vying works to elevate the management level in the state and collective sectors. This journalist even makes the argument that, rather than contributing to inflation, as bureaucrats claim, the small peddlers keep prices stable. For, he reasons, without the petty merchants there to collect the surplus products in the villages, scarcities in the markets would force prices up.

And while not even marketeers deny that the individual economy can produce bad apples, on the whole they urge the use of the state's economic controls to deal with any difficulties that may come up: "Naturally, if their income gets too high, we can collect business income tax according to the tax laws and regulations."[26] Another marketeer writer suggests that the state can use credit and price levers, as well as taxes, to redirect any trading with a harmful effect onto a path that will meet social needs. According to his opinion, probably a characteristic enough response from a marketeer to his challengers, "it's very hard to have something without flaws; . . . we should strengthen management, but not give up eating for fear of choking."[27]

Bureaucratic

It is hard for the outside observer to distinguish between self-interest and philosophy, fears and values, pretexts and genuine motives, in the reasonings offered by defenders of the bureaucratic line. The most likely explanation here is that fear, habit, and interest intertwine with long-ingrained beliefs, so that excuse and true intent are closely joined even in the mind of the bureaucratic speaker.

On the less rational side, probably the greatest fear entertained by those bent on preserving the place of the state bureaucracy comes across in this quotation from a *People's Daily* article of mid-1982: "Some comrades think the market is already too lively, that the individual economy has developed to saturation; some people even think that state commerce is surrounded by the collective and individual economy and that business is hard to do."[28] Or, even more explicitly, a letter to the newspaper complaining about obstructions set up against the private sector about a half year later quotes a district-level leading comrade to this effect: "I fear the individual economy . . . they earn so much money—what is the limit on the degree to which they can get rich?"

Another official is purported to have observed that "Developing individual firms amounts to thinking of crowding out state enterprise."[29] Others worry that letting the peasantry and individual merchants and peddlers engage in long-distance trade will create market "chaos" and that speculators will then be able to take advantage of the resultant mess.[30] Thus, the emotional disposition of professors of the bureaucratic tendency contains a mix of anxieties: apprehension that state-run trade will suffer, concern that wealthy tradespeople will escape the state's control, and dread of disorder in the marketplace.

Habit reinforces this mind-set. Some supporters of bureaucratic modes of operation, used to the monopoly position enjoyed by state commerce for decades, continue to rely on "old systems" and "old practices and regulations."[31] But, since such systems serve to shore up the dominant role of those who staff the bureaucracy, is it really just a "pretext," as the writer claims, when "some localities" emphasize the planned economy, as their cadres attack private operators for being "criminals in the economic sphere?"[32]

A certain proportion of those standing for bureaucratic principles may well have a genuine philosophical preference for the planned approach to distribution in a socialist economy. For those whose thinking follows this line, competition between sectors is not a positive situation as marketeers believe, but a dangerous precondition leading to serious shortages in state-dominated circulation channels. In this view, when other avenues of trade siphon off scarce and popular goods, state plans go unfulfilled, which negatively influences price stability rather than enhancing it, as marketeers maintain.[33]

Relatedly, the Theoretical Education Editorial Office of *Red Flag* journal published a long analysis of Chen Yun's early 1950s opinions on the state monopoly over the purchase and marketing of grain and other major products. This article draws parallels between that time and the present, warning that "If we fail to solve a problem of serious imbalance in grain purchase and marketing, we'll have no possibility of guaranteeing the people's livelihood, stabilizing market prices, maintaining social order, and ensuring the fulfillment of plans for socialist construction."[34] This manner of connecting state control with the people's sustenance links bureaucratic values and methods with positive state power in a way that seems to go beyond the self-interest of the writer.

The bureaucratic tendency proposes two sorts of strategies for dealing with free markets: implementing better management and organization of them by state offices, in order to incorporate them more closely into the state sector; and urging state departments to benefit financially from their activities through the collection of extra income from the taxes and management fees (*guanli fei*) their participants must turn over. The first of these, the organizational strategies, include establishing fixed cooperative relations between state market management departments and "keypoint" and "specialized" households in the countryside. Through such connections state concerns can call on these households to supply scarce commodities at reduced-fee rates while offering them transportation, in order to undercut individual merchants who are trying to buy up scarce goods cheaply to resell at a killing.

Other state-managed organizational strategies include setting up state-run wholesale markets to facilitate the interdistrict exchange of small commodities, as a way of retaining state control over the adjustment of supply and demand between areas; having state-managed general-goods companies organize individual firms to send foods to the countryside (under the aegis of the state, of course) by setting up a wholesale department within the company just to handle these concerns; and creating district-level private traders' federations in cities, which in turn are subdivided first into branch federations and then into small groups, and which are guided by the municipal industrial and commercial administrative departments in the regular study of relevant policies.[35]

An interesting contrast of two different organizational approaches to private commerce appears in press stories on Lanzhou and Harbin. Lanzhou boasted that its industrial and commercial administrative departments changed the "dirty, chaotic" situation in the city's markets by rearranging all individual firms to work in a certain district. Only a few months later, however, an article reporting on conditions in Harbin cites as a *problem* the fact that some departments, in the process of strengthening state control over the small firms, forced all the mobile merchants in the city to locate themselves on several designated streets, thereby obliterating their special feature of operating in a scattered and flexible manner.[36] Comparing these two articles reveals the differences across the country in handling petty traders, even at one given moment.

The second sort of bureaucratic strategy for handling private-sector trade stresses the economic benefits for the state of such commerce. The national press, often anxious in the past few years to promote freer trade, has made mention of some incentives that should encourage state-run enterprises and departments, concerned with their obligations to the planned economy, to accept and even nurture these new enterprises.[37] For instance, one article in praise of the private sector notes how fifty-two peasants who pooled their capital in a Fujian commune to form four long-distance trading teams were able to turn over some 30,000 yuan in management fees, some of which went to their brigades and some to the local industrial and commercial administrative departments. The business of these same teams also yielded over 40,000 yuan in taxes, paid to the local tax bureau (the fee rate was 1 percent; the tax rate 3 percent). Another story is from Shangshui County, Henan, where the state-run general-goods company managed to expand its own purchase and sales business, and to reduce its stockpiled goods by cooperating with the small firms, thereby increasing its total annual sales volume by 17.7 percent and its profit by 24 percent. Apparently, some local departments need to be convinced that there is something in it for them when the private sector flourishes.

Radical

Radical beliefs, now quickly identified by the reader by the terms *leftist* or *ossified thinking,* have their source in the radical attachment to egalitarianism in society, and to a strain in Marxism that disparages commercial activity for its parasitic, nonproductive nature.[38] Those holding such beliefs are charged with being "accustomed to using the concept of natural economy to view commodity production and the division of labor emerging in the countryside," who, "from the bonds of leftist thinking see this as 'abandoning agriculture for commerce.' " Considering agriculture and commerce as being in opposition one to the other, they deem the one absolutely good, the other totally bad. Moreover, even if some leftists manage to accept the possibility of some peasants improving their income, they think that producing grain, cotton, and oil and raising pigs, chickens, and rabbits is the only proper path for doing so, while engaging in sidelines such as handicraft, service, or transport, and especially commercial work, is crooked in contrast.[39] Radicals have their own fears about the private sector, but these are tied more to their horror of capitalism than to bureaucratic-style worries about the weakening of state-managed offices and controls per se. Qualms labeled "leftist" noted in the press include a "fear that as some individual laborers get rich first, polarization will occur; ... terrified by the sight of the restoration and development of the individual economy, some link it up with capitalism." This kind of analysis is coupled for radical thinkers with a sense of disgust that the national economy is retreating back to a state of rampant capitalism. For, in their estimation, socialist society ought not to permit some people to obtain large incomes (such as those gained in long-distance trade); and radicals see "public" as the only proper type of economic activity under socialism. These people are now blamed for continuing, at the present stage of development, to castigate as "speculators" merchants acting as middlemen, even as the critics of these "leftists" admit that such views were orthodox in China for decades.[40]

Because radicals regard nonstate commerce as "inferior" and take collective enterprise as merely an "elementary form" of public ownership, they feel justified in urging (or, as in the Cultural Revolution, engaging in) drastic action against it.[41] As for the individual economy, they try to crowd it out, or, at best, merge its little firms with state enterprises. Though the language differs, the effect for the collectives is the same: to "upgrade" this low-level specimen into the general "pattern" of government operated trade. This has entailed toppling a number of them or changing them into state-run enterprises, appropriating their assets in the process.

The foregoing has taken note of the kinds of reasoning to which representative lobbyists for each of the three lines resort in their arguments about the private sector, and the corollary action programs they push to realize their values. The presentation here, however, should not obscure the fact that throughout the period of the early 1980s only bureaucratic- and marketeer-type arguments have been promoted positively by the press. The general line from the center in these years has been to permit "free" trading activity, with the degree of controls on it varying over time and place along with the shifting balance between marketeer- and bureaucratic-based thinking in policy councils. The next section will connect local-level activity with the three lines, as it grounds the activities of economic actors in their disparate interests and resources.

Economic Actors in the Localities and Three Lines

Local Cadres and Their Units

Attempting to discover how the three lines cut across the population outside the top decision-making circles necessarily involves making inferences from the press. Interviewing local cadres, not to mention petty peddlers and peasants, about their own personal views on the private sector in more than the most indirect or casual manner would be either prohibited, hedged in with restrictions, or, because of reticence on the part of the subjects, otherwise ultimately unfruitful in China today. On top of this, the news media itself rarely quotes such people in their own words, but offers only tales of their activities, usually in the form of positive models or negative lessons for other, similarly placed readers to learn from.

Yet despite these obstacles, approaching the press reports through the lenses afforded by our threefold categorization helps to give meaning and order to the data there. And, in fact, the behavior described in these reports can indeed be collapsed into the classification scheme under utilization here.

It will become clear in the following discussion, however, that the same cadres may at one time follow one line, but, given changes in the incentives presented by shifting central policy, as well as changes in the resources in their own hands, they may under altered circumstances become proponents of other lines. Relevant resources, as the analysis will suggest, include position as well as powers and material goods; pertinent incentives may be either opportunities or threats.

Marketeer. At the grass roots, as at the top of the political system, there are cadres (and their enterprises and departments) who are prone to let markets flourish. But here, at the level of daily life, the personal enrichment markets can afford, more than the grander notion of national prosperity, seems most often to be the motivating factor. An economic goal, then, as in the case of marketeer central policy makers, informs cadres of this stripe, cadres, that is, who are poised and inclined to take advantage of the opportunities markets offer. Their enthusiasm for markets is backed up emotionally by some greed; in terms of resources, it is generally those cadres working in the state commercial sector who draw on the goods under their control to garner bribes and divert scarce commodities and precious foodstuffs in directions where payoffs lie. Marketeer-type cadres respond to the incentives presented by the liberalization policies—the chance for units to retain a percentage of profits over a base level and thus enhance their personal bonuses; the existence of negotiated prices, which allow them to bargain and obtain prices higher than those once set down by the state; the personal responsibility contract system, which rewards individuals for their own sales volume. As the head of the seafood group at the now infamous Chongwen market in Beijing openly boasted, "I want to take advantage of the present contract system to make more money." This statement was backed up by one of his female salespersonnel who had been involved in that market's recent large-scale illicit resales for profit, when she retorted under inquiry: "Policy or no policy, if there's money to be made, we sell."[42]

Aside from commercial-sector officials, the only other local cadres mentioned in the papers working in support of liberalization policies are local party unit leaders.[43] Presumably it is their charge more than anyone else's to promote the policy of the central elite. Perusal of the press reports of local-level activity during the early 1980s uncovers an interesting trend. Media criticism of markets in 1981 and 1982 focused particularly on the bureaucracy-mindedness of cadres, that is, on their discriminatory treatment of private enterprise and their preference for routing the best goods to retailers belonging to their own bureaucratic system. Their purpose then was to ensure that their own state-run company successfully met its targets for sales. By early 1983, however, the collusive dealings state cadres engaged in wholly outside the bounds of the state plan were more often the brunt of attack.

Generally these deals were struck between cadres and individual—most often, unlicensed—peddlers; or between state wholesalers or market officials in one place and units such as transport and catering companies from other localities (with which they ought not to have been doing business, according to the state plan's design, at least not before state targets were met); or even between cadres and the collective enterprises set up by unemployed youth with whom they had special relations. As one food company manager is quoted as having quipped, "We can't treat other enterprises the same way we treat enterprises connected with us when we wholesale beef. Because we want to let the staff and workers in our own department's enterprises and the unemployed youth increase their quota of fast-selling goods so they can earn a little more income."[44]

In one such episode in Harbin, a municipal fruit procurement and supply station let private merchants monopolize the market in sugar cane brought in from Canton. Because of that monopoly not even one *jin* of sugar was distributed through proper channels to the state retail shops, but over 54,000 *jin* was wholesaled to fifteen fruit merchants from other districts, while the rest was given over to a youth-run shop connected to the station for the young people to sell on commission.

This kind of story could be a sign that, as nonplanned, market modes of operation receive official endorsement over a longer stretch of time, state personnel are taking advantage of the opportunities offered in ways they did not dare to do before. In the process, the temptation to respond to market-type incentives may have become stronger than the old çalls to meet state-plan targets, with at least part of the private sector benefiting—at least until the law catches up. That such behavior can indeed deplete state markets is something I can verify from personal experience: as recounted in a late June *People's Daily* article, fruit disappeared in the Jianghan district of Wuhan in the spring of 1983. According to the article, the cause was the sort of activity described above.[45]

Bureaucratic. In contradistinction to marketeers (those with goods in their hands who want to see the markets flourish), many state cadres and their work units as a whole follow the bureaucratic line. These individuals pursue strategies which shore up the dominance of the state bureaucracy. Drawing on their main resource, the authority of the state and its offices, and motivated to hold on to their own primacy and positions, they work to fulfill the state plan, that framework for their ascendancy and guide for their responsibilities. Where marketeers focus on economic goals and use economic resources, the bureaucratic-liner both utilizes and aims to retain or build his or her power of command.

Despite the efforts noted above of bureaucratically inclined central-level politicians to get local state firms to coopt the business of the small enterprises, most bureaucratically based behavior at the local level appears to draw on two other sorts of tactics in handling this sector. Both of these involve maintaining the dominance of the state sector, and a given cadre is likely to pursue both strategies simultaneously: to keep the merchants too poor to pose any serious competition to state-run trade, they restrict merchants' activities and interfere with their business, through enforcing onerous regulations and exorbitant fees, and by making nearly impossible their obtaining capital, sites, and supplies. At the same time, though, they do let some petty entrepreneurs set up business, as the state cadres recognize them as a fertile source for squeeze. As one commentator writing in Hong Kong put it: "In general the local cadres have this kind of concept: 'Only let the individual firms open shop, but don't let them earn any money'; they thus see them as fat meat to be arbitrarily cut up."[46] For these cadres, suspicion, envy, and competitive feelings fuel their actions, as they respond to the incentives presented by the planned economy, and as they try to meet their own business volume targets and sustain their own units' historical monopoly of the market.

The motives of some state-run commercial firms in attacking and obstructing the trade of the private sector is obvious: in the words of one typical news article,

"Some people fear others operating business well, getting rich first; they worry that collective and individual commerce will develop quickly and the state's monopoly in commerce will break down."[47] In one Hebei commune in Leting County, the business of the individual firms only accounted for 5.9 percent of the total volume of retail sales. But, at the same time, the county supply and marketing cooperative system found that its own operations volume continuously fell over a period of several months. It was able, through its complaints that individual merchants were stealing its business, to convince "certain leading persons" in the county government to "cut off" more than 900 of the small firms, according to a reader's letter to the *People's Daily*.

In other parts of Hebei Province, not only commercial units, but local offices in charge of public health, public security, urban construction, city appearance, neighborhood organization, and taxation frequently confiscate licenses of the firms seemingly on a whim. As of early 1981, Jinan reported that the number of firms had been reduced by one-half in 1980 through such practices.[48]

Similarly, in Chengde County, Hebei, just to get the license in the first place an independent operator needs approval from five different organs (commerce, grain, supply and marketing, public health, and public security). In this county of over 400,000, only seven private merchants had received permission to ply their trades in the cities as of early 1983, while more than one hundred were still waiting to be allowed to do so.[49]

State firms trying to thwart the private sellers' success in sales have been charged with trading them commodities at higher prices to increase their costs, forcing them to buy wholesale-sized quantities that tie up their capital, selling them spoiled food or unpopular, low-quality manufactured items mixed in with the goods they want, or charging them at retail rates for replenishing their stocks.[50]

Other forms of harassment include forcing the firms to change their sites, ransacking their shops and even destroying their materials, and summoning them for interrogation. State-run units causing difficulties for the petty private sector include the police and the public security, transport companies, produce inspection stations, banks, tax collection and finance departments; and, frequently enough, the industrial and commercial administrative offices, overzealous in their enforcement of market order.[51]

In depicting the anger and discrimination the little firms arouse in local officials, one journalist mused ironically that the cadres seem to prefer vagrants on the streets (which some of the unemployed youths who try to open shops previously were, or which they would become without the chance the firms offer to earn a livelihood) to the individual enterprises, as the cadres shut down the firms in the name of "urban appearance." Another writer noted, similarly, that "concerned departments" don't accuse state-run enterprises setting up breakfast stalls with obstructing traffic and harming the city's appearance, but do so attack the private vendors, even though their booths take up less space.[52]

While some state departments make life difficult for the private firms by interfering with their work and confiscating their licenses, other units view them as providing an opportunity for extortion.[53] The various fees collected and the units involved are wide-ranging and multifaceted: for sanitation by public health units; by neighborhood offices, for managing sideline activities; by metrology departments, for checking on weights and measures; by traffic and urban construction committees, for occupying space in the streets and maintaining the city's appearance; for market supervision by the industrial and commercial administration departments; by epidemic prevention stations, for the examination of foodstuffs; by housing offices, for real estate fees; and by the public security, for overseeing public order. In addition, there are a range of other miscellaneous fees billed to the new enterprises for such things as slaughtering, the approval of seals, and for holding "unscheduled meetings." With each of these fees costing a small firm several yuan a month, plus income tax rates for businesses ranging from five to over 80 percent of total business volume, it is not particularly surprising to read that in Changchun 755 firms returned their licenses voluntarily in the first half of 1981, and that in Dalian over 1,000 closed down during 1981 and in the first half of 1982.[54]

Radical. As distinct from cadre activity that checks private sector trade by being excessively bureaucratic, or that milks the firms through fees and fines, the behavior of radically inclined cadres appears motivated by a specifically ideologically rooted distaste. For them the only solution is the outright abolition of private entrepreneurship. Though no one speaks openly in the press in favor of class struggle, many articles reveal that anxiety over income polarization is not uncommon in China today. Moreover, 1983 saw for the first time in decades some material in the papers charging "market overlords" with bullying the smaller merchants out of business;[55] concern also mounted about speculation, profiteering, and cheating of various sorts in the markets.

Units cracking down on these practices are intent on preserving features of socialism, with its guarantees of a decent and equitable life for all. When the basic ideological tenets of this system seem threatened, radicals draw attention to the negative aspects of freer business. Units involved with the private sector and representing this tendency are the civilian police, the public security, and the party's Discipline Inspection Committee at the lower levels, to judge from accounts of their behavior retold in the press.[56]

In one egregious case in Beijing, the army's civilian defense personnel and the sanitation civilian police beat up a retired woman who was helping her unemployed daughter sell fruit and tobacco in the city street, after the old woman refused to turn over their selling cart. The police used the pretexts that this business interfered with the city's appearance, that the selling was being done in a lane not designated for the private sector, and that the girl had given to her mother a license issued only for her own use. Police harassment eventually caused this poor girl, already unemployed for four years after high school graduation, to shut down her little business.[57]

Commenting on the mentality of obstructive local cadres, a Hong Kong journalist charged these officials with "ignorance, degeneracy, bureaucratism, and leftism."[58] In our terms, these designations represent the range of behaviors alluded to here in connection with the three lines: "degenerate" cadres are taking advantage of markets (and so are "marketeers"); "bureaucratic" cadres' harassment aims to uphold the dominance of the state system; and "radical" cadres oppose the private sector purely on "leftist" or ideological grounds. But just what any of these cadres may be "ignorant" of is unclear. For each group can be understood to be rationally pursuing the realization of its values or of what it takes as its interests.

The Private-Sector Practitioners

Laid atop this foundation of state cadres' activities, the story of the private-sector merchants can be told much more concisely. Given the officials' proclivities to collude with (marketeer); coopt, control, squeeze (bureaucratic); or eliminate (radical) the business people in the markets and stalls who are pushing carts or carrying poles, the peasants and peddlers wishing to take part in the new, more commercialized economy have several options. They may try their own luck as entrepreneurs, either individually or in partnerships, opening shops with borrowed capital and stocks garnered from who-knows-where, or collecting surplus agricultural produce for shipping to districts where goods are scarce. Obviously those rural households and the educated but unemployed youths who have sufficient labor power, funds, supplies, and skills are managing to succeed at such ventures.[59] For them, and, according to official statistical reports, many farm families across China, freer markets have spelt higher consumption standards in recent years.

With all the barricades set up by the bureaucrats, however, being an honest business person in China today seems to require not only the array of assets just listed, but some luck as well. Several front-page reports in the *People's Daily* in summer 1983 indicate that the numbers preferring to take risks by operating dishonestly, usually not registering for licenses but collaborating with state-run shops and wholesalers in getting stocks, have reached rather staggering proportions in some cities. For instance, in Lanzhou, where 200 merchants holding licenses dealt in vegetables, some 3,000 others were found to be operating covertly in June of that year.

Wuhan's market investigators turned up 1,200 spots where small stall peddlers were working without licenses (two service personnel I encountered there in May 1983 must have been members of this group, one of whom tried to charge me fifty cents—twenty-five times the usual cost—to stand on his scale; the other wanted to be paid five yuan for gluing on my shoe sole). And in

Shanghai more than 2,500 instances were uncovered involving unlicensed business and other forms of illegal exchange in the first half of June alone.[60] These gamblers as well as those dealing legally can all be counted marketeer, as they thrive on the presence of markets and so of course favor them.

Other private salespeople must be allowing themselves to be coopted or incorporated into the state system. For the object-lesson articles cited above propagating the value of state trade organs working with private merchants contain tales in which keypoint and specialized households and small vendors sending goods to the countryside have indeed cooperated with state-run organs.[61] Since their own business will succeed or fail depending on the extent to which they manage to comply with state-set procedures, vendors choosing this path fall into the bureaucratic category.

Others who are also thinking bureaucratically, in that they are preserving their faith in the system that has existed in China for three decades, are unemployed young people who prefer not to take advantage of the new system, choosing instead to wait for a state-sector job rather than operating in the free-market economy. They make this choice for several reasons: because the individual laborer's social position is still low in China's socialist society, because such a laborer's income is unstable, or because they feel that participating in this sphere may influence their opportunity for landing a "proper" job in the state economy later on.[62]

It is hard to pinpoint the background of the individuals still cherishing radical values in the stories in today's generally promarket press. Nevertheless, because of the efforts to control, squeeze, and remove the private sector's little firms, many of which in cities are run by youths, it seems reasonable to speculate that the frustrated young people thrown back into vagrancy and unemployment after taking a chance in the private sector may eventually, if not at present, form a contingent supportive of the radical solutions of the past.[63] That some people in China expect policy to shift back in this direction is revealed by the fact that some refuse to participate in the private sector out of fear that policy may change.[64] Thus, in the walks of daily life, as well as among opinion and decision makers, three attitudes toward the marketplace and its private-sector activity can be identified in China today, along with a range of behaviors that can also be categorized along the parameters of this trichotomy. The remaining part of this chapter will detail how the conflicts and excesses growing out of these attitudes and behaviors may play a role in producing policy changes.

Incentives, Excesses, and Conflicts: Triggers for Policy Change

"In historical context, it's often occurred in trade fairs that 'popularization leads to activity, activity to chaos, chaos to control, and control to inactivity.' "[65] This apt summation of the cyclical process characteristic of China's experience with a domestic private sector over the past several decades describes a pattern whose dynamics our model helps unravel. There are several steps in this repetitious interaction for which the foregoing analysis provides a framework.

First of all, any given new policy has attached to it certain incentives. Those who, because of their resources and powers, are in a position to respond to these incentives will do so, provided that they are in general agreement with the aims of the policy, and that they perceive it to be in their interests to align themselves with it. In the case of the policy of economic liberalization, central-level encouragement of small traders, the institution of negotiated prices (in essence, legalized bargaining), the right to retain a part of enterprise profits in state firms, and all the other aspects of this policy detailed above awoke responses, especially in households with extra labor power and business skills, and, within the state sector, in those firms that trade in scarce and popular goods.

Among the cadres, many preferred at first to cling to the dictates and structures of the planned economy to which they had become accustomed over a period of three decades. With time, however, the new incentives seem eventually to have counteracted or at least weakened the incentives attached to the old procedures. By 1983 more and more local bureaucrats had chosen to collude with the private sector rather than to control it.

Within the private sector, peddlers and peasants opting to associate with the practices of the private economy often "reacted with a vengeance . . . not always favorable to the state," as one economist put it.[66] Meanwhile, this system-in-transition (or mixed system) became one supporting a range of activities, each of which in different ways bespoke clashes between some two of the three tendencies or lines. These clashes occurred as various social groups/economic actors pursued the disparate rewards offered respectively by the several lines in conflict, often going beyond the limits of officially allowed activities as they did so.

These various sorts of excesses and conflicts in turn produced economic and social effects that central-level policy makers could not fail to note. And once the elite turns its attention to this feedback from their policies, their opinions fall into the three-line paradigm, from the perspective of the analyst. For all along there have been these different tendencies, if not rigidly dividing up the leadership into unchanging factions with constant stances, at least available to any given individual or group for consideration.

No doubt at times negative social and economic feedback from a currently pursued tendency provides those supporting a tendency that was out of favor with an opportunity to push their own policies. In other instances, it may be the case that the majority of the leadership as a whole finds such feedback a sufficiently significant trigger that a near consensus can be reached to shift policy back toward one of the other two tendencies.

This model of change can be fleshed out a bit through some examples of the kinds of excesses and conflicts that have led to shifts of emphasis in central policy in recent years. These new emphases occurred despite the generally continuous profession of the creed of economic liberalization.

Excesses

Many of the forms of overresponse (from the perspective of China's socialist leadership) that market incentives have produced in the early 1980s were alluded to above. Already in the summer of 1980, dubious rural cadres were "discovering that they were unable to stop the markets."[67] At that point, however, the press at most targeted adulteration of foodstuffs for sale or short-weighting in bazaars as the kind of behavior that should be censured and corrected. Then, by mid-1981, small-scale merchants were elevating the prices of such common items as brown sugar, wine, and tobacco anywhere from three cents to ten yuan per unit amount, as compared to state-set charges for the same items.[68] Within a couple of more years, however, thousands of private vendors, presumably by then more certain of the durability of the policy favoring them, were prepared to exploit this policy by taking risks on a far larger scale. Thus, they were daily rushing without licenses to the fields to snatch up big lots of vegetables; in free markets along the roads purchasing for resale what should go to the state; and even buying up large batches of goods right at state-run counters, by forming liaisons with official trade personnel.[69]

Adulteration of food had reached the extent of causing a "dramatic increase in intestinal infections" in Guangji County, Hubei, in late summer 1981. Some peddlers added water to wine, and, worse yet, mixed the water used to wash the milk pails in with the milk for sale. Others hawked dead pork and hare that food-poisoned the customers; while still others combined such rotten peanuts into peanut seed (for processing into oil) that eggs cooked in it smelled too foul to eat.[70] Also, official sources more and more grew concerned about the taxes going uncollected from individually and collectively run firms and at fairs, often enough because of intentional swindling and misrepresentation of accounts.[71]

Besides these illegal practices on the part of the members of the private sector, the press increasingly focused on illicit dealings between these wily merchants and state trade personnel. State shops and wholesalers by mid-1983 were even turning over rationed goods to private retailers, who would then withhold them from the market until prices rose; or letting store clerks privately buy commodities in short supply to resell at higher prices. Even the crucial commodity, grain, was being shipped to other localities for resale at a profit through nonstate channels.[72] In other words, the incentives to be nonbureaucratic were apparently gradually outweighing those linked to the state plan and its organized hierarchies.

A particularly flagrant case recounted in installments in the *People's Daily* was that of the Chongwen market in Beijing, one of the city's four largest state-run retail markets for vegetables. Here careful on-the-spot investigative reporting uncovered a group of state-market personnel, incited to action by the institution of the responsibility system, and using the slogan "enliven operations" as their pretext, in the act of shipping truckloads of food to outside units and local "connections firms" (*guanxi hu*). With the market's party branch secretary and its manager personally directing the action, nearly 400 *jin* of dried squid and over 90,000 *jin* of vermicelli, among other things, left the market in the dark of night just in the three months of April through June 1983.[73]

In these kinds of episodes at first the private sector participants, but eventually state personnel as well, responded to incentives and even stretched their meanings in a manner that already in 1980 was beginning to be hard to halt. The similarities are striking between the behavior described in these articles, on one hand—corruption by private merchants and cadre collusion with such merchants and with other cadres—and activities recounted in the press of the early 1950s, before the socialist transformation campaign of 1956, on the other.[74] It may be that the continuing incantation by central leaders of the policy of invigorating the domestic economy is not just weakening state controls in general terms. It may also be leading to the actual disruption of bureaucratic hierarchies, and of the incentives to follow bureaucratic procedures, as the lure of the market makes undercover dealing with the private sector more profitable than the bureaucratic forms of corruption more customary over the past few decades—the hoarding of goods within one's own unit, region, or functional system.

Conflicts

Nonetheless, especially during the earlier period of the market initiative, but later on as well, many cadres working in state-managed offices and enterprises continued to orient their behavior in bureaucratic ways. Conflicts within the state sector, between levels in the bureaucracy, between public and private sectors, and ultimately between tendencies or lines, were the result. One article from early 1982 spoke of what it termed "tangled warfare" (*hun zhan*) within the state sector, in addition to the competition going on between private and public channels for trade. In its account, state plans for purchasing fast-selling, scarce goods were not being fulfilled, in part because of contention between factories rushing to production sites to procure raw materials, shopworkers traveling directly to rural areas to buy up goods, and even some foreign trade departments participating in the melee, all without any concern for whether or not the local purchase task for state commerce had been completed. The commentator concluded that prices were rising because state channels for goods were becoming depleted.[75] In this case, the promarket policy induced competitive behavior within the state sector, but the various units involved maintained their loyalties to their own, state-run units.

Another form of bureaucratic behavior exhibited by public departments that caused contention showed up in the several stories in the press of unanswered appeals when private entrepreneurs who were wronged sought the aid of superior, but still subcentral offices.[76] Some press reports suggested that the upper-level units (at the city, district, or even provincial levels) simply turned a blind eye to these infractions; one analysis from Hong Kong, though, voiced the suspicion that the local cadres must be incited by higher-level officials, or they would never dare to cause such obstruction.[77]

While bureaucratically oriented units at various echelons below the center seem often to have closed ranks in opposition to the private sector, such behavior also constituted the contravention of promarketeer central-level policy, thereby activating another line of conflict. As this same Hong Kong writer put it, "despite full state support [for the policy of liberalization toward the private sector], there's pressure from the local cadres."[78] That is, regardless of marketeer-type directives from the capital, marketeer-inclined merchants have frequently to contend with bureaucratically biased cadres at home. Many of the newspaper stories speak of local officials drawing on "old documents" or on their responsibility for market control, or using the campaign to "strike at serious crimes in the economic sphere" all as excuses to affix fines, confiscate goods, and withdraw licenses, despite orders from Beijing to relax trade restrictions.

In one case in Xiu County, Hunan, a youth vending fish with a hand-pulled tractor lost over 600 yuan as a result of harassment from a tax collection unit and the local meat procurement station. Although the county party committee ruled that the boy should be compensated for his loss, it refrained from assigning responsibility to the departments involved. This was because, so the party committee reasoned, the units were merely implementing the "original policy regulations," which just happened to be inconsistent with then-present policy, a "normal phenomenon" it said, "in a period of change."[79]

References to counterattacks by bold members of the private sector offer some indication that the harassment has not been all in one direction in this battle between two lines. Thus, commercial regulations issued in June 1983 by the Tianjin Municipal Industrial and Commercial Administrative Control Bureau threatened strict punishments by the public security and judicial departments for "those who have beaten or cursed personnel in charge of market management."[80]

And, finally, one last form of conflict brought on by the new marketeer policy lies within the private sector itself.[81] One such case involved a gang of fish-peddling market despots who intercepted goods, raised prices, and resold for profit, while they also bullied and oppressed both the owners of cargo and properly operating individual stall peddlers in the largest market of Shanghai. Since this gang controlled the prices in the market as a whole, those whose prices were lower than the gang's were forced out of business.

In another account, "black sheep" were said to "lurk" among the individual enterprises in Beijing, verbally abusing and beating up buyers, and even carrying concealed weapons threatening the lives of the customers. According to the reporter, these are unlicensed merchants, some of whom are hoodlums and persons released from prison, but others of whom are merely jobless youths or even workers holding jobs. They force customers to buy when they examine and price the merchandise. Disputes in business transactions with such merchants have reportedly led to violence and murder. And besides attacking and threatening customers, these businesspeople also harass market management personnel. The article relating this information hinted at the larger social implications of the actions of such traders in its warning: "if this situation is allowed to develop, 'northern overlords' and 'southern overlords' will surface again." Apparently, the marketplace of today contains the seeds of incipient class struggle.

Overall, then, incentives presented by marketeer policies induced cadres in some state organs, still true to their bureaucratic upbringing, to become more competitive, but still strictly along the lines created by the hierarchies and systems of the state plan; reinforced loyalties among the several lower echelons beneath the center, as they set those faithful to the bureaucracy against both marketeer-prone central officials and members of the private sector; caused local cadres to fall back on old documents and pretexts in their efforts to shore up their wonted role on China's economic stage; and brought on what appears to be the beginnings of a certain degree of class warfare within the marketplace.

The last stage in this explanation is to examine the way this conflict along with the excesses noted above, both of which issue from the incentives of the new marketeer initiative, trigger reevaluations and reemphasis among the central policy-making elite.

Conclusion: The Dynamics of Policy Change

With the exception of the period surrounding the December 1980 Central Party Work Conference, when grave concerns about inflation and state budgetary deficits made it possible for the elite to come to a general agreement on the need for a price freeze and for intensified controls over the markets, liberal, marketeer policies toward the private sector have been more or less continuously in force since early 1979. But, as noted near the outset of this chapter, fine shadings of variation, such as whether or not long-distance trade is permitted; whether private traders may engage in wholesale as well as retail trade; whether first-category goods can be sold on free markets; the number of apprentices permitted in the small urban enterprises; and the range and scope for negotiated prices, came and went in the first four or five years of this policy's life covered here.

Also, as discussed in different places above, only at certain times were speculation, resale for profit, short-weighting, swindling, adulteration, tax evasion, and operating without a license the subject of press accounts. State cadres in the localities sometimes were censured for ignoring or harassing the petty traders; but at other times were charged with coddling and colluding with the worst of them, those peddlers operating on the fringes of the system without having properly registered with the authorities. At some points the central elite directed local party and government units to strengthen market and price controls; while only a few months later local departments were castigated for hampering the business activities of the individually and collectively owned firms. With the analysis of the three lines laid out here, it is possible now to set this changing policy in an analytic context.

It is always difficult in reading the Chinese press to know definitively whether certain sorts of stories appear at a given juncture because there is indeed more of the type of activity they delineate occurring in society at that time; or whether such tales are brought to the surface because reporters have been instructed to ferret them out, in order to represent a viewpoint then current within the central elite. Without pronouncing on either side of this researcher's dilemma, it is still possible to draw some conclusions about the connection between the three tendencies and economic actors' excesses and conflicts, on the one hand, and shifts in the policy mix at the center, on the other.

Three general types of behavior designated dysfunctional by central policy-makers have been highlighted and censured in the news about markets in the early 1980s. These are, first, their diverting of goods, so that scarcities arise in state-trade channels, the plan is upset, and, so the reasoning goes, inflation occurs; second, their merchants' tyrannizing of customers and of other sorts of petty traders; and, third, their harming the interests of consumers, through unsanitary and polluting practices, tricks with weights and measures, price manipulation, and the like. Each of these kinds of activity has genuine social and economic consequences; each is brought on by the conflicts and excesses described above; and each is viewed as especially heinous by policy-making proponents of one of the three tendencies. If at some point behavior of these sorts can be shown to be excessive, making it possible for those most incensed by it to build a winning coalition or create a consensus around their displeasure, policy with new emphases is soon issued, designed to skew popular marketing practices back away from the particular excess at hand.

To spell this out more fully, diverting goods, at least in the interpretation typically offered in the Chinese papers, is brought on by private entrepreneurs "wantonly" grabbing goods before state quotas are fulfilled, acting too marketeerly, as it were; and by state organs, sometimes from bureaucratic motives, sometimes from marketeer ones, competing either among themselves, against private traders, or in collusion with these merchants, to get hold of commodities in demand. This kind of behavior particularly outrages bureaucratically inclined policy-makers, and its appearance makes it possible for such individuals to shift the line at least for a time to one of tighter controls over markets, along with directing more official attention to problems of fulfilling state plans and of ensuring state domination over the supply of goods.

The second kind of excess, tyrannizing small merchants, results from local cadres' concerns about their obligations to and own power base in the state-run economy. The primary conflict here is one between the bureaucratic line pursued by such officials on the one hand, and the marketeer activities that the merchants are trying to carry out, on the other. The occurrence of this activity particularly troubles promarketeer central officials, and, when these individuals believe that it is happening to an excessive extent, it seems that they can shift official opinion toward concern over this, as the papers soon emphasize the importance of invigorating the economy, and of giving a freer hand to the private-sector business people.

Then, third, damaging the interests (and the wallets) of ordinary customers brings out the radical strain in many central leaders, and, by late 1983 even legitimized the return of radical-type language in the press, as the term "class struggle" reemerged after a few years of having been put to rest.[82] In radical logic, behavior of this sort comes about as an effect of the excesses of marketeers, in their chasing after profits, money, and wealth. At several points in the early 1980s, this concern appeared in the press as a recurring strain, a fact that indicates a certain hesitancy, a kind of unease with capitalistic practices under socialism, despite the wish of many leaders to let the economy prosper. Reportage stressing disorders and illegalities in the markets was generally accompanied and followed by stricter regulations, sometimes promulgated nationally, sometimes broadcast locally.

At the time of this writing, nearly half a decade has passed since the Third Plenum of the Eleventh Party Central Committee of December 1978 authorized a policy already enunciated ten months previously at the Fifth National People's Congress—to let the individual economy operate legally once again in China. And yet only recently, the State Council still found it necessary to issue a set of "supplementary regulations" on the nonagricultural individual economy in the cities.[83] This document's final substantive ruling in a list of fourteen of these was this: various levels of the industrial and commercial administrative management organs must do three things: strengthen administrative management over the individual firms, guarantee their legal operation, and ban their illegal activities. This study of the three lines and the petty private sector has uncovered many of the reasons why Chinese leaders today believe that (bureaucratic) administrative management still needs to be emphasized over the little firms; why their (marketeer) operations are seen to require legal guarantees; and why and how their entrepreneurs engage in illegalities, that is, in illicit acts repugnant to radicals.

Notes

1. *Renmin ribao* (Beijing) (People's Daily) (hereafter *RMRB*), January 9, 1983, p. 1.
2. These terms are borrowed from my book, *Chinese Business Under Socialism* (Berkeley: University of California Press, 1984). Chapter 2 of that book introduces these terms and their content at some length.
3. I use the term "petty private sector" to refer to the very small-scale commercial activity that individual peasants, peddlers, young people without state-sector jobs, and retired persons (or small groups of each) engage in at fairs, on city streets, or as itinerant hawkers in the rural areas. I am not planning to deal with the vastly more capitalized and complicated businesses being initiated by the one-time wealthy capitalists in China's major metropolises in recent years.

4. See Franklyn Griffiths, "A Tendency Analysis of Soviet Policy-Making," in *Interest Groups in Soviet Politics*, ed. H. Gordon Skilling and Franklyn Griffiths (Princeton: Princeton University Press, 1971), pp. 337, 363–64. Griffiths uses the concept of "tendency" to explicate policy making and conflict over policy, and he notes that a given tendency contains three elements: a value or goal; an analysis of the situation in which the individual or organization is to pursue the given value; and a recommendation or demand stating how the given value should be allocated in a given situation.

5. *RMRB*, August 29, 1980, translated in U.S. *Foreign Broadcast Information Service* (hereafter *FBIS*), September 11, 1980, p. L58.

6. See Solinger, *Chinese Business Under Socialism*, chap. 6.

7. Ibid.

8. See *Peking Review*, no. 10 (1978): 22, for Hua's report; and no. 11 (1978): 7, for Article 5 of that constitution.

9. Cotton rationing was terminated, "temporarily," according to the State Council order that decreed this, as of the end of 1983. See *FBIS*, November 23, 1983, p. K9; and November 28, 1983, p. K17. Presumably cotton would be legally sold on free markets beginning in 1984.

10. These developments are traced and referenced in *Chinese Business Under Socialism*, chaps. 4, 5, and 6.

11. For a comparison of the two regulations, see Dorothy J. Solinger, "The 1980 Inflation and the Politics of Price Control in the PRC," paper prepared for the workshop on "Policy Implementation in Post-Mao China," cosponsored by the Joint Committee on Chinese studies of the Social Science Research Council and the American Council of Learned Societies, and the Mershon Center of the Ohio State University, Columbus, Ohio, June 1983, pp. 24–25.

12. See Market Management Bureau of the Central Bureau of Industrial and Commercial Administrative Control, "How to Regard Merchant Activity in Rural Non-Staple Commodities," *Hongqi* (Red flag) (hereafter *HQ*), no. 2 (1981): 29–30.

13. See *RMRB*, July 16, 1981, p. 2, on individual laborers; and *FBIS*, August 12, 1981, pp. K3–6, on agricultural products.

14. Reported in the *New York Times*, November 24, 1981, and in *RMRB*, November 11, 1982, p. 1, respectively.

15. See *RMRB*, November 11, 1982, p. 2; November 18, 1982, p. 1; November 29, 1982, p. 3; January 6, 1983, p. 2; January 7, 1983, p. 5; January 29, 1983, p. 2; and February 7, 1983, p. 5, for a few examples.

16. In *FBIS*, April 26, 1983, pp. K8–11, and April 27, 1983, pp. K9–12.

17. *RMRB*, May 25, 1983, p. 1.

18. *FBIS*, April 25, 1983, p. K18.

19. For news on Tianjin, see *FBIS*, June 16, 1983, p. R1; on Wuhan, see *RMRB*, June 29, 1983, p. 1; for Shanghai, see *RMRB*, March 4, 1983, p. 1, and July 6, 1983, p. 1; and for Beijing (typically clamping down on free trade sooner and more harshly than other places), *RMRB*, March 13, 1983, p. 2.

20. These figures and those that follow are in *RMRB*, March 10, 1981, p. 2, and *FBIS*, March 24, 1983, p. K11. My hesitations about them derive principally from the fact that, especially in 1983, there were many articles on unlicensed peddlers, tax evasion, and illicit diversion of goods. Obviously this subterranean part of the private sector cannot be accurately counted in official statistics. The data on the percent of total retail sales occupied by free markets come from Nai-Ruenn Chen, "China's Inflation, 1979–1982: A Quantitative Assessment" (draft).

21. He Jianzhang, "Actively Support, Appropriately Develop Individual Economy in Cities and Towns," *HQ*, no. 24 (1981): 14; *Beijing Review* (hereafter *BR*), no. 17 (1983):

4; *Far Eastern Economic Review*, April 28, 1983, p. 40; and *FBIS*, February 24, 1983, p. K14.

22. *RMRB*, November 11, 1982, p. 2; November 18, 1982, p. 1; January 7, 1983, p. 5; January 18, 1983, p. 2; and January 29, 1983, p. 2.

23. *RMRB*, January 12, 1983, p. 1, and *FBIS*, March 2, 1983, p. P2.

24. *RMRB*, January 6, 1983, p. 2, and July 24, 1982, p. 3.

25. *BR*, no. 17 (1983), p. 4.

26. *RMRB*, July 24, 1982, p. 3.

27. He, "Individual Economy," p. 15.

28. *RMRB*, July 24, 1982, p. 3.

29. *RMRB*, February 27, 1983, p. 5.

30. *RMRB*, January 12, 1983, p. 1.

31. *RMRB*, November 11, 1982, p. 1, and January 25, 1983, p. 1.

32. *RMRB*, July 24, 1982, p. 3.

33. RMRB, January 8, 1982, p. l.

34. *HQ*, no. 9 (May 1, 1983): 41–45, translated in *FBIS*, June 8, 1983, pp. K10–18.

35. *RMRB*, June 13, 1983, p. 3; November 30, 1981, p. 2; January 11, 1982, p. 2; August 9, 1982, p. 2; and *FBIS*, July 3, 1983, p. Q6.

36. Contrast *RMRB*, April 23, 1982, p. 2, with July 2, 1982, p. 2.

37. *RMRB*, January 12, 1983, p. 1; June 12, 1982, p. 3; January 7, 1983, p. 2; and January 28, 1983, p. 3.

38. On this theme, see Dorothy J. Solinger, "Marxism and the Market in Socialist China," in *State and Society in Contemprary China*, ed. Victor Nee (Ithaca: Cornell University Press, 1983), pp. 194–219.

39. *RMRB*, April 3, 1983, p. 5; February 7, 1983, p. 5; January 6, 1983, p. 2; and January 9, 1983, p. 1.

40. Xue Mou, "How to Accurately Understand Small Production after Socialist Transformation Is Basically Done," *HQ*, no. 21 (1981): 43; He, "Individual Economy," p. 15; *RMRB*, January 7, 1983, p. 5; and *RMRB*, November 18, 1982, p. 1.

41. *RMRB*, January 9, 1983, p. 1, and December 12, 1982, p. 2.

42. *RMRB*, August 4, 1983, p. 2. More on this market appears later in this chapter.

43. Examples of articles showing the party committee, usually at the county level, urging support for the private sector are in *RMRB*, November 11, 1982, p. 2; November 18, 1982, p. 1, and March 3, 1982, p. 2. In these reports, the party committee is often shown in opposition to or in instruction of other units.

44. *RMRB*, May 29, 1983, p. 2. Other similar stories are in *RMRB*, July 7, 1983, p. 1, and *FBIS*, July 12, 1983, p. R2.

45. *RMRB*, July 25, 1983, p. 2 (for Harbin); and *RMRB*, June 30, 1983, p. 1 (on Wuhan). I was living in that district at that time and found virtually no fruit for sale. Of course, I have no way of knowing just who was responsible, but the leadership group has been found guilty and replaced, according to the *People's Daily*.

46. Xiao Xiangzi, "Obstacles to the Development of China's Economy," *Zheng Ming* (Hong Kong) (Contention), no. 48 (October 1981): 74.

47. *RMRB*, January 27, 1983, p. 4.

48. *RMRB*, February 27, 1983, p. 5.

49. See *RMRB*, March 28, 1981, p. 2, on Jinan; *RMRB*, February 27, 1983, p. 5, on Chengde County.

50. See *RMRB*, July 5, 1981, p. 5; Xiao, "Obstacles," p. 74; and *RMRB*, January 9, 1983, p. 1, for a few articles representative of dozens containing such stories.

51. Press accounts about these various departments' obstructive activities are in *FBIS*, April 25, 1983, p. K18; *RMRB*, November 18, 1982, p. 1; March 3, 1982, p. 2; January 9,

1983, p. 1; January 27, 1983, p. 4; February 27, 1983, p. 5; January 20, 1983, p. 2; and April 30, 1983, p. 5.

52. Xiao, "Obstacles," p. 73; and *RMRB*, January 9, 1982, p. 1.

53. Accounts of the kinds and amounts of fees, taxes, and fines levied can be found in Ch'en Ting-chung, "Individual Economy on the Mainland," *Issues & Studies*, no. 17 (August 1981): 6–7; Xiao, "Obstacles," pp. 73–74; and *RMRB*, February 27, 1983, p. 5.

54. *RMRB*, October 11, 1982, p. 2; and Xiao, "Obstacles," p. 74.

55. E.g., *RMRB*, July 6, 1983, p. 1.

56. The public security is depicted as driving them away or detaining and fining them at will in *FBIS*, April 25, 1983, p. K18, and as taking away their licenses for obstructing traffic in *RMRB*, January 9, 1983, p. 1. The discipline inspection committee in Fengnan County, Hebei, was reported to have brought a lawsuit against an individual peddler for buying cloth to process into clothing for sale in *RMRB*, February 27, 1983, p. 5.

57. *RMRB*, January 27, 1933, p. 4.

58. Xiao, "Obstacles," p. 74.

59. See *RMRB*, November 11, 1982, p. 2; and November 29, 1932, p. 3, for rural success stories; and Zhang Xinxin, "How Did a Small Stall Peddler Get Rich?" *Jing bao* (Hong Kong) (Mirror), no. 8 (August 1981): 20–22.

60. *RMRB*, July 7, 1983, p. 1 (Lanzhou); June 9, 1983, p. 1 (Wuhan); and July 6, 1983, p. 1 (Shanghai).

61. See note 35 above.

62. He, "Individual Economy," p. 15; Xiao, "Obstacles," p. 74.

63. Xiao, "Obstacles," p. 73, offers a story of one such youth.

64. Ibid., p. 74, is only one place among many where such a fear is noted.

65. *RMRB*, August 29, 1980, in *FBIS*, September 11, 1980, p. L59.

66. Robert F. Dernberger, "The Chinese Search for the Path of Self-Sustained Growth in the 1980's: An Assessment," in Joint Economic Committee, Congress of the United States, *China Under the Four Modernizations, Part 1* (Washington, DC: U.S. Government Printing Office, 1982), p. 50.

67. *FBIS*, September 11, 1980, p. L58.

68. *RMRB*, April 12, 1981, p. 3.

69. *RMRB*, July 7, 1983, p. 1.

70. *RMRB*, July 11, 1983, p. 2; February 20, 1982, p. 5; and September 5, 1981, p. 3.

71. *RMRB*, July 16, 1983, p. 3, and February 8, 1982, p. 2.

72. *FBIS*, July 16, 1983, p. R1, and July 3, 1983, p. O6.

73. The facts of the case are set out in *RMRB*, August 4, 1983, p. 2.

74. For a discussion of the types of activities going on in southwestern China in the early 1950s, see my article, "State Versus Merchant: Commerce in the Countryside in the Early People's Republic of China," *Comparative Studies in Society and History* 21, 2 (April 1979): 168–94.

75. *RMRB*, January 8, 1982, p. 1.

76. Reference to this kind of situation is in *RMRB*, January 7, 1983, p. 5; August 4, 1983, p. 2; and January 27, 1983, p. 4.

77. Xiao, "Obstacles," p. 73.

78. Ibid. Why is commerce different from agriculture? According to an article by David Zweig, "Opposition to Change in Rural China: The System of Responsibility and People's Communes," *Asian Survey* 22, 7 (1983): 885, in some rural areas, "pressure from above meshed with support (for the system of contracting land to individual peasant households) from below, squeezing the middle-level bureaucrats who opposed the policy. . . . This policy has relied on an unofficial coalition between reformers and peasants from the poor areas. Caught in this vise, middle level cadres could do little but accept the

changes." Probably the traditional and Marxist hesitations about the worth of trade—and the positive valuation that old attitudes put on agricultural production—weaken the hand of rural cadres who are trying to obstruct the responsibility system, a policy that is being associated with increasing agricultural productivity. At the same time, such views strengthen cadre efforts to place controls over commerce. However, *FBIS*, August 16, 1983, p. P7, contains a report indicating that "more than 500 peasant households in a Hunan county [or 10 percent of the local peasant households] have asked to reduce the contracted rice fields, because cadres have placed 'excessive charges' on the contracted land."

79. *RMRB*, March 3, 1982, p. 2. See also August 29, 1980; January 18, 1982, p. 1; January 6, 1983, p. 2; January 7, 1983, p. 5; and January 20, 1983, p. 2.

80. *FBIS*, June 16, 1983, p. R1. For similar attacks on those enforcing price control regulations, see *FBIS*, January 13, 1981, pp. L6–7, and February 9, 1981, p. L19.

81. *RMRB*, July 6, 1983, p. 1, and *FBIS*, July 20, 1983, pp. R2–3, report the two accounts that follow.

82. See, for example, *FBIS*, August 1, 1983, p. K11, in the "Report on the Work of Striking at Serious Crimes in the Economic Field," where Party Chairman Hu Yaobang's report to the Party's Twelfth Congress (in September 1982) is quoted thus: "Grave criminal offenses in the economic sphere . . . are important manifestations of class struggle under the new historical conditions in which we are pursuing a policy of opening to the outside and taking flexible measures to invigorate our economy domestically."

83. *RMRB*, April 25, 1983, p. 2.

11
Urban Entrepreneurs and the State:
The Merger of State and Society

Urban economic reform in China has not yet led to the emergence of what is popularly labeled "civil society,"[1] among the business class. Nor has it hewed out any sharp and novel borderline between the "state" and a distinctive sphere of "society" among its subjects in this particular realm. No "repluralization"[2] can be said to have issued from some genuine formation of a "private" realm truly separate from the still enveloping "public" one for those who make their lives in the marketplace. Instead, the essential economic monolith of the old party-state now shapes official and merchant alike; both have become dependent, mutually interpenetrated semi-classes, even as both share a new kind of dependence on the state. As a Chinese commentator described the situation:

> China's private economy has developed . . . during the transformation from a product economy of unitary composition into a planned commodity economy of coexisting multiple economic sectors . . . because the strong socialist public sector occupies the dominant place in the national economy, the private sector developing in this situation cannot but be related to, as well as influenced and restricted by, the public sector. . . . Hence it must be dependent on the socialist public economy and at the same time supplement it.[3]

Thus, in contrast to Eastern Europe, it is yet difficult to speak of any real "autonomy" of social forces from the state,[4] at least where what might be called the bourgeoisie is concerned.[5]

This chapter was presented at the conference on "State and Society in China: The Consequences of Reform, 1978–1990," the Keck Center for International Strategic Studies, Claremont McKenna College, February 16 and 17, 1990.

Reprinted from *State and Society in China: The Consequences of Reform*, ed. Arthur Lewis Rosenbaum (Boulder: Westview Press, 1992), by permission of the publisher.

This joint dependence—on the state and on each other—fosters collaboration in some instances but also intense competition in many others, as merchant and bureaucrat both battle over but also at times jointly participate in the expansion of a single pot of state resources, state-owned supply channels, and state-dominated sales outlets.[6] The complexity of the concept of "entrepreneur" and its applicability to a range of actors within what is typically termed the "public sector" as well as within the new so-called private sphere in the cities exemplifies this pattern.

Since there are no clear indications of where this historical formation is heading in the short run, any assumption that we are witnessing an ultimately predictable "transition" from a planned to a market economy may skew the analysis away from considering this particular period as sui generis and as potentially quite protracted. It is neither plan nor market although it partakes of both. Consequently, agents of the plan and practitioners in the market are, respectively, no longer fully bureaucrat nor yet true merchants operating autonomously.

The most dominant and determining characteristic of this stage is what may by this point be termed a prolonged decomposition of the hereditary monolithic elite mobility channel once constructed by the party-state at its peak. Under the regimen of that totalistic channel, all commercial and industrial social forces were steered toward and absorbed within the all-encompassing net of orthodox associations. This absorption was first accomplished for the business class through the socialist transformation of the mid-1950s, and soon thereafter anchored into place by the assimilation of that class into such institutions as the *danwei* and the trade union federation for the lesser fry, and the Chinese People's Political Consultative Conference and its associated All-China Federation of Industry and Commerce and "democratic parties" for the bigger fish. Positioned atop that rigid structure and holding it firmly together sat the mighty *nomenklatura.*

Ironically, however, the party-state's imposition of an organizational and leadership framework that obliterated the operational and political autonomy of once private social formations actually *emphasized* rather than having erased or made more "porous" the boundary[7] between what may be called "state" and "society" in the business world in the cities. In fact, despite the single route to power, influence, and status for the elite under the socialist system, and regardless of the absorption of the business sector into elite-contoured and commanded collectivities, there was a *sharper* demarcation line between "state" and urban "society" (understood as what is commonly called "the private sector," the capitalist class) in the prereform era than has developed since the reforms began. That is, there was in those times an absolute bar against entering the preferred "state" sectoral jobs and obtaining their perquisites, plus an impenetrable restriction against party membership for formerly "bourgeois" social forces, who were, in essence, ascriptively excluded from these privileges.[8] Thus, one might speak of a "society" of former business forces that was at once detached, even barred, from the state even as it was submerged, encompassed, even locked up within the bonds of that state's very institutions.

The onset of reform has begun to shatter this singularity of the path to power, just as it has seemingly freed nonstate actors, by opening opportunities for new occupational alternatives for the members of the long isolated society. Nonetheless, the differentiation of social forces that is accompanying the reform is quite a partial one, so that categories that were previously discrete and unrelated have instead become in some senses symbiotic. The result is a continuation if in quite altered form of the state's social hegemony, under which a business sector that is still largely incorporated and captured has appeared. The presence of this new sector has recast officialdom as well.

Thus, as the monolith of the party-state's elite stratum breaks apart, freeing both official and merchant from the fixity of the former party-controlled frame, the pieces chipping off it are all different amalgams of that monolith. It is as if forces that were once incapable of combination have merged, even if often in complicated, uncongenial, and competitive fashions.

Most importantly, except in the southeast coastal region where overseas remittances and joint ventures with Hong Kong partners provide a foundation for a capital formation which is truly separate from the state, there is as yet no true autonomy of economic power for a "private" sector, nor any genuine division of labor between economic and political power in the cities. The state and its institutions remain for the Chinese urban entrepreneur who operates on a scale of some size the principal source of start-up capital; in addition, entré to the state's means of production and guidance through its regulatory and informational labyrinth has been the *sine qua non* for business activity. All of these constraints keep the new merchant force dependent. The new "bourgeoisie," such as it is, is one, then, whose members usually lack their own means of production, independent capital, material supplies, and modes of operation.

Simultaneously, officialdom—party cadres, state bureaucrats, and state enterprise managers—have engaged in exchanges with, and constantly essayed to collude with and incorporate, or simply to take their squeeze from the profits, skills, connections, and time of the incipient merchant force, rendering officialdom dependent now not just as before on the state but sometimes on the new "private" sector as well. The outcome to date has been a stratum of people exclusively pursuing business who are inextricably entangled with cadredom, and an official class increasingly corroded by commercialism. Both are "entrepreneurs."

Consequently, given this overlap of social forces, concretized in a sometimes intentional, sometimes constrained collaboration among mutually dependent semi-classes, the bribery, extortion, corruption, and bargains that have frequently been the object of at least rhetorical opprobrium do not, at the analytical level, really occur between two distinct groups. One could rather claim that, since "doing business" often involves the participation of both formations, such exchanges in fact take place within one blended class to which they both belong.

This complex class, much like the "bureaucratic capitalists" at the apex of the imperial order in late dynastic times or the "gentry-merchants" who inhabited its base in the localities,[9] is the paradoxical product of a splitting off of new, officially sanctioned professions from the formerly monolithic elite mobility channel. In the late Qing as in the recent PRC, diversification of the economy (in both cases initiated at the peak of the polity) and a crisis in the orthodox ideology together brought into being new occupations or helped to legitimize trades disparaged when the regime was stronger and more authoritative, the economy less elaborate.

What appears as a liberation of society has actually at both times (though more so today) been an incorporation of society, albeit under grossly altered terms. As Fairbank expressed this situation in writing of the late Qing, "The line between landlord-gentry and merchant was blurred; merchant-gentry now acquired degree status, just as the roles of official and merchant became homogenized in bureaucratic entrepreneurs."[10]

Taking a long view, it is possible to see the present moment as one in which a familiar historical cycling has so far repeated itself. This cycling is one in which in a kind of dialectical interaction state and business class recurrently merge and come apart. The start of the Communist party regime in the early 1950s, as with the period of consolidation of KMT power in the late 1920s, saw the state gathering its power and mustering all available social capital as it placed itself in blatant opposition to the business class.[11]

Both new regimes treated this class as a force to be first milked and preyed upon, but ultimately conquered. The outcome was to force what had been separate and potentially competing classes into a monolithic order in which the bourgeoisie was emasculated, having lost its ability to defend its interests, whether political or economic.

A second stage in this dynamic matches in a structural sense the long years of essentially unbroken party economic power in the People's Republic after 1956 on the one hand with the heyday of dynasties, on the other. During such eras, the state, with its power, confidence and hegemony at their peak, was able to impose upon society a monolithic mobility channel, sometimes excluding and other times subsuming, capturing, coopting, and incorporating within itself alternate, unofficial, or unorthodox economic forces in society.

True, Communist party hegemony was far more encompassing and exclusive than anything attempted or even intended by the Qing. In its most benign guise, as in the high Qing tax farming out to the merchants described by Mann[12] or the self-managing guilds depicted by Hamilton,[13] this was merging that admitted of some autonomy and entailed in some spheres a form of official-societal collaboration sanctioned by the state. But the primary impulse of all money-holding families in this era was to prepare the conditions for at least one of their offspring to enter the elite stratum, and the monolithic dominance of just one channel of real prestige sustained the hegemony of the state.

The third and final phase of this process is the one in which the PRC finds itself today: This is a time of partial state withdrawal, of state admission that society has become too large and too unmanageable and that the state's tasks have turned too complex and massive for the more or less totalistic controls—or the attempt at them—of the past. In such periods the state begins to shuffle off its multitude of responsibilities. New channels of mobility emerge as the old one cracks apart under the strain, enabling alternate professions to emerge. This is the overwhelmed state, the state in decline or collapse. The emergence of merchants after 1980 bears a vague resemblance to the appearance of urban activists in late nineteenth century Zhejiang as delineated by Rankin[14] and to the guild federations that arose to manage social life in Rowe's Wuhan in this period.[15] The era of the most pronounced flourishing of a separate bourgeoisie, from the mid-teens until the consolidation of power by the KMT in 1927, however, was exceedingly brief, only possible in a period when there was no national government at all.[16]

Certainly the merchants of the 1980s were an altogether far more dependent class than those of earlier eras, issuing as they did from a vastly more hegemonic central power, a power that even as it falters continues through the ownership structure to command a weighty proportion of the national material resource and capital base. Still, structural similarities in the dynamic of alternation in the balance between state and societal business forces over time in China provide insights about the relation of one to the other.

To underline these historical parallels in social structure between former eras and the present, this chapter will adopt the labels "bureaucrat" and "merchant" in referring to the members of what is conventionally termed "public" and "private" or "state" and "society," respectively. For the Chinese urban "entrepreneur" of today is neither wholly a private operator nor a member of the state; to be financially successful in the cities, he/she must become involved in both of these spheres. This perspective provides a way of understanding those cadre "obstructions" of the private sector that have been impossible to wipe away despite a decade of nearly continuous regime injunctions against them; the ambiguity in the application of the incentives offered to the merchant sector; the merchant's preference for registering its ventures as "collective" rather than "private" or "individual"; and the inconclusiveness and ambivalence in the political elite's debates over the role of the "private" sector in the reform era.

The durability and indeed so far the stasis of this historical juncture is buttressed by the interpenetration and interdependence of elites. This period which is witnessing the cracking apart of the monolithic mobility channel has been marked by the birth of a set of institutions new to the socialist political economy of the People's Republic. These are institutions that have issued from the reforms and that aim either explicitly or implicitly at coopting either the bureaucrats or the merchants into the process of "reform." A number of them generate that blur between social forces described above.

In short, the breakdown of the single-stranded elite mobility pathway under conditions of continuing state ownership of the overwhelming bulk of national resources has not sharpened or clarified but rather has blurred the borderline between state bureaucrat and private merchant. This decline of central power—over resources and in overall capacity, and, attendant upon that, over mobility channels open to aspiring elites—is a recurring theme. The merger, interpenetration, and sometimes dependence of occupational strata that ensues may take the form of collaboration or, alternatively, may find expression in open competition.

The following sections use this perspective to explain some features of the ambiguity in the relationship between bureaucrat and merchant, and to show how the institutions of the "reform" period have so far served to perpetuate the stasis of that relationship. The paper concludes with some speculation about the prospects for abandoning this pattern.

Ambiguities and Mutual Dependency in the Bureaucrat–Merchant Relationship

The most common themes that repeatedly appear in discussions of the interaction of the bureaucratic and merchant strata can be analyzed in light of the argument above, in order to make that argument more concrete. Probably the most prominent of these themes concerns the obstructions that some bureaucrats have been posing to private business.

Paradoxically, these efforts at obstruction[17]—which it seems would, if successful, eliminate the practitioners of market activity—are accompanied by bribery, corruption, and extortion forced on the merchants,[18] activities that would seem to imply that bureaucrats should value merchants for their ability to generate capital. Other areas that have received attention are the contradiction between the appeal that private sector jobs are having for those in state jobs since about 1984 or 1985,[19] and the periodic decline in numbers of operators and firms over the same years.[20]

In the late 1980s there have also been increasing reports of subterfuge. First the individual firms (those allegedly employing no more than seven workers in addition to the owner) and later the newly authorized private enterprises (those officially permitted after July 1988 to hire eight or more workers) have been registering themselves as "collective" or even state-related firms instead of as private.[21] Finally, the framework laid out above can help to elucidate the seemingly endless and ultimately inconclusive disagreements among political elites over the extent to which the economic reforms should be permitted to go. In all of these activities we may find evidence of new forms of dependence and symbiosis between bureaucrat and merchant.

Obstructions against private sectoral activity have been present right from the start of its appearance in the cities after 1980. Indeed, such obstruction reflects long-standing ambivalence toward this activity present in China since the birth of the PRC. As ever, it has been fueled by a mix of rivalry between state and private sectoral practitioners and by ideological scruples among the cadres.[22]

Stories aimed at giving this interference bad press in order to discredit it told of cadres wrecking the little shops' equipment, stealing their tools, ransacking their premises, ruining their materials, and delivering to them only leftover, spoiled products to sell. Licenses, difficult to obtain in the first place, were later confiscated and customers threatened; merchants themselves were barred from operating in certain sections of town.[23]

Alongside this apparent urge to abolish competitors in the marketplace, another sort of cadre behavior has appeared: a collusion between the two strata, one that is however by no means always witting on the part of both parties. This is the bribery into which merchants are coerced by extortionate cadres; the not uncommon requirement that merchants offer a bribe simply to obtain a business license or a loan;[24] the higher prices (often retail prices for wholesale quantities) they must pay to procure scarce state-owned and managed materials and supplies;[25] the higher tax rates;[26] and the myriad of fees and assessments (in addition to the basic assessments called "management fees") levied at will, often in transgression of central governmental policy, by local departments in charge of sanitation, urban construction, public security, transportation, and weights and measures.[27]

As one informant put it, not just the major private entrepreneurs but the *getihu* as well "need to lubricate all the joints from the police station to the tax offices to the market control commissions to the neighborhood committees; . . . all those working in the hierarchical levels of the bureaucracy must be bribed."[28]

Though these practices may fleece the merchants, bureaucrats who manage such squeeze, who connive for a share of the profits,[29] or who in effect pull the private traders into "protection rackets"[30] have become to some extent dependent on the private sector, as they plainly benefit from its continued existence. There are cases where local governments "have found it more profitable to coordinate with private traders than to rely on state markets";[31] in other instances local governments encourage the expansion of private economic activity in the interest of fostering local industrialization, expanding the tax take, and solving problems of local unemployment.[32]

On a grander scale, the central government published in early 1986 its intention to incorporate collective and individual investments into the overall state plan for fixed assets investment. The opportunism in this project is apparent in the announcement's calculation that, over the previous four years, these investments had accounted for almost one third of the total social investment in fixed assets nationwide, terming it "an important means for expanding reproduction in society."[33]

For these reasons, it is inadequate to picture local bureaucrats as simply *opposing* privatization as a threat to their power and privilege or as a betrayal of socialist values,[34] though certainly such attitudes do exist. The simultaneous presence for cadres of new chances for gain (whether for themselves personally or for their cities—there is no way to measure or weigh the proportions) underlines the symbiotic connection into which reform policies have thrust cadre and merchant, with both groups dependent on some of the same inputs but both also to some degree dependent on each other.[35] If some merchants lose from harassment and squeeze, surely others have thrived on collusion.[36]

A second contradiction lies in the appeal of the private sector even for people with secure jobs and the generous state-conferred benefits that go with them, alongside the periodic decision of some merchants to relinquish business licenses already acquired, and the opting by others to hide their firms under more orthodox registration as collectives, a phenomenon dubbed wearing a "red hat."[37]

The proposition of symbiosis illuminates this paradox as well. The private sector even with its risks has attractions for those seeking a chance to develop their talents and a freer environment in which to work. Personal growth is not the only motive for breaking one's tie with a state-run unit, however. Some do so in response to the state's use of material incentives. These incentives include special loan funds allocated by the Industrial and Commercial Bank, higher interest rates on business deposits, tax holidays, and the right to inherit private property (written into the 1982 state constitution).[38] It is clear that the state at the policy-making stratum has nurtured private business, thereby acknowledging its dependence on the tax revenues its ventures can yield.[39]

This contradiction illustrates not just the state's new willingness to draw upon privately garnered profits, but also the merchants' ultimate dependency on the state. For those who give up their right to work as traders on their own find the political climate and the economic environment in which they must operate often to be hostile. Problems of discrimination, low status, difficulties in securing supplies from the bureaucracy, and general harassment plague nonstate sector entrepreneurs who lack an entré into the bureaucrats' world.[40] The weakness of these individuals who try to move without the crutch connections provide offers glaring proof of their reliance on officialdom.

The estimated nearly 50 percent of private firms who register themselves as affiliated with collective or state-owned enterprises or as themselves collectively owned do so for reasons which, again, illustrate the symbiotic relationship that exists for many successful merchants.[41] According to such arrangements, the private enterprises can obtain preferential tax rates and cheaper raw materials; receive political protection; and find it easier to conduct their business, since often receipts from the private firms are not recognized by public units. The existence of these deals, however, shows that it is not just the merchant firms that need the public ones. A mutually beneficial exchange is struck, as merchants present a portion of their profits as "management fees" to their state-sector partners.

These various contradictions are rooted first of all in competition between bureaucrats and merchants as rivals in a market where state resources and those able to command them still hold dominion, but are also based in a set of mutually dependent ties between the two. This paradox explains as well the difficulty of pinning down the respective stances of "conservatives" versus "reformers" on the issues of political and economic reform.

Those most firmly ensconced within the party hierarchy—those with the richest network of cronies—should be those best placed to take advantage of the opportunities today's distorted market can offer. Self-interest may dictate that they attempt to throttle challenges to the power structure, but not that they eliminate a market that so clearly can be made to work on their own behalf.

By a similar logic, many merchants ideally would like to cut the tie between old political and new economic power which remains so strongly entrenched. But it is that very bond that has generated this class in the first place and that sustains it economically, as the supports offered by the old framework continue to help many opting for the private sector to get their start and go on to prop up their daily dealings. Thus, cadres of all cuts have been the beneficiaries of economic reform, just as large numbers of merchants are the beneficiaries of the bureaucracy.

A return to a regime based purely on planning would undermine new-found opportunities now enjoyed by cadres; while a leap to fully open and unobstructed markets would deprive the most successful merchants of their special inside channels. As a result, there is an implicit pact to preserve the monolith, and a stasis in the symbiotic tie between bureaucrat and merchant.[42]

The Institutions of the Reform and Their Role in Prolonging the Transition

As noted above, new institutions have emerged in the 1980s that all manage to coopt either the bureaucrats or the merchants into dependent relationships. Their combined effect has been to prolong the decomposition of the monolithic position of the state and to entrench a symbiosis between the two groups. These institutions are of several types. One category contains institutions established by the state bureaucracy to incorporate the private sector. Second, there are those institutions formed by the merchants themselves, albeit with assistance from the state or its assets. And a third variety includes institutions that are generated directly by the reforms. All three facilitate deals across the now more-than-ever blurred boundaries between sectors. They do so in a way that serves to freeze the transition such that this amalgam of classes persists.

Institutions to Control the Merchants

In this category we find such institutions as the associations of private entrepreneurs formed at the urban level and the new business guilds brought together under official aegis. There has also been in the past decade an effort to encourage merchants to join the Communist party, and to make models of them by nominating them to serve in local and even the National People's Congress.

Individual workers' associations first arose locally in 1980, under the party's auspices; in 1986 they were united into a national body. The state bureaucracy's Industrial and Commercial Administrative and Management Bureau monitors these groups, and its cadres serve among their board members, insuring that the merchants imbibe pertinent state and party policies and the political ideology of the moment.[43] There is nothing secret about the state's concern to keep these organs under its mantle: Wang Zhongming, the secretary-general of the national Association of Individual Laborers of China, was announced in late 1989 as being also the director of the Individual and Private Economy Department of the State Administration for Commerce and Industry.[44]

The associations are charged with mobilizing the merchants to pay their taxes, and with helping them to maintain the quality of their service and sanitary conditions.[45] Supposedly they are also to provide assistance to the members, and to the extent that they meet this obligation, merchants no doubt find themselves falling into a dependence on these bureaucratic bodies. Among their other responsibilities is to foster mutual aid among the merchants, protect their legal rights and represent their opinions and demands, help them to solve problems in their operations, and offer technical training, legal advice, and information.[46] But the dependence, it turns out, is mutual: criticism has held that the offices meant to assist the associations often treat them as the commercial and industrial departments' own appendage, in effect turning them into their own little branches.[47]

Other, related types of cooptation also provide for mutual penetration and control. The first provincial congress of private entrepreneurs held in Guangdong, for example, met in late 1989. In attendance were the vice-chairman of the provincial people's congress's standing committee, the provincial vice-governor, and the director of the department in charge of individual and private economic affairs under the State Administration for Industry and Commerce. The congress had the ambitious goal of absorbing into the state's networks all the private entrepreneurs in the province, as it plans to send out an appeal to them all to become members of a provincial association of private entrepreneurs now in the midst of formation.[48]

Not only were the merchants permitted and even encouraged to join the Communist party after 1982[49]—one source claims that as of late 1988, 15 percent of the owners of private enterprises were party members[50]—and to become representatives of both local and, in 1983 for the first time, the National People's Congress. Going further, in 1989 the first party branch within a private enterprise was created in a Shenyang factory in the food industry. Of the eighty-two persons in the factory, a full nine of them were party members.[51]

In the latest development, at the end of 1989 the All-China Federation of Industry and Commerce announced its revival of 150 business guilds, operating now as "nonofficial bodies." These associations are obviously designed to be far more closely linked to the bureaucracy than those that Rowe and Mann studied from the nineteenth century: "The Federation pledges to give full support to the development of guilds . . . [which are] to bridge businesses with the government and provide services," read the notice.[52]

All of these new corporations bond merchant with state, in part to limit the competitive threat merchants pose as they draw largely upon the same capital, equipment, and supplies the state and its bureaucrats do. These associations' presence also embodies the state's effort to bind the merchants into a dependency upon its offices; in the process these corporate agencies bolster the bureaucracy's ability to play out its own dependence by helping them more readily to tap the skills and profits of the merchants.

Dependent Institutions Formed by Merchants

In this category are technology development centers and corporations, the most notorious of which is the Stone Group; joint ventures that merge merchant skills and needs with bureaucratic connections and supplies; small-scale collective firms that are tied to the state's neighborhood committees; and moonlighting practices that involve the use of state-owned facilities, equipment, and assets.

The Stone Corporation is China's leading high-technology firm. It was brought into being in 1984 by the famous entrepreneur Wan Runnan, who is now one of the four top democracy leaders abroad. The advantages that undoubtedly launched Wan on his successful career exemplify once again the centrality of ties between bureaucrat and merchant.[53]

Wan, exiled to the countryside with other Cultural Revolution victims (in part for his audacity—perhaps even perceived in that era as his criminality—in marrying the daughter of Liu Shaoqi in 1970), made his comeback into Beijing in the late 1970s through his choice for his second wife. This was the daughter of Li Chang, then the party secretary of the Chinese Academy of Sciences (CAS). Once in the capital, Wan quickly became a software engineer in the computer center under CAS (one suspects with help from father Li), where he studied diligently. By the early 1980s, Wan had been named director of that center. Soon he was assisting IBM, invited into China by the top political elite to train ministry-level personnel, in running its training classes.

The economic reforms' encouragement of a commercial spirit elicited a boom in company formation by government offices of all sorts. Wan grabbed the chance to put into practice a pet idea of his, to join laboratory research with money-making ventures. Borrowing 20,000 yuan from the Agricultural Bank of China, he set up a joint venture with a township government in the Haidian district of Beijing, and began to adapt a U.S.-made printer to Chinese market requirements, with the help of the Mitsui Corporation. Wan went on to manufacture custom-made typewriters and printers, including electronic typewriters capable of printing in both Chinese and English. By the time Wan left China in

1989, the Stone Corporation had cornered 80 percent of the domestic market, managing some 600 stores, 40 wholesale centers, and 100 maintenance and training centers, plus running joint ventures with Japanese and Hong Kong companies.

Wan's group is representative of the thousands (no one knows how many) of hi-tech collective enterprises known as *minban* companies across the country, of which there are three main types: those, like his, which are supposedly owned and managed by "people" (*minyou-minban*); those owned by the state but managed by "people" (*guanyou-minban*); and those jointly operated and owned by the state and "people" (*guanmingongyou*). Wan's type is in the minority. Indeed, of the top ten computer companies in China in terms of 1987 sales, only Stone was *minban;* all of the others were offshoots of the Ministry of Electronics, either wholly so or through joint ventures with "people," even though they all are classified as *minban.*

Nonetheless, despite its alleged "collective" status and the supposed absence of state capital in its portfolio, Wan was forbidden to claim any of the property as his—or his employees'—own. In fact, any attempt to withdraw funds from the venture would have brought on a criminal charge: *sifen jiti caichan* (privately dividing up collective property). For this reason, before the Tiananmen massacre, Wan had essayed to set up a share system (*gufenzhi*) and to sell his stock, chiefly in order to clarify the ownership rights of the firm. Zhao Ziyang's backing for this scheme sent it the death knell after June 1989.

In doing business, Stone, just as any other company interested in importing, needed more than funds to do so. In addition and perhaps even harder for non-state firms to come by is the precious importing license. Since only governmental ministries legally have this privilege, connections with bureaucrats are essential for the undercover purchase that is the only way to obtain the license.

Stone's work was also greatly expedited by the attention the firm received at least indirectly from Zhao Ziyang in early 1988. For it was very probably Zhao who delegated Wen Jiabao (then director of the Central Work Office [*zhongyang bangongting*]) and Rui Xingwen of the Party Secretariat to investigate Stone, and who later wrote out instructions for the creation in May 1988 of the Beijing New-Tech Industrial Development Experimental Zone. In this zone where Stone was located, firms received a three-year tax exemption, another three years of tax reduction, and permission to retain a sizable percentage of the foreign currency they earned also over a three-year period, plus promises of help in solving problems with visas, electricity supply, and the local bureaucracy. Similar parks for other such companies exist in Shenzhen and three other cities.

Firms of this sort are sometimes distrusted, resented, and even harassed (Wan himself got into legal hassles on two occasions between 1985 and 1988). Some have found themselves entangled in more red tape than are ordinary state-owned firms despite promises that this will not be the case. But it is clear that those who succeed on a large scale must combine their skills with bureaucratic backing.

In addition to this very blatant and well-publicized kind of collaboration, there are other forms of combination that grow out of a merger of funds and thus an overlap of interest between merchant and bureaucrat. Many smaller individual firms got their start with loans or grants from their neighborhood resident committees, again making use of capital from the state. Another variation is ventures that began to appear in the late 1980s between private enterprises and state-run firms and between private and collectively run enterprises. Shareholding arrangements also bring together bureaucrat and merchant capital in mutually beneficial ways.[54]

And one more example is the "moonlighting craze" that has sprung up in Chinese cities as the monolithic mobility channel decomposes.[55] A common pattern is for a person to labor in a state firm during working hours, and in leisure time to perform the same services for other units introduced to him by friends. In large cities like Guangzhou, the state's estimate is that about 30 percent of workers and staff hold supplemental jobs. One survey showed that nearly half of those taking on extra employment were workers, teachers, doctors, and scientific and research personnel, with managers constituting the other half. It is likely that these people ply their second trades with either direct or indirect help from bureaucrats or with state assets.

All of these opportunities for "private" achievement are only accessible to those able to anchor their activities with bureaucratic bargains and blessings. Thus, one could say, these opportunities coopt the new-style merchants into the state's own structure and thereby perpetuate its monopoly on economic power.

Reform-Generated Institutions

This set of organizational forms and practices permits bureaucrats to utilize the resources of the state system—connections, information, credit, supplies—to amass market power. Probably most significant of these is the double-track price system, which makes specially advantaged insider salesmen out of any bureaucrats with control over or even access to valued supplies in demand. In this class I would also place the multifarious supply and trading "companies" set up by bureaucrats, their offices, and their offspring in recent years, newly forming enterprise groups forged among state firms, share companies, materials exchange markets, and wholesale trade centers.

The double-track price system was initiated in the mid-1980s. The idea behind it was to allow market prices to coexist with administered ones, in order to placate interests potentially threatened by further price reform while allowing market-like transactions to go forward. This obviously created an open field for arbitrage that bound bureaucrats to the state and their privileged access more firmly than ever before. Officials found that they could enjoy reform immensely so long as the system it introduced remained frozen. And any merchant who was not to be shut out of the market by this arrangement was forced to ally him/herself with these now doubly-empowered bureaucrats. On several occasions since 1985 there have been campaigns publicized to eliminate and cashier the uncountable hordes of "companies" that sprang into existence once the economic reform program legitimized making money.[56] These are companies put together with the assets of state offices and are backed up by networks of favors and mutually granted access to scarcities among bureaucrats. Movements to wipe them out have never succeeded, no doubt because the numbers of people favored by their existence and the clout of these individuals both far outweigh the numbers or the influence of those who might have an interest in their abolition.

Though officials in the materials supply bureaucracy have probably been the chief offenders, those in commercial wholesaling and foreign trade work have also benefited mightily from the establishment of such concerns; even the public security, judicial departments, and the army have formed their share. The tight linkage between the bureaus and their commercial activities is captured in the phrase "one shop with two signboards," which symbolizes that most of these companies are at once internally government institutions and externally business companies.[57]

Enterprise groups constructed to free up the movement of materials and commodities once entrapped within the constraints of the vertical bureaucracies that administered the state plan have spawned their own bureaucratic trappings. They do this by gathering under one much more massive unit far more assets than any one firm ever mustered in the old days. At their head sit powerful officials well connected with local party and state bureaucrats.[58]

Similarly, share companies, markets for the means of production, and wholesale trade centers all heighten the sway of officials whose influence was already notable before the reforms. These bureaucrats now can make use of fractures in the planning system and imperfections in the market to capitalize on whatever assets and connections they command, earning extra commissions as they do, all to a degree unimaginable in days of tighter controls.[59]

To the extent that bureaucrats may have had misgivings about the reform program and its potential for undermining their own potency, institutions and measures such as these coopt them into the transition but continue to tie them to the state as they do so. They also encourage their joining forces with merchants when to do so would enhance the capabilities of the ventures they now are managing.

All three of these kinds of institutions, then, draw either merchant or bureaucrat into the transition and create vested interests that prolong that transition. Through this cooptation, they also serve to bring the two forces into more explicit dealings and closer confrontations with each other—whether it be through competition or collusion—than they experienced in the time of the planned economy.

Conclusion: Prospects for Change?

The argument in this paper has reiterated the point that the arrangements of the reform era have merged, if under vastly shifted conditions, the entities we call "state" and "society." The monolithic mobility channel has begun to decompose, but its dominance is far from totally shattered. The result is the further solidification of the old bond that has always tied bureaucrat to the perquisites offered by state employment. What is new is a bonding and incipient interdependence between bureaucrat and the merchant with whom he/she competes for state funds, supplies, and markets but with whom he/she also bargains and colludes.

What prospects for change lie latent in the present scenario? There are two sources, interestingly the same two that eventually and finally split apart the long-decaying imperial order. Both of these are tied to the forces that pushed both that order and the present one on its downward spiral: the diversifying economy and the discredited belief system.

In the current era we see these at work in the pressures for political liberalization that merchants were backing even before the Tiananmen demonstrations which they financed from behind the scenes (probably with tacit support and encouragement from Zhao Ziyang and his advisers, one may surmise, in light of the link that later became public between Yan Jiaqi and Wan Runnan).[60] Given what was explained above about the constraints on ownership under which the *minban* hi-tech firms are forced to operate today, it is clear what the larger merchants have to gain from a freeing up of political structures. Similarly, in the decade before 1911 merchants—in those days it was merchants in the provinces—were also at the forefront of the demand for loosening the autocratism at the political center.

The other possible source potentially capable of smashing the monolith, then as now, is groups whose source of finances comes from outside the system. At the turn of the century there was Sun Yat-sen with his overseas communities; today it is those living in the southeastern coastal provinces who have relatives abroad or who have managed to underwrite their new economic ventures with investment from those places and so have become released from the hegemonic dominion of the state economy. Interestingly, a late 1988 Chinese analysis of the owners of private enterprises as "a new social stratum" speak specifically of a federation of entrepreneurs in Fuzhou which publishes its own newsletter, lives by its own regulations, and conducts direct business negotiations with foreign merchants.[61]

It is hard to claim there are any immediate grounds for hope of change. In the aftermath of June 4, we find the chief merchant—and probably many of his lesser colleagues—resident abroad, and the southeast coast largely going its own way, cut off from the larger concerns of the country. Still, the existence of these two pockets of potentially potent protest and autonomy within the merchant stratum suggests the likely points at which the stasis that has been the dominant pattern to date will one day be halted. In the meantime, the cords that connect merchant to bureaucrat and both to the state continue to tighten.

Notes

1. Thomas B. Gold, "The Resurgence of Civil Society in China," *Journal of Democracy* 1, 1 (Winter 1990): 18–31.
2. See John P. Burns, "China's Governance: Political Reform in a Turbulent Environment," *China Quarterly* (hereafter *CQ*), no. 119 (September 1989): 481–518, for a statement of this claim.
3. *Beijing Review* (hereafter *BR*), May 8–14, 1989, p. 25.
4. See Ivan Szelenyi, "Eastern Europe in an Epoch of Transition: Toward a Socialist Mixed Economy?" in *Remaking the Economic Institutions of Socialism: China and Eastern Europe*, ed. Victor Nee and David Stark (Stanford: Stanford University Press, 1989), pp. 222, 225.
5. Here I must emphasize that this chapter concentrates purely on the relationship between the state and the sector of society that deals in business. I would not venture to extend its conclusions to other classes or social groups.
6. Here I am speaking of the entrepreneurs managing sizable enterprises. But the *getihu*, even if they own their own assets, must still compete and collaborate with the state to survive.
7. David Stark and Victor Nee, "Toward an Institutional Analysis of State Socialism," in Nee and Stark, *Remaking*, pp. 1–13, speak of "reforms . . . (as) redrawing the boundaries between state and society and shaping new patterns of transaction, mediation, and bargaining across them," on p. 16; and of "porous state-society boundaries" during the Maoist era on p. 23. Now, they claim, we see "a system in which state and society are insulated from each other to a greater degree," also on p. 23.
8. Though since about 1983 private entrepreneurs have been encouraged to join the party, and party officials have been enjoined to enlist them, this is a fragile arrangement. In autumn 1989 that trend was terminated, at least for the time being, when party chief Jiang Zemin spoke out against it. See *Foreign Broadcast Information Service* (hereafter *FBIS*), October 23, 1989, p. 19.
9. On this, see Susan Mann, *Local Merchants and the Chinese Bureaucracy, 1750–1950* (Stanford: Stanford University Press, 1987), pp. 21–23. See also Wang Jingyu, "The Birth of the Chinese Bourgeoisie," *Social Sciences in China* (hereafter *SSIC*) 3, 1 (March 1982): 220–40; and Editorial Board for Modern and Contemporary Chinese History, *Historical Research,* "Chinese Historical Studies on Early Modern China's Bourgeoisie," *SSIC* 5, 1 (March 1984): 9–31, for discussions on the complexity of the overlapping class formations in the late nineteenth century.
10. John King Fairbank, *The Great Chinese Revolution, 1800–1985* (New York: Harper and Row, 1986), p. 147.
11. For the study that sets out this thesis quite sharply for the KMT, see Parks M. Coble, Jr., *The Shanghai Capitalists and the Nationalist Government, 1927–1937* (Cambridge: Council on East Asian Studies, Harvard University, 1980).
12. Mann, *Local Merchants*.
13. Gary G. Hamilton, "Why No Capitalism in China? Negative Questions in Historical Comparative Research," *Journal of Developing Societies* 1 (1985): 187–211.
14. Mary Backus Rankin, *Elite Activism and Political Transformation in China: Zhejiang Province, 1865–1911* (Stanford: Stanford University Press, 1986).
15. See William T. Rowe, *Hankow: Commerce and Society in a Chinese Society, 1796–1889* (Stanford: Stanford University Press, 1984).
16. See Parks M. Coble, Jr., "The Kuomintang Regime and the Shanghai Capitalists, 1927–1929," *CQ*, no. 77 (March 1979): 3; and Marie-Claire Bergère, *The Golden Age of the Chinese Bourgeoisie* (New York: Cambridge University Press, 1989).

17. Two examples of work emphasizing obstructions are Linda Hershkovitz, "The Fruits of Ambivalence: China's Urban Individual Economy," *Pacific Affairs* 58, 3 (Fall 1985): 427–50, and Dorothy J. Solinger, "The Petty Private Sector and the Three Lines in the Early 1980s," in *Three Visions of Chinese Socialism*, ed. Dorothy J. Solinger (Boulder: Westview Press, 1984), pp. 73–111. Thomas B. Gold, "Urban Private Business in China," *Studies in Comparative Communism* (hereafter *SCC*) 22, 2 and 3 (1989): 187–201, refers to this problem on p. 187. See Chapter 10 in this volume.

18. The following articles deal specifically with corruption: Alan P. L. Liu, "The Politics of Corruption in the People's Republic of China," *American Political Science Review* 77, 3 (1983): 602–23; Connie Squires Meaney, "Market Reform in a Leninist System: Some Trends in the Distribution of Power, Strategy and Money in Urban China," *SCC* 22, 2 and 3 (Summer/Autumn 1989): 203–20; Athar Hussain, "Chinese Economic Reforms, Irregularities and Crimes," paper prepared for Conference on Social Consequences of the Chinese Economic Reforms, Fairbank Center, Harvard University, May 13–15, 1988; and James T. Myers, "Modernization and 'Unhealthy Tendencies': Toward a Definition of the Problem," paper presented at 1985 Sino-American Annual Conference on Mainland China, Columbus, Ohio.

19. Thomas B. Gold, "China's Private Entrepreneurs," *China Business Review* (November–December 1985): 46–50, makes this point.

20. In both 1986 and 1989 the numbers of private firms dropped. See *Renmin ribao* (People's daily) (hereafter *RMRB*), November 25, 1986, overseas edition. This article states that in the first half of 1986 the numbers of private firms fell for the first time in the previous several years. Compared with the end of 1985, there were 360,000 fewer (registered) private firms and 470,000 fewer private entrepreneurs. *BR*, November 6–12, 1989, p. 11, states that the 23.049 million individuals working in private business as of the end of 1988 had dropped to 19.43 million by the end of the first half of 1989. The specific cause for these declines in a long-term rising trend were not given in the data. However, we must assume that since the appeal of the private sector has by and large been a secular trend over the decade, it has generally been unaffected by periodic attempts to intimidate or tax its practitioners or by times in which credit has been scarce, causing some merchants to be at least temporarily forced out of business.

21. Ma Jisen, "A General Survey of the Resurgence of the Private Sector of China's Economy," *SSIC* 9, 3 (September 1988): 78–92, claims that only 115,000 of the 225,000 private enterprises in China have properly registered themselves as private.

22. I elaborate on this my *Chinese Business Under Socialism* (Berkeley: University of California Press, 1984), especially in chap. 4.

23. Ibid., pp. 201–02. See also Gold, "Urban Private Business," p. 197.

24. Hussain, "Chinese Economic Reforms," p. 9; Ma Jisen, "General Survey," p. 89.

25. Ibid.

26. Before 1986 the private sector was only made to pay a business tax. Regulations in force as of 1981 left it to urban regulatory agencies to work out procedures for taxing. In 1986, a 10-grade progressive income tax scale was promulgated for the private sector, whose rates were pegged much higher than those for state-sectoral business. The highest taxes reached a rate of 84 percent. See Hershkovitz, "Fruits of Ambivalence," p. 444; *China Daily* (hereafter *CD*), January 27, 1986, p. 3; and Ma Jisen, "General Survey," p. 89.

27. Hershkovitz, "Fruits of Ambivalence," p. 447.

28. Interview, February 2, 1990.

29. Hussain, "Chinese Economic Reforms," p. 9.

30. Meaney, "Market Reform," pp. 210–11, came up with this helpful characterization.

31. *FBIS*, July 22, 1988, p. 49.

32. Some of this is suggested in the early research of Jian Yuan, as stated in her dissertation proposal to the Department of Political Science at Yale University ("Private Property and the Socialist Economy, Dissertation Prospectus (draft)," December 1989. I thank Susan Woodward for showing me this draft.

33. *BR*, March 31, 1986, p. 26.

34. For this argument, see Thomas B. Gold, "Stimulating Initiative in Urban China's Private Sector," prepared for the Association for Asian Studies Annual Meeting, San Francisco, March 25–27, 1988.

35. This perspective resolves what otherwise would appear to be two mutually contradictory statements in Meaney, "Market Reform," on pp. 203–4: "Market reform threatens the party's organizational base by creating spaces for actors . . . outside the purview of the *nomenklatura* system"; and, "Market reform in Leninist states creates new opportunities to make money, but access to these opportunities tends to favor party cadres and their networks of connections." This is an excellent article, but it does not explicitly come to grips with this internal contradiction.

36. Here again we find an instructive historical parallel. See Rowe, "Hankow," pp. 177–81, for a thoughtful and thorough analysis of four different, not altogether mutually incompatible approaches that scholars have taken in assessing the stance of the traditional Chinese state toward commerce: what he calls the " 'repression,' 'neglect,' 'collusion,' and 'stimulation' theses." As Rowe admits in settling for the stimulation thesis to describe the situation in nineteenth-century Hankow (the idea that the state primarily encouraged commerce in order to increase state revenues and to benefit the populace), "the other[s] [theses] [also] have some validity as the Qing administration's role in commerce was complex and at times contradictory." This is on p. 180.

37. See Ma, "General Survey," pp. 87–88, and *CD*, June 25, 1988, p. 4.

38. See Gold, "Urban Private Business," pp. 194 and 199, and Gold, "China's Private Entrepreneurs," p. 47. In the early 1980s, there were also selective incentives for specific sectors, such as the waiving of commercial taxes for two or three years in the service and repair trades and a two-year period of income tax exemptions for unemployed young people who opened individual enterprises. This is recounted in Charlotte Hart, "Urban Private Businesses in China, 1978–1984," Asian Studies Program, Dartmouth College, May 6, 1985.

39. Gold, "China's Private Entrepreneurs," p. 47.

40. Gold, "Urban Private Business," p. 197.

41. See *CD*, November 7, 1989, p. 1, and June 25, 1988, p. 4, and Ma Jisen, "General Survey," for discussion of this issue.

42. See the conclusion for a qualification of this claim.

43. Gold, "Urban Private Business," p. 199.

44. *CD*, November 7, 1989, p. 1.

45. Hu Guohua, Liu Jinghuai, and Chen Minzhu, *Duosediao di zhongguo geti jingyingzhe* (Many-hued Chinese individual operators) (Beijing: Economic Academy Publishing Co., 1988), pp. 195–96.

46. Wang Hui and Guan Mi, eds.,*Geti jingying yishu* (The art of individual management) (Tianjin: Tianjin Social Science Academy Publishing Company, 1989), p. 216.

47. Hu et al., *Duosediao di zongguo geti jingyingzhe*, p. 197.

48. *FBIS*, December 26, 1989, p. 38.

49. See note 8 above. In 1989 this effort was terminated, at least temporarily.

50. *FBIS*, December 7, 1988, p. 36 (a translation from *Jingji cankao* [Economic reference], November 14, 1988, p. 4).

51. *RMRB*, January 6, 1989, p. 4.

52. *FBIS*, December 7, 1989, pp. 32–33.

53. The material that follows comes from an interview with an insider who worked with one of the hi-tech companies for some years; and from Marc Abramson, "Minban Science Firms in China," *China Exchange News* (hereafter *CEN*) 17, 4 (December 1989): 12–17; Richard P. Suttmeier, "Chinese Scientific and Technology Reforms: Toward a Post-Socialist Knowledge System," *CEN* 16, 4 (December 1988): 7–13; Adi Ignatius, "Fast-Growing Chinese Electronics Firm Emulates IBM," *Wall Street Journal*, June 3, 1988; "Zhongguancun: A Look at Five Companies," *Asian Venture Capital Journal*, July 1988; Tai Ming Cheung, "Stone Keeps on Rolling," *Far East Economic Review*, October 13, 1988; Seth Faison, "Stone Group Could Set Trend of Share Ownership in China," *South China Morning Post*, October 27, 1988; and Dori Jones Yang, "Can Chinese Computers Survive in the Wild West?" *Business Week*, December 26, 1988.

54. Ma Jisen, "General Survey," p. 90.

55. On this, *BR*, November 6–12, 1989, p. 25.

56. For one example among dozens of such announcements, see *RMRB*, November 8 and 9, 1989, both on p. 1.

57. *BR*, November 13–19, 1989, pp. 18–23.

58. An example of such an official entrepreneur is Yu Zhi'an of Wuhan, who stood at the core of several such enterprise groups in mid-1987, managing vast holdings of raw materials, energy sources, and commodities.

59. I have written of these various "reforms" in my article, "Capitalist Measures with Chinese Characteristics," *Problems of Communism* 38 (January–February 1989): 19–33. See Chapter 6, this volume.

60. See Meaney, "Market Reform," p. 216.

61. Ibid., pp. 216–19; and *FBIS*, December 7, 1988, pp. 32–36 (a translation of an article from *Jingji cankao*, November 14, 1988, p. 4).

Afterword

Beginning in autumn 1988, China's program of economic reforms was jolted by two sudden blows in succession. First there was the autumn 1988 somber stock-taking of the reforms themselves. What had been the mainstay of policy through the 1980s abruptly seemed to many to have produced startlingly ominous effects. Then the Chinese were compelled to cope with the imposition of economic sanctions by the Western powers and Japan that followed the Tiananmen massacre of June 1989. In the wake of these shocks, the leadership installed and implemented an austerity program, which, in turn, spawned its own set of drawbacks. The net effect, as of mid-1991, was to drag the reform policies through a period of stalemate, in which little was explicitly canceled and nothing novel was attempted.

The Thirteenth Party Congress of the Chinese Communist Party, held in October 1987, provided the final podium on which then-Party General Secretary Zhao Ziyang held forth as the chief promoter of economic reform, a cause he had been championing from his successively more prominent and prestigious positions in the party and state since the late 1970s. That meeting seemed to outside analysts to represent a culmination of the by-then almost decade-long campaign to sever the strictures of the planned economy. Its slogan—that China was still just in the "primary stage of socialism"—appeared to serve as an alibi for, indeed, to presage, all manner of experimentation with market-type practices. The reasoning popularized with this plenum was that any measure that stimulated the economy would, at least theoretically, prime the productive forces for an eventual transition to a later, more orthodox stage of socialism. Thus in 1987 and 1988 the trials of enterprise bankruptcy, stock markets, enterprise mergers and "enterprise groups," and materials exchange markets discussed in chapters 5, 6, and 8 began to flourish within the state-run economy. These were accompanied in the unofficial sphere by an all-too-healthy out-of-plan marketplace, with its double-track pricing system for goods of all types. That is, middlemen with the right contacts were profiting from diverting key commodities away from the official track and reaping profits from the differential between the prices at which they could purchase them and the prices they could go on to command for them on the open market. At this time a wide berth was given to the private and collective sectors of the economy; the larger-scale urban entrepreneurs delineated in chapter 11 had their heyday then.

On top of this leeway in the domestic economy, in early 1988 a pet plan of Zhao's, the "coastal zone economic development strategy," opened several coastal provinces to foreign investment and technology, giving a boost to the labor-intensive, non-state-owned processing industries so prevalent along the southeast coast, especially in Guangdong and Fujian provinces.[1]

This policy added extra energy to the already explosive development of these processing ventures, as Hong Kong capitalists moved their operations over into the mainland to take advantage of preferential tax rates, cheap labor, and more plentiful land than they had access to at home. These firms were able to pay higher prices for the raw materials they needed than state concerns, constrained to charge state-set prices for their goods, could afford. Because of their flexibility, the nonstate firms were then able to siphon off supplies the government intended for its larger and more essential factories.[2] The most common way of describing the dislocations that ensued was to say that "the development of the processing industries far surpassed the capacity of the energy, transportation, and raw materials industries."[3]

Yet one more risky innovation introduced in 1988 was the decision made in the spring, reportedly by Deng Xiaoping but pushed ahead by Zhao Ziyang, to free up the prices for many commodities formerly regulated by the state. Rumors of this plan reached the populace in force in the ensuing months, causing immediate inflationary shocks.

So on top of a decade that had seen much official speculation feeding off the double-track pricing system, and which had also witnessed both mass incomes (wages and bonuses in state industry, profits in the private sector, and profits from free market and other entrepreneurial activity in the countryside) and state subsidies (for prices and for enterprise losses) steadily rising way beyond productivity,[4] by late summer a racing inflation rate—already appraised to be in the neighborhood of 20 percent—shot up even higher than ever.[5] Some estimates ran as high as 50 percent for principal foodstuffs in the major cities; a more likely unofficial evaluation put overall figures at 30 percent by year's end.[6] Bank runs and hoarding of staples broke out in alarming proportions in August to accompany and further feed the inflationary spiral.

Combined with a continuously climbing deficit in the state budget,[7] these developments triggered among the majority of the leadership a rapid rethinking of economic strategy followed by a swift reining in of the economy. By September 1988, a rigorous austerity program, called an "economic adjustment" or "economic rectification," was put into place. Its measures included a sudden and severe freezing of prices, a transferal of the power of approval for foreign trade activity back to the central level, an effort, as in the past, to guide economic behavior through setting quotas and norms in the capital, a closing off of credit, large cuts in currency issuance, a scaling back of capital construction targets, and the cancellation of projects already conceived.

Thus, many reasoned, all the "economic reform" and "opening to the outside world" which had been the hallmark of the 1980s had exceeded the bounds of what the economy could sustain. It had thrown the system seriously out of balance, causing excess demand, an inadequacy of supplies, resources, and financial power, and rampant price rises.

But not surprisingly, this draconian plan bred its own array of difficulties. In the succeeding months the sluggish market, capital shortage, closure of some enterprises (with an attendant rise in unemployment which reportedly doubled to about 4 percent by the end of 1989[8]), and general slowdown in economic activity only heightened the state deficit, pegged at 9.535 billion yuan for 1989.[9] The deficit increased as enterprises found themselves unable to meet their bills and inter-enterprise debts skyrocketed to 100 billion yuan in 1989.

State subsidies used to compensate enterprises suffering losses amounted to 60 million yuan, and, combined with other price subsidies granted to state firms and foreign trade subsidies, the central government was compelled to invest a total of 100 billion yuan in state enterprises that year.[10] Within a year of the onset of the austerity program, the economy had fallen 2.1 percent below its level one year earlier;[11] profits of state-owned enterprises continued to drop into the first half of 1990, diminishing state returns even further.[12]

These troubles coincided with, and, of course, were exacerbated by the foreign economic sanctions that came in the wake of the killings of June 1989. Just as the Chinese political elite had been struggling to "rectify" what in the eyes of many of its members had been an overly liberalized economy, the international reprisal against the Tiananmen massacre rendered their job of making do on a tighter string much more challenging. Cut-offs of foreign loans and investment and a drop in external trade added to the already present lack of working capital. Simultaneously, the state's demand for foreign firms to rely on local sourcing became harder than usual to fulfill with the by then generalized stagnation of domestic production.[13]

In short, over the last two years of the decade the leaders in China had to come to grips with two major economic challenges. One of these was a deeply disquieting realization that, by their form of reckoning the reform program which had seemed so rosy only recently had wrought difficulties too massive to ignore; the other was an international pariahhood perhaps even more severe, at least temporarily, than the one from which their country had recovered not much more than a decade before. Both of these crises resulted in economic contractions, one chosen and the other in part imposed. The chill they cast upon reform still lingered into 1991 and reinforced and even exaggerated the persistent statism that lay at the core of the reform program itself.

As the contraction began to presage disaster, the regime reacted in statist fashion. Already by March 1990 a new policy granted concessions to what were entitled "double-guarantee" enterprises. For some four or five dozen large-scale state-owned concerns in the northeast, presumably all in some financial diffi-culty, the state promised to ensure the delivery of energy, raw materials, commu-nications, and transportation in exchange for these firms' agreement to meet fixed targets for a supply of finished products, profits, and tax payments to the state.

The enterprises involved accounted for about 90 percent of the coal and steel output, and all the petroleum, electrical power, nonferrous metals, motor vehi-cles, and electrical-generating equipment produced for distribution by the state from the three provinces of Liaoning, Jilin, and Heilongjiang.[14] In the same spirit, more than 55 billion yuan in loans were issued between January and April 1990 to help large and medium-sized enterprises purchase materials needed to produce daily necessities and items for export.[15] As this approach continued, a year later the *Far Eastern Economic Review* reported that "Over the past year most bank loans have been directed to loss-making state enterprises with little prospect of ever meeting their debt obligations."[16] Such bail-outs were made in lieu of reviving the bankruptcy proposals outlined in chapter 6 in the face of the near collapse of many firms.[17]

Experiments with securities markets went forward, at least superficially. But at the July 3, 1991, opening ceremony of the Shenzhen exchange (succeeding the birth of one at Shanghai in December 1990), Vice-Chairman of the National People's Congress Chen Muhua announced that stock market reforms that con-flicted with socialism would be rejected, and the central government set an aggregate ceiling on listings for the year.[18] Around the same time it was calcu-lated that only about 7 percent of the shares publicly traded in all of China's securities markets were held by individuals.[19]

On the Shanghai market, up to 95 percent of trading was done in bonds into 1991, since the local authorities were reluctant to promote share trading, and the government was in control of as much as 75 percent of the shares on the ex-change as of early in the year.[20] It is also notable that stock companies and exchanges were not given much of a role in the Eighth Five-Year Plan nor in the Ten-Year Economic Program drawn up at the end of 1990.[21]

The survival throughout the reform decade of the problem of bureaucratic inter-vention into the firms, and therefore of the patterns of control and checks on autonomy elucidated in chapters 4 and 8, is suggested in a reform document publicized in mid-1991, the "Main Points on Reform of the Economic Structure in 1991," drafted by the State Commission for Restructuring the Economy. For there we come upon words that have echoed over the years: "Enterprises' right to independently deal with their production and businesses should be ensured in accord with the 'Enterprise Law.' . . . Meanwhile, governmental organs' administrative interference in enterprises' production and businesses should be reduced."[22]

These various continuities—both intended and unintended—sustained the state-centered proclivity of the entire program. They were only bolstered by the leadership's deepening paranoia against what it perceived as conspiracies perpetrated by the West to ensure China's "peaceful evolution" toward capitalism as the nation entered the 1990s. In this vein, top politicians insisted more forcefully than anytime since the 1970s upon China's rock-bottom commitment to socialism.

Thus, it came as no surprise to find Party General Secretary Jiang Zemin pronouncing on the occasion of the seventieth anniversary of the Communist party on July 1, 1991, that, "A socialist economy with Chinese characteristics requires that we adhere to socialist public ownership of the means of production as the main form of ownership";[23] to discover an article in the *People's Daily* of late May 1991 entitled, "China's Reform Should Never Take the Path of Privatization and Market Orientation";[24] or to come upon a spring 1991 speech to the Chinese Planning Society by Song Ping, a member of the Politburo Standing Committee, in which he proclaimed that, "The aim of combining the planned economy with market regulation is [in the first place] to maintain the proportionate development of the national economy, to ensure the rational allocation of resources and to regulate income distribution, while [in the second place] invigorating the economy through market regulation."[25]

With these declarations, the decade of reform closed upon itself full circle. China's political economy had to await the southward inspection journey of its dominant leader, Deng Xiaoping, in early 1992, before more of the capitalistic ventures the first decade of reforms had presaged could go forward once again. It is likely that the shape they will take as they unfold will be stamped by the nature of the reforms as documented in this volume.

Notes

1. *Japan Economic Journal,* May 19, 1990, translated in *Foreign Broadcast Information Service: China Daily Report* (hereafter *FBIS*), June 4, 1990, annex, p. 10.

2. Martin Weil, "China's Exports: On the Edge," *China Business Review* (hereafter *CBR*), January–February 1990, p. 43.

3. One place among many where this phrasing may be found is in Liu Zepu, "China's Economic Rectification and Sino-U.S. Economic and Trade Relations," *Foreign Affairs Journal* (Beijing), no. 16 (June 1990): p. 4.

4. *Beijing Review* (hereafter *BR*), no. 6, 1989, p. 22, states that there was an 80 billion yuan gap between purchasing power and goods available in 1988; another report noted that the purchasing power generated by excess issuance of currency by the state had exceeded the supply capacity by more than 20 percent as of late 1988 (*Renmin ribao* [People's daily], December 8, 1988, translated in *FBIS*, December 20, 1988, p. 32).

5. In 1987, an additional 20 billion yuan in banknotes were issued to cope with rising demands for cash (*FBIS*, December 16, 1988, p. 26). By December 1988, it was estimated that the currency in circulation could rise by another 35 percent for that year (*FBIS*, December 20, 1988, p. 32).

6. According to *BR*, no. 6 (1989): 23, in 1988 retail prices rose by 18.5 percent and the

consumer price index by 20.7 percent, figures, the magazine claimed, "never witnessed since the founding of New China in 1949."

7. The deficit went from 7.06 billion yuan in 1986 to 7.95 billion in 1987 and 80.5 billion in 1988. These figures are in *Zhongguo tongji nianjian 1989* (Chinese statistical yearbook) Zhongguo Tongjiju (China Statistical Bureau), ed. (Beijing: Zhongguo tongji chubanshe, 1989), p. 657.

8. *South China Morning Post* (hereafter *SCMP*), June 3, 1990, reprinted in *FBIS*, June 5, 1990, p. 29.

9. This figure is from a Xinhua report, given in *FBIS*, March 22, 1990, p. 12.

10. These figures came from an interview with noted Chinese economist Li Yining published in the *Hong Kong Standard*, March 29, 1990, and reprinted in *FBIS*, April 4, 1990, p. 36.

11. *Japan Economic Journal*, May 31, 1990, in *FBIS*, June 4, annex, p. 9.

12. *New York Times*, July 30, 1990.

13. Richard Brecher, "The End of Investment's Wonder Years," *CBR*, January–February 1990, pp. 28–29.

14. Robert Delfs, "Promises, Promises," *Far Eastern Economic Review* (hereafter *FEER*), March 22, 1990, p. 51.

15. This was in a Xinhua report dated June 2, 1990, translated in *FBIS*, June 8, p. 33.

16. Tai Ming Cheung, "Coy Capitalists," *FEER*, May 9, 1991, p. 43.

17. Other pieces of the period that underline the continuing commitment to enterprise bail-outs by the state and which similarly shun bankruptcy appear in *FBIS*, March 28, 1990, pp. 36–37, on the Liaoning Province governor's efforts to revive failing firms by speeding up enterprise mergers and allocating relief funds; *China Daily*, April 12, 1990, p. 4, reprinted in *FBIS*, April 20, 1990, p. 48, on the determination to "help" enterprises which had stopped production as a result of the austerity policy and the Shanghai city government's collection of funds for this purpose; and the recovery through "cooperation" with a successful firm of a garment factory in Liaoning which had been on the verge of bankruptcy two years earlier, in *FBIS*, July 10, 1990, p. 35.

18. Elizabeth Cheng, "Small Leap Forward," *FEER*, July 18, 1991, p. 69.

19. Paul Schroeder, "Rebuilding China's Securities Markets," *CBR*, May–June 1991, p. 21.

20. Elizabeth Cheng, "Share of the Action," *FEER*, January 31, 1991, p. 34.

21. May 7, 1991, p. 12, reprinted in *FBIS*, May 7, 1991, p. 55.

22. As translated in *FBIS*, June 21, 1991, pp. 34–35.

23. In *FBIS* Supplement, July 5, 1991, p. 5.

24. The author is Jiang Xuemo, a professor at Fudan University, and the article is translated in *FBIS*, June 19, 1991, pp. 41–42.

25. As translated in *FBIS*, May 7, 1991, p. 55.

Index

Media *(continued)*
  reports on private sector, 226
  See also specific publications
Merchants
  decline in number, 272*n.20*
  dependent institutions formed by, 266–68
  institutions to control, 264–66
  relationship with bureaucrats, 5, 10, 260, 261–64, 267–68
  taxes, 89, 262, 263, 272*n.26*, 273*n.38*
  trade, 225–55
  See also Bourgeoisie; Petty private sector
Mergers of state enterprises. *See* Enterprise mergers and takeovers
Metcalfe, J. L., 83
Minban companies, 267, 270
Mining, coal. *See* Coal industry
Ministry of Commerce, 76, 79
Ministry of Electronics, 267
Ministry of Light Industry, 116
Ministry of Machine-Building, 116, 179
Ministry of Metallurgy, 116
Mitsui Corporation, 266
Monetary system. *See* Currency
"Moonlighting craze," 268
Municipal Commission for the Restructuring of the Economic System (Wuhan), 137
Municipal Economic Commission, 96

Nanjing Automobile Company, 99
National Association for Industry and Commerce, 15
National Conference on Learning from Daqing and Dazhai in Finance and Trade, 37
National Conference on Learning from Daqing in Industry, 156
National Industrial and Communications Work Conference, Zhao's speech to, 62*n.93*
National People's Congress
  role in party decisions, 27–62
  Standing Committee, 130, 181
  See also specific congresses
Naughton, Barry, 90, 160
Neoclassical contracting, 109–10
Networks, 9, 175, 187–88
  formation of, 212–13
  place of central cities within, 205–22
  See also Information channels

New China News Agency, 128
New Economic Policy, 43
News media. *See* Media
No. 2 Bicycle Factory (Wuhan), 187, 189, 191
No. 3 Radio Factory (Wuhan), 182
Nomenklatura, 257
Nonstandardization of design, 7, 108, 110, 110–11, 112, 113, 116–17, 118
Nove, Alec, 155, 166, 167
NPC. *See* National People's Congress; specific congress numbers

"Observe Economic Laws," 37, 157
Obstructions, against private sectoral activity, 5, 54, 75, 243, 249, 261–62
Oil industry, 34, 45
  Bohai Gulf disaster, 43
Olson, Mancur, 83, 166
Ossified thinking, 225, 237

Party cadres, 9, 226, 250
  attitudes toward private sector, 238–44, 245, 249, 258, 262
  job identification, 86
  See also Bureaucrats
Party Congress. *See* specific congress number
"Pass-hands" trade, 229
Paternalism, state socialist, 8, 87, 153–70
Peng Zhen, 45
People's Bank, 135, 186, 187, 188, 191, 213
People's Daily, 18, 20, 29, 37, 42, 43, 44, 56, 66, 69, 93, 134, 139, 195, 211, 225, 230, 234, 240, 243, 279
Per capita income, 145*n.9*
Personal relationships. *See Guanxi*
Petroleum Faction, 35, 41–42, 43, 59*nn.32, 35*
Petty private sector, 9, 225–55
  policies, 229–31
  practitioners, 243–44
  size, 231–32
  views of population on, 238–44
Pigs, marketing of live, 74
Pingheng (balancing), 93, 94, 99
Pizhun. See Plannng and approving
Planned economy. *See* Command economy
Planned management, reducing, 17, 18
Planning and approving (*pizhun*), 93

Dorothy J. Solinger is Professor of Politics and Society at the University of California, Irvine. She is the author of *Chinese Business Under Socialism* (1984) and of *From Lathes to Looms: China's Industrial Policy in Comparative Perspective, 1979–1982* (1991), and the editor of *Three Visions of Chinese Socialism* (1984). Her work on the Chinese economic reforms of the 1980s is based in part on ten research trips to China between 1978 and 1990.